Portrait of New Canaan

Portrait of New Canaan

The History of a Connecticut Town

MARY LOUISE KING

NEW CANAAN HISTORICAL SOCIETY

Copyright © 1981 Mary Louise King
All rights reserved under International and Pan-American
Copyright Conventions.

Library of Congress Catalog Card No.: 81-80612
ISBN 0-939958-00-7

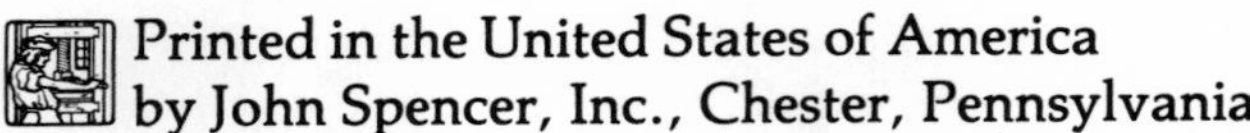
Printed in the United States of America
by John Spencer, Inc., Chester, Pennsylvania

Preface

I am a writer of history, not a historian. Given the same materials, someone else might have written a quite different book, though I think I have interpreted the records correctly. However, some of my information probably is inaccurate, and for resulting errors I apologize.

I happen to have been born in New Canaan, and when I returned in 1958 after an absence of 22 years, I resumed the work I had formerly done for the New Canaan Historical Society—title searching old houses. But a straight chain of title has never interested me. I have always wanted to know who were the people who occupied a house or a store, what they were like, what they did, and so I went farther afield than land and probate records. After publishing some of my research in pamphlet form, I began eight years ago to write a history of the town. No one previously had completed a full history of New Canaan; Samuel St. John's "Historical Address" of 1876 is brief and more than 100 years out of date; book-length histories of the churches are church and not town histories, while other publications deal with limited subjects.

I don't pretend to know all about New Canaan history, but I know it is not true to say "nothing ever happened in New Canaan"; something was happening every day, and in any period of time someone was making local history. At first it was the Congregational ministers, with the authority of their office and college education; next it was the civil and military leaders of Revolutionary days; then the "landed gentry" with their sense of *noblesse oblige,* followed by the enterprising 19th-century men of commerce, who were responsible for the town's temporary growth. After 1870 the summer residents, though few in number, exerted pressure for change, as did the 20th-century "commuters," who made their money elswhere. Two World Wars, the Depression, and corporate mobility produced the men and women who have made more recent New Canaan history.

Over the years I have had generous help from many people, in particular my friend the late Lois B. Bayles, whose research was always available to me. The late Mrs. Elsa Dannenberg of Fairfield provided me from her files on Fairfield County shipping records of New Canaan masters and ships, while the late F. Clerc Ogden of Wilton permitted me to copy all the journals of his great uncle, the Rev. David Ogden. Always the New Canaan Historical Society allowed me full access to its library and files. Special thanks go to Marshall H. Montgomery and Joseph C. Sweet, who took the time to read my manuscript and make helpful suggestions and improvements; to Jean E. Crego, who proofread the galleys; to Mrs. Mary Ritter, New Canaan's town clerk, and her staff, who were unfailingly cooperative; and to my husband John King, who designed and helped to illustrate this book and encouraged me whenever I despaired of finishing it.

Except where the context requires otherwise, I have used today's names and spellings for streets—Elm Street instead of Railroad Avenue, Oenoke Ridge instead of Haynes Ridge, Silvermine instead of Silver Mine, although old timers vehemently insisted that the road, area, and river be spelled as two words. Some surnames vary in spelling, but appear as in original documents. At the end of the book I have listed my sources, but I have omitted footnotes, in order to make the pages more readable. However, a completely annotated copy of this book is on file at the New Canaan Historical Society for those who wish the specific references for facts and statements.

New Canaan, Conn. — Mary Louise King
February 26, 1981

Contents

Foreword viii

Part I—Canaan Parish 1731-1801

Illustrations 2
1.—In the Beginning 3
2.—The First Two Decades, 1731-1751 28
3.—Fighting and Feuding, 1751-1771 46
4.—The Revolution, 1771-1781 67
5.—From Parish to Town, 1781-1801 98

Part II—New Canaan 1801-1951

Illustrations 118
6.—The Benevolent Despots, 1801-1825 119
7.—The Shoemaking Boom, 1826-1850 149
8.—The Best Laid Plans, 1851-1875 183
9.—The Changing Scene, 1876-1900 217
10.—Growing Up—Slowly, 1901-1931 261
11.—A Sense of Community, 1931-1951 301
Sources 324
Index 330

Foreword

New Canaan is a town of 18,000 persons situated in the southwestern part of Connecticut's Fairfield County. Depending on where one measures, its southern border, crossed by the Merritt Parkway, is some four to seven miles north of Long Island Sound. Its northern border is the easternmost jut of New York's Westchester County, at Pound Ridge and Lewisboro. To the east are Norwalk and Wilton, to the west is Stamford, Connecticut. New Canaan's area of 22.2 square miles is made up of north-south running ridges and valleys, drained by brooks that courteously are named "rivers." Sloping gently northward, the land reaches a peak elevation of 580 feet near the head of Oenoke Ridge, providing that "healthful climate" old timers stressed when they wished to ignore the poor quality of the soil and the dearth of economic opportunity.

Lacking natural resources to exploit, devoid now of any industry, connected with the main line by a single-track branch railroad, New Canaan would seem to have little to recommend it. Yet today it is one of this country's most desirable residential communities, home of leaders of business and the arts.

This book, therefore, is an effort to explain New Canaan to itself and to others. It is, unsentimentally, a tribute to the individuals who, in every decade of the 250 years of Canaan Parish's and New Canaan's history, guided community destiny. I hope it will make everyone who lives in New Canaan aware of their inheritance.

PART I

Canaan Parish 1731-1801

Illustrations

	PAGE
The Perambulation Line stone wall	9
A field on Canaan Ridge	23
Map showing Canaan Parish superimposed on the townships of Stamford and Norwalk	26
The Rev. John Eells' house	30
A shoemaker's bench and tools	40
Fireplace in the keeping room of the Hanford-Silliman House	44
Map showing the location of Daniel Keeler's tavern and the houses of the counterfeiters	49
Five Mile River harbor	59
The Rev. William Drummond's parsonage	72
Captain John Carter's commission	84
Major Benjamin Tallmadge	90
Mementos of Revolutionary days	97
A typical sloop	102
School District No. 2 schoolhouse—Rock School	113

CHAPTER 1

In the Beginning

Necessity made town planners of the founders of most early Connecticut villages. Laying out four short streets around a common pasturage, the first settlers assigned themselves homelots according to a priority, based on importance or contribution to the venture, and along those streets built their houses one next to another, so that each family would have the help and protection of everyone else. Then they drew up rules and regulations for governing themselves and those who joined them. Without official permission, no new family could move in and no man could settle outside the village. Beyond the settlement, the surrounding acres were "zoned" into fields and woodlots for the founding families—the Proprietors—while the rest of what usually was a huge township remained undivided. Sometimes, as defense against Indians, parts of the earliest villages were palisaded (as at Windsor), while elsewhere only the meeting house was protected (as at Stamford). Then, as dangers decreased and local ordinances removed certain domestic animals from the center of town, larger dwelling houses replaced the first small ones, and the common pasture became the village green—so dear to the hearts of today's antiquarians and the eyes of photographers.

Not so New Canaan. No founding fathers set out to build a town or to form a government. No one planned anything. The first settlers, early in the 18th century, simply scattered their homesteads haphazardly over a wide countryside, made up of some 14,000 acres, two thirds of which then lay in the northwestern part of the town of Norwalk and one third in northeastern Stamford. These people were moving north from their home towns on the shore to such sites "in the country" as they could afford. Until 1801, they and their descendants and successors would remain inhabitants and taxpayers of either Norwalk or Stamford, depending on where their landholdings were.

When enough families to warrant consideration had settled, they petitioned the colonial legislature in 1731 to let them establish Canaan Parish, so that they might build a convenient meeting house and form a Congregational church. No one in Norwalk or Stamford then foresaw that 80 years later the "suburb" of Canaan Parish, which was solely a religious entity, would break away to become the town of New Canaan. But it did, and so the how and why Canaan Parish was formed, though a rather long story, is a vital part of New Canaan's history.

Background History

No two Connecticut towns were or are exactly the same. Wilton and Darien also began as religious parishes, but New Canaan is like neither one. In 1731, the lands that made up Canaan Parish not only belonged to two adjoining towns on Long Island Sound but once had belonged to two different colonies (making New Canaan unique). Norwalk was settled in 1651 by the Colony of Connecticut, while Stamford began 10 years earlier under the Colony of New Haven. Although the two colonies were merged long before anyone settled in Canaan Parish, Norwalk and Stamford had quite different histories, and the differing inheritances of the two sides of Canaan Parish were to survive well into the 20th century and affect local history.

The first three townships that were the nucleus of the Colony of Connecticut—Hartford, Windsor, and Wethersfield—were founded in the Connecticut River valley in 1634-36 by settlers who came overland from Massachusetts, primarily from Dorchester and Watertown. Few of these men had been in the Massachusetts Bay Colony five years when they set their sights on the rich Connecticut valley and highhandedly appropriated what had been claimed by the Dutch and by Plymouth Colony and already was occupied by Plymouth men. Strengthening their hold on what would later be a part of Connecticut, other Bay Colony men built a fort at Saybrook to control the outlet of the Connecticut River into Long Island Sound. Then, in 1637, Connecticut settlers were recruited in support of Massachusetts troops to fight the Pequot War—with unforeseen results. Before the Pequots were defeated in the famous Swamp Fight (a little west of what is now Fairfield), men from Hartford, Windsor, and Wethersfield had ranged over considerable unoccupied lands and shores and found them to their liking.

The news spread, and in 1638 Theophilus Eaton and the Rev. John Davenport bought an area called Quinnipiak from the Indians. Bringing settlers from Cambridge, Mass., they founded the Colony of New Haven, extending inland from their town of New Haven toward Meriden and along the shores of Long Island Sound. Religious differences accounted partly for the earlier exodus from Massachusetts to Connecticut, and these differences were renewed when New Haven founded a theocracy wherein only male church members had a vote in colony affairs. And New Haven intended to develop a trading center, whereas the Colony of Connecticut was engaged in agriculture.

No love was lost between the rival colonies. In no time at all the two were in competition for more lands and more settlers, and the first move was made by Connecticut.

Remembering the island, harbors, and lands he had seen during the Pequot War, Roger Ludlowe of Windsor in the spring of 1639 acquired from the Indians for the Colony of Connecticut a plantation stretching westward from present Stratford to Saugatuck and laid out the town of Fairfield. Returning to the colony seat in Hartford, Ludlowe was accused of exceeding his orders, but was let off with a small fine for having missed the September session of the General Court. Connecticut Colony was well aware that Ludlowe's unauthorized purchase had blocked the Colony of New Haven's plans to buy the coastland and had gained for the colony new ports on Long Island Sound from which to confront Dutch threats.

The year 1640 saw three more acquisitions of Fairfield County land by the two colonies. On April 20, one day after the Dutch council in Manhattan had ordered its secretary to buy what now is Norwalk, Capt. Daniel Patrick, Windsor's paid military commander, acting for Connecticut bought from the Indians not only what would be the western part of Norwalk but, going farther west, also bought Greenwich. The Dutch were too late and got nothing at all. Between Patrick's two tracts lay Rippowam, which on July 1, 1640, was bought for the Colony of New Haven by Capt. Nathaniel Turner. Rippowam would become the town of Stamford (first spelled Stanford). Almost rounding out what now is the shore front of Fairfield County, Ludlowe on February 26, 1641, bought from the Indians the land between the Saugatuck and the Norwalk rivers, including part of present-day Westport and Weston and the eastern part of Norwalk. (Norwalk acquired Rowayton in 1651, while Stamford bought what is now Darien from the Indians in 1645.)

With such large tracts of unoccupied land, the problem was to find families to settle there, and this time the Colony of New Haven made the first move. Wethersfield had barely survived the Pequot War when a majority of four of its seven voting church members wanted to move out. The dispute was irreconcilable, and the clergymen called in to mediate agreed that the only solution was for some Wethersfield families to emigrate. So the dissident families of Wethersfield accepted New Haven Colony's offer of a plantation, and for £33 (half of which was paid with 100 bushels of corn) purchased Rippowam in 1640. Agreeing to the rules New Haven laid down, the next year they founded Stanford, or Stamford. In 1650, with the blessings of Connecticut's General Court, the Ludlowe and Patrick purchases were bought by a company of Hartford men, who founded the town of Norwalk in 1651.

Both the Connecticut and New Haven colonies prohibited individuals from buying land from the Indians, and much as present-day owners might like to say they can title search their property back to an Indian sachem, they can't. The only exception is an island in Norwalk harbor. This was deeded by a sachem to the Norwalk minister who had Christianized him, and the minister was permitted to keep the island. Otherwise, land was purchased from the Indians in large blocks, either by an agent or a committee of one or the other of the two colonies or by a group acting for a would-be town.

Once Stamford and Norwalk were founded, local Indian sachems kept right on selling land to both towns or they renewed previous deeds signed by their relatives, thus causing all kinds of confusions and involving what would be New Canaan lands.

Every Indian deed to Stamford and Norwalk has been preserved—if not the original, then a contemporary copy—and all are vague to the extreme about the boundaries of the lands changing hands. Grants overlapped; tribal land sold by one sachem was resold to the same town by his descendants; different sachems sold the same tract of land to different towns. The last deed was drawn in 1702 wherein the Chief Katonah sold to men from New York Colony land that had been deeded to Stamford 30 years earlier. More than the names and numbers of the many Indian and white players in the land game are needed to unsnarl the tangle the Indians made quite unintentionally. And a fair size piece of what would be New Canaan was snagged in the mess.

The colonies of Connecticut and New Haven had no dispute over the original purchases of Norwalk and Stamford, although the vague northern boundary of both would involve Connecticut later in a long legal battle with New York. Stamford's grant included (besides present Bedford and Pound Ridge, N.Y.) the western third of New Canaan; Norwalk bought what would be the eastern half. In between the two purchases was a long strip of land lying between the mouths of Goodwives and Five Mile rivers and extending some miles northward from Long Island Sound. This would become a large piece of Darien and the center strip of New Canaan, and this tract had been sold by one Indian tribe to Stamford in 1645 and by another tribe to Norwalk in 1651.

The Perambulation Line

There is small point in giving here the details of the prolonged feuding and skirmishing, both armed and legal, that went on between Stamford and Norwalk over this land. The two-colony aspect of the dispute came to an end in 1662, when John Winthrop, Jr., returned from London with a charter from Charles II for the whole of what now is Connecticut. During the next three years the Colony of New Haven was phased out (and as a belated sop to New Haven, from 1701 until 1873 Connecticut had two capitals—New Haven and Hartford—where the colonial and then the state government sat alternately). Then, in 1685, when Connecticut faced the possibility that James II would merge it into New York, the Colony ordered all its towns to describe their boundaries, list the names and claims of their proprietors, and apply for official patents to town lands—all of which was to strengthen Connecticut's charter claims. Thus it became vital that Stamford and Norwalk once and for all establish their common boundary, and the General Court appointed a committee to make sure the job was speedily done. Norwalk lost out on its claim to Goodwives River as its western boundary and had to settle for Five Mile River (which is so named because it is five miles west of the Saugatuck River, which was Norwalk's eastern bound). After this decision, the Norwalk-Stamford boundary for the first time was officially surveyed during the winter of 1685-86.

Beginning at the mouth of Five Mile River—putting one side of the harbor in Norwalk and the other in Stamford—the surveyors followed the river inland to what now is Old King's Highway North in Darien. From there, they ran a course 37½ degrees west of north until they came to the colony line, paralleling the boundary already established between the towns of Stratford and Fairfield. In that day the colony line was considerably beyond New Canaan's northern border (which is the New York State line), but not until 1731 was Connecticut forced officially to relinquish to New York the northernmost acres of Greenwich, Stamford, and Norwalk—called the Oblong—to give Westchester County its odd panhandle shape.

Once established, the common boundary between Norwalk and Stamford was called the Perambulation Line, a familiar term to most settlers. If not actually seen, many had heard of the "perambulation of the bounds" in an English parish, and the "beating of the bounds" when a young lad was whipped by a parish official so that in later years he would have no doubt as to just where the boundary was in some specific spot. But from the time it was run in 1686, the Norwalk-Stamford Perambulation Line was no vague bound; more than a line on a map, it was an honest-to-goodness stone wall. As you went north from the shore, all the land on the right side of the wall lay in Norwalk; on the left, in Stamford. With the Perambulation Line as one of his boundaries, no later Canaan Parish landowner was ever in doubt as to the town in which he filed his deeds and to which he paid taxes.

In present-day New Canaan terms, the part of the Perambulation Line that ran through Canaan Parish began at the southern boundary on Brookside Road. Following its 37½-degree-west-of-north course, the Line crossed South Avenue a little north of the Merritt Parkway, ran through the junction of Park Street, Bank Street, and Old Stamford Road, crossed Mead Park and Elm Street and Weed Street on a diagonal, and then ran almost parallel to West Road—putting two thirds of what would be Canaan Parish into Norwalk and the western third into Stamford.

When New Canaan was incorporated in 1801, the Perambulation Line ceased to have meaning, since all land then lay in one town. Landowners whose adjacent fields had been on either side of the Line tore down their sections of the dividing wall, but bits and pieces still remain. One short stretch of the old Perambulation Line stone wall, hidden from public view, runs behind the house lots on the west side of Kimberly Place; another angles through the woods just east of Lapham High School's lower parking lot.

The Perambulation Line stone wall undoubtedly has been rebuilt many times since 1686.

Settlement

In 1686, when the Perambulation Line was run, all the acres that now make up New Canaan were part of either Norwalk's or Stamford's common land and lay undivided—that is, they belonged to the Proprietors of those towns and had not been deeded to individuals—with one exception. Samuel Finch on February 18, 1684, had registered with Stamford his claim to four acres of land on Ponus Ridge. This is the earliest recorded land record pertaining to New Canaan real estate. The first private purchase on the Norwalk side was made in 1699—to land at Silvermine hill.

As I have already said, when a new town was being settled, the founding fathers parceled out only such acreage as they needed, leaving the rest undivided. Calling themselves "Proprietors," the original 30 men who bought Stamford for £33 from the Colony of New Haven, drew up a "List of Estates," setting down how much each man had paid in cash, corn, and necessary supplies toward the original costs of settlement. In other words, the 30 Proprietors were the equivalents of stockholders who had invested varying amounts in the "company" of Stamford. At their first Proprietors' meeting, each man's original holdings—homelot, meadows, salt marsh, woodland, and such—were decided on. In this way, a total of 276 acres of Stamford's land were parceled out in a rough semicircle, with Long Island Sound on the south. The arcuate boundary of the original town was called the "Sequest Line," beyond which lay hundreds of undivided acres held in common by the Proprietors against the day when they would need more land.

While Norwalk's Proprietors did not follow Stamford's arrangement to the letter, in general each new Connecticut town held and developed its lands the way Stamford did. Occasionally, an important newcomer was voted a right in the Proprietors' lands, and in this way in 1705 William Haynes of London acquired from Norwalk 93 acres along New Canaan's Oenoke Ridge (which for nearly 200 years was called Haynes Ridge until an irrelevant Indian name was pinned on it). Otherwise, the rights to commonage passed by inheritance from the original Proprietors to their sons. And Proprietors' rights to common land were never part of a man's taxable estate; only his actual land holdings were on the town's List of Estates, which was the base for colony, town, and church taxes.

Before they could think of expanding much beyond the village green, the original settlers of Stamford and Norwalk had to establish towns and develop farmlands. Newcomers and a second generation brought demands for more land. Disease, poor diet, crudely handled childbirth, and high infant mortality took their tolls, but still many settlers raised large families. Their estates, divided among six, eight, ten children (and married daughters with their husbands shared in the distribution of a father's land), were never enough to support so many second-generation families. (Except that the eldest son, in certain situations, received a double portion, Connecticut never followed England's primogeniture, whereby the eldest son inherited all his father's land.) And as towns grew, newcomers needed to buy more land than the original settlers had for sale. So, periodically and methodically, the Proprietors of Norwalk and Stamford moved their Sequest Lines outward, opening up new "tiers" of land.

Once a new "tier" was authorized, a man on the Proprietors' list could pick out a certain number of acres in fixed proportion to his "investment," his opportunity to choose having been determined by a "pitch" or lottery. After his new land had been surveyed and recorded on the land records, he was free to sell if he wished. In this way, Stamford and Norwalk slowly opened up their common land.

Because the acres that would make up Canaan Parish were so far from the shore—in the uppermost "tiers"—it was almost 100 years before they stopped being Norwalk or Stamford's common land and passed into private hands. But once Norwalk had moved its Sequest Line northward in 1705 and Stamford had opened its last "tier" in 1711, private ownership began in a hit-or-miss way. You might suppose that, for security or some other good reason, a man would buy just north of the land he'd already taken up, but this was not so, and large tracts of common land often separated one man's choice from his next. Mill sites and hayfields were important to the earliest buyers, who built a few barns but never built houses in Canaan Parish. By 1715, Stamford men had bought far out on Ponus Ridge (probably mill sites), on West Road and Weed Street, in Talmadge Hill, and on Flat Ridge (where New

Canan's Waveny Park is now). Norwalk settlers, beginning in lower Silvermine with mill sites (north of Silvermine Tavern), scattered their purchases just as widely—on Clapboard and Canoe hills, out Smith and Oenoke ridges, and in lower White Oak Shade—wherever they thought the land might be productive. Flat Ridge, upper Oenoke, and (probably) Bushy Ridge are Drumlinoid ridges, and as such were less wooded than land elsewhere. This meant that they were easier to work into good hayfields, offsetting their inaccessibility, which may be the reason that tracts on these ridges were among the first deeds to be recorded by individuals.

After 1715, settlement of what would be Canaan Parish began, and the first known dwelling (long gone) was built by Theophilus Hanford of Norwalk in 1719—on the east side of Main Street where today Hoyt Street begins. The paths to settlement were the river valleys and the ridges, along which a few "highways" had been laid out.

As one family after another in Stamford and Norwalk packed up its worldly goods and moved northward with their animals, no sense of urgency impelled them. No one was being transferred; no man had need to rush off and buy a house his wife had not seen. All men knew the lay of the land and the courses of the rivers, for they and their fathers had hunted freely (until in 1698 Connecticut enacted its first game law, forbidding the killing of deer between January 15 and July 15 of each year). Summer after summer, complying with ordinances that forbade swine to be at large in the town centers while crops were growing, men and boys had driven Norwalk's pigs to pasture on "Marvin's Hog Ridge" or "Smith's Hog Ridge." Some men had searched for and supposedly found a bit of silver where the Indians—according to legend—had mined on Silvermine Hill, and iron ore had been found in the same ridge farther north near the Colony line (now under the waters of the upper Grupe Reservoir). Others had located, felled, and dragged back to town the great white oaks that went into building British as well as colonial ships. (Because of the straightness of the trees felled on the Upper Clapboard Hills, what is now Carter Street was called "the mast path.") And any man knew where good cropland could be found. So the first settlers picked out acreage that suited their plans for the future, waited until convenient sawmills were operating, and then tackled the job of building a house and a barn. Those first families probably never thought of themselves as pioneers opening up a wilderness; they simply were building new houses on less developed land than that closer to the towns to which they would keep their ties.

As Canaan Parish, New Canaan thus began in a very different way than had either of its parent towns. Stamford in 1641 and Norwalk ten years later were started from scratch, settlers hurrying to fell trees and plant crops, lest they freeze or starve to death during the first winter of settlement. Each built a town along the shores of a harbor that provided access to a water "highway" as well as fishing grounds, and each clustered its houses for protection from Indians, Dutch, wolves, and other dangers. Coming from the new towns in the upper Connecticut River valley, those people had had to be almost entirely self-sufficient, doing without nails and bullets, shoes, clothing, and some kinds of food until the uncertain arrival of a vessel—possibly out of England but more likely out of Boston—or an overland ox cart with needed goods.

Sixty-five years later, when the settlement of Canaan Parish began in earnest, everything had changed. Wolves still had to be reckoned with and so did rattlesnakes, but the Dutch no longer were a menace nor were the Indians. Although some people prefer it otherwise, tales of red savages in Canaan Parish are purely a myth. No one was ever scalped by an Indian lurking in the bush. Indians came here as summer campers until the early 19th century, but no Indians were living in this area when the land was being settled, and the Indians who passed through or camped were peacefully inclined. There was a very good reason why.

Stamford's first settlers did have Indian troubles, and one Stamford man was murdered by an Indian, who was surrendered by his sachem to the white men. Stamford and Greenwich were the closest Connecticut towns to the Dutch in New Amsterdam, and Dutch-Indian relations were notoriously bad. So when the Dutch in May 1643 ambushed and beheaded Myanos, an Indian chief, Stamford had good reason to fear an Indian reprisal. None came, but rumors persisted, and so on February 3, 1644, the Dutch landed an army of 130 soldiers from New Amsterdam at Stamford harbor. That night, those men, led by Capt. John Underhill, Stamford's paid military commander, attacked the Indian stronghold near what is now Bedford, N.Y. In the first hour of fighting, 130

Indians were killed; then the stockade was fired and perhaps 400 more, including women and children, were burned to death. Understandably, after this ambush many of the small Indian tribes in the area moved northwestward toward the Hudson, to put themselves under the protection of the Iroquois. (Although the atrocities called King Philip's War occurred outside Connecticut, Fairfield County towns participated by sending quotas of troops. When that was ended, December 17, 1675, at Kingston, R.I., in a holocaust worse than the Bedford one, a local soldier belatedly "seriously inquired whether burning their enemies alive could be consistent with humanity and the benevolent principles of the Gospels.")

Despite the Bedford slaughter, small tribes of Indians did remain in Fairfield County, and although the early settlers never quite trusted them, Norwalk avoided trouble far more successfully than Stamford did. The sagamores who sold land to the English were chieftains of semiagricultural tribes, well known for their tobacco growing and the wampum they made from oyster shells. Now and then, because England prohibited the export of coins, this wampum served the earliest settlers as a medium of exchange. But as Norwalk and Stamford opened up their common land, the few remaining Indians were forced inland away from the shores. Either these Indians died out or drifted toward the Hudson, because by the early 1700's no settled tribe remained in this area.

Sea Trade

Rather than a lack of Indians, impetus for the settlement of Canaan Parish came from the development of Norwalk and Stamford into thriving port towns. Those who built the first houses in Canaan Parish knew that they had only to go to the wharves and stores in their home towns to fill their needs. More important, they had markets there for surplus farm produce and whatever wares they made—and most of the settlers followed a trade.

From the beginning of settlement until after the War of 1812 and the coming of the steamboat in 1824, the economy of southwest Fairfield County was anchored in the small trading fleets on Long Island Sound that sailed out of the harbors of Norwalk, Old Well (as South Norwalk was called), Five Mile River, Rings End,

Shippan, and Stamford. Although surviving documents are few, what exist suggest that Stamford and Norwalk lost little time after settlement in building a shallop or a pinace to trade up and down the Sound. Surplus crops, a few fur skins, Indian tobacco, hops, and fish could be sold or exchanged with other Sound ports, while demand for timber, ships' masts, and certain marine supplies for the British navy eventually led to larger sloops and longer voyages.

Connecticut's official colonial records point to Boston as the shipping center for the colony's British trade, but Stamford and Norwalk seem early to have sent their sloops to the west. At first the Dutch were a problem, having established a sea trade on the Sound and up the Connecticut River which they wanted to maintain, but Fairfield County vessels did trade with the Dutch in New Amsterdam—though this was against colony law. Once New Amsterdam became New York, Long Island Sound became an English sea, and those who lived in southwestern Fairfield County turned their backs on the rest of Connecticut to focus on New York. It has been so ever since. (The western part of Fairfield County was so different from the rest of the colony, and later the state, that it is largely ignored in printed histories of Connecticut. Local historians today jokingly refer to "Fairfield County, N.Y.," as a couple of old land records actually termed it!)

The three bars to colonial shipping were the bitter cold winters, when the Sound froze; the inability of towns to build ships easily; and British laws. Neither the Colony of Connecticut nor the towns of Norwalk and Stamford thought that England should know too much of what went on, so records and statistics are hard to come by. Officially, for British consumption, in 1680 the town of Stamford was credited with only a 10-ton sloop and the 80-ton *Punch,* but Stamford earned an early reputation for shipbuilding and you can find the names of other vessels in the land records and elsewhere. In 1673, when the Dutch again temporarily controlled New York, a Stamford vessel belonging to Capt. Jonathan Selleck was captured off Stamford by the Dutch, and in May 1689, a different Captain Selleck, on a voyage out of Stamford for England, was captured by the French.

The Stamford town meeting minutes for 1692 note the problems one resident was having in building a ship for a New York Dutchman. That shipbuilder was John Leeds, whose family had had a shipyard in New London and whose descendants would be wealthy settlers in Canaan Parish. Norwalk, too, was building ships, and when in 1700 that town granted permission to Eli Darbe to build a vessel at Five Mile River, the record says his was not Norwalk's first shipyard. No statistics can be found for the size of the ships or the lengths of their voyages, but Norwalk and Stamford men traded regularly up and down the coast, across the Sound to Long Island (settled by Connecticut families), to New York, the West Indies, and still farther from home.

What affected Fairfield County's economy most was England's Navigation Acts. As early as 1660, England sought to restrict colonial shipping to English-built and/or English-owned vessels, and followed this with more restrictive Navigation acts, which provided for colonial customs commissioners, posting of cargo bonds, and payment of duties at ports of clearance—anything to prevent intercolony trading and evasion of tariffs. In common with other New England towns, Stamford and Norwalk lacked money to buy goods in England, so, to have credit and cash, some men developed a trade with the West Indies, in particular with the non-British islands. This was strictly against Crown law, but once they were able to put vessels on the high seas, the colonists learned to outsail British ships and avoid being stopped and searched. In the West Indies they sold lumber, horses, grain, and other local items, bringing back sugar, salt, molasses, and rum. More often, though, they sailed their goods and produce to New York for transshipment in larger vessels to the Islands or England, and in New York they bought their foreign imports.

Norwalk was growing into the sixth largest town in the Colony, but it was Stamford which in 1702 was made one of Connecticut's eight ports of clearance, with a "Navall office" to collect "such fees as have been accustomed." One way of avoiding the law and the payment of duties on imported goods was to deal with pirates and smugglers—though pirates were not an unmixed blessing since they preyed on colonial shipping on the Sound as well as on vessels on the high seas. Stories of Norwalk's and Stamford's dealings with pirates or their activities as smugglers cannot be verified, but the stories persist, and almost any summer will find treasure hunters along the coasts of those towns or their surviving islands in the Sound. The only specific "evidence" is a letter written by the Earl of Bellomont on November 28, 1700, when he was governor of New York, accusing Major Selleck of Stamford of receiving "at least £10,000 worth of treasure and East India goods" from the famous Captain Kidd. Bellomont was trying to justify his participation in William Kidd's dealings, so this letter may be a false statement the Governor prepared for Kidd's trial in London—which historians now consider to have been rigged to make Captain Kidd the scapegoat for a number of embarrassed Englishmen who had expected to share in Kidd's success.

Although Queen Anne's War (1702-13) saw such bloody incidents as the massacre at Deerfield, Mass., the coastal towns were less affected by the frontier warfare than by New England's economic depression brought on by the strict enforcement of the Navigation Acts. Norwalk and Stamford sent a few men to the Connecticut militia contingent, which marched to the defense of Albany, but everyone at home suffered because the West Indies trade was almost shut down. With the end of the war and a change of monarchs, sea trade revived, and the fortunes of the Fairfield County port towns improved. By the 1720's when Canaan Parish was about to be formed, the day of the "pioneer" was over. Norwalk and Stamford were old, settled towns, whose residents were interested in accumulating some "wealth" by trade as well as landholdings. The local economy had stabilized when third-generation Stamford and Norwalk families began to move "to the country," and these settlers knew that what they grew or made might well find markets far beyond the town trading centers.

The Congregational Church

By 1730 enough families were living in what would be Canaan Parish to put substance behind earlier vague grumblings that no one should expect them to go all the way to Norwalk or Stamford to attend Sunday worship services. Bedford had been set off as a separate town from Stamford in 1682 and Ridgefield from Norwalk in 1705, but the settlers in this area had no wish to form a new town. What they wanted was permission to organize as a Congregational parish as Wilton, within Norwalk's bounds, had been allowed to do in 1725. To form a parish it was necessary to have the sanction of Connecticut's General Assembly, because, until the constitution of 1818, government and the Congregational church were closely entwined.

The founders (1635) of Connecticut's first three towns brought with them from Massachusetts the Puritan church. First called "Separatists," because they had "separated" themselves from the Church of England, these people were soon known as Congregationalists, and the Congregational Church was "established" early as the official church of Connecticut colony. This union of Church and State is implied in the preamble of the Fundamental Orders (1639), by which the early Connecticut towns governed themselves, and in Connecticut's Code of Laws (1650) is the power to tax all property owners for the support of Congregational clergymen. Everyone unless seriously ill had to attend Congregational services each Sunday, but Connecticut—unlike the Colony of New Haven—stopped short of imposing religious tests for the franchise. Little was changed when in 1662 the Fundamental Orders were replaced by the colonial charter obtained from Charles II, though that charter did say that Connecticut's laws could not be "contrary to the laws of this Realme of England"—which some were.

Many of the founding fathers had left England to be free to worship God in the ways they believed were those of the early Christian church. In particular, Separatists objected to the episcopacy of the Church of England and had seen imitation of the Roman Catholic church in the new emphasis on ritual. For Separatists, the only two important sacraments were baptism, especially of infants, and communion; instead of ritual and ceremony, they wanted long, erudite sermons and Bibles instead of prayerbooks. Yet, once on their own, these early settlers were as intolerant of those with differing religious beliefs as Bishop Laud and the Church of England had been of them. Quakers were especially anathematized, because they denounced baptism as "a relic of popery," and Connecticut's law against "Heretics, Infidels and Quakers" (1657) was an invitation to the downright persecution of Quakers that became widespread in the colony.

With no hierarchy and no common creed, each Congregational church was autonomous—and still is. This is both a strength and a weakness, because the congregation controls everything from the choice of its minister on down, and a Congregational church is only as effective as the majority of its members decides. A colonial Congregational church was founded by the acceptance of a covenant—a compact with God—which the members and the minister drew up (often copied from that of another church), each member having made satisfactory public testimony to his or her regeneration or conversion to unsinful ways.

Early Connecticut Congregationalists believed that all men were sinners who could be saved only by the grace of God. Rejecting the doctrine of good works, as had Martin Luther when he accused the Roman Catholic church of "selling" salvation, Congregationalists believed that a man should go on doing good deeds in this world, but that good works were no guarantee of salvation. Like John Calvin, they believed in predestination—that from birth an unknown elect few were destined to be saved while all others were damned for their sins. A pious people, believing that the sole purpose of this life was to prepare for the life to come, whether or not they would be saved, the early Congregationalists carried their religious beliefs into civil and social dealings, with a minister directly behind them to make sure that they did. Although Congregational clergymen could not hold public office, they exerted enormous influence on those who did.

Congregationalism held that the individual had the right to worship according to his own conscience, developed by a strict interpretation of the word of God, found only in the Bible, and expressed through a congregation of like-minded men and women. (This matter of individual interpretation would come to the fore almost immediately after the Canaan Parish Congregational church was formed.) Hence, Congregationalists considered public education an absolute necessity; before any person could understand the teachings of the Bible for himself, he or she must at the very least be able to read and write. Accordingly, the 1650 Code of Laws provided that every town with 50 householders must have a schoolmaster to teach all the children. In practice, this put education into the hands of the local Congregational Society (the financial arm of a local church), which paid the schoolmaster's salary.

With its emphasis on the individual, Congregationalism was also responsible for Connecticut's town-meeting form of government, wherein every tax-paying citizen, who met the qualifications, had a voice in his local government. And, similarly, for untold years each Connecticut town had its individual representative in the General Assembly of the colonial and then the state legislature.

Long before Canaan Parish was thought of, both Congregationalism and the Colony of Connecticut had relaxed somewhat. As early as 1657, those unable or unwilling to testify publicly to conversion sought modification of church membership so that they might have their children baptized and, hence, perhaps "saved." After years of dispute, the General Assembly in 1669 authorized the now-famous Halfway Covenant for Congregational churches, which created a new class of church members. Those not "in full communion" might get "halfway" into the church by "owning" their baptismal covenant—that is, by reaffirming their own baptism as infants—and thus gain the privilege of having their children baptized. (These terms on church registers cause considerable confusion among amateur genealogists searching for ancestors.) Then in 1708 the Assembly ordered all Connecticut Congregational clergymen and lay representatives of the churches to meet at Saybrook and restate church discipline. With their powers and privileges (after 1699 no clergyman could be taxed), some ministers had become so high and mighty that they had hopelessly divided their congregations. The results of this meeting were the three documents that made up the Saybrook Platform. One of the three was the "Fifteen Articles," which provided for regional "Associations" of churches and regional "Consociations" of pastors and elders. While only the Congregation had the right to discipline its members, Consociations could be called in to advise local churches. I emphasize this here because the Consociation and the Association of Fairfield County West were frequently on the Canaan Parish scene settling disputes.

Meanwhile, before the Saybrook Platform was adopted, Connecticut had had some religious toleration forced upon it. A 1675 law temporarily relieved Quakers of fines for nonattendance at Congregational worship services, but stopped persecution only briefly. Fourteen years later, in England William and Mary proclaimed freedom of worship for all Protestant sects—except the Unitarian. Connecticut officially ignored this proclamation, but a

Methodist church was founded in Groton in 1705 and a Church of England church at Stratford in 1707. But Connecticut went right on taxing every property owner for the support of the Congregational churches, and complaints of intolerance grew.

In the fall of 1705, Queen Anne meeting with her Privy Council annulled the colony's 1657 law against "Heretics, Infidels and Quakers" (which all along had run "contrary to the laws of this Realme) and on receipt of this dictum Connecticut had to repeal the act. Then, in May 1708, it went a step farther by acknowledging the existence of William and Mary's 1689 Toleration Act. "Such as soberly dissent from the way of worship and ministrie established by the antient laws of this government" were granted the liberty to worship God in their own way—provided they proved their sober dissent in a county court and continued to pay their Congregational taxes. Finally, as head of the Church of England, George II had heard enough of Connecticut's partiality to the Congregational Church. On orders from London, the colony's General Assembly in May 1727 passed a law admitting "the professors of the Church of England" to equal status with the Established (Congregational) Church. This meant that any man who proved he could "conveniently" attend (and actually did attend) a Church of England church could have the tax he paid to support the local Congregational minister turned over by the county collector to the nearest Church of England church. And a Church of England Society was given the power to levy taxes on its members for the support of its rector. Although none then existed, Quaker congregations were excused from contributing to the support of the established ministry, and exemption was extended to the Baptists in 1729. Hence, when Canaan Parish was formed in 1731, the Congregational was NOT Connecticut's only recognized church, and despite what has been published heretofore in New Canaan, all Canaan Parish residents did NOT have to attend local worship services.

As Congregationalism made concessions and religious tolerance was enforced, first Norwalk, then Stamford, broke one of the ties between Church and State. The freeholders of Norwalk in 1723 voted to separate town matters from those of the Congregational church, to set up for the first time two separate minute books, and to build a town house (a town hall) where the civil authorities and the voters could meet. In return (or revenge), Norwalk's Congregational church voted to exclude town meetings from its meeting house, where they had always been held. Stamford followed suit in 1731 (the year Canaan Parish was formed). But in both towns, the schools continued to be run by the Congregational societies.

Plans for a Parish

In this shifting scene and murky religious atmosphere, plans for Canaan Parish were formulated. The parish would have to be Congregational; the law made no other provision then. This was the Colony of Connecticut, not England, and although the Church of England and the Baptists could form churches, a parish could be set off within a town—two towns in the case of Canaan Parish—only for support of a Congregational church and a Congregational minister.

When the people living in northwestern Norwalk and northeastern Stamford came up with a definite proposal for parish status, Norwalk raised no objections; Stamford voted "No," apparently not wanting to lose any church revenues. That was in December 1730. Despite the negative, the settlers went ahead and in the next four months precisely plotted the area they proposed to include in the new parish they planned to call Canaan. Neither then nor in later years did anyone record when, how, and why "Canaan" was chosen as the parish's name. Despite their heavy reliance on the Old Testament, Congregationalists were not obliged to give parishes Biblical names—witness Middlesex (now Darien), Stanwich (part of Greenwich), and Wilton, three nearby parishes which took English names.

In 1731 "Canaan" was just one of several easily identifiable regions within the proposed parish bounds. With few roads and no maps or large surveys, the earliest settlers described their land holdings by region rather than in degrees, rods, and feet. Upper Clapboard Hill, Silvermine, Merry Hill, Bald Hill, Upper Ponasses, Kellogg's East Ridge, Flat Ridge, Canoe Hill—all were definite geographical regions and not the vague designations you might suppose. As a regional name, "Canaan" first appears in 1713 on the Norwalk Land Records, Book 4, page 113. There John Abbott recorded the 35 acres laid out to him by the Proprietors "at

Benedict, John Fitch, Ebenezer Carter and "sundry others" in the northwest part of Norwalk and the northeast part of Stamford, the legislature granted "parish privileges and liberty of forming themselves into a society under the name of Canaan Parish." This meant that the heads of families within the parish bounds (a trifle larger than present New Canaan) were obligated to organize the Society of Canaan, composed of all Parish landowners, which had the right to tax every Society member to cover ecclesiastical expenses. That was all. The residents of Canaan Parish remained for all other purposes under the civil authorities of Norwalk and Stamford.

The founding of a Canaan Parish Congregational church was a matter for those men and women who, when the time came, would subscribe to a church covenant and join the church. But the Society's control of the church's purse strings (and hence a say in who would be minister) was to cause trouble, because ownership of Canaan Parish land, not church membership, determined who could vote in Society meetings, and by no means did all landowners become members of the church.

The Society of Canaan was organized on July 1, 1731, no one knows where, with 25 men on hand. The first order of business was to elect a three-man Society Committee—two chosen from Norwalk and one from Stamford, the proportion that would be almost always maintained. The next matter was to ask Norwalk and Stamford to provide the clerk of the Society with copies of their Lists of Estates that pertained to ownership of Canaan Parish land. Without this combined record, the Society could not know the total of the individual land valuations on which Society taxes would be laid.

John Bouton, one of the petitioners, lived on Weed Street on the Stamford side of the Parish; John Benedict lived in Silvermine, Ebenezer Carter on Clapboard Hill, and John Fitch at the foot of Canoe Hill, on the Norwalk side. But how many families made up the "sundry others" is something of a guess. One man who had seen the Society records before they burned in 1876 (they had been borrowed by Professor Samuel St. John to prepare his Centennial address of July 4 and were still in his house when it burned to the ground in October 1876) said Canaan Parish began with 47 families, 30 of whom lived on the Norwalk side. I think the figure was a bit above 50 and the Parish population 300 plus, but it's a hopeless job to sort out the early land, house, and genealogy records and come up with accurate figures for 1731.

Ten years later the 93 members of the Canaan Parish Congregational church came from 46 families with 27 different surnames—Benedict, Bouton, Carter, Davenport, Eells, Finch, Fitch, Green, Gregory, Hanford, Hoyt, Keeler, Lockwood, Marvin, Parkington, Prindle, Reed, Rusco, Seely, Seymour, Slauson, Smith, Stevens, Talmadge, Tuttle, Waterbury, and Weed. (You can find 21 of these surnames in the current telephone directory, but few are descendants of the original settlers.) Missing from this church

Canaan Parish was superimposed on parts of Stamford and Norwalk.

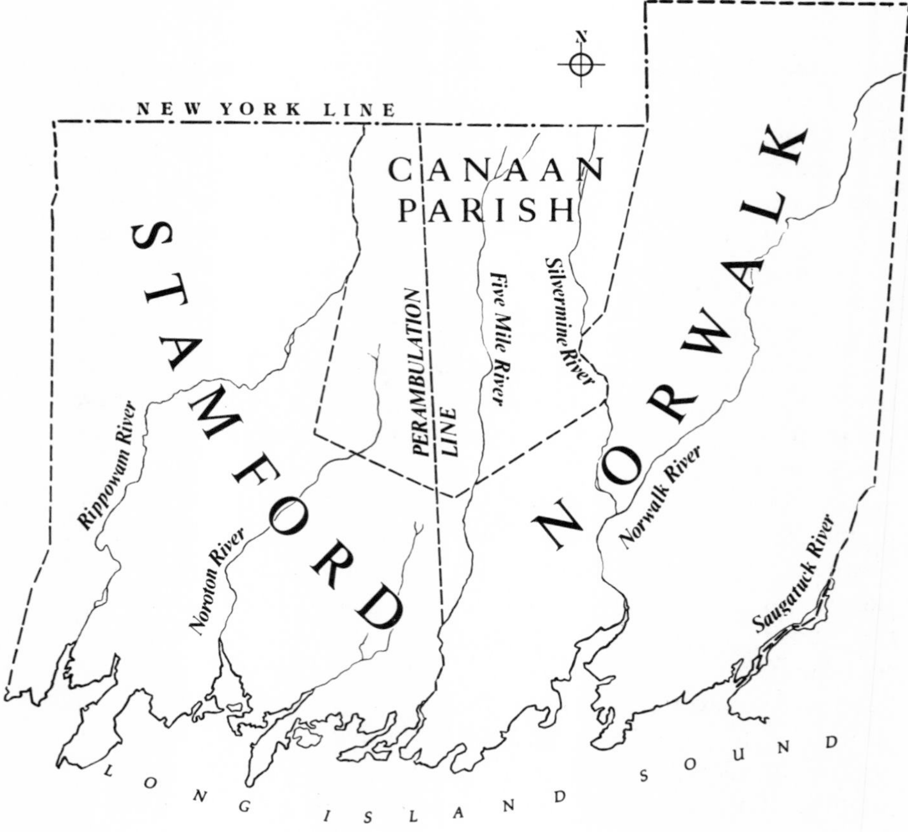

list were the Betts, Bolts, Comstocks, Kelloggs, and some other families who definitely were living in Canaan Parish in the earliest days.

These families, on the whole, were young couples in their 20's or early 30's, just starting their families, though John Bouton, one of the memorialists was in his 70's and John Fitch was 54. They were little different from the people who live in New Canaan today; they simply lived different kinds of lives. They loved and they hated and they vehemently took sides. They gossiped, they cheated, and they did many good deeds. Some people were kinder than others; some were physically or mentally handicapped; some, like Thomas Seymour, would live to a ripe old age; many would die young. Men followed a variety of "careers"; women had only one. There was no such thing as "made work"; from babyhood on, every member of a household had his or her chores to perform, so that the family might survive. Houses lacked our "modern conveniences," and in particular much chance for privacy. If to us the life led by the early settlers seems difficult and uncomfortable, they did not think so. Life in 18th-century Canaan Parish was no cruder than in the older shore towns, where many people imported small luxuries, some traveled by sea or land to trade, and a very few sent their sons to Yale.

As stated earlier, Stamford and Norwalk did not share a common religious, political, or economic inheritance, and the differences were to disrupt the Parish time and again. Other factors, too many to explain here, entered in, so I will generalize and say that the families on the Stamford side of Canaan Parish were the larger landowners, often by inheritance, and were likely to be prosperous farmers or mill owners; those on the Norwalk side were often craftsmen following a trade and lived on smaller farms that they had bought for themselves.

With only ecclesiastical matters to bring them together, people largely went their separate ways, and Canaan Parish quickly became a scattering of small regional settlements, each with its shoemaker, weaver, cooper, and carpenter, possibly a blacksmith, and perhaps a joiner and plasterer. Where water power was available, a region had both a grist and a saw mill. Most neighborhoods had a cider mill (in time some would have a still), and eventually there would be eleven regional or "district" schools.

CHAPTER 2

The First Two Decades, 1731-1751

When the General Assembly authorized Canaan Parish, it left nothing to chance. On the same day in May 1731 that the Parish was authorized, the Assembly passed "An Act directing how to proceed when it shall be necessary to build a Meeting House for Divine Worship," spelling out what steps were to be taken. Accordingly, in the fall the Society of Canaan petitioned the General Assembly to send a committee "to appoint, fix and ascertain" a suitable place on which Canaan Parish should erect its meeting house. The committee which the Assembly sent appeared on October 26 and apparently did nothing but put its stamp of approval on a site already chosen by the Society by a vote of 20 to 6. That site was a piece of common land belonging to Norwalk at the lower end of Haynes' Ridge, as lower Oenoke Ridge was then known. In today's terms, the first Congregational meeting house was located a few feet west of Park Street where St. John Place intersects.

Next, the Society voted on November 5 to build a 30 x 30-foot wooden meeting house "of a suitable heighth for one tere of galleries," and to pay for this laid a tax on all property owners of 10 pence on the pound—though Norwalk and Stamford had yet to provide Lists of Estates. The meeting house was promptly begun, yet in his annual report to the Assembly, the Society's Clerk stated on October 10, 1733, that while the walls were lathed and the doors hung, only the lower windows had been glazed. On hand was lime for plaster, glass for the windows, and timber "for ye seats and pulpit"—all of which suggests that after nearly two years of work the meeting house was an uncomfortable and drafty place in which to worship.

Previously, on April 3, 1732, Norwalk had granted "to the Inhabitants of Canaan Parish all ye common land where their Meeting House standeth, Thirty Rods from the meeting house, that is common and highway" for as long as they supported a meeting house "in said place." No one saw fit to draw up a deed describing accurately this 30-rod square, and as a result title to and the boundaries of this now unintelligible grant have been squabbled over a number of times by the Congregational Church, the town of New Canaan, and private citizens. All you can be sure of is that part of the northern boundary of the grant is beneath the south sill of the present (third) Congregational meeting house, and the sill was deliberately laid there so that the Church could retain title to the original grant of land. The western boundary seems to have been the stone wall that runs south from the meeting house to Seminary Street (in front of the present Christian Science church), while the east and south bounds are probably covered up by the paving on Park and Seminary streets.

God's Acre was never a part of Norwalk's grant of common land. Hence it was never a Parish common around which a village would grow. It was purchased on Jan. 26, 1773, for £3 from William Boult and Jonathan Husted, two Canaan Parish men, and deeded to the "Proprietors of the Parish of Canaan" to be a cemetery for "public benefit for the whole community." (Since there never were any "Proprietors" of Canaan Parish, this deed also has produced confusion about ownership of the land.) The money to buy God's Acre came from the Proprietors of Norwalk, to whom Capt. Samuel Hanford, then the Canaan Society's clerk, had applied for an addition to Canaan Parish's "burying place." In other words, some part of Norwalk's 1732 grant of common land had been used as a churchyard cemetery. And on that grant also stood the "House for the Entertaining of persons seized with infectious Distempers" (meaning smallpox), which Norwalk had ordered built when the meeting-house site was a half mile from the nearest dwelling house.

On the advice of the Fairfield West Consociation, the Rev. John Eells (1703-1785) of Milford arrived in May 1732 to preach on probation to the people of Canaan Parish. Ten months later he was "called" by the Society to become minister at a yearly salary of $313, according to a 100-year-old document. The Church of

Christ in Canaan Parish finally was formed on June 20, 1733, when Mr. Eells was ceremoniously installed by his brother clergymen, a covenant (long lost) was approved, and 13 men and 11 women transferred their memberships—13 from the Norwalk and 11 from the Stamford Congregational church. Two deacons—John Bouton and Thomas Talmadge—both from the Stamford side of the Parish were elected for life. Although a fair number of people joined the church later in the first year, for a variety of reasons other Canaan Parish adults chose not to become members of the new chuıch. The well-to-do Moses Comstock of Silvermine Hill worshiped in Wilton, while John Kellogg, who lived near the present Silvermine Tavern, was able to have the southeast bound of Canaan Parish moved a few feet north so that his house would be in Norwalk, where he attended church.

John Eells was 30 years old, a Yale graduate (class of 1724), married and the father of one child when he was installed as Canaan Parish's first minister. For the next 60 years, he and his successors would be the only college graduates in the community, looked up to on the score of their learning and office if not their

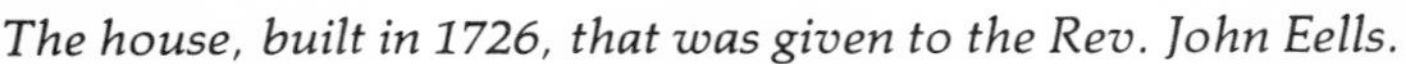
The house, built in 1726, that was given to the Rev. John Eells.

theology. On the same day the church was formed, the Society's Committee deeded to Eells the house that today is No. 477 Carter Street, the oldest house standing in New Canaan that can be documented. Together with 8½ acres of land, it had been given on Feb. 27, 1726, by John Benedict, Jr., to his son John, 3d, and house and land had been bought by the Society for £260 in the fall of 1732.

With a minister in residence, the people of Canaan Parish not only could listen to long Sunday sermons in their own meeting house, but they could be married and buried and have their children baptized by a clergyman even if they were only Halfway members of the church. And they could send their children to school. Since Canaan Parish had more than 25 families, at least one school must have been started and a schoolmaster hired at this time, though no record survives as to where that school was. All one knows is that by the 1730's school expenses were partly paid by a county tax of £2 on each £1,000 of a town's List of Estates as authorized by the Colony, and a receipt dated 1743 acknowledges Canaan Parish's share of the colony school funds paid over to Norwalk. This seems to prove that at least one school was functioning at that time on the Norwalk side of the Parish.

The Train Band

Besides Sunday services and Society meetings Parish men were brought together by the semiannual militia training day. Hard on the heels of the church's formation, the General Assembly in October 1733 approved the organization of a Canaan Parish Train Band—a trained militia company.

As the Congregational Church was formed by people transferring their memberships from the Norwalk and Stamford churches, so Canaan Parish's Train Band was made up of men who had drilled with Norwalk or Stamford militia companies. Since militia companies had the right to elect their officers, what the Assembly did in 1733 was to confirm the choice of Ebenezer Carter (from the Norwalk side of the Parish) as lieutenant and Ebenezer Seely (Stamford side) as ensign and order them to be so commissioned. When the Train Band was up to full strength in 1737, Carter was commissioned its captain.

Born in Deerfield, Mass., in 1697, Ebenezer Carter was one of the eight children of Samuel Carter captured by the Indians during the Deerfield massacre of 1704 and the only child to return and join his father in Norwalk. Set up in a home on Clapboard Hill, Ebenezer Carter became a large landowner on both sides of the highway now called Carter Street. He was one of the four named memorialists who petitioned for Canaan Parish, and he may have had a trade other than farmer, for he amassed considerable wealth for that day. When he died in 1775 he owned three slaves. (Ensign Ebenezer Seely also owned a slave.) It may come as something of a shock that Connecticut Congregationalists owned slaves, but many of the wealthier Canaan Parish families bought black men to help with the farm chores and black women to work indoors. Free Negroes as well as slaves also lived in the Parish, and though it took a town authorization, free blacks did own Parish land. Just to the north of Ebenezer Carter lived Robert Jacklin, a free Negro of Norwalk, who built his house in 1735.

By colonial law, every settlement had to have a Train Band to which all able-bodied men over 16 years of age supposedly belonged. Only magistrates and church officials were excused from the start, but in 1750 certain other occupations would be excused—justices of the peace, presidents and tutors and students at collegiate schools, physicians and surgeons, schoolmasters, mariners, and one grist miller in each town. This form of military "conscription" was accepted by the Canaan Parish men as a customary obligation for the protection of their land; after all, their ancestors had done the same for generations.

Although knowing only the threat of the Spanish Armada, England after the accession of Elizabeth I had maintained some national preparedness with her "trained bands" of civilians rather than a standing army—which would have had to be paid. Muster rolls were made up in every English shire, and the shire's lord lieutenant, a Crown appointee, was responsible for the turnout on appointed days of every man on his muster roll, properly armed according to his station in life. Plymouth and Massachusetts Bay colonies brought this kind of train-band preparedness to New England, sending with their first shiploads of settlers professional soldiers (Miles Standish was such) to organize and train the men in each new settlement in defense against menace from land or sea.

Connecticut adopted Massachusetts' procedure, and both Stamford and Norwalk had a Train Band organized and drilled by a resident paid professional captain. For a time, all Fairfield County Train Bands were in readiness more to defend their shores from the Dutch than to fight off Indian raids. Later, when the Colony of Connecticut called for troops to fight in King Philip's War and for the defense of Albany (1692), Stamford and Norwalk had quotas to fill, and men in the local Train Bands saw service a long way from home. Hence the Canaan Parish men knew they were being trained for possible military service outside their area, should a threat to the colony arise.

Following the military reorganization of 1740, only seven years after the Parish Train Band was formed, the Train Bands of Norwalk, Stamford, Greenwich, and Ridgefield were designated Connecticut's 9th Regiment of Militia, officered by a colonel, lieutenant colonel, major, and the captains of its 12 companies. Canaan Parish's Train Band became the 9th Regiment's 9th Company. Every four years a regimental muster was held, and a fine of £5 was levied against the captain of any company that failed to appear. Each local company, after three days' warning from its captain, trained twice a year—in March, April or May and in September, October or November. Canaan Parish (and later New Canaan) favored May and September, but where its militia trained is a mystery until, in 1778, it was deeded the parade ground on Parade Hill. What one does know is that Training Days were second only to Thanksgiving as a public holiday. (Christmas was not celebrated until the next century.)

Even under John Winthrop, that strict colonial governor, the early Massachusetts settlers had been able to turn Training Day into something akin to the fairs they had known in their English home towns. After drill ended, tugs-of-war, wrestling matches, and other exhibitions of strength by men and boys drew crowds of onlookers; stalls of goods for sale were set up; and despite official and clerical frowns, hard liquor could be had.

The Problems of John Eells

The Canaan Parish church was barely two years old when the elderly John Bouton, the senior deacon, began telling everyone who would listen that the Rev. John Eells preached false doctrine. Bouton claimed that what the minister preached could not be proven by Scripture. He was within his Congregational rights to interpret the Bible for himself, but few people who listened to his reasoning agreed. As a result, in January 1736, a Consociation of nine clergymen and eight "messengers" from other Fairfield County churches met to hear Mr. Eells' complaint that his character was being disparaged in such a way as to frustrate his ministry and foster "Destructive Divisions" among his parishioners.

As witnesses, John Eells summoned 22 people—both men and women—to testify as to what, when, and where Deacon Bouton had said against him. Person after person had his say until it came to James Hait, whose testimony Deacon Bouton wanted to have ruled inadmissible. James Hait, three previous witnesses had said, "seemed to be in a passion" every time Bouton's charges against Eells were repeated to him. Calling the Deacon "a Treacherous & falsehearted man and like unto Judas," Hait, it was said, had sworn he would kill Bouton "as soon as he would a rattlesnake." For good measure, Hait had added that John Bouton "was a very sorry dog." The "Reverent Sirs" of the Consociation, sitting at Caleb Benedict's house (near the top of Brushy Ridge), must have had quite a day.

I wish I knew more about James Hait, for he sounds like a colorful person. When and where he died is unknown, but he was born in 1708, a son of Joshua Hait, who was one of the earliest and largest landowners on the Stamford side of Canaan Parish. James Hait soon after his majority began acquiring hundreds of acres, mainly between West Road and Ponus Ridge, and he owned at least one saw and one grist mill. Never a Congregationalist, he would become an Anglican and his sons would become Loyalists, forfeiting their lands to Connecticut after the Revolution began. James Hait owned a slave, Cesar, who was on Oct. 7, 1744, admitted to full communion in the Canaan Parish church. Just before Cesar joined, the church had admitted James and Samuel Jacklin, free Negroes, to membership, and to them James Hait sold a 132-acre farm out of his Ponus Ridge tracts.

Back in 1736, after James Hait was allowed to testify, the Consociation ruled in favor of Mr. Eells, declaring Deacon

Bouton's interpretation of Scripture was "very uncharitable and forced," and ordered Bouton disciplined. Nevertheless, John Bouton continued his attacks on John Eells, and in 1738 the minister responded by barring Bouton from communion. This meant that Bouton had to resign as deacon. Then Mr. Eells barred all the Bouton sons from communion, insisting that he had the ministerial power to debar any parishioner when he thought fit without giving his reasons. (Whether it had any bearing on the situation, I don't know, but John Eells had lost his first wife in 1736 and shortly afterward married Abigail Comstock, the daughter of the wealthy Moses Comstock, and began a second family.) Twice more the Canaan Parish church summoned the Consociation to reconcile the differences, and then in 1741 the Society brought its weight to bear, the majority of its members insisting they were "dissatisfied with the Ministerial performance and conversation" of Mr. Eells. It could be that "evil-minded people" in the Society saw in the Church's dispute an opportunity to hire a younger minister at a lower salary, as Norwalk had once done. Or John Eells may well have decided that Christian ministry in Canaan Parish was a thankless job.

This time there was no reconciling of differences. The Consociation in June 1741 accepted John Eells' resignation and dissolved his ties with the Canaan church. While it said John Eells would do well to humble himself, the Consociation gave the whole Parish a good verbal dressing down. What now sounds like a tempest in a very small teapot in reality was something else. The "Great Awakening" was disrupting Canaan Parish, as it was the whole of Connecticut, with effects no one foresaw.

The Great Awakening

In the winter of 1734-35 the religious revival known as the "Great Awakening" swept across Connecticut from the Northampton, Mass., Congregational church of the Rev. Jonathan Edwards. Whatever the state of religion in individual churches, everyone soon was aware of the revival of Calvinist doctrines, as Edwards preached the need for spiritual rebirth, gruesomely describing the hell that awaited the unregenerate. Here was a call to return to the principles that the Congregational church had forsaken when it authorized the Halfway Covenant. And there was more to come.

Connecticut in 1740 was treated to the preaching of the English evangelist George Whitefield, a Calvinistic Methodist, who unlike his first mentors the Wesley brothers did not consider free will and good works as means to salvation. Like Jonathan Edwards, the sponsor of his Connecticut tour, Whitefield believed that spiritual rebirth came only by the free grace of God and by faith. As he had in England, Whitefield had tremendous appeal for unsophisticated rural people, who flocked to hear him. Before his effect wore thin, he had brought about many a spiritual rapture and physical swoon, which were thought to be manifestations of true conversion.

As a result of Edwards and Whitefield, Connecticut's Congregationalists became badly split. The newer rural parishes broke away to become the "New Lights," supporting the Awakening; the older, more settled and wealthier parishes became the "Old Lights," retaining the Halfway Covenant and scorning revivalism. (Of the "New Light" pastors, not one was a college graduate.) Everywhere, responses to revivalism were mixed, and for the first time in colony history congregations divided along class lines, which would have political effects.

In this part of Fairfield County the Congregational churches remained "Old Light," and Deacon Bouton, as I interpret the records, was trying to swing the Canaan Parish into the "New Light" ranks when he attacked the preaching of John Eells. It is very small proof, but some of John Bouton's children left Canaan Parish eventually to settle in Stockbridge, Mass., where Jonathan Edwards had gone as minister after he was ousted by his Northampton church.

If Congregational clergymen once had prayed for a true revival of religion, they were appalled by the excitement and unrest that now disrupted their parishioners. Connecticut was sufficiently alarmed by religious irregularities and fanatical excess to pass laws against such. And one man who was jailed for "great disorders" was the Rev. James Davenport, a follower of Whitefield, son of the late Stamford divine and half-brother of John Davenport, one of the 24 founders of the Canaan Parish church. This brought the Old Light—New Light controversy rather close to home.

Another religious development also affected both the Canaan Parish Church and the Society of Canaan. One quite unforeseen result of the "Great Awakening" was the rapid growth of the Church of England, in which the Anglican forms of worship offered peace and quiet instead of noisy revivalism, and the liturgy counteracted spiritual unrest.

In the winter of 1727-28, less than a year after Connecticut had granted the Church of England equal status with the Congregational church, two Anglican missionaries began preaching in Stamford and Norwalk. One of these was the Rev. Henry Caner, a Yale classmate of the Rev. John Eells. Then in 1734 (one year after the Canaan Parish church was formed), the Proprietors of Norwalk gave to the "Professors" of the Church of England, one rood of common land as a site for a meeting house and a burying ground, and there St. Paul's Church was founded in 1737 with Henry Caner as its first rector. St. John's Church would be formed by the Stamford Anglicans in 1741.

St. Paul's early records were burned when the British set fire to Norwalk in 1779, but the baptismal and marriage records from 1749 on survive for St. John's. And if the number of Canaan Parish families who appear on St. John's records is a valid clue to the numbers attending St. Paul's, then something between a fifth and a quarter of the Canaan Parish people became Anglicans. According to the 1727 law, this meant that these landowners could no longer be taxed to support the Canaan Parish Congregational church, and therefore the Society of Canaan had to increase its rates for support of the minister and the meeting house. Although his successor would bear the full brunt of this financial situation, it could well be that the Rev. John Eells was partly the victim of the Society's penny-pinching.

The Rev. Robert Silliman

To these "quarrelsome & contentious People. . . of difficult tempers and Disposition" in September 1741 came the Rev. Robert Silliman of Fairfield, another Yale graduate (class of 1737) to preach on trial. The Church and the Society had turned down two earlier candidates recommended by the Consociation, and though he was called by both in December, Mr. Silliman turned them down. Canaan Parish, he said, was badly divided, with many parishioners loyal to John Eells (who would live on in his Carter

Street house until he died in 1785). It took all the persuasion the area ministers could muster to make Silliman change his mind.

Robert Silliman was 25 years old when he came to Canaan Parish with his wife and baby son and was ordained as Canaan Parish's second minister on Feb. 2, 1742. Besides an annual salary of £100, he was given a "settlement" of £500 to be paid over five years. With £250 of this he bought two acres of land and a dwelling house close to the meeting house (the site of the present New Canaan firehouse) plus a tract of land across the highway (near Husted Lane) and more land with a barn (about where the Union Trust bank building stands on Main Street).

Years later, Mr. Silliman reported that, a little more than a year after he had been installed, "such tumults" arose that he was obliged to "send abroad" for assistance to quell them. No church, Society, or Consociation minutes survive to suggest what happened in Canaan Parish in 1743; all you have is the minister's statement that a "Party" thereafter "ransacked his character" and tried to prejudice people against him. Despite this, Robert Silliman was launched on a 30-year ministry that would see 156 men and women join the church and 290 become Halfway members by "owning their baptismal covenants." Nine hundred and seven children were baptized and 173 couples joined in marriage during Mr. Silliman's pastorate.

Years of Growth

The first two decades of Canaan Parish saw a certain amount of backing and filling. Despite the house for persons with "infectious Distempers," a number of the early settlers died in an epidemic thought now to have been flu. Even in those days people didn't stay put, and some of the first settlers moved away—to greener fields in Westchester County and to the new towns being formed in Litchfield County. One of these was Canaan, Conn., incorporated by the legislature in 1739. (The parsonage Mr. Silliman bought was the house built *c.* 1734 by David Marvin, who with his wife joined the church in 1737 but by 1741 had gone off to Goshen, N.Y.) But then, as now, new families were continually moving in, and the population of Canaan Parish rose to about 600 by 1751.

One impetus to settlement was the "Upper Division," the last distribution of Norwalk's common land, which began in 1738 and ended in 1745. During those seven years, all those people listed as having Proprietors' rights "pitched" on hundreds of acres of common land in what is now New Canaan, Wilton, Norwalk, and Westport. (When their turns came to choose the acres they were entitled to, many men found themselves with land far from home, and their exchanges and sales take up pages in Norwalk's land records that often have been misinterpreted as land speculation.)

In Canaan Parish about 900 acres of common land passed from the Proprietors of Norwalk into private ownership in the course of the "Upper Division." Depending on its location, an acre as valued by the Proprietors ranged from 5 shillings to £2, and a man could take up as many acres as his credit on the Proprietor's list allowed. About 360 of these common-land acres lay in three almost adjoining large tracts along and on both sides of Five Mile River, running through the heart of present-day New Canaan from East Avenue north to the reservoir. Here were sites for three saw, one grist, and one bark mill, which were built once the Five Mile River acres passed into private hands. As further encouragement to settlement, Norwalk during the seven "Upper Division" years laid out eight "highways" on its side of Canaan Parish, including Seminary Street, North Wilton Road, Silvermine Road from Valley Road to Canoe Hill, and Parade Hill, leading from Haynes (now Oenoke) Ridge down to a grist and a saw mill on Five Mile River.

During the "Upper Division," the Society of Canaan in 1743 belatedly claimed the six acres of common land Norwalk had voted in 1729 be granted whenever a minister was settled in his work. Known as the "Parsonage land" for nearly a century, this tract lies west of the intersection of West Road and Oenoke Ridge on the north side of West. It was sold by the Society to Mr. Silliman in 1746 as his personal property, just one more of the several tracts that he acquired.

Then and for decades to come, land was the measure of a man's wealth, and the amounts of land some early settlers acquired through purchase, Proprietors' rights, and inheritance was considerable. Most of the early settlers owned enough acres to suggest they were large-scale farmers, but very few were. Every settler, even the minister, farmed if he wanted to eat, and consequently each family had to have much more land than we do. Soil in most parts of the Parish was rocky and poor, and with 18th-century husbandry the yield per acre was low, obliging every man to work as much land as he could with whatever help he had from his sons, hired workmen, or slaves. Almost everyone kept animals, which needed pastureland, and every family had its woodlots where trees were felled for timber and, most important, for firewood. Consequently, each Canaan Parish settler hoped to own enough kinds of land to be almost self-sufficient. Each farmed, gardened, and raised poultry and animals in order to have staples to eat. Some, of course, farmed for profit, raising animals for sale and shipping butter, cheese, salted meat, and garden produce to market in Norwalk or Stamford. One crop the settlers did not raise for sale was wheat; Connecticut's export of this grain had been ruined some years before by the "wheat blast." Not until the 20th century was the contemporary "hunch" confirmed that the presence of barberry bushes caused the disease.

Although this bench in the Historical Society's Tool Museum belonged to a 19th-century shoemaker, some tools and one of the lasts date from the 18th century, when no distinction was made between a shoe for the left and the right foot.

Professor Samuel St. John in his Historical Address of July 4, 1876, stressed farming as Canaan Parish's 18th-century mainstay and thereby created a myth. Even for the first two decades of Canaan Parish history, there is good evidence that most men had a trade. David Marvin, whose house went to Mr. Silliman, was a shoemaker. So, too, was John Fitch, one of the four petitioners for the Parish and a founder of the Church. In 1737, "for love and affection" he deeded to his son 38 acres of farmland on Upper Clapboard Hill, including in his gift "my shoemaker's shop." This son, Theophilus, was not only a shoemaker but started a tannery. Eliphalet and Eleazer Slawson, on upper West Road, were grist millers; so were the Benedicts of Brushy Ridge. The Bolts, the Stevens, and later some of the Hanfords were weavers. Perhaps the most unusual trade was that of Samuel Bartlett, a grandson of William Haynes, who made a business of buying or rounding up horses—this area was famous for its wild horses—which he drove to ports as far off as Newport, R.I., to be shipped to the West Indies.

A weaver might pay for his family's shoes with some cloth that he wove and vice versa for the shoemaker, but the families in early Canaan Parish never subsisted on barter alone. Money would be scarce during periods of inflation, but hard money changed hands regularly. Not only land but church rates, town taxes, court fines, and probate fees had to be paid in coin. One paid a carpenter, a blacksmith, a plasterer, the schoolmaster, and the minister with cash, and it was money from sales of butter or shoes in the port towns that went to buy such luxuries as tea, books, ribbons, and gin. But the value of money was about to be dealt a blow.

The Louisburg Expedition

In 1744, when the Canaan Parish Train Band was 11 years old, Governor Jonathan Law promised 500 Connecticut men for the military expedition being planned by Governor William Shirley of Massachusetts against the French fortress of Louisburg. Built by France at enormous expense as a North American Gibraltar, Louisburg on Cape Breton Island, Nova Scotia, had also become the base for French privateers that preyed on colonial fishing and trading vessels. The English settlers in North America had good reason to say "Capture Louisburg and you capture Canada." Convinced that as long as Louisburg was in French hands, the very existence of the New England colonies was at stake, Shirley won support for a daring attack, although England could spare none of her troops since she was busy fighting the War of the Austrian Succession. Hence, what came to be called King George's War, the third of the French and Indian campaigns, was strictly a New England affair.

Settlers in the northern colonies saw the proposed expedition as a religious war—their chance to avenge neighbors cut down earlier by the Roman Catholic French and the Indians. Connecticut settlers were lukewarm. Col. Jonathan Hait of Stamford could report to Governor Law on July 5, 1744, that he had "enlisted & Imprest one Hundred good Effective men" from the companies of the 9th Militia. Actually only 27 of these men had volunteered; the other 73 had been impressed—including all eight Canaan Parish men who made up the quota for the 9th Company.

Daniel Benedict, Person Bishop, William Bolt, John Finch, Jr., Elijah Green, Ebenezer Smith, David Stevens, Jr., and Daniel Tuttle were young men in their twenties and unmarried, except Green, when they set off from Canaan Parish to attack Louisburg. In the wake of the main fleet out of Boston, Connecticut troops sailed in April 1745 for a rendezvous at Canso, Nova Scotia, and it may well be that the Canaan Parish militiamen were aboard the *Jane,* a vessel out of Norwalk, which was one of the seven Connecticut transports under escort of the *Defence,* the colony's armed sloop. Despite support from a fleet of British merchantmen, commanded by Sir Peter Warren, the *Jane* was later sunk in an engagement off Louisburg, and her three Norwalk owners subsequently had to be indemnified.

Bombardment and attack began in May and seven weeks later, on July 17, 1745, Louisburg fell to the small force of poorly equipped colonists. Norwalk celebrated by firing a cannon when news finally reached here; British army officers were unbelieving. It was the first military engagement the American colonists had won on their own, and as far as the colonists were concerned, they had preserved New England and colonial shipping for the mother country.

All eight men from the Canaan Parish Train Band returned unharmed, though they were gone from home for more than a year. England was so short of troops that they had been forced to stay on through the winter at Louisburg, helping to garrison the fort they had captured. You can imagine the anger aroused by the news in 1748 that England had returned Louisburg to France by the Treaty of Aix-la-Chapelle. To Connecticut men, this meant that their mother country had simply written off their military prowess and they were back where they had started, trying to build up their trade under the guns and ships of the French fortress. Bitterness against England ran deep and was the base upon which were piled resentments at later British acts, leading to the American Revolution.

For Connecticut, the cost of the Louisburg expedition in lives lost, provisions, and money was considerable. To pay her share, the colony had issued thousands of pounds of paper money, and although a special tax was laid at the time of each printing, revenue from the tax was never enough to retire an issue when it came due. When the total of Lists of Estates for all the Connecticut towns was less than £1,000,000, Connecticut had some £166,000 of new bills on top of £340,000 public debt in old tenor bills. When England finally paid the colony £28,000 in gold toward its Louisburg expenses, she stipulated the money must be used to call in the paper currency. By the time the bills were paid off at 11 percent of face value, a depression had set in and inflation was rampant. Prices rose much faster than wages, and in Wilton the minister's salary was raised from £55 to £650 to give him his old purchasing power. In Canaan Parish, the Rev. Robert Silliman in 1749 was paying £21 per acre for land, whereas in 1741 he had paid but £14.

Connecticut was also fast losing its overseas trade as merchants in England and Ireland refused to accept colony bills in payment of goods. As a result, Rhode Island with her sound currency bought up Connecticut goods for sale overseas and also syphoned off much of Connecticut's intercolony trade—all of which affected Stamford's and Norwalk's trade, and hence the people in Canaan Parish.

Houses

Like the others who were children when Canaan Parish was organized, the veterans of Louisburg soon married and started families of their own. The houses they built were, by and large, two-story dwellings in the Colonial or Georgian Style, perhaps with a lean-to addition at the rear. Rectangular in shape and made of shingles or clapboards, such houses were built around a central chimney, which allowed for three fireplaces on the ground floor and two in the bedrooms on the floor above. In larger houses, the front door was centered on the long side, which faced the road, with two windows on either side and five above. On the ground floor were at least three rooms—a parlor, a master bedroom, and the keeping room (the kitchen which doubled as a family room)—

Fireplace in the keeping room of the Hanford-Silliman House, built c.1764.

but their layout depended on the location of the family's well, which usually was on the south side of the house, just outside the keeping room.

Whether it was to one side of the front door or across the back of the house, the keeping room was the center of family life. There mother and daughters prepared and cooked food, did the laundry, made the wearing apparel, dipped candles, spun yarn, and made butter and cheese. There the father and his sons repaired harnesses and cared for their tools after tending to the livestock and bringing in the daily supply of water and wood. Until well into the 19th century, the two sessions of the district schools were geared to planting and harvesting, when all children were needed at home. Girls as well as boys worked in the fields, drove cows to pasture, collected apples for cider-making, and gathered nuts, and girls helped their mothers tend the family garden as well as learning to cook and sew.

Perhaps as many as 35 houses survive in New Canaan from the pre-Revolutionary days, though few resemble their original states. Men who grew wealthy from the shoe trade added a third story to a Colonial house, complete with Gothic Revival trim and, of course, porches. The advent of indoor plumbing and electricity (and the need to build closets) resulted in much interior remodeling, which often eliminated the original center chimney. Still, when an inventory exists in the 18th-century probate records, one can determine how many rooms a house originally had, because a deceased man's personal estate was inventoried and priced room by room—parlor, bedroom, kitchen, storeroom. From such inventories one knows whether a man was well-to-do or not—items of silver as well as pewter and wood, looking glasses, diapers (linen tablecloths)—and what trade he followed—looms for a weaver, grain and flour for a miller, charts and spyglass for a mariner—though the Colonial house on which we set such store today was likely as not to be valued at no more than $150. Land carried a quite different figure.

By 1750, when Canaan Parish's population was approaching 600, the first Congregational meeting house was proving too small for the growing number of parishioners, and construction of a larger one was about to begin.

CHAPTER 3

Fighting and Feuding, 1751-1771

In 1752 the new year began on January 1, when the British dominions adopted the Gregorian calendar as ordered by Parliament the year before. Theretofore, the new year began on March 25, Lady Day, causing the awkward doubledating of records between January 1 and March 24 of any year—for example, Feb. 16, 1733/34. The Julian or Old Style calendar by 1752 had accumulated an 11-day lag, so to bring it abreast of the astronomical year, 11 days had to be "suppressed." This was done in September, when September 2 was followed by September 14, so that in 1752 no one was born or died and no deed was dated on September 3 through September 13.

Also in 1752, after two years of work, the second Canaan Parish Congregational meeting house was ready for occupancy. Built a little north and east of the first small structure and facing what now is God's Acre, this meeting house was 50 feet long and 40 feet wide, of sufficient height to hold one tier of galleries, though neither galleries nor steeple were built for several decades. The second meeting house had large double doors on the front and two sides, with one window on either side and three above the front portal, two to the sides and five above the doors on the sides. Since the meeting house was unheated, a 21 × 16-foot Society House had been built nearby. In it was a fireplace at which worshipers could warm themselves between the long morning and afternoon services and heat whatever food they had brought for a midday meal.

Norwalk and Stamford, and hence Canaan Parish, of course adopted the New Style calendar, but precious little survives to tie either town to the larger history of the day. Nevertheless, as I interpret the records, everything of importance that occurred in Canaan Parish between 1751 and 1771 stemmed from outside events. This is certainly true of the most bizarre episode to happen in Canaan Parish (or in New Canaan), and it began the summer of 1753.

By then, Norwalk's selectmen had elected Daniel Keeler one of the town's tavernkeepers, sworn to uphold the laws, with bond posted with a colony official to make sure that he did. Tavern-keeper was a post and something of an honor for a man or a woman of good character (both Norwalk and Stamford had widow tavernkeepers), and Daniel Keeler was an upright man who had been a founding member of the Canaan Parish church. By law, a tavern had to be located on a through road, to provide food and lodging for travelers and feed and stalls for their mounts. Keeler's house (now gone) was well situated for a tavern, standing on Smith Ridge near where North Wilton Road leads eastward to Wilton and near where Michigan Road, like Smith Ridge, led to the Province of New York.

Daniel Keeler and the Counterfeiters

It was in August 1753 that Daniel Keeler was approached by David Sanford, who lived over the colony line in Salem, N.Y., and asked to ride to Noroton with an extra horse to "carry" a stranger he would meet there to Sanford's house. That man was named Zephaniah Stevens. From Stevens' conversation on the long ride and from something he observed at Sanford's house, Daniel Keeler returned home suspicious that a gang of counter-feiters was at work in Salem, practically on the Canaan Parish bounds.

Keeler was well aware that counterfeit bills, especially 20- and 40-shilling New York notes of the 1737 issue, were the bane of the Colony and of every man in trade. Ever since the Louisburg expedition and devaluation of Connecticut money, counterfeiting of bills of other colonies had become a profitable if risky "trade." And Daniel Keeler knew from the general talk that, outside the port towns, taverns were the favorite butts of counterfeiters. A man could pay his bill with a bad note and ride off without leaving a trace. The name of Zephaniah Stevens meant nothing to Keeler, nor did the name Sullivan Brown, who Keeler soon learned was also at Sanford's house. "Sullivan Brown," so it turned out, was just one more alias of Owen Sullivan, and Keeler and everyone else who read a newspaper had heard of him. New York City had a price on his head.

Said to have fought with Massachusetts troops at Louisburg, Owen Sullivan was a Boston jeweler until his wife got drunk and let it be known that counterfeiting, not goldsmithing, was responsible for their living in high style. Sullivan was arrested, Aug. 31, 1748, tried and acquitted, though he was made to stand for two hours in the Boston pillory and given 20 stripes (lashes with a whip). Understandably, Sullivan removed himself to Rhode Island, where he developed a complicated system for distributing his wares. A skilled engraver, Sullivan could easily duplicate a set of two plates (one for each side) for whatever bill he was counterfeiting. Then, making use of a number of accomplices, he gave each man just one set of plates. The result was that each accomplice, after providing his own ink, paper, and crude press, had notes of a different denomination to pass off. (How Sullivan made his profit, I'm not sure.) Thus it wasn't long before Rhode Island, New Hampshire, and New York counterfeits in various denominations and of various issues were turning up everywhere. (With their declining face value, Connecticut bills were not counterfeited.)

Not until August 1752 was Sullivan caught in Rhode Island with nine of his accomplices, one of whom turned King's evidence. That man and Owen Sullivan were convicted on October 9 and sentenced according to the law—which meant they were to be branded with a huge "C" on each cheek and have their ears cut off. (Connecticut's penalty for counterfeiting was the same.) Sullivan must have been a man of considerable charm—of "good address" the old records say—for so many people "favored" him that he had the freedom of the Providence jail. So, while his accomplice was being "cropped," Sullivan walked out. But for no given reason, he soon turned himself in and suffered the penalties, which made him a decidedly marked man.

Early in 1753 Sullivan broke jail and disappeared. By August he was holed up at David Sanford's in Salem, using his Sullivan

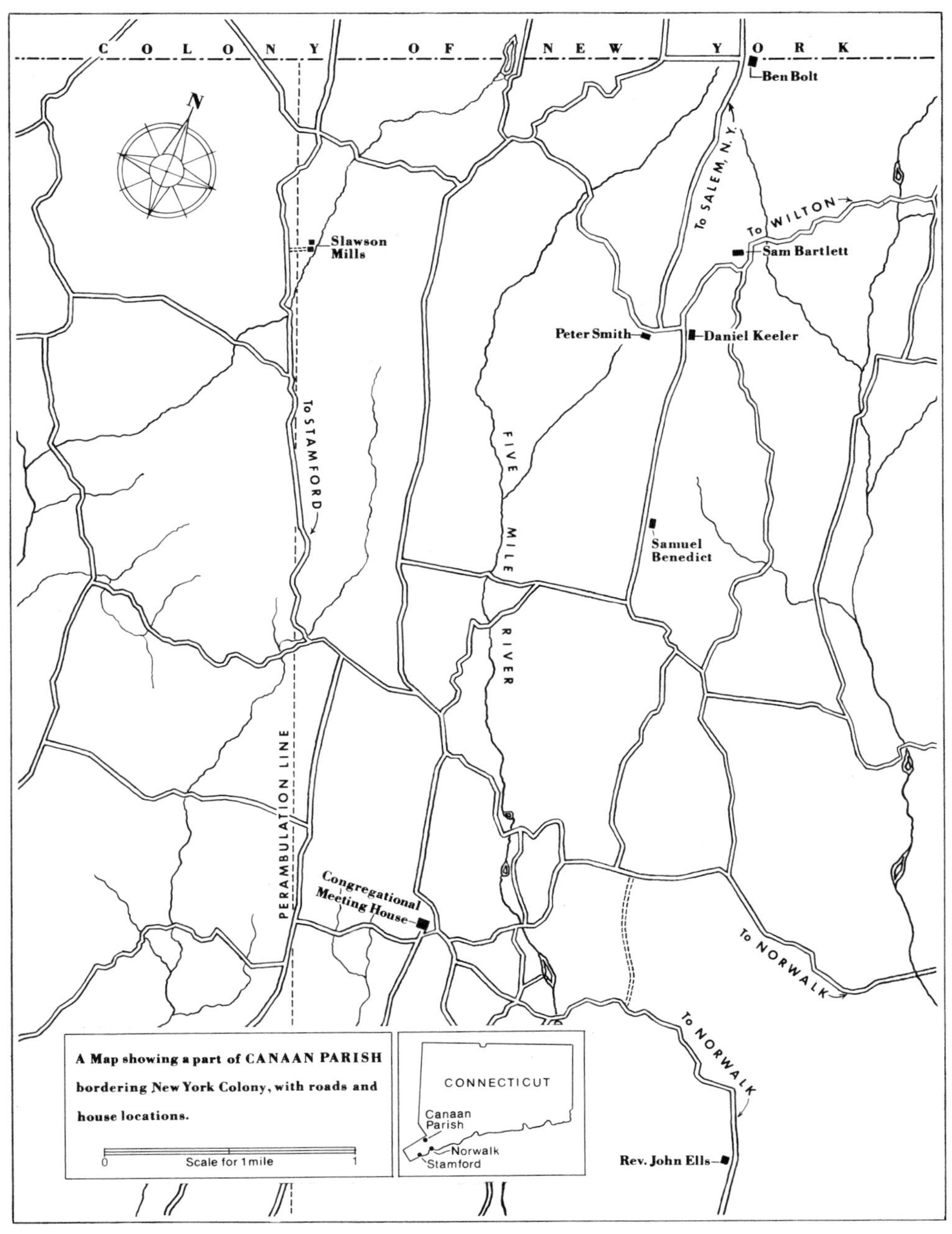

Daniel Keeler's house stood on present-day North Wilton Road and Peter Smith's house still stands on Michigan Road.

Brown alias, and counterfeits were turning up at Woodbury, at Greenwich, and at Danbury, where bills were passed through a tavernkeeper. Then Daniel Keeler was approached by Zephaniah Stevens. If Keeler would rent him a room in which to work, Stevens would make him a partner in counterfeiting. Keeler refused—a tavern, he said, was too public a place and the scheme would become known—but he was soon aware that the counterfeiter was somewhere in the neighborhood. What Keeler did not know was that Owen Sullivan had cleared out of Salem and his accomplices had scattered, Stevens bringing to Canaan Parish his set of plates for £8 Rhode Island notes.

Daniel Keeler took his knowledge and his suspicions to the Norwalk authorities, who assured him it was his duty to his King to run down the criminals. But, he was warned, counterfeiters were dangerous men who would stop at nothing if their suspicions were aroused, and if he were not careful Keeler might be risking his life and his family's safety. And, not fully convinced, the authorities told Keeler he must produce positive evidence or he would bring the law on himself if he accused innocent men.

Asking questions, keeping his eyes open, picking up gossip at his tavern and in Norwalk, Keeler learned that Zephaniah Stevens was being concealed by Peter Smith, a weaver, who lived at what is now No. 64 Michigan Road. Two frequent visitors at Smith's were Eleazer and Eliphalet Slauson, brothers from the Stamford side of the Parish, who owned much land and two prosperous mills off West Road. Somehow involved in the scheme also was Ichabod Doolittle, a Norwalk blacksmith, who regularly bought rum at the tavern. One man who declined to join the "club," as they called it—and consequently had his life threatened—was Keeler's son-in-law, Abram Hoyt, a schoolteacher.

Then, on Dec. 25, 1753, seeing Peter Smith ride away, Keeler dared search Smith's house. What he found were Stevens' saddlebags, paper, lampblack to make ink, and in the fireplace, only partially burned, a stack of counterfeit bills. Since Stevens was nowhere in hiding, Keeler had to guess that Peter Smith had lost his nerve, tried to burn his share of the bills, and was on the point of turning Stevens out.

When he went to Norwalk to be reelected a tavernkeeper on the first Monday of January 1754, Daniel Keeler privately informed a

Norwalk judge of what he had discovered, stressing that Stevens was set to flee if he hadn't already gone.

Since counterfeiting was a crime against the colony, the sheriff of Fairfield County then took charge. That is why on Jan. 8, 1754, the sheriff's Norwalk deputies seized Stevens and Peter Smith at Smith's house on the Norwalk side of Canaan Parish, while the Stamford deputy sheriffs arrested the Slauson brothers over on West Road. (Unfamiliar with Canaan Parish history, some writers have reported the arrests as two separate cases of counterfeiting.) With relatives and friends to post bond, the three Canaan Parish men were soon free on bail. Stevens, as a "foreigner" to Connecticut, was not entitled to bail and so was jailed at the county seat in Fairfield. Daniel Keeler was the key witness at the trial held the next month.

From what you can read in old papers at Congregational House in Hartford, the trial must have been a disorderly shouting match, with accusations flying between prisoner and witnesses. Because he had repented and burned his counterfeit bills (and because he was the son of a wealthy man), Peter Smith was let off with a £100 fine; the Slausons lost much of their real property, which (as you can read in the Stamford land records) was confiscated and sold to repay those whom the brothers had defrauded with counterfeit. Stevens was convicted, branded, and cropped. But the story doesn't end there.

David Sanford and the others who had continued the counterfeiting at Salem had been captured elsewhere in Connecticut and punished for defrauding the colony. By March 1754 all had broken out of their respective jails and resumed work at Sanford's place. They were also bent on revenge against everyone who had helped to turn them in. In short time they had Ridgefield and Wilton terrified by nightly raids, some along the Canaan Parish-Wilton border, which saw fences and fields set afire and barns burned to the ground with the cattle inside. The whole countryside was worn out from night watches and fire fighting until a posse of young men, ignoring the Colony line, ran Sanford and some of his gang to earth in Salem. When Wilton petitioned the General Assembly in May 1754 to capture the rest of the "club," that parish estimated her damages at £4,000 and valued the time her men had lost from "spring husbandry" at £100 per day.

Once David Sanford was again in jail, Peter Smith and the Slausons sought their revenge on Daniel Keeler. The tavernkeeper, they insinuated, was as guilty as they and had been one of Zephaniah Stevens' counterfeiting ring. Since all three were convicted men, by law they could not give evidence to a grand jury, so instead they accused Keeler of breaking church law. He had, they kept saying, broken the 8th and 9th Commandments—as a counterfeiter he had stolen and he had borne false witness against his neighbors. The Rev. Robert Silliman, as Canaan Parish's minister, tolerated no lawbreakers, and more than once he had reported to the grand jury those he suspected of flouting civil law. Since he could not ignore charges of this sort against a parishioner, he laid the rumors before a church committee. Once the committee had decided that the charges should be pressed, Daniel Keeler was summoned in October to defend himself before the whole Canaan Parish church.

The first hearing was quite an occasion. Some 20 persons testified for or against Keeler, including several from outside the Parish, while Mr. Silliman, acting as scribe, took down their "evidence." (The records still survive.) Nothing conclusive came from this or a second hearing, and so many people lost interest in the case that when a third hearing was held in December the church members on hand considered themselves too few to decide Keeler's guilt or innocence. On Keeler's insistence, the Consociation of Fairfield County West was called to Canaan Parish in January 1755. It convicted him on both charges, ignoring the evidence in his favor and relying on statements made by David Sanford's wife, which Mr. Silliman had ridden to Salem to take down. (These were later proved to be a pack of lies.)

As punishment, Daniel Keeler was denied his church rights until such time as he made public confession of his sins—which he was not about to do. Presumably, he lost his good character and hence his tavernkeeper's post, though the records aren't clear about that. One year later, in January 1756, after patient persistence, Daniel Keeler was able to reconvene the Consociation and get into the record the letter he had from the Norwalk man who had advised him how to proceed against the counterfeiters. The man who wrote the letter was Thomas Fitch, and Thomas Fitch was then governor of Connecticut. The Consociation was not about to question the Governor's testimony, and Daniel Keeler was promptly cleared.

The French and Indian Wars

Before this second Consociation hearing took place, Canaan Parish had become involved in much larger concerns than the possible falsehoods of one resident. The French and Indian wars had resumed, and 15 men from the Parish Train Band had been campaigning hundreds of miles from home.

The muster rolls of the companies Connecticut raised during the later French and Indian wars are not always complete, and except for officers they do not include the names of the towns from which men came. Adding to the problem of who served from where is the duplication of names, so that without exhaustive research who can say at this late date which, if any, of the several John Benedicts, James Haits, and Nehemiah Benedicts, for example, were Canaan Parish men. Hence my lists have been pieced together roughly from a variety of sources.

Connecticut, in March 1755, had raised 1,000 men, organized in two regiments of six companies each, as its quota of colonials to support the British expedition against Crown Point under the command of Sir William Johnson. But defeats and ambushes mounted, and by August of that year Governor Fitch was calling for 500 additional troops. Early in September 14 Canaan Parish men enlisted (or they may have been "impressed") in the newly formed 5th Company, which was sent north to be attached to the 4th Connecticut Regiment.

In command of the 5th Company was Captain Samuel Hanford, who had been elected ensign (1747) and captain (1750) of Canaan Parish's 9th Militia Company. Born in 1710, Hanford was a grandson of the Rev. Thomas Hanford, Norwalk's first Congregational minister, and of William Haynes, who had once owned so much Canaan Parish land. By the time of the French and Indian wars, Hanford families were solidly settled on Hanford acres, which extended along Main Street from present Maple Street to Old Norwalk Road, running eastward to take in two mill sites on Five Mile River and even, in places, as far east as Carter Street. For the

1755 expedition, Samuel Hanford was commissioned captain of the 5th Company in August, his first lieutenant being Joseph Hait of Stamford and his second lieutenant, a Danbury man.

Arriving too late for the Battle of Lake George, the 5th Company possibly was sent to Fort William Henry, which Johnson had begun to build. Cold weather soon set in; supplies, especially bread, were low; and morale among the colonial troops was poor. When ordered to begin the advance on Crown Point, Connecticut troops, according to Johnson's account, refused to march. I can find no record of just where the 5th Company went or whether it refused to attack. Since no winter campaign was to be undertaken, the bulk of the Canaan Parish men received their discharges between December 7 and 12, 1755, two others having been allowed to return home earlier.

In 1756, when the war spread to Europe and the planned campaign in America failed to take place, only two Canaan Parish men saw service, again with the 5th Company. Though there was little military activity except the fall of Oswego to the French, his Majesty's troops were in the news as victims of counterfeiting. Owen Sullivan was again at work, duping the British regulars into exchanging the bills in which they were paid for his New York counterfeits. (Later he would brag that he had passed off £1,600 in bad bills in this way in one day.) But the Owen Sullivan story was about to end.

Two months after Daniel Keeler had been cleared, Sullivan was at last captured, in March 1756. Eliphalet Beecher, a New Haven man returning from New York colony on private business in December 1755, had come on a gang of counterfeiters, all cropped, operating in Dutchess County on Connecticut's western border. Convinced that the leader, who called himself Johnson, was Owen Sullivan, Beecher went to New York City and on December 29 obtained arrest warrants signed by Chief Justice James Delaney and two other judges of the Supreme Court. With these in hand, he obtained from Connecticut's General Assembly authority to track down Sullivan and the funds to pay the men whose help he would need. When a Dutchess County justice of the peace contested Beecher's two impressive papers of authority, the Connecticut General Assembly had Governor Fitch write to Sir Charles Hardy, governor of New York, insisting that Hardy direct all local

New York authorities to cooperate with Beecher. Canaan Parish learned all the details from the Norwalk and Stamford deputies to the Assembly, whom they had helped to elect.

Not until March 13, 1756, did Beecher flush Sullivan from his hiding place—a minute room under the dirt floor of a house at Dover, N.Y. (Small as his quarters were, Sullivan had fitted them up with a tiny fireplace, which he vented with a flue into the house's chimney.) By the day of the arrest, Beecher had been in the saddle 95 days in pursuit of his quarry, and among his 11-man posse was Timothy Delavan, one of the witnesses at the Daniel Keeler hearing, who recently had moved from Canaan Parish to Courtland Manor, N.Y. This manhunt cost Connecticut £134:3:0, but it put an end to serious counterfeiting—and to Owen Sullivan.

Taken by Beecher to jail in New Haven, Sullivan was then sent under heavy guard to New York City, which twice had publicly accused him of crime. There he was sentenced to be hanged. He was "turned off" on May 10, 1756, but not before he had charmed "reporters" for the *New York Gazette: or the Weekly Post-Boy* and the *New-York Mercury*, both of which printed some rather lurid accounts of the case. Sullivan freely named the currencies he had counterfeited, amounting to some £40,000, but when asked which issues of New York bills he had copied, he would say only "You must find that out by your learning." Loyal to the end, he refused to name even one of his 29 accomplices, though he advised them all to destroy their plates and "quit the Money-making business." These and other details of the Sullivan story could be read in one or two Norwalk and Stamford shops, where weekly issues of New York papers were hung up for customers to read.

In 1757, when campaigning against the French was resumed, John Campbell, Earl of Loudon, was in command of the British forces, and Connecticut in the spring had sent 1,400 men in one regiment of 10 companies to support his regulars. Early in August came urgent appeals from the commanders at Albany and Fort Edward for reinforcements—Fort William Henry, which Johnson had built, was under seige by the French. Responding to Governor Fitch's "Alarm for the Relief of Fort William Henry and Places adjacent," 25 Canaan Parish men went off in Captain Samuel Hanford's 5th Company, while seven others joined two other Alarm companies. All told, nearly 5,000 Connecticut militiamen were rushed to upper New York.

Of the 102 men in Hanford's company, the record says that 100 rode horses out of Norwalk. Since this was August when horses were needed at home and since the 5th Company were militiamen, not cavalry, three men were dispatched to bring back the horses (probably from Albany, which seems to have been their first destination). One of the three was Stephen St. John (perhaps of Canaan Parish), who was credited with nine days of service. The men in the 5th Company were on active duty between 16 and 18 days, for Fort William Henry had surrendered on August 9, before reinforcements could reach it.

Waiting for orders to attack Louisburg, that northern fortress, the Earl of Loudon brought some of his regulars to winter on the Connecticut coast. In November 1757 Stamford had 250 of Colonel Fraser's Highland Battalion quartered on it (plus 17 women and 9 children), while Norwalk had another 350 regulars wintering there. The expense to the two towns for some 600 extra persons was considerable, and each had to vote to lay a new tax of 1 penny to the pound on their Lists of Estates to pay the costs. Though no troops were quartered in Canaan Parish as far as anyone knows, the Parish people had to shoulder their share of the tax along with all other landowners. The money was used to buy firewood, bedding, and candles, to pay the rent of the houses where the troops were lodged, and in each town the British also commandeered buildings for a guardroom and a hospital. For all that it did, Stamford later collected from the Colony £369:13:4½ plus an extra £5:15:7, and Norwalk a total of £348:13:4½. Considerably higher bills were presented to Connecticut after the winter of 1758-59, when Norwalk and Stamford had the 48th Foot Regiment of British regulars quartered on them.

In addition to being reimbursed for expenditures by the Colony, the people of Norwalk and Stamford, including those in Canaan Parish, had profited for two winters from the needs of the British officers and troops for food, goods, and services. And for two winters the townsmen had rubbed shoulders with men from the mother country, though I can find no direct evidence of such contacts.

Long before the 48th Foot moved into winter quarters, some 30 Canaan Parish men had served for seven or eight months—from March or April into November 1758—in three companies of Connecticut's 4th Regiment. Under General Amherst (not Loudon) the British captured Louisburg, while the Connecticut 4th, assigned to James Abercrombie, Loudon's replacement, took part in the disastrous attack on Fort Ticonderoga. By then, a dozen of the Canaan Parish militia were veterans of earlier campaigns.

When in 1759 the British at last met with success and Quebec fell, only three Canaan Parish men seem to have been in service (April to December). Though some Stamford men were among the Connecticut troops with the British at Montreal when the war ended on Sept. 8, 1760, the two or three enlisted Canaan Parish soldiers were elsewhere. (The rolls and records for 1760 are very incomplete.) Simeon Hanford, Hezekiah Davenport, and Peter Finch (who may not be Canaan Parish's Peter Finch) belonged to the 9th Company of the 3d Regiment, captained by Thaddeus Mead of Norwalk. They saw action at Oswegatchie, N.Y., near the St. Lawrence, where in August Captain Mead died (perhaps killed in action) and Finch "in the trenches" had his right hand shot away by "a ball from enemies cannon." For this, the Connecticut General Assembly voted him £50 compensation the next year.

If he was indeed from Canaan Parish, then Finch is the only casualty I can discover among the possibly 80 Parish men who saw military service betweeen 1755 and 1760. Joseph Hoyt, who would be Canaan Parish's highest ranking officer during the Revolution, was wounded at Ticonderoga in July 1758, but he had yet to move to the Parish from Stamford. Although men of the same name lived here, the Jonathan Slauson and Ebenezer Weed "of Stamford," who were lost while serving in "the Navy," probably lived in Middlesex (Darien).

Who can say now what new ideas the Canaan Parish troops brought back from hitherto unknown places and men? And who knows what effects the wintering British troops had on the townspeople of this area? For whatever cause Canaan Parish by 1761 was ready for change, and one catalyst was Captain James Richards, master mariner.

Maritime Trade

Thanks to large British reimbursements in sterling, the Colony of Connecticut came through the French and Indian wars with sound currency and a small debt. By 1761, according to one authority, the New England and Middle Atlantic colonies were developing faster than any other Christianized area, with growth coming in all fields of endeavor. It was at this time that Connecticut shipbuilding took a spurt, as did overseas voyaging.

Although most people in southwestern Fairfield County lived a simple, work-a-day life (except the governor and the clergymen), a small wealthy class, such as had existed in the South, was making its appearance—the Leeds and Sellecks in Stamford, the Lockwoods in Norwalk, and in Canaan Parish the Carters and the Comstocks, into which the Rev. John Eells had married. Though £5,000 then was a large estate, such wealth was not based solely on land but included bills of exchange and stocks of goods. And in most instances it was maritime trade that provided both cash and credit. Not only staples but luxury goods were being imported and advertised, with retired sea captains often being the prominent local merchants. Philadelphia was still the port with the largest foreign commerce, but New York was growing faster than Boston, and the economy of southwest Fairfield County was now strongly linked to the shipping in and out of New York.

With some half-dozen good small harbors, Stamford and especially Norwalk had a part in this maritime trade, as men invested money in sloops carrying goods to New York for sale or transshipment and in ocean-going ships and their cargoes. Hence, when Captain James Richards of Rowayton, on the Norwalk side of Five Mile River harbor, moved in 1762 to a 270-acre homestead on North Wilton Road, Canaan Parish in effect acquired its own port. For almost a century afterward, most Canaan Parish and New Canaan exports and imports passed through Five Mile River harbor.

Born in 1723, James Richards was the fifth of 10 children of Samuel Richards, of Staffordshire, England, who came to America as a soldier, settling in Norwalk on his marriage in 1714. Family tradition holds that Samuel became a successful weaver before he began acquiring land on the east side of Five Mile River harbor, including the site of a former shipyard. Before he died in 1761, three of his sons—Samuel, Jr., James, and Daniel—had become sea captains, and alongside their harbor wharf the two elder brothers in 1753 had founded a store from which to sell the imported goods that they brought back from their voyaging. Still standing, the store bears on its front a National Historic Landmark plaque.

So few port records survive prior to 1789, when the new United States regularized record-keeping, that it is impossible to learn where Richards' ships went. One does know that at this time horses and oxen were two exports sent to the West Indies, and Madeira was a profitable import for captains sailing to the "Wine Islands." The Richards had their own shipyard north of their store, but there is no record of the early vessels built there. The yard went out of existence early in the 19th century, while the store remained Richards' property until it was sold in 1823 to another New Canaan man.

Five Mile River harbor as it looks today, with Richards' store out of sight on the left.

By 1761, despite an epidemic of smallpox that year (there was another in 1768), Canaan Parish's population continued to grow, with no evidence of the population pressures affecting Connecticut in general. Children of the first settlers were grown up and married, and in both 1760 and 1761 the Rev. Robert Silliman baptized 36 infants. There is no direct proof, but by this time Canaan Parish seems to have at least three district schools. Although the two sides of the Parish went their separate ways, a sense of community seems to have grown up on the Norwalk side —larger in area, more populated, and more given to trade than the Stamford side.

Daniel Keeler, the tavernkeeper, before he died in 1764 had paid for apprenticeships for three of his sons: two as shoemakers, one as a weaver. During the 1760's these two trades would come to the fore as Canaan Parish "cottage industries." On Brushy Ridge, the Benedict family, for one, began its long connection with shoes, and Stephen Hanford set himself up as a weaver on Oenoke Ridge where, south of a shoe-making family, he built what is now the Historical Society's Hanford-Silliman House. But some young men were going to sea and a very few were finding employment with the merchants and traders who were becoming the capitalists.

Along with these developments, alcoholism gets into the records. Five Canaan Parish men in 1766 and 1768 were hauled before Justice of the Peace Theophilus Fitch of Carter Street, confessed to being drunk, and were fined, usually 8 shillings. (Fitch had been made one of the colony's justices in 1754, entitled to call himself "Esquire," and his book of court cases survives.) Stephen Hanford had been drunk on March 25, 1766, and three of the others on March 26, 1768, so perhaps the old New Year's Day hadn't yet died out. Despite his arrest, Stephen Hanford would soon be elected one of Norwalk's tavernkeepers and have a tavern in his Oenoke Ridge house until the end of 1775.

That Canaan Parish artisans were dealing outside the area can be proved by a series of deeds that from 1762 on appear on the land records. Misinterpreted in later years as land speculations by New York City men, these warranty deeds to Canaan Parish homesteads were actually mortgages, given as security for payment of such raw materials as leather bought by Canaan Parish men from New York merchants or of goods purchased for resale.

Though Canaan Parish would have no store until 1772, it was quite familiar with traders, who bought and sold on commission, often putting together enough small shipments of produce or wares to make up a cargo for overseas. Such a trader was Nehemiah Benedict, who began married life in 1752 in the new house his father built for him on what is now Country Club Road, and whose store was at Norwalk harbor. Eventually Benedict was prominent in the affairs of the Canaan Society, was perhaps a tavernkeeper, certainly employed at least two apprentices, and owned Robin, a slave.

Once again, nothing specific ties Canaan Parish to the critical situations created between England and her American colonies by the passage of successive Parliamentary bills designed to produce revenues for the mother country. All the colonies were suffering an economic depression and everyone was feeling the pinch, so that England's Sugar (1764), Stamp (1765), and Townshend (1767) acts, laying a variety of taxes, aroused opposition in all the colonies. Connecticut was so divided about complying with the laws that, for the first time, the colony had two distinct political parties: Conservative and Radical. In addition, the Sons of Liberty was formed in opposition to the Stamp Act, though there is no evidence of their activities in this area.

In the main, Norwalk and Stamford, and hence Canaan Parish, were Conservative. A Norwalk town meeting of Nov. 12, 1765, went so far as to express "utter abhorrence and detestation" at the "routs and riotous assemblies of disorderly people" opposing the Stamp Act; Stamford's town meeting was silent about these and later disturbances. Despite what his home town thought, Connecticut was sufficiently Radical by 1766 to oust Thomas Fitch as governor, because he had reluctantly taken an oath to execute the Stamp Act, as he felt his gubernatorial oath of loyalty to the King obliged him to do.

The Church of England

Loyalty to the Crown was being taught by the Anglican missionaries wherever they had a church, and by May 1764 Canaan Parish saw the beginning of a small Church of England meeting house. This was on West Road on the Norwalk side of the Perambulation Line, just east of Weed Street. Two months later, in a deed dated July 18, 1764, title to the land on which "the frame for a church now standeth" was given to "Samuel Belden, Gideon Leeds, Ebenezer Smith & his son Ephraim Smith & the Rest of the Professors of the Church of England" by James Hait, that earlier opponent of Deacon John Bouton. His gift of 55 rods at the north end of his farm was made, Hait said, "in Consideration of the Good Will & Respect" which he had "for the Professors of the Church of England Dwelling in the Towns of Stamford & Norwalk & in Canaan Parish." The building was gone before 1830, and all that survives is Church Hill Burying Ground, occupying the whole tract that was James Hait's gift, now used and maintained by St. Mark's Church.

Beyond this deed, little is known about Canaan Parish's Church of England church. In 1760 there were only 14 Anglican missionaries in Connecticut, and none was available for the little new

St. Mark's burying ground on West Road occupies the tract of land originally deeded to the professors of the Church of England.

church. These missionaries labored under difficulties, for their principal support came from overseas—from the Society for the Propagation of the Gospel in Foreign Parts. Any young man from America who desired to enter the Church of England ministry had to pay his way to England to be ordained, receiving his canonical authority as priest from the Bishop of London. In England he had also to take the oath of allegiance to the King (which would lead to difficult decisions for the American Anglican clergy during the Revolutionary War). Despite the 1727 law, Connecticut firmly opposed a colonial Church of England bishop, and without a bishop the Anglicans here could neither ordain priests nor confirm members of the church. Apparently, the Canaan Parish Anglicans were only irregularly served by the rectors of St. Paul's Church in Norwalk and St. John's in Stamford, which about one quarter of all Canaan Parish families attended. Occasional services may have been held in the West Road meeting house, but more likely the building was used only for funerals and lay worship.

Problems for Mr. Silliman

Nothing in existing records suggests that the building of an Anglican meeting house was the cause of any of the difficulties that beset the Rev. Robert Silliman during the 1760's. Certainly the Church of England gained a foothold in Canaan Parish at the time this part of Fairfield County was becoming an Anglican stronghold, but dissent from the Established Church had been spreading as the New Lights in general supported the Radicals and the Sons of Liberty. Congregationalists still took their religion seriously, but by now Puritans had become Connecticut Yankees and piety was tainted by profit-making.

Mr. Silliman's troubles with the Congregational Church officially began in 1761. In that year and again in 1762, the ministers of the Association of Western Fairfield County were called to Canaan Parish to settle "unfortunate misunderstandings" that were never explained. As today, no pastor then could please all his parishioners, and opposing stands on political issues, wounded vanity—anything but religion—may have led to the attacks on the minister. Possibly the two oldest Silliman children were responsible for the second complaint heard by the Association, because on Jan. 21, 1762, 21-year-old Samuel Cooke and 18-year-old Rhoda Silliman admitted in a Justice of the Peace court that they "broak one penall Law of this Colony by playing at Cards." Each was fined 13 shillings, 4 pence—almost double the fines paid by the men who were drunk. Theophilus Fitch, the presiding J.P., was not only clerk of the Society but since 1760 had been a deacon of the Church, so this "crime" was not to be hushed up.

In the prolonged feuding between minister and Parish, the only religious complaint ever made against Robert Silliman was that he spent too much time in his sermons proving indisputable doctrine. He was variously accused of not showing proper sympathy when a parishioner was drowned, of causing "a grievancy to Sundry Brethren" at Deacon Thomas Talmadge's house on the "Sabbath Day Knight" before Talmadge died, and of reporting Eleazer Bouton, Jr., a grandson of Deacon John, to the grand jury for unspecified violations of civil law. Matters came to a head in 1766 when Nathaniel Bouton, one of the former Deacon's sons, bypassed the church and complained directly to the Western Fairfield County Association that Mr. Silliman had broken the 9th Commandment by bearing false witness against several Parish men (though the charges were withdrawn two years later).

Adding fuel to the fire, Bouton and others in the spring of 1767 went behind Mr. Silliman's back and invited the Rev. Samuel Sacket of Compounds, N.Y., to come to Canaan Parish and preach to them. The "Old Light—New Light" controversy was back in Canaan Parish in full force, for Samuel Sacket was a New Light evangelist of the extreme left, called "one of the most enthusiastic Methodists" by his detractors. From the day he was licensed to preach in Westchester County, in 1743, he and his fellow clergymen differed over doctrine and discipline.

Once the matter came before them, the ministers of the Association of Fairfield West took an Old Light stand and sent a stern letter to Sacket, condemning his unauthorized appearance in Silliman's parish. They were acting under the colony's "itinerancy law," which forbade any minister to preach in a town without the prior permission of both the resident pastor and the congregation. This was one of the laws the Congregational ministers had gotten the General Assembly to pass in 1742, at the height of Whitefield's evangelism. Since the New Lights believed in itinerant evangelism, they were bitterly opposed to the statute, and it would soon quietly be dropped from the Code of Laws as they became political factors as Radicals.

New Light sentiments in Canaan Parish seem to have been concentrated on the Stamford side, especially in the families living along Weed Street. Political feelings were deepening, and it is possible that some of the Stamford families leaned toward the Radicals, who in 1769 would elect Jonathan Trumbull governor despite heavy support for Thomas Fitch, who was again the Conservative candidate.

Whatever the real reasons for taking sides, the people of Canaan Parish were so divided that on Feb. 15, 1768, the Society voted 44 to 26 to dismiss Robert Silliman. Weather may have accounted for the small number of voters, because three weeks later 64 men subscribed their names to a petition supporting him. "We are Unwilling," they wrote, "for Mr. Silliman's Dismission, as we have no objection against Him but are Satisfyd with his ministerial Performances And Personal Conduct. And also with our Present Constitution in Church government Which we Apprehend Several of the Desirers of Mr. Sillimans dismission are desirous also of overturning." The 64 men who signed the subscription came almost equally from both sides of the Parish; fewer than half were church members, and along with the two church deacons were a number of Church of England men.

Meeting at the house of Abraham Weed (on Weed Street near present Wahackme Road), the Association of area ministers found no grounds for dismissal in the complaints made against Mr. Silliman, but they were acutely aware of dissension in parish and church. Therefore in November 1768 they proposed that for six months Robert Silliman should go as a missionary to the Synod of New York and Pennsylvania, while they took turns supplying the Canaan Parish pulpit.

Mr. Silliman served at churches in New York City, Newark and Elizabeth, N.J., and Abington and Carlisle, Pa., but this cooling-off period proved nothing. Silliman returned to alienate still more members of his Canaan Parish congregation by excluding some of his opponents from communion and denying baptism to two children of another, the powerful Abijah Comstock. The Society of Canaan countered with Norwalk's old weapon: they withheld the minister's salary. Then a group in the Society, led by Abraham Weed, proposed to break away from Canaan Parish and form a parish and church of its own. Sitting in May 1770, the Association censured Silliman's conduct, concluded that the break could never be healed, and "for the future peace and edification of the People" recommended the minister be dismissed. But this could not be accomplished immediately, because the General Assembly had before it both the division of Canaan Parish and the matter of Mr. Silliman's unpaid salary.

The petition to divide Canaan Parish had been presented to the Assembly in May 1770 by Abraham Weed and others, mostly men from the Stamford side. When the committee appointed by the Assembly came to Canaan Parish, "all parties" were heard, and all agreed that the proposed division would "ruin said Society." Should those living in northwestern Canaan withdraw, neither the new parish nor the old would be able to support a church and a minister. Canaan Parish remained intact, for in May 1771 the General Assembly voted against Abraham Weed's proposal. It further ruled that Mr. Silliman could not be dismissed until the Society of Canaan paid him his salary to the day of dismissal and gave him an additional £85 as severance pay.

It took the Western Fairfield County Association two days—Aug. 28-29, 1771—to bring the matter to a close. With his salary paid in full, Mr. Silliman tendered his resignation as minister and the Consociation dissolved his pastoral relation with the people of Canaan Parish. He left with the Consociation's good wishes and expressions of high esteem and soon became pastor of the Congregational church at Chester, Conn. He would return frequently in the years to come, occasionally to preach, for he left behind him in Canaan Parish his eldest son, Samuel Cooke Silliman, soon to come into prominence, his daughter Rhoda, already widowed, and another son Thomas, who was one of the Parish schoolmasters.

CHAPTER 4

The Revolution, 1771-1781

How anyone in Canaan Parish knew that a Church of Scotland missionary serving in Canada was seeking a pastorate is a mystery. But someone did, and the Rev. Robert Silliman had barely been dismissed when the Society's Committee—Theophilus Fitch, John Benedict, David Stevens, Jr., Eliphalet Seely, and Nehemiah Benedict—sent off an invitation to the Rev. William Drummond (*c.*1740-*c.*1778) to come to Canaan Parish to preach on trial.

The Third Congregational Pastor

Thanks to a surviving diary, one knows that William Drummond had sailed from Greenock on Apr. 8, 1770, and arrived at Prince Edward Island, then known as St. John Island, on June 2. Just the year before, St. John Island had been made a separate British colony, and among the variety of experiences Mr. Drummond recorded during his stay was a visit to the governor. Besides preaching in the wilderness, he also paid calls on the captain of a British man-of-war and to an Indian chief, who staged a war dance in his honor. Despite pages of entries, his diary gives no clue to a Canaan Parish connection, but there must have been one. Hence, when the Fairfield West Association sought to recommend a candidate to the Canaan Parish church in its "present destitute circumstances," the Society's committee on December 24 replied it did not wish to consider another candidate; though it had yet to hear from Mr. Drummond, it "had some expectation of his coming."

The Rev. William Drummond arrived in Canaan Parish on Saturday Feb. 1, 1772, and the next day preached in the meeting house. Within a week he was settled as a boarder of Nehemiah Benedict on present Country Club Road, and by the end of the month he was acquainted with the area ministers, had spent a night with former Governor Fitch, had conducted two funerals, paid 12 shillings for a new spring for his watch, and passed three days with the Rev. Robert Silliman, sharing the pulpit with him on one Sunday. Mr. Drummond was well on his way to calling on all the important church members in Canaan Parish, who catechized him closely over dinner or tea.

On March 9, 1772, the Canaan Society called Mr. Drummond as minister at an annual salary of £100, although eight men registered their objections. Before he accepted on April 14, Mr. Drummond made a four-day visit to New York, riding there on horseback in one day. When he did accept the Society's call, although he had no wife, he asked to be provided with a parsonage, "agreeable to ye general practice of the cuntry," and the Society agreed. As the weather improved, Mr. Drummond indulged in a bit of sport, participating in a fox hunt (he got four) and several times riding to Middlesex (Darien) to go fishing on the Sound with the Rev. Moses Mather and Capt. Samuel Richards, a brother of Canaan Parish's Captain James. Finally, on June 25, the Canaan Parish Church called Drummond as minister, and his installation was arranged for July 15.

When the Council of the Western Fairfield Consociation assembled on July 14, it was presented with written objections from seven church members—Abraham Weed, Eliazer Bouton, Jr., Joseph Davenport, Silvanus Hait, Nathaniel Crissy, Hezekiah Davenport, and Deodate Davenport, all men from the Stamford side, two of whom were Church of England and most of whom earlier had opposed Mr. Silliman. Mr. Drummond, they wrote, (1) had not been recommended by the Consociation and so his call was contrary to the Church's covenant; (2) his preaching was vague and rarely touched on the "Great & Essential Doctrines, Necessary to the Conversion & Salvation of men"—including the total depravity of mankind and the sovereign grace of God in conversions; (3) his life and private conversation did not "savor of Religion"; and (4) his conduct when questioned on important questions of divinity was harsh, severe, and forbidding. (Among other things, Mr. Drummond had called the men in this group "Clandestine Backbiters.") To these complaints the next day were added two more: Mr. Drummond, in conversation with a Ridgefield physician, had made an "impious Jest," and alleged proof existed that while in New York Mr. Drummond had been seen "drinking intemperately."

In the two days of examination of Mr. Drummond and the seven complainants, the minister presented his credentials, and these survive at Congregational House in Hartford—the originals, not copies by the clergyman acting as scribe. These are a certificate from the College Hall of Edinburgh stating that Drummond had been awarded the degree of Master of Arts in April 1761 and two testimonials dated in Glasgow in 1769 commending his preaching and his character to the "highland congregation" there before he went to Paisley. To the Council Mr. Drummond showed an attested copy of his ordination by the Presbytery of Ochterarder, "one of ye Presbyteries of ye Church of Scotland within ye Bounds of ye Provintial Synod of Perth & Sterling." This did not survive.

So few facts are known about William Drummond that I tried, with the help of a friend living in Scotland, to learn something more. But despite the cooperation of the Church of Scotland, the University Library, Old College, Edinburgh, and individual ministers and librarians, all I could establish was that one man who signed one of the Drummond references did live in Glasgow at the time. Otherwise, no College Hall of Edinburgh seems to have existed nor did the "clerk" who signed the M.A. certificate; no Drummond, let alone a William Drummond, was ordained by Auchterarder (Ochterarder) within a hundred years of a possible date; no Drummond was a minister at Glasgow or Paisley in the late 1760's, where no church names fit those Mr. Drummond was said to have served. But, whether or not his credentials were forged, the Council denied the objections, and William Drummond was installed as the third Congregational minister in Canaan Parish on July 15, 1772. Among the messengers from the nearby churches for the occasion were the Hon. Thomas Fitch of Norwalk and Capt. Samuel Richards, Drummond's fishing companion from Middlesex.

Mr. Drummond's Pastorate

On Dec. 7, 1772, Mr. Drummond began his "Journal of Family Visitation" (now in the Historical Society's vault), listing his almost daily calls on families of the Parish and his comments thereon. By Jan. 29, 1773, when he ended his journal, he had called on 132 families living in 126 houses and listed 792 individuals, including 449 children and 12 slaves. Although it was long considered such, this "Journal" is not a census of Canaan Parish; it is not even a census of Congregationalists, for Mr. Drummond failed to call on a number of church members and included two families of Anglicans. After a careful study, made in 1972, of church records, existing lists of names, land records, and other documents, Lois B. Bayles, then historian of the Historical Society, could place 238 families in Canaan Parish in Mr. Drummond's time: 176 Congregational, 52 Church of England, and 16 unknown church affiliation. Because Mr. Drummond's figures averaged 6 persons to a family, Mrs. Bayles used the same multiplier to obtain a 1773 census figure, but because of possible errors she considered the figure of 1,428 too high. It seemed more likely that Canaan Parish's population in 1773 was somewhere between 1,300 and 1,350.

The increase in the number of Parish families perhaps accounts for the need of a new cemetery, which resulted in the purchase of God's Acre on Jan. 26, 1773. Or deaths by smallpox may have been on the rise. Certainly smallpox was much in the news, and just a year before two Stamford physicians, Dr. Nathaniel Hubbard and Dr. Platt Townsend, had been tried and acquitted for innoculating eight Stamford residents at Dr. Townsend's house "to ye terror. . . of ye inhabitants." Though Platt Townsend would perform Canaan Parish's first known operation before the year was out, Canaan Parish already had two resident doctors. One was Samuel Baker, who as his second wife would soon marry the widowed Rhoda (Silliman) Weed, oldest daughter of the Rev. Robert Silliman; the other was Dr. Azor Betts, who lived in the house now numbered 643 Oenoke Ridge. Connecticut law punished smallpox innoculation with heavy fines on physician and patient, and Doctor Betts fled hastily to New York City after he was accused on Feb. 11, 1773, of innoculating John Hickox (of 914

Valley Road) and others unnamed. Inoculation was legal in New York—and, furthermore, it was successful—so with more and more people believing in preventing smallpox, more than one person in this area crossed the Colony line. Nathan Olmstead of Norwalk, according to Fairfield County Court reports, was fined £20 and costs of £12:16:5, because on Jan. 4, 1774, he "did go to a certain house in Salem called Rogers Hospitals and voluntarily took injection of the Distemper called smallpox. . .soon was sick with it. . .came back to Norwalk less than 20 days after being cleansed."

Apparently acting as a Society's committee, Jonathan Husted and William Bolt deeded the rocky, sloping half acre that is God's Acre to the people of Canaan Parish (not the Church) on Jan. 26, 1773. Three days later Mr. Drummond called on Jonathan Husted, former captain of the Train Band, and his wife Mary at their home (now No. 16 West Road), noting in his "Journal of Visitation" that the other members of the household were two slaves: Candace and the child Onesimus (probably Candace's son). Six days later, on Feb. 4, 1773, Captain Husted sold his new dwelling and considerable land to Moses Comstock and, unexplainably, left Canaan Parish, while his wife, after 29 years of marriage, went home to her aging father, Capt. Ebenezer Carter. (Carter promptly cut Husted out of any inheritance through his wife.) Husted seems to have gone to Brookhaven, Long Island, because in a deed dated there on Aug. 9, 1773, he sold Onesimus for £39 to Moses Comstock's aunts, Sara and Phebe. (Onesimus was to leave his mark on New Canaan history; hence this mention here.)

It was the year after Captain Husted sold Onesimus that the General Assembly passed Connecticut's first anti-slavery law, stating that no Indian, Negro, or mulatto slave could be brought or imported into the colony "from any place whatsoever to be disposed of, left, or sold within this Colony." This was the first small step toward ending slavery, but it had no effect on the slaves already in Connecticut. Among the 37 baptisms Mr. Drummond recorded in 1772 was that on December 29 of Idea, a Negro child, "property of James Youngs." Among the 37 deaths he entered in 1774 was that of June, the 23-year-old "Negro wench" of Ebenezer Carter, who died of consumption, that all-encompassing term that often meant tuberculosis but could mean diabetes, cancer, or another unfamiliar disease. And to this period belongs the last will and testament of Cesar, who had been James Hait's slave when he joined the Congregational Church in 1747. Cesar belonged to Abijah Comstock when in 1773 he willed to his master's children and his fellow slaves a variety of possessions that included money, silver shoe buckles, beaver hats, several books, and two traps.

Meanwhile, on July 8, 1773, Mr. Drummond had acquired as his much-wanted parsonage the house that is now No. 18 Seminary Street. This had been built in 1766 by the Rev. Robert Silliman for his son Samuel Cooke Silliman, who had mortgaged it to Daniel Phoenix, a New York merchant. But instead of moving in immediately, Mr. Drummond began an addition and did not occupy the house until the next spring.

While the entries Mr. Drummond made in his account book do not add up to a full picture of Canaan Parish in the 1770's, they supply some details. From it you know that Benjamin Brown was a mason and Samuel Hanford, Jr., a teamster. Josiah Weed and Abraham Youngs both were plasterers and glaziers, each working with two apprentices. Despite the number of Canaan Parish saw mills, Mr. Drummond had Daniel Finch bring him pine boards and

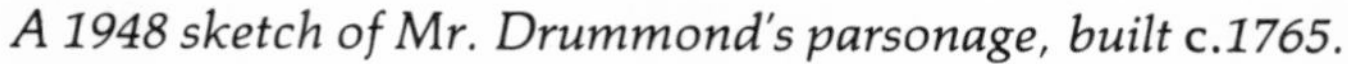
A 1948 sketch of Mr. Drummond's parsonage, built c.*1765.*

planks from New York City, probably by sloop, where he also bought a brass lock for his new front door. Two Canaan Parish blacksmiths were Timothy Reed and David St. John, while Samuel Crissey was a carpenter who in 1776 worked with an apprentice to repair the meeting house. Sugar was £6, then £7 a barrel, and the price of a two-day stay for a man, his servant, and two horses was £1:2:11 at Stephen Hanford's tavern (now the Historical Society's Hanford-Silliman House).

On separate pages for the Norwalk and Stamford sides of Canaan Parish, Mr. Drummond meticulously entered the "rates" each of his parishioners paid him directly toward his yearly salary and the sums turned over to him by the two "Collectors of Rates," which give a good idea of the relative financial standing of the many families. Except for a load of wood and a bushel of oats and an occasional day's work, all rates were paid in cash.

As the minister, what Mr. Drummond spent and what he did was typical of only the well-to-do in the Parish. His accounts show that he bought a suit of clothes for £4:2:7 at Thomas Benedict's store in Norwalk and paid 3 shillings 6 pence for a silk purse. He bought a quire of paper on which to write his sermons, ordered a case of gin from a sea captain, and through a New York agent subscribed to a newspaper, complaining that several issues were never received. A sixpence given to a lame sailor is just one incidence of his charity.

Once he had acquired his own mare (who in the course of time produced two colts), the largest sums Mr. Drummond spent were on his frequent travels. May 1773 saw him in New York City; in June he journeyed to Hartford to observe the General Assembly and then went to Saybrook and New Haven. He went again to New York in late June, this time to see one of his two brothers who had followed him to America, and in October he made a two-week's journey to Boston. All the while others in Canaan Parish also made trips outside the Colony, but usually for the purpose of trade.

Preliminaries to War

Less than two months after Mr. Drummond's return, Boston staged its Tea Party on Dec. 16, 1773, and the people of Connecticut heard the news with admiration and alarm. They had not long to wait before England's retaliation: the three Coercive Acts of March and May 1774 closed Boston's port to all traffic, quartered British troops in the town, and virtually repealed Massachusetts' charter.

No one recorded what life was like in Canaan Parish during the Revolution, though from the beginning to the end Canaan Parish people were more involved than one might expect since no battle took place here. Canaan Parish was not a town, but from the records of Norwalk and Stamford one can pick out a number of facts about Parish people and not simply draw on imagination to describe the local situation.

In the colony of Connecticut, sympathy for the plight of the Bostonians ran high, with the eastern and northern Radical towns plumping for nonimportation of British goods. Connecticut sent delegates to the First Continental Congress, convened in Philadelphia in September 1774, and the next month, foreseeing possible military encounters, the General Assembly raised four new regiments, increased the number of militia training days, and ordered the towns to double the supply of powder, bullets, and flints they were storing, which affected the Canaan Parish Train Band.

Meanwhile, on Oct. 7, 1774, Stamford had called a special town meeting, which was so largely attended that the men (including those from Canaan Parish's western side) could not fit into the town house and had to adjourn to the Congregational meeting house. The meeting then recorded its sympathy for the people of Boston and authorized the collection of money for Boston's poor. On the committee to collect these funds was Charles Weed of Weed Street.

The resolution that was adopted, while acknowledging "our subjection to the laws of Great Britain," supported the actions of the Continental Congress. "We are determined," the resolution read, "in every lawful way to join our sister colonies resolutely to defend our just rights & oppose all illegal & unconstitutionel [*sic*] acts of the British Parlement that respect America."

Stamford's greatest concern, however, was the Quebec Act that, though not one of the Coercive Acts, had also been passed on May 20, 1774. The Act provided Canada at last with a civil government, but in the concessions it made to Roman Catholics the people of Stamford found "an open declaration that our religious privileges which our Fathers fled their native country to enjoy are very soon to be abolished." The return of Louisburg to France after the 1745 expedition and the losses during the French and Indian wars had not been forgotten. On all these matters the freemen of Norwalk were silent, and there is no reason to believe that Stamford's resolution was adopted unanimously. In this politically Conservative part of Fairfield County, with its high proportion of Anglicans, the question of loyalty to the Crown was dividing people, and on either side feelings were beginning to rise.

Both Norwalk and Stamford, however, in line with the 11th article adopted by the Continental Congress, elected at their annual town meetings a Committee of Safety to keep in touch with the situations in other towns. Norwalk's 20-man Committee, elected on Dec. 5, 1774, included Capt. James Richards and Lt. John Carter of Canaan Parish; Stamford named no Canaan Parish man to its Committee chosen December 15.

Beginning of the Revolution

News of the battle of Concord reached Norwalk and Stamford, and hence Canaan Parish, on Apr. 22, 1775. Four days later the legislature in special session called up all militia companies in response to the "Lexington Alarm." Norwalk did not comply; Stamford produced only a partial company, which with other Fairfield County militia units was rushed to New York to defend that port. In command of Stamford's 43 men and officers was Capt. Joseph Hait, the French and Indian Wars veteran, who had moved to Canaan Parish and was living at the south corner of what is now Oenoke Ridge and Parade Hill. When it was obvious the British would not attack New York, the men were sent home.

In 1775 Canaan Parish seems to have had about 80 men in its Train Band, the 9th Company of the 9th Militia Regiment, though many more were of eligible age. In the eight years that the Revolution lasted, young men as they turned 16 enlisted, so that approximately 225 Canaan Parish men saw military service on the Continental side of the conflict, almost 20 percent of the population. (Perhaps 20 more fought with the British.) But in May 1775, when Ensign Jacob Selleck was recruiting, only 25 men and officers from the Train Band enlisted for seven months in Connecticut's "Continental Regiments." Except for Captain Hait, then 50 years old, most of the men were in their 20's and were unmarried. Captain Hait was given command of the 4th Company in the new Connecticut 7th Regiment, which after helping to fortify coastal towns was sent in September to the Boston area. With him were nine Canaan Parish men (counting 14-year-old Warren Hait, who went as his father's "waiter"), who were gone from home until August 1776—five months after the British evacuated Boston and one month after the Declaration of Independence had been signed.

The other Canaan Parish men who enlisted in May were assigned to the 5th Connecticut Regiment, which was sent to New York. There the fortunes of war soon saw this regiment attached to the new Northern Department of the Continental Army and on its way north in the campaign against Canada. Marching through Maine with Benedict Arnold's prong of this badly planned Canadian attack were four more Canaan Parish men: James Ambler, Squire Dan, Ashahel Kellogg, and Brush Weed. Before enlistments ran out in December, Canaan Parish learned of its first war casualty: young Ezra Stevens of Ponus Ridge died on Oct. 7, 1775, in the disease-ridden military hospital of Ticonderoga. Levi Tuttle had been wounded in August at the siege of St. John's but recovered and came home. Much later Canaan Parish would have news of the death in Canada of Brush Weed, an employee of Nehemiah Benedict and fellow boarder with the Rev. Mr. Drummond when he lived at Benedict's.

Before the remnants of the 5th Connecticut came home in December, when their enlistments expired, Canaan Parish had learned what war was about. Abraham Weed, James Youngs, Deodate Davenport, and Hezehiah Davenport, on the Stamford side of the Parish, now served on Stamford's Committee of Safety, while Norwalk's Committee included Capt. James Richards, Moses Comstock, and Samuel Cooke Silliman, the former minister's eldest son. These Committees of Safety were charged with ferreting out treason, meting out punishment to Loyalists, and handling any town matter related to the war.

By no means were all people in Norwalk and Stamford wholehearted partriots, and though percentagewise Canaan Parish had fewer Loyalists than its parent towns, 41 Parish men eventually were listed as Loyalist. In 1775 only a few of these had gone over to the British, the first being Joseph Hait 5th, eldest son of Capt. Joseph Hait. As a lieutenant colonel in the Continental army, his father would become Canaan Parish's highest ranking officer, while Joseph Hait 5th, after serving in the British army, would emigrate to Nova Scotia at the end of the war.

Squire Dan was one of the few who reenlisted at Quebec, when his first term of service expired, but his brother Nathan, after a brief stint with the 5th Connecticut Regiment, went over to the British. Though he was an avowed Loyalist, their father Nehemiah Dan was allowed to remain in his Ponus Ridge house. It seems odd today that, even after Connecticut became a state, suspected Tories were not interned. Stripped of their firearms, they were allowed to live at home under the surveillance of the Committee of Safety. In time, most Tories were restricted to their home towns, as was Wyx Seely of Old Stamford Road. Minus his guns, he was prohibited from leaving Canaan Parish—and then fined several times for refusing to march with the Train Band when it was called for duty elsewhere.

In January 1776, when the British were known to be planning to evacuate Boston, Gen. George Washington issued the call to arms that the local militias had been expecting. This time 35 Canaan Parish men enlisted or were drafted, but they did not march as one unit. The local Train Band was oversize, too large for one company but not enough for two, so the 9th Company in 1776 served as a pool of men from which the militia companies in nearby towns filled their ranks. As a result, Canaan Parish's Capt. Daniel Benedict, 55 years old and an important miller, became captain of the 4th Company (Norwalk's), with 31 Canaan Parish men serving under him. The other four men served in other companies.

As part of a new Connecticut militia regiment, the 4th Company was sent to join New York and New Jersey militia regiments in building defenses for New York City. But New York was not prepared for an influx of some 5,000 soldiers, and the Canaan Parish men had to camp out in the open in winter weather, trusting their families at home to send them some of their food while they built gun emplacements. In March, their enlistments expired, all came home in good time to plant crops. Meanwhile, Canaan Parish families had been selling food and fodder to Norwalk and Stamford, where military units passing over the Post Road to and from New York were in need of overnight quarters and meals.

In May, when Connecticut reorganized its military, the Canaan Parish Train Band, along with all local militias, was assigned to back-up emergency duty, to be called out for a few days or a few weeks of service in the immediate area—something that had little meaning for Canaan Parish men as time went on. Behind the Train Band was the Alarm List, made up of older men, former Train Band officers, and those recovering from wounds, who were to be called upon in extreme emergencies. Twenty Canaan Parish young men, however, signed up for one-year enlistments in what, after the Declaration of Independence, were called State Troops. These were intended to be on continuous duty within Connecticut but in 1776 were attached to the Continental service.

Despite the restriction on where Connecticut Train Bands were to serve, after Washington decided to defend New York City, the Canaan Parish Train Band was called up on August 12 as the 9th Company of the 9th Militia Regiment and sent to New York. Of the 45 men and officers who marched under Capt. Daniel Benedict, 36 had done no military duty before and were typical of the militiamen on whom Washington had to depend as troops during the first two years of the war. Though they had trained twice yearly at home under the officers they elected from their ranks and had participated in regimental reviews, they did not take kindly to orders from "foreign" colonels and generals. On the whole, the militiamen made poor soldiers when a part of an army, many deserting if the going was tough, and most being ready to go home as soon as their enlistments were up, no matter where they were. It's no wonder Washington later wrote to the Continental Congress: "If I were called upon to declare under oath, whether the militia had been most serviceable or hurtful upon the whole, I should subscribe to the latter."

When the 9th Company reached New York City, camps were crowded, dysentery was rife in the summer heat, and after a few days some of the men were sent home as unfit for duty. Though other Canaan Parish men with other regiments were to be in the thick of battle, the entire 9th Company had been discharged by September 13, the day before the British landed in New York.

Sylvanus Hait died of dysentery two days after his return, while before the year ended Captain Benedict was dead from the same cause. John Green died of causes unknown. John Carter was elected in Benedict's place as captain of the Train Band, while in time Andrew Powers, who came to Canaan from Middlesex, bought the Benedict grist and saw mills from the Captain's heirs.

In the May reorganization, the 7th Connecticut Regiment became the 19th Connecticut Continental Regiment, in which Capt. Joseph Hait and his seven Canaan Parish soldiers served until the war's end. Transferred from Boston to New York, these men took part in the defense of and retreat from New York, as did Wadsworth's Brigade of State Troops, in which the 20 Canaan Parish enlistees were serving. When Fort Washington fell, 11 of the men in Wadsworth's Brigade had been shifted across the Hudson River for the defense of Fort Lee, but the other nine Canaan Parish men were taken prisoner on November 16.

One of those captured at Fort Washington was Stephen Weed (1753-1821), a veteran of the 1776 Northern campaign. Tradition has long held that Weed was so deranged by his imprisonment in the Sugar House that, to prevent a British attack along the Noroton River valley, he singlehandedly built a small stone fort off the south side of Frogtown Road. There he was said to have kept a daily vigil until well after the war was over. Yet Weed, in his pension application of 1818, wrote that after just two months' confinement in the prison ship *Jersey,* he was returned home on a year's parole, married in May 1778, and in 1779 served under Capt. Reuben Scofield in the 9th Militia Regiment. Later Weed followed a shoemaker's trade, and one has to wonder if his insanity was part of a fanciful explanation for the "fort."

Meanwhile, after Washington had retreated from Harlem Heights to make a stand at White Plains with the small force under him, the 9th Militia Company was called out again. Under Lt. John Carter—he had yet to be made captain—69 Train Band officers and men, including 30 who had been in New York with Captain Benedict, were sent to Westchester County on October 25. There they remained for three months, participating in minor skirmishes, and there Aaron Abbott, for one, was wounded and Samuel Seely died. From a bill submitted to the Continental

Congress, one learns that Timothy Reed was sent to North Castle (Armonk) to bring home the wounded, who were cared for by Dr. Samuel Baker in Reed's West Road home.

Except for the cheering news of the Battle of Trenton on December 26, Canaan Parish ended the year 1776 with grim statistics. Almost 90 of its men were under arms outside the state; the known dead from war-related causes now numbered seven; nine men were British prisoners. Of those, one would die in prison and one on his way home, for such were the appalling conditions in New York prisons and prison ships. Almost every Canaan Parish family by now had been affected by war.

Ministerial Problems amid Military Turmoil

On December 23, three days before the Battle of Trenton, the Society of Canaan called a meeting that elected a four-man committee to "treat with Mr. Drummond Wheather he Would be Willing to unight with the Society in taking a Regular Dismission." One week later, "by a majority vote"—22 to 21—the Society offered to pay the minister his salary until February if he would resign. Taking advantage of the number of absent members, the anti-Drummond faction from the Stamford side of Canaan Parish saw its chance to get rid of the minister it had always disliked.

Mr. Drummond was not about to oblige and objected strongly to being pressured by a "majority" of 1, pointing out that the Society had some 160 legal voters, many of whom "were engaged in the business of the country" on the day the vote was taken. December, he noted, had been "a sickly time," so some voters had been unable to attend; still others were so "disgusted with the conduct of the now prevailing party" that they refused to sit with "party" members in Society meetings. Nevertheless, the "prevailing party" pushed ahead, inviting the Association of Fairfield County West to hear its complaints. But before the ministers assembled at Samuel Cooke Silliman's house on March 26, the people of Canaan Parish were in turmoil again.

Armies must eat, and once Washington quartered part of his troops in the Hudson Highlands, commissary agents were hard put to find food and supplies for the Continental army. In New York City, the British army needed more food for its men, more fodder for its horses, and more firewood than could be supplied by Long Island and the greater New York area under British control. Hence, as Connecticut began to fill its vital role as the "Provision State," Westchester County, across which most supply routes ran, became the "Neutral Ground," fair game for raiding parties on both sides, who looted crops and animals throughout the countryside. And from across Long Island Sound, British and Loyalists in small boats, led by former residents of the area, raided the Connecticut coasts almost nightly, plundering cattle, grain, firewood, and valuables. Coast guard duty became the chore of the local militia companies, which apparently rotated duty at the many potential landing spots.

Thus it happened that 14 men from the Canaan Parish Train Band, on the night of Mar. 13, 1777, were part of a 48-man contingent of Norwalk militia on duty on the east side of Five Mile River harbor. The night was bitterly cold, and, ignoring duty, some of the men had gone inside the "hotel" of Capt. Samuel Richards to get warm. There a Tory raiding party surprised them, carrying 14 prisoners to Long Island, including Captain Richards and nine Canaan Parish men. Eventually, all the prisoners were taken to New York, where six of the nine Canaan Parish men died.

At that time, a prisoner would be exchanged only for a man of equivalent rank. For Samuel Richards, a prominent civilian, the British demanded the release of a Tory in jail in Boston. (Richards' family tradition holds that the man was "Ned Davis," but no such name appears on modern lists of Loyalists and may have been remembered incorrectly.) Consequently, Capt. James Richards had to obtain permission to ride to Boston and bring back the Tory before he could effect his brother's release. But as a result of prison conditions, Capt. Samuel Richards died June 25, 1777, age 60, one day after he was returned to his Rowayton home.

Once the Western Fairfield Association met on March 26, it found the charges against William Drummond so scandalous that it promptly convened the Consociation. With seven ministers and 10 messengers from Fairfield County churches, the Consociation met in Canaan Parish for three days, April 8 through 10. To the two 1772 charges against Drummond—that his preaching was general and vague and that his behavior toward some parishioners was "harsh, invective, and forbidding"—two more had been added: Mr. Drummond used "spiritous Liquor to excess," and he showed an "unfriendly Disposition to ye Rights and Liberties of ye United States of America."

Convinced that he was not to be given a fair hearing, the minister blamed his drinking on the "sore sickness" from which he had been suffering for more than two years. Beyond quoting from a sermon or two, he declined to defend his preaching, and he pointblank denied the right of the Association to try him for his political opinions. That was the concern of the civil Committee of Safety.

On its last day, the Consociation dismissed the charge of disloyalty (contrary to what so many times has been put into print), saying that the evidence was out of date and that Mr. Drummond had become "more friendly to the cause of America" since then. But the Consociation found William Drummond guilty of the first three charges, suspending him there and then from his pastoral duties in Canaan Parish and from all privileges of the Association and Consociation. The ministers and messengers then went on to state that Mr. Drummond should be excommunicated—"debarred from communion with the visible church"—but they were reluctant to act without giving the minister the opportunity to show satisfactory "penitence to all parties concerned." For this they set the last Tuesday in May, but before May 27 arrived, the British army had made the first of its four invasions of Connecticut.

On Friday April 25, under the command of Gen. William Tryon, former British governor of New York, 26 ships anchored at Compo Beach (then part of Norwalk) and landed 2,000 British and Loyalist troops. Led by former residents of Fairfield and Danbury, this force marched inland and made camp for the night. News of the British landing was rushed to Fairfield, from where Brig. Gen. Gould Selleck Silliman, commander of the 4th Militia Brigade, sent out the alarm to the local Train Bands. (Since it was night, bonfires as well as musket shots were likely to have been the signals of alert.) From New Haven came Gens. David Wooster and Benedict Arnold with a handful of Continental troops, so that by morning the three Generals had a force of perhaps 600 Americans. Not until the British marched northward toward Bethel was anyone sure that their destination was Danbury, the seemingly safe place the Continental army had chosen to store military and medical supplies. Word of the British destination was passed along to the alerted Train Bands to the west, while the American generals set off in pursuit with the small force of militiamen and regulars on hand.

Exhausted from their forced march, the Americans camped at Bethel late Saturday night. The British, meanwhile, had already raided Danbury, collecting all the materiél and supplies. But unable to procure carts to carry away the stores and aware of the Americans nearby, Tryon early Sunday morning burned the booty and some 20 Danbury buildings and marched his men off to the west. When the Americans started again in pursuit, they did not know whether Tryon was heading for the Hudson River or taking a roundabout route back to his ships at Compo—until the British turned southward toward Ridgebury. Then General Wooster with 200 men set out to harry Tryon from the rear, while Arnold and Silliman rushed down the more direct regular highway to reach Ridgefield before the British did.

The Canaan Parish Train Band must have received the alarm on Saturday, because by Sunday noon Capt. John Carter had put himself and his 40 men under Arnold's command. Fruitlessly, they helped built a barricade of trees, rocks, and overturned carts across a narrow spot in the road just north of Ridgefield town. News had yet to reach them that General Wooster had been mortally wounded during a delaying action he had ordered outside Ridgebury and was not in command of the detachment behind Tryon's men. Once the British reached Ridgefield, they flanked Arnold's barricade. Arnold's horse was killed under him, but he escaped capture, while the badly outnumbered Americans could only snipe at the British from cover behind trees. When the brief Battle of Ridgefield was over, two Canaan Parish men lay dead: Nathaniel Gray of Seminary Street, who had done duty in Westchester County, and Lt. Hezekiah Davenport, a veteran of the Boston campaign, member of Stamford's Committee of Safety, and one of the original objectors to William Drummond.

As the British moved south toward Wilton to camp overnight, someone must have taken word back to Canaan Parish, because (so legend says) residents along the eastern Parish borders hastily drove their livestock to the "hidden meadow" above Valley Road, determined the British army would not feed on Canaan Parish

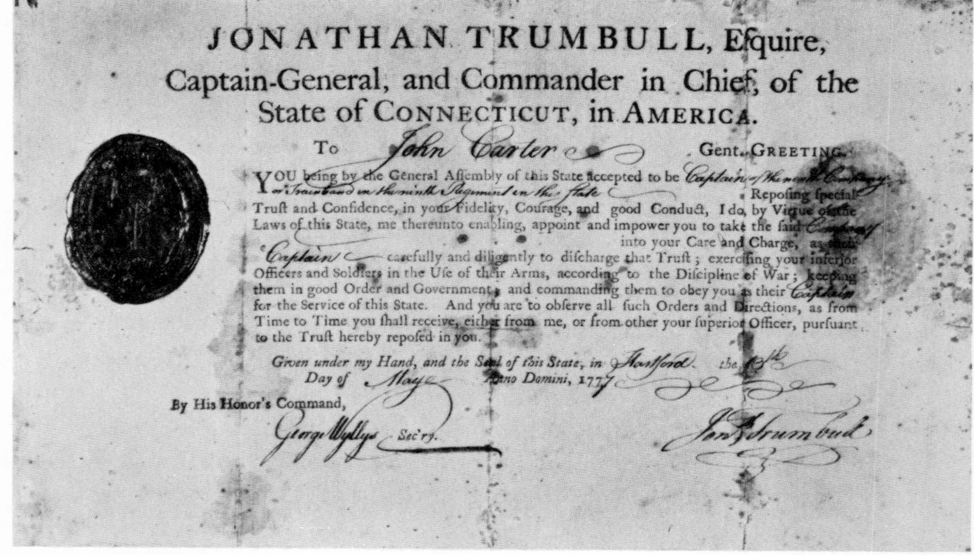

JONATHAN TRUMBULL, Esquire,
Captain-General, and Commander in Chief, of the
State of CONNECTICUT, in AMERICA.

To John Carter Gent. GREETING.

YOU being by the General Assembly of this State accepted to be Captain of the ninth Company or Trainband in the ninth Regiment in the State. Reposing special Trust and Confidence, in your Fidelity, Courage, and good Conduct, I do, by Virtue of the Laws of this State, me thereunto enabling, appoint and impower you to take the said Company into your Care and Charge, as their Captain carefully and diligently to discharge that Trust; exercising your inferior Officers and Soldiers in the Use of their Arms, according to the Discipline of War; keeping them in good Order and Government, and commanding them to obey you as their Captain for the Service of this State. And you are to observe all such Orders and Directions, as from Time to Time you shall receive, either from me, or from other your superior Officer, pursuant to the Trust hereby reposed in you.

Given under my Hand, and the Seal of this State, in Hartford *the* 13th *Day of* May *Anno Domini*, 1777.

By His Honor's Command,

George Wyllys *Sec'ry.*

Jonth Trumbull

John Carter's commission as Captain of the 9th Company or Train Band, 9th Regiment, signed by Gov. Jonathan Trumbull, May 13, 1777.

animals. Monday saw some if not all the Canaan militiamen helping to harass the British on their way back to Compo, where, after two more skirmishes, Tryon's forces reboarded their ships late on Monday April 28.

When the Consociation met on May 27 it formally dissolved the Rev. Mr. Drummond's ties to the Canaan Parish church, though the minister was ill and failed to appear. Instead, he sent the Consociation a note insisting its judgment of him was both unfounded and severe. Again, the ministers postponed excommunication—until June 24 and then until June 1778. William Drummond certainly did nothing to bolster his defense, but by then he was probably too ill to care what happened and too disappointed by the failure of his important friends on the Norwalk side of the Parish to come to his defense. By July he had sold his parsonage back to Daniel Phoenix of New York, and, though he remained in the Parish, no one knows where he went to live, except that it was on the Norwalk side.

Once Drummond was dismissed, the Canaan Parish church was without a minister for almost five years. No candidates were to be found, and in this low period one Fairfield County Congregational church after another closed. (The Church of England rectors of St. Paul's and St. John's were under house arrest or in jail.) Norwalk had been without a Congregational clergyman since 1772, when the Rev. William Tennent was dismissed; Stamford had not replaced the distinguished and patriotic Noah Welles, who died in 1776; the Rev. Jonathan Ingersoll would die in 1778, leaving Ridgefield without a minister; while Jonathan Murdock of Horseneck (a part of Greenwich) would flee to the British as a Tory. Nineteen Canaan Parish couples in 1778-1780 were married in Wilton by the Rev. Isaac Lewis, who with the Rev. Moses Mather of Middlesex carried on in this area. (Whether they preached outside their own parishes is not known.) Yet even Moses Mather was not always on hand; twice he was captured by Tory bands that included some of his parishioners, and both times he was imprisoned for several weeks in New York.

The Home Front

Though they had no way of knowing it then, after the Danbury Raid the people of Canaan Parish settled into the uneasy way of life they would follow for the next five years. Having seen former neighbors in British uniform, the last of Canaan Parish's 22 ardent Loyalists fled, including James Hait, Jr., and his brother Silvanus, sons of the James Hait who had given the Anglican church its West Road land. (All the Tories on the Stamford side of Canaan Parish had connections with St. John's Church.) As Connecticut stiffened its penalties, the houses and lands of all Loyalists who fled were confiscated, and those families who had been left behind soon became destitute and so they too left.

Spurred by the Danbury Raid, 13 Canaan Parish men enlisted for the duration in the Continental army, including the veteran Joseph Hait and a number of boys just turned 16. Before the year was out, one would desert when Washington moved part of his army to Pennsylvania, one would die defending Mud Island in Philadelphia's harbor, and one would die during the severe winter at Valley Forge.

In the course of the Revolution, the Danbury Raid was of small consequence, but it had proved that Connecticut could be invaded, and the towns now were reluctant to see their Train Bands sent off to support the Continental troops. They wanted the militia at home, to respond to the more-and-more frequent alarms as the British as well as the Tories raided the coastal towns, especially Greenwich.

Nevertheless, by September 1777, when Burgoyne was threatening from the north and Clinton moved his army out of New York City to go to Burgoyne's support, a special regiment of six Connecticut militia companies was sent to Fishkill, N.Y., to aid in the Hudson River defense, where Joseph Hait and other Canaan Parish Continentals were stationed. Though on coast guard duty at Horseneck, Edmond Richards of Canaan Parish was so fired by the call for more volunteers that he went off to Albany to join General Gates. As a result, he saw Burgoyne surrender at Stillwater, N.Y., on October 17. Perhaps his father, Capt. James Richards, then in command of Canaan Parish's Alarm List, also witnessed this historic event. Just one surviving court record places Captain James at Stillwater, though it seems unlikely that the aging and incapacitated men on the Alarm List would have marched that far.

Stories persist, with no proof for or against, that the weavers of Canaan Parish made uniforms and the shoemakers made shoes for the Continental army. Taking military service and the many alarms in stride, the people of Canaan Parish seem to have been hard at work, while protesting that they had "many times left our homes and Farms and Businesses under very disadvantageous Circumstances to our Private Injury and great Hurt [and] gone forth in defense of our Country." Certainly by the end of 1777 a number of men on both sides of the Parish were filling important posts in the towns of Norwalk and Stamford as well as serving in the Train Band or Alarm List and carrying on their trades. Besides the Committees of Safety, busy prosecuting Loyalists, each town had a committee to provide care for the families of the men who enlisted; each had a committee to supply clothing to the Continental commissary; and each had "Inspectors of Provisions" to certify to the quantity, quality, and price of what was forwarded to the commissary. On all these committees were Canaan Parish men, and I think it entirely possible that Canaan Parish crops and "manufactured" goods were among those carted across Westchester

County's "Neutral Ground" year after year. Certainly Caanan Parish men in the service were provided by their families with homemade uniforms and shoes.

The Canaan Parish man with the greatest authority was Samuel Cooke Silliman. As a sergeant of Canaan Parish's 9th Militia Company, he had served for four months in Westchester County in 1775-76. On his return in January 1776, he had been elected to Norwalk's Committee of Safety and as Canaan Parish's new tavernkeeper, so he hired a substitute to serve in the militia in his stead. Then 35 years old, S. Cooke Silliman was also a Justice of the Peace and clerk of the Canaan Society. Besides the tavern, he was conducting a trading business in his father's former parsonage on the present Firehouse site. In a letter dated Feb. 26, 1776, he complained to his brother in Chester that times were bad, money was not circulating because the soldiers had yet to be paid for the previous summer's duty, and he was unable to collect the money owed his brother for fish that had been traded earlier.

In May 1776 S. Cooke Silliman was elected one of Norwalk's two representatives to the General Assembly, an office to which he would be reelected every year except four until his death in 1795. Thus Silliman was one of the legislators who acted on the petition which the Rev. William Drummond sent to the General Assembly in October 1777, saying he was in poor health and asking permission to return to Scotland where relatives would care for him. Drummond wanted to go to New York City, in enemy hands, where he could procure passage, and either to take out of the state his "books, wearing apparel, and Bedding" and three horses or to "broker" them in Connecticut for flaxseed or another commodity of no advantage to the enemy that he could resell in New York to pay his passage.

Though permission was granted in January 1778, Mr. Drummond again petitioned the legislature in February. This time he wanted permission to take out of the state provisions for a four-month voyage. Except that a letter written by the Rev. Moses Mather in May 1778 was addressed to William Drummond in Canaan Parish, no one knows exactly what happened to him after that. He may have reached New York and died there or nearby. What is certain is that in 1782 when his brother Robert went to New York to settle the affairs of their deceased brother John,

Robert Drummond took back to Catskill, N.Y., the various journals the minister had kept, making notes in one of them. Robert Drummond had married Theophilus Fitch's daughter Anne, and their son William Drummond inherited Fitch property on Carter Street. When he moved to New Canaan and about 1830 built the Greek Revival house that is No. 587 Carter Street, the second William Drummond brought with him his uncle's journals, using one of them for years for his farm accounts. This is how the 18th-century journals of Canaan Parish's third minister happen to be in New Canaan today

In 1778 morale was boosted by word that Congress had signed a treaty with France and boosted still more by news of the battle of Monmouth Courthouse on June 28-29—what turned out to be the last large battle in the north. But word soon followed that Ebenezer Benedict, one of the Parish's Continental soldiers, had died of wounds received during that battle.

The Train Band

No one ever recorded where the Train Band had drilled before Sept. 1, 1778, the day on which the "inhabitants of Canaan Parish" paid Joseph Blatchley £14 for an acre of his Oenoke Ridge farm to be "a military parade." The Continental army had been successfully reorganized and trained, but the Train Band still needed regular drilling and a centrally located parade ground where the militiamen could assemble when an alarm was heard. There had been no lessening of raids, and one militiaman later wrote that the Canaan Parish Train Band was called out 19 times between 1779 and the end of the war, while a second said the Train Band served in 15 campaigns in 1781-83.

Canaan Parish was too far from the shore of Long Island Sound for raiding parties of Tories to rob farms and get back to their boats with cattle, valuables, and grain under cover of night and in the face of alarms. While there are no records of what or how much Canaan Parish farmers were producing, local storage of grain was enough to tempt not the Tories but Sheldon's Light Horse Infantry, a branch of Washington's defense in the north.

After Monmouth, the left wing of the Continental army and Sheldon's troops wintered at what is now Putnam Memorial Park at Redding, Conn., where deplorable conditions made it a second Valley Forge. Men came close to starving, but the dragoons on horseback could range far afield in search of feed for their mounts. A 1778 petition, addressed to Gov. Jonathan Trumbull, recounts how the dragoons "frequently come into the Parish of Canaan... and by force and violence enter the inhabitants' barns, and at will and pleasure, with the same force, take their oats and carry them off...without ever applying to any authority." The dragoons not only helped themselves without payment or receipt, but their collecting methods were so destructive that the Canaan Parish people feared they would be left with no oat seed for the next crop and, if the oats ran out, the dragoons would take their wheat and corn for horsefeed.

In the midst of these forays, S. Cooke Silliman reported to a fellow legislator that a Mr. Comstock, on objecting to the strong-arm tactics of Capt. Josiah Stoddard's troop of dragoons, had been threatened with death and the burning of his house and barns. Whichever of the several well-to-do Comstocks this was, he did not take kindly to threats and obtained a writ against two dragoons, had them arrested, and brought to trial before Mr. Silliman, sitting in his capacity as justice of the peace. As Silliman wrote, court was in session in his tavern, the room was crowded with bystanders, when "in a great fury" Captain Stoddard burst in at the head of armed troops. Pointing their swords at the justice, the dragoons collected their two offending comrades and dragged Mr. Comstock and one of his sons from the room. Captain Stoddard forced the Comstocks to mount their horses and ride off with the dragoons but released them after two miles with nothing more harmful than abusive language. From repetition of such goings-on, Silliman demanded state protection.

In a few months, when Major Benjamin Tallmadge began camping his troop of dragoons in the vicinity of Ponus Ridge, Canaan Parish reversed its opinion of Sheldon's Light Horse. They may have been a drain on provisions, but off and on for the next four years Tallmadge's dragoons were a protection to the Parish and a support for the local militias as well as the Continental army.

In the 20th century it has been humorously said that nothing happened in Canaan Parish during the Revolution. That's not true. While battles took place elsewhere, from June 1779 until the war's end Canaan Parish was headquarters and home for Col. (later Gen.) John Mead. Mead commanded the 9th Militia Regiment, made up of the 13 Train Bands in Greenwich, Stamford, and Norwalk. Since the Canaan Parish Train Band was the 9th Company in this Regiment, it became more or less Mead's mainstay. After the sixth attack in 1779 on Greenwich, Mead had had to flee with his family to avoid Tory harassments, and thereafter he issued his orders and wrote important war correspondence from Canaan Parish with Parish militiamen guarding him.

I don't wish to overstate Canaan Parish's place in history, but from his despatches one knows that Major Benjamin Tallmadge made Canaan Parish his base for weeks at a time in 1779, 1780, 1781, and 1782. Very few besides George Washington then knew that Tallmadge was the originator and first chief of the United States secret service. What was called the "Culper Spy Ring" began operating in 1778, getting military intelligence in New York City and forwarding it by code or invisible writing to Setauket, Long Island, and then across the Sound to the Connecticut shore, from where Tallmadge or another agent transmitted it to General Washington. In Tallmadge's words, Ponus Ridge, with its then open

Sketch of Benjamin Tallmadge by John Trumbull, son of Connecticut's Gov. Jonathan Trumbull.

view of a long arc of the Sound, was a good station from which "to watch the enemy, either up on the lines, or across the Sound on Long Island." But before Tallmadge made his first encampment here in September 1779, Canaan Parish found itself near the geographical center of a well-planned British campaign.

With Washington's army camped in the Hudson Highlands, the British had been contained all winter and spring in New York. Because Connecticut's armed whaleboat service on the Sound was now well organized, British supply vessels from Newport were prevented from reaching New York, while the illicit trading across the Sound was somewhat restrained. Greenwich and Westchester County, however, remained fair game for British-led raids seeking supplies.

On June 1, after months of inactivity, Gen. Sir Henry Clinton sent an expedition up the Hudson that captured Stony Point and Verplanck's Point, the forts guarding the southernmost ferry crossing for Continental supplies from New England. As Clinton hoped, Washington called to the Highlands the bulk of his left wing that, camped at Redding, had protected the Connecticut coast as far east as New Haven.

With these troops removed from the scene, on June 17 came the sixth British attack on Greenwich, which forced Mead to flee. On June 23, Mead at Canaan Parish ordered the militias back to Greenwich on receiving word that the British cavalry was threatening Bedford nearby. Next, early on July 2, the Canaan Parish Train Band was rushed to Pound Ridge. Near dawn, after a night ride from Mile Square, near Yonkers, N.Y., British cavalry under Col. Banastre Tarleton descended on Major Tallmadge, who with his mounted dragoons was camping at Pound Ridge. A lookout spotted the British just in time for the dragoons to scatter in two directions. Tallmadge escaped capture but Tarleton got his saddlebags, in which Culper papers identified one of Washington's spies. So swift was the morning raid that the Canaan militia could not arrive in time to help prevent the British burning the house where Tallmadge had been staying or the meeting house nearby where his men had tethered their horses. At that time, two Canaan Parish men were serving in Tallmadge's troop, and one of them, Jared Hoyt, was wounded in the foray and became one of the four men Tallmadge lost as prisoners.

Then, on July 4, in a fleet of 48 vessels, Gen. William Tryon, of the Danbury Raid, sailed up the Sound from New York and attacked New Haven on July 6. Ordered to the relief of that town, the Canaan Parish Train Band had marched as far as Stratford when word came that Tryon had put out to sea. The men had barely time to reach home when news came on July 8 that Tryon's force had landed at Southport. Off the militia went again, not in time to prevent the destruction of Fairfield but in time to harass the British retreat to their ships on July 9. Finally, on the night of July 11 the alarm guns sounded again: the British had landed at Norwalk. Though a company of some 50 regulars under Capt. Stephen Betts of Canaan Parish was sent to Norwalk from the Continental left wing, the Americans were too small a force to make a stand against Tryon, even after Tallmadge's regrouped dragoons rode to Norwalk to join the weary Train Bands. On Tryon's orders, on Sunday July 12, Norwalk was systematically set afire, while the Americans could only protect the fleeing residents by occasional sniping and skirmishing. As Sunday ended, the British sailed away, taking with them some 20 Norwalk Loyalist families and the rector of St. Paul's Church, which also had been burned to the ground.

Called out six times in three weeks through a terrified countryside, the men of the Train Bands were exhausted. But with the burning of Fairfield and Norwalk, British raids on Fairfield County towns came to an end. Tory raids would go on and on. The business at hand for Canaan Parish now was to provide for some of Norwalk's destitute families, and many a home opened its door to take in relatives and friends.

In the village of Norwalk only 11 houses remained standing, 80 houses, 87 barns, and two meeting houses having been burned. But that was not all. Tryon had planned the destruction of Norwalk well, and his men also burned 22 stores, 17 shops, four mills, and five ships tied up in the harbor—all this at a time when such trade as there was was plagued by the declining Continental currency. Four of the 17 men on the Committee to inquire into Goods Plundered were from Canaan Parish, and though claims were filed with the state, settlement was years in coming and Norwalk was slow in rebuilding. Fifteen months after the burning, the legislature in October 1780 granted Norwalk's petition to be allowed to load a 50-ton vessel with specified quantities of pork, tallow, flour, and grains "to export by water to Massachusetts or New Hampshire—the embargo notwithstanding." With the sale of this produce, Norwalk was allowed to bring back the boards, shingles, glass, and what else was needed to finish building new houses and shops.

The Illicit Trade

With the British in New York and Newport, R.I., trade outside Connecticut had been severely curtailed, lest useful goods fall into enemy hands. Like everyone else, the people of Canaan Parish had little opportunity to trade with any but their neighbors or agents for the Continental commissary. And the commissary paid in Continental paper money, the same currency that was the despair of the regular troops because its value fell constantly. To pay taxes and debts, to settle estates, simply to know where they stood financially, everyone wanted sound money—if not hard coin then Connecticut bills. And they wanted foods and goods they had long done without. So many a man, patriot as well as Loyalist, succumbed to the temptation to drive cattle across Westchester County to sell to the British, who paid in coin, or as seller or buyer to participate in the illicit trade that flourished back and forth across Long Island Sound. It was against this trade as well as the marauding Tories that Maj. Benjamin Tallmadge moved in 1779, although it would take him three more years to stamp out the last of it.

The recapture of Stony Point on July 15, 1779, had boosted morale generally, although locally it was lowered by the capture of the Rev. Moses Mather and four of his sons by a party of Tory raiders later that month. Then came the first raid on Long Island that Tallmadge planned from Canaan Parish.

Through the spies in his ring, Tallmadge had accurate information about the fortifications and British garrisons at Long Island harbors and the numbers and locations of the men and boats involved in the illicit trading and raids. For his first expedition, he picked Lloyd's Neck, a point of land outside Oyster Bay. With 50 of his dismounted light infantry, about 30 Continentals, and 50 boatmen and volunteers, Tallmadge left Shippan Point at Stamford at 8 o'clock on the night of September 5. After a two-hour sail, they landed on Lloyd's Neck, where they destroyed the houses and huts of "the whole gang of marauders and plunderers. . .which have for so long a time infested the coast of the Sound." To Tallmadge's chagrin, about 50 of the raiders were away in their boats on an expedition of their own, but his men destroyed every other boat they could find. With the alarm given, Tallmadge did not dare attack the nearby British fort. Before sunrise he was back at Shippan with a number of important prisoners and without the loss of a man.

The next month, writing from Canaan Parish to Gen. Robert Howe, Tallmadge reported that after three men had deserted from his troop two had been speedily caught with the help of the "well-affected inhabitants" of the Parish.

Tallmadge was again camping in Canaan Parish when, early in September 1780, he received a letter from Gen. Benedict Arnold, asking him to provide an escort for John Anderson, a merchant who would be visiting West Point. At the same time, Tallmadge's intelligence in New York informed him that Major John André of the British Army was arousing suspicions because he was receiving letters addressed to "John Anderson." So, when André and his incriminating papers were brought on September 23 to North Castle, where Tallmadge had just been transferred, he had a good idea of what was happening, and that night he took charge. Unable to prevent word of André's capture from reaching Arnold, who promptly fled from West Point, Tallmadge was able to intercept André, whom the commanding colonel at North Castle had earlier allowed to leave. (By coincidence, one of the men assigned to guard André that night was a Canaan Parish soldier. And one of the military court that tried Joshua Smith, André's unsuspecting companion, was Canaan Parish's Col. Joseph Hait. Though Smith was acquitted of treason, he was jailed as a Loyalist.)

Meanwhile, after the bitter cold winter of 1779-80—so cold that at least one deserting Hessian walked across the frozen Sound from Lloyd's Neck to Shippan Point—part of the British army had been moved south, from New York City to South Carolina, and the Tory raids on Connecticut had begun again.

Unless you have read every dispatch, letter, petition, claim for damages, and town meeting minute, you cannot believe today how many times the coastal towns of Greenwich, Stamford, and Norwalk were raided, how great were the losses the people suffered, and how often the militia was called to the scene. It was the man in the Train Band who bore most of the physical brunt of the Tory raids year after year until 1783—called at any hour of the day or night from his farm or his trade to march or ride to some part of the shore. When the Revolution ended, 190 Parish men knew what militia service meant. Writing from Canaan Parish on the same day Major André was captured, Gen. John Mead summed up the situation for Gen. Gould Selleck Silliman, just released as a British prisoner. Stating that the 9th Militia Regiment had seen more duty than any other two regiments, Mead went on: "We are now twelve days without bread, only what they have found themselves. Greenwich is completely ruined [the civil authorities had been forced to move to Stamford]. . . Stamford will soon be in the same state as Greenwich. The inhabitants are greatly discouraged."

Although some aid came from the State Troops and the coast guard was stepped up, the situation only worsened. Fifty-one Canaan Parish men, in a petition to the state legislature on December 11, summarized the damage done to the Middlesex part of Stamford in three recent raids. "This plundering is done," they wrote, "by those Refugees that have gone from this State, joined our Enemies, with the assistance of those that are Suffered to live a Moung us & allowed Protection of Law." They asked that the losses to their Middlesex neighbors be reimbursed out of the estates of the "inimical persons" still living among them. Despite the work of the Committees of Safety and the prosecution of suspected Loyalists, stepped up after the burning of Norwalk, Canaan Parish knew that it still had some of the enemy in its midst.

The year 1781 began for Canaan Parish with Samuel Cooke Silliman presiding over the trials of three men and a woman who had been trading with the enemy. While on coast guard duty, officers and men of the Canaan Parish Train Band had intercepted boats from Long Island attempting to land, and they produced in court the "foreign and India goods" they had captured as evidence that their neighbors were involved in illicit trade. In April four men from West Road were caught trying to smuggle cattle to the British in Westchester County. Tried for a state offense by the

Superior Court, sitting in Danbury, all four served jail sentences in Litchfield. That same month, William Reed, Jr., of White Oak Shade, fled to New York City. Apparently unsuspected before, Reed had concealed and then assisted a number of Tories to get to safety inside British lines. Next, on May 30, the Alarm List was rushed to Compo to repel an enemy landing. There Capt. Daniel Bouton, then in command, took a bullet in his shoulder (some accounts say he lost an arm), disabling him for life. Then, on Sunday, July 22, came the second capture of the Rev. Moses Mather. Two armed vessels had put in at Ring's End harbor, and 44 men and boys from among those attending service were captured at the Middlesex meeting house, to be carried off to Long Island and then to prison in New York. One of the leaders of that raid was Joseph Smith, who formerly had lived on Oenoke Ridge. A notorious raider, he had been captured and jailed earlier in the year but managed to escape.

Although the harbors of Norwalk and Stamford were fortified, obviously long stretches of the coast and the smaller harbors were open to raiders. So to protect both the coast and the interior, Gen. David Waterbury, one of Stamford's heroes, proposed building and manning a back-country fort, and with Governor Trumbull's approval, Fort Stamford belatedly was begun in August 1781.

Located three miles back from the Sound (one mile south of the present Merritt Parkway on Westover Road), Fort Stamford's garrison was able to move east, south, and west to the defense of the coastal towns and north to inland Greenwich and Bedford. Dr. James Cogswell, stationed in Stamford, could write on Sept. 19, 1781, "I do not consider our situation so much exposed at present as it has been. General Waterbury with near six hundred men lies about four miles west [Fort Stamford]. Maj. Tallmadge with a body of Continental Horse & Infantry [is] at Canaan ready to march to our assistance at the shortest notice, besides one or two companies in town." Three days earlier, Tallmadge had written to Barnabas Deane, his merchant friend, that Gen. William Heath had also stationed a battalion of infantry at Canaan Parish. The Parish, by then, was well accustomed to companies of soldiers and to supplying provisions for them.

In August, Washington had moved a large part of his and the French army south to Virginia, and in October news filtered back of Cornwallis's surrender at Yorktown on Oct. 17, 1781. Not for two years would families learn the details directly from the Canaan Parish men who participated in that battle. They already knew that young Ebenezer Hickok had died in Virginia before the fighting began, bringing to 22 the number of Canaan Parish men who lost their lives because of military service. Of the 213 men from the Parish who bore arms, 23 had enlisted for the duration in the Continental regiments, while 45 of the 190 militiamen served with Continental regiments for briefer times. The war was not over yet for Caanan Parish families.

CHAPTER 5

From Parish to Town, 1781-1801

Yorktown was the last major engagement between the British and Americans, but the Revolution did not end until Sept. 3, 1783, when a peace treaty was signed in Paris. So, until the British put an end to hostilities on Feb. 4, 1783, the illicit trade continued across the Sound and Connecticut men continued to go into Westchester County to protect people from cowboys and other raiders. Stamford had to bear the brunt of the expense of the State Troops stationed at its fort, and the unpaid and restless Continental soldiers, back in the Hudson Highlands once more, still had to be supplied. Nonetheless, the feeling was spreading that independence had been won, and at the end of 1781 Canaan Parish was giving thought to its church, which had been without a minister since March 1777, when the Rev. William Drummond was dismissed.

In May 1781, the General Assembly had authorized creation of the Parish of North Stamford along Canaan Parish's west boundary, and the North Stamford Congregational Church would be organized on June 4, 1782, with Dr. Samuel Hopkins as its first minister. Hopkins had left his church at Newport, R.I., when the British occupied that town, and eventually settled at Stamford where he ministered unofficially to the Congregational parishioners of his deceased former Yale classmate, Dr. Noah Welles. Hopkins, perhaps, also served the Canaan Parish church, because on widely scattered Sundays in 1781 and early 1782 some clergyman, now unidentifiable, admitted 22 persons to church membership.

In May 1782 Canaan Parish asked the Consociation of Fairfield County West to suggest names of possible ministerial candidates. One of those recommended by the Consociation was the Rev. Justus Mitchell (1784-1806), who since 1779 had been serving the Congregational church at Ridgefield on an irregular basis, following the death of the Rev. Jonathan Ingersol. Born in Woodbury, Conn., Justus Mitchell graduated from Yale College in 1776 and seems not to have served in the war. In 1779 he was ordained by the Litchfield South Association, and in September of that year he married Martha Sherman of Woodbridge, Conn. Martha (always called Patty) was the daughter of the Rev. Josiah Sherman, pastor of the Plymouth Church at Milford, Conn., who had been chaplain of the 7th Regiment, Connecticut Line, and she was a niece of the Hon. Roger Sherman, one of Connecticut's signers of the Declaration of Independence, who would soon sign the United States Constitution and be one of Connecticut's first Senators.

On Nov. 25, 1782, Justus Mitchell was called by the Society of Canaan—the Church apparently was not functioning officially—and on Jan. 21, 1783, the Consociation assembled in Canaan Parish, to spend the night in the house (now 46 Park Street) of David St. John, blacksmith and Train Band sergeant. The next day, in the meeting house across the road, Justus Mitchell was solemnly installed as Canaan Parish's fourth Congregational minister. The laying on of hands was performed by three neighboring clergymen, and the sermon was preached by the Rev. Isaac Lewis of Wilton. Should you care to read it, that sermon is in the Historical Society's Document file, having been published in book form in Hartford in 1784.

Between the call of Justus Mitchell and his installation, the business of war had again come close to home. For three nights in early December, Maj. Benjamin Tallmadge, back at his old stand, had attempted to transport the large force under his command from Shippan Point to Long Island, and each night a severe storm had made embarkation impossible. Thus ended Washington's plan to take his army down the North River for a two-pronged attack on the British in New York, while Tallmadge pressed in from Long Island. Instead, Tallmadge turned his attention once more to the illicit trade, and before Justus Mitchell's installation had captured vessels at Norwalk and elsewhere on the Sound.

It was on May 3, 1783, at Newburgh, N.Y., partly for morale purposes, that Gen. George Washington awarded the first three Purple Heart decorations, then given as Badges of Military Merit. All three went to Connecticut men: Sgt. Elisha Churchill, one of Tallmadge's Light Dragoons, who had participated twice in assaults on Tory strongholds on Long Island, and Sgts. Daniel Bissel and William Brown, for gallantry in action during the battle of Yorktown. William Brown, raised by his uncle Capt. John Carter of Train Band renown, had enlisted from Canaan Parish as a private in the Continental Army in 1777, at age 16. At Yorktown on Oct. 14, 1781, "with great bravery propriety and deliberate firmness" he had conducted a "forlorn Hope," a surprise attack by a small group on a small British stronghold.

William Brown came home to Canaan Parish in July 1783, following the informal discharge of most Continental troops. (Passing through Stamford, he "casually" lost his pocketbook containing the government notes that were all his earnings for six years in the service. On his petition, the Stamford town meeting the next year voted to make good the whole sum.) But home was not the Canaan Parish William Brown had left. Besides his fellow soldiers who had lost their lives in the war, his Carter Street neighbor Theophilus Fitch, shoemaker, tanner, and justice of the peace, was dead, and his uncle John Carter, no longer in the Train Band, was about to take Fitch's place as a deacon of the Congregational church. Also the Rev. Robert Silliman, while on a visit to his son, had died and been buried in Canaan Parish in April 1781. Some 75 Loyalists from perhaps a dozen Canaan Parish families were gone, their houses and lands confiscated and sold. Most of the Tories who had participated in the raids on Connecticut shores had sailed in the the Loyalist fleet for Nova Scotia, though a few who had fought in the British army had attempted to return home after the surrender at Yorktown. In both Stamford and Norwalk they were met with petitions for their punishment and majority votes against their return. Of the 19 "inimicals" Canaan Parish had permitted to remain in their homes, at least eight were able eventually to clear their names, by proving they had not been guilty of unpatriotic acts. Their confiscated estates were returned, but, despite the General Assembly's order to do so, the selectmen of Stamford refused to reopen the cases of other inimicals or to return monies and land that had been taken from them.

Exodus

Before the summer of 1783 was over, the last of the Continental soldiers had come back to Canaan Parish, and in December the British evacuated New York. The regular soldiers had fought from Massachusetts to Virginia with men from the other twelve states (one had served with the French under Lafayette), and besides towns and terrains outside Fairfield County they had learned something about foreigners and European ideas. Whereas the older soldiers and the militiamen were content to settle down and try to resume trades, the younger veterans, newly married, began moving away. By 1789, with the formation of the United States, good farmland in New York was selling for $1 per acre and Vermont was about to become a state—two inducements to migration. Kelloggs and Seymours, to name a few, settled at Ballston, N.Y., Boutons at Genesee, Benedicts at Greenfield, and Amblers and Slausons in Vermont. So many young families went to Walton, N.Y.—Benedicts, Eells, Hoyts, Fitches, St. Johns, Seymours, and Weeds—that that town became known as New Canaan's "daughter," to which the Congregational Church in 1829 would present its original communion service. In the 1790's would come the moves to Pennsylvania, Ohio, and farther west with the opening of the Western Reserve, so that by 1800 some 120 Canaan Parish families had moved away, taking their trades to the new towns they helped to found and leaving home markets to their older established relatives.

Transportation in the late 18th century was no different from what it had been when Massachusetts families settled Connecticut in 1635. Men, women and children walked, rode on horseback or in ox-drawn carts, or they traveled by water. When the time came to move, Canaan Parish families simply packed clothing and bedding, picked out a few utensils and tools, gathered up their seed and their herbs, and left most of their furniture behind. Before the settlement of Walton, several young Canaan Parish men had made a preliminary trip west in the summer of 1789 to look over the possibilities, buy land, and start building a house or two. One pioneering shoemaker did a winter's work in New York state before returning home for the final move, sending back word of his whereabouts by those who returned in the fall. Then the next spring, several related families set out together to move to the chosen site.

One wife, left behind to await the birth of a child, packed herself, her four children (including the new baby), and her goods on board a sloop at Five Mile River landing and sailed to New York. Aboard another sloop, she went up the Hudson River to Catskill, N.Y., where her husband had promised to meet her on Aug. 1, 1790. Coming overland from Walton with borrowed horses, he arrived eight days late.

Not everyone who left Canaan Parish was young. Dr. Samuel Baker, who had married Rhoda (Silliman) Weed, was nearing 60 when he bought 1,000 acres of land at Middle Island Creek in "the County of Ohio in New Virginia"—what would become West Virginia. A 1789 letter tells how he was farming the land with the help of only his young son. And Capt. James Richards was 65 when, after losing his first wife, he set out in the fall of 1788 with Judge John Cleves Symmes of New Jersey and two other men for Ohio. There Captain Richards spent the winter in the only house that had been built at the settlement called Lozantiville, which would become Cincinnati. Captain Richards had lost at least one of his vessels to the British, and he had lost heavily by accepting Continental money during the war, but pioneering was not for him. He soon returned to Canaan Parish, married twice more, and took to sheep-raising and weaving on a rather large scale. Sgt. William Brown, however, became a proprietor of Cincinnati. After moving to Ballston, N.Y., he received bounty land in the

18th- and 19th-century sloops were fast sailers, capable of carrying more cargo and passengers than their size suggests.

Northwest Territory in 1789, and soon afterward settled in Cincinnati, where he raised nine children and became a justice of the peace and a lieutenant colonel in the county militia.

New Churches

Some historians have characterized the period immediately following the Revolution as a time of free thinking, much drinking, materialism, and vice. Justus Mitchell recorded in 1787 Canaan Parish's first suicide—a young lady of 29 who was "attended with a melancholy"—and in 1790 the first death "by alcoholism"—a man. Materialism can perhaps be evidenced by the acquisition of more land by a few of the already large landowners, but the pattern of land sales was much as it had been all along. Of local vice, nothing is known. And, contrary to what may have been going on elsewhere, Canaan Parish was thinking hard about religion.

Immediately after his installation, Justus Mitchell drew up a new Confession of Faith and a new Covenant for the Canaan Parish Congregational Church, which were said to have been very close to the originals of 1733. (This, plus the fact that he was called by the Society only, suggests that the Church had to be reinstituted or re-formed.) After nearly six years with no minister, the Parish settled down to regular Sunday services, attended by so many people that in 1787 the meetinghouse galleries, planned in 1752, at last were built. In 1797 a steeple was added and the first church bell hung there. It weighed 519 pounds and for years was rung every evening at 9 P.M. No serious religious dispute would mar Mitchell's ministry; such spats as necessitated Consociation hearings were caused by civil suits among church members over real property.

Late in 1787 the Congregational Church voted down a proposal to consider as members in full standing all those who had "owned" their baptismal covenants. This left the old Halfway Covenant in force and the full-communion members in control, thus pitting the exclusive Congregationalists against Baptists and Methodists.

Connecticut in 1784 had passed a General Toleration Act. Thereafter, anyone who presented the clerk of a Congregational Society with a certificate that showed he was a member of a religious society now recognized by the law had to be excused from paying the abominated Congregational tax. Eagerly, the Baptists and Methodists, emphasizing rebaptism, set out to found churches and convert anyone who even mildly dissented from the Established church, and in Canaan Parish after the Revolution they found quite a few.

Two months before the Methodist Episcopal Church was formally organized at Baltimore in December 1784, Norwalk was listening to the preaching of the Rev. William Black, an English Methodist. Tradition holds that as early as 1785 another Englishman preached Methodism at Pound Ridge and that as early as 1787 the Rev. Cornelius Cook conducted Methodist services in Canaan Parish. That was the same year when the Rev. Samuel Q. Talbot of the New Rochelle Circuit formed a "class" at Dantown (named for the Dan family) in northwestern Canaan Parish—and this is the base for New Canaan's claim that it was the place of origin of New England Methodism. (Officially, Stratfield, Conn., is credited with the first New England Methodist Society, formed in 1788.) What is known for sure is that Jesse Lee, the great pioneer Methodist preacher, held services in Canaan Parish in June 1789, and at Dantown (he made the distinction) on Feb. 27, 1790, he took charge of the quarterly meeting of the recently formed Stamford-Redding Circuit. Lee recorded these facts in his diary, adding that at Dantown he was joined by Elder Jacob Bush and two preachers: George Roberts and Daniel Smith. In another diary entry, Lee noted that on Oct. 21, 1790, he baptized a child at Dantown, the first baptism there. He was to return again, since Canaan Parish soil was good for Methodism, but when the Dantown Methodists built their first meeting house in 1795, it was located a few yards over the state line in Pound Ridge, N.Y. Canaan Parish had to wait until 1808 for its first Methodist Society, formed in Silvermine.

Meanwhile, Canaan Parish had been a bit reduced in area by a change in its western boundary. Nineteen Congregational families living between Dantown and Davenport Ridge had in May 1788 petitioned the General Assembly to be put under the new North Stamford Society; it would be more convenient for them "to attend preaching in North Stamford," since they lived closer to that meeting house than to the Canaan Parish one. Provided all had paid "any Parish taxes already laid by Canaan Parish," the petition was granted, and Canaan's western boundary was moved eastward so that, roughly, it ran 20 rods east of Ponus Ridge road. Not only was the highway but a good 5,300 acres of land transferred to the North Stamford Society, which land, the petition claimed, was assessed at less than $3,000 (or about $2.83 cents an acre, not counting any dwelling house). Some but not all of these acres later would come back to New Canaan.

Information about the Baptists is neither complete nor clear. Without bothering to say who the man was, someone carefully recorded the fact that the first Canaan Parish Baptist was baptized in New York City by Elder Gano in 1775. Gano, however, had been baptizing and preaching in Stamford in 1769-70, and in 1772 the Stamford Baptists built the first Baptist meeting house north of New York City. So perhaps the first Canaan Parish convert was baptized by Gano in Stamford, rather than in New York, although lists of early Stamford Baptists contain no Canaan Parish names.

Soon after the 1784 Toleration Act, a Baptist revival produced surprising results in Connecticut, and about then Canaan Parish seems to have formed an independent group of Baptist converts. (No records of this survive.) This was contrary to Fairfield County as a whole, where the itinerant, often illiterate, Baptist preachers had far less appeal than they did in other counties of the state. Democratically inclined, the Baptists and Methodists blamed the poor social and economic conditions of the post-Revolution days on the aristocratic and academically snobbish Congregationalists, whom they accused of dominating all living and learning. (Although it's getting ahead of the story, out of this period of dissent with the Established Church came Connecticut's 1818 Constitution and complete religious liberty—a victory for the Republicans, supported by the newer denominations, over the Federalists, backed by the Congregationalists.)

One Canaan Parish man who "got religion" and felt called upon to become a lay Baptist preacher was Justus Hoyt, a shoemaker, who had been a sergeant of the 9th Militia Company during the many alarms of 1779. He was the father of many later prominent Hoyts, and his house, which stood opposite where the New Canaan Library stands, was moved in 1964 to become 32 East Maple Street. Two of Hoyt's converts were Enoch Comstock, another Revolutionary veteran, and his wife Anne, only child of Abraham Weed, that thorn in the flesh of two Congregational ministers. Some time in the 1790's, a reminiscence holds, Justus Hoyt was to preach at a Baptist service in the Comstock's house (now gone from the south corner of Weed Street and Wahackme Road). He arrived late, in his shirt sleeves, dissheveled and perspiring. He had, he said, been having "a dreadful time in running away from the devil," who had tried to persuade him to shave, dress up, and wear a coat. Although she had said not a word, Miss Deborah Abbott (later to be housekeeper and practical nurse for Congregational Deacon John Carter) must have looked askance, for "Preacher" Hoyt asked "sister Abbott" what was on her mind. "I thought," Miss Abbott replied, "The Good Book said when Peter went a-fishing, he girded on his fisherman's coat." Instead of records, it is anecdotes like this, repeated years later, that characterize New Canaan's recollections of the earliest Baptists.

To give the people of Canaan Parish still wider choice and add to the problems of the Rev. Justus Mitchell, the old Church of England church was re-formed on Nov. 15, 1791, as the Episcopal Society of Canaan Parish, which reopened the West Road Anglican meeting house. The Protestant Episcopal Church in the United States of America had been founded two years earlier, and the first Episcopal bishop was the Rt. Rev. Samuel Seabury of Connecticut. (Though not until 1851 would a priest visit New Canaan, 1789 was also the year in which the first Roman Catholic bishop for the United States was appointed, and the whole of Connecticut was put under his See of Baltimore.) In October 1791, Connecticut had granted the right of free incorporation to all churches, and shortly afterward the Episcopal was recognized as the second church in the state. Forty-two Canaan Parish people were listed in 1791 as founding members of the Episcopal Society—among them Crissy, Raymond, Seely, Smith, Talmadge, and Weed families—some of whom had been "inimicals" less than a decade before, while others had been leading patriots. In the next decade, their numbers would be increased by former Congregationalists. Still, Canaan Parish seems to have had enough people to support four religious denominations, while a few more supported no church at all.

New Parish Leaders

Religion, of course, was not all that was on people's minds. Earning a living probably was uppermost. With the end of hostilities and the opening of the Sound, everyone demanded the goods they had so long done without. The people of Canaan Parish went back to their trades, especially shoemaking and weaving, and even before New York was rid of the British, farm products again were being shipped there by boat. While the farmers on the east side of Canaan Parish used Norwalk's ports and those along Ponus Ridge went to Shippan, such large farmers as the Lockwoods on Oenoke and Abijah Comstock at the north end of Smith Ridge sent their produce to Five Mile River harbor at Rowayton. There Andrew Powers had the brig *Sally,* and there Comstock's new neighbor, Capt. Isaac Richards, was both master mariner and part owner of a store.

Isaac Richards (1759-1825) was only 23 years old when in May 1782 he purchased from Nehemiah Benedict, his father-in-law, the 186½-acre farm where Mr. Drummond had boarded on present Country Club Road. (When his great-grandchildren sold to the Country Club in 1905, the land was still called "the Isaac Richard farm" and was still 186½ acres in size.) Isaac Richards twice had done military service with two different Middlesex companies before he was wounded at the battle of Ridgefield in 1777. Shot in the left leg, he avoided being bayoneted by the British by playing dead, and in later life he drew a small pension for his injury—not that he needed it.

A third-generation master mariner, Isaac Richards was the younger son of Capt. Samuel Richards, Jr., of Rowayton, who had died on June 25, 1777, the day after his brother, Captain James, had brought him home from a British prison in New York. His estate, not probated until 1782 in Fairfield, is the largest I have come upon for this period. Among some 40 listings of real estate Capt. Samuel Richards, Jr., owned were several houses, five farms, a mill, a wharf and a store at Five Mile River harbor, and one fifth of the shipyard there. Isaac Richards inherited a third of this considerable property, and like his brother-in-law, Capt.

Gershom Richards, became a successful master mariner. His first wife, Hannah Benedict, died in February 1786 at age 26, leaving three small children, and in December of that year he married Eunice Taylor of Middlesex.

In the Richard's genealogy, Captain Isaac is described as "a man of rare strength of both body and mind and remarkable for self-government. . . . When rudely treated and assaulted, his defense was never in blows, but in hugging, at which he was as formidable as a bear." Once he had a man in his grip, he allowed him only enough breath to cry quarter, releasing him "more thoroughly tamed than he could have been by a bloody mauling, and yet without ability to prove an assault." By "strength of mind" and not brute force, Isaac Richards was to put his mark on Canaan Parish and New Canaan.

Until the new United States government ordered ports to keep records in 1789, little information is available about ships and shipping, and nothing is known about the revival of the Richards' fleet immediately after the Revolution. The port book for Fairfield, where County vessels were registered, shows that in 1789 Capts. Isaac and Gershom Richards were owners of the *Two Brothers,* a 32 69/95-ton sloop, which because of her small size probably plied the Sound between Five Mile River harbor and New York. In 1793, however, the two Captain Richards owned the 91 87/95-ton schooner *Washington,* which had been built for them by Henry Johnson of Greenwich. Registered at Fairfield, the *Washington* with Capt. Naphthalie Raymond as master, made a voyage in 1794 to St. Thomas and Martinique, bringing back for the Richards a cargo of molasses, sugar, copper, limes, and tamarinds.

The *Washington* made history, but not until after the Richards had sold the schooner to various Lockwoods and Sellecks of Norwalk. With Capt. Henry Chichester as master, the *Washington* was captured by a French privateer in 1799 and taken into Guadalupe, where vessel and cargo were condemned by the French, no longer the friends of the United States. Chichester and his crew eventually came home, but out of this and similar captures of American ships grew the French Spoliation Claims. Renewed by successive generations of descendants of the original owners, the claims were finally settled by Congress in 1906, at which time a share went to a Selleck descendant, who, when she came to live in New Canaan, had some of the papers relating to the *Washington*.

Meantime, in 1798 Isaac Richards had become owner and master of the sloop *Delight*, a costal vessel which, on one of its voyages, took a cargo of Connecticut stone from Rowayton to Philadelphia. One of the bondsmen then was Samuel St. John, who had just married Capt. Isaac Richards' only daughter and was living in the house (now 46 Park Street) of his deceased father David. Only ten years different in age, the two men thereafter were closely associated in business and public affairs. In 1800 they had the brig *Charleston* built for them by Henry Johnson, who had moved from Greenwich to Rowayton (from whence his descendants would move to New Canaan). At the time Canaan Parish became New Canaan, the firm of Richards & St. John not only had a general store near Samuel St. John's house but also acted as a private bank, loaning money on mortgages, since land was the only security available to most men in those days.

Until he died unexpectedly in 1795, Samuel Cooke Silliman went right on being one of Norwalk's two representatives to the legislature. In 1792 he married as his second wife Dinah, a daughter of Abijah Comstock, whereupon he retired from business, selling the Main Street house that had been his tavern and store to Gould and Stephen Hoyt, sons of the Baptist lay preacher Justus Hoyt. Although it would soon put him into bankruptcy, Gould Hoyt acquired the distillery near the East Avenue millpond where he made fruit brandies for such Canaan Parish men who had developed large orchards. It wasn't long before Jesse Richards, Captain James' son, and Samuel Comstock, son of Abijah, were operating a distillery on upper Smith Ridge; the Weed family began one near Cascade Road, and the Stevens family another in Talmadge Hill, while the many existing cider mills, owned in shares by neighborhood families, went right on making cider, both sweet and hard. Rum, gin, and whisky had to be imported, but the cheaper products of local stills encouraged the intemperance that became a real problem.

As Canaan Parish began to grow, after the exodus of people who moved west, it had in the person of Dr. Joseph Silliman (1756-1829) both a new resident physician and a surveyor. As a boy of 15, Joseph had gone to Chester when the Rev. Robert Silliman, his father, became minister there in 1771. Somewhere (quite possibly in Canaan Parish under his brother-in-law, Dr. Samuel Baker) Joseph Silliman studied medicine and seems to have established a practice in Canaan Parish by 1785, when he married Martha, a daughter of the well-to-do Elisha Leeds. Although his forebears had been Stamford master mariners, Leeds owned the prosperous farm that today is the western part of New Canaan's Waveny Park, and for his daughter and son-in-law he bought in 1789 the Oenoke Ridge property that had been Stephen Hanford's tavern and house (now the Historical Society's Hanford-Silliman House). Possibly because, as Joseph wrote a brother in Chester, "in general time of health. . . physicians have but a little business to do in visiting the sick," Joseph Silliman sought a second source of income. Through the influence of his eldest brother, S. Cooke, he was appointed surveyor for Fairfield County in 1787, and after his brother's death, Dr. Joseph was elected by the legislature to suceed Samuel Cooke Silliman as one of Fairfield County's justices of the peace. He also farmed on a small scale along Oenoke Ridge, where his neighbor to the north was the Rev. Justus Mitchell.

With the death of S. Cooke Silliman in 1795, a new generation of Canaan Parish men came to the fore. Abijah Comstock, then 74 years old, was interested only in extending his already large farm on upper Smith Ridge over the line into New York state; Justice of the Peace Abraham Weed had filled many important war posts in Stamford, but at 67 now was content to manage his property. (He had set a precedent when in 1783 he freed his female slave Tamar.) Lt. Col. Joseph Hait, nearing 70, farmed the Ponus Ridge lands that had been given him in lieu of back pay for his eight years in the Continental army, though he had served in 1789 as one of Stamford's representatives to the legislature. Andrew Powers, the mill and ship owner, had died in 1785, aged 38, and young Capt. Stephen Betts devoted himself to the very new Episcopal Church, of which he was first warden, while farming on upper Oenoke Ridge. Thus the leadership of Canaan Parish affairs passed to the Rev. Justus Mitchell, Dr. Joseph Silliman, and Capt. Isaac Richards, who in 1795 were, respectively, 40, 38, and 35 years old.

No one ever described Justus Mitchell's appearance, and no portrait survives. When he died suddenly on Feb. 24, 1806, leaving a wife, four married children, and some two dozen handwritten sermons, he passed into local history as "the beloved Pastor," whose sorrowing parishioners planted a weeping willow beside his tombstone on God's Acre. Yet the Rev. Justus Mitchell not only was a well-known clergyman; he was the founder of Canaan Parish's first private school and first library, and he was called "the brains" behind the incorporation of New Canaan.

In 1783, with £165 of the money he received from the Society for "settling" as minister, Justus Mitchell bought 22 acres from Stephen Hanford and built the house that is now the front section of No. 195 Oenoke Ridge (the Roger Sherman Inn). Soon he acquired much more acreage on the west side of the highway, which Dr. Silliman surveyed for him. In his house Mitchell promptly established a private school, expressly to prepare young men for Yale. The first of his pupils to graduate were Eliphalet St. John and Daniel Smith, both in Yale's class of 1791. St. John temporarily returned to the Parish to found his own school, while Daniel Smith, son of that Peter Smith who had been a counterfeiter, became Stamford's Congregational minister. For the first time in its history Canaan Parish knew college graduates other than the minister. Later Yale graduates whom Mitchell prepared went on to other sorts of professional careers. Among the day pupils were one of the clergyman's own sons, who became a lawyer, and two sons of Doctor Silliman, while as boarding pupils he educated two of his wife's relatives: Roger Minot Sherman, a prominent Fairfield County judge, and Roger Sherman Baldwin, who became governor of Connecticut in 1844.

In the Library of Congress are three letters that passed between Justus Mitchell and his uncle by marriage, the Hon. Roger Sherman, pertaining to the founding of a library. (Sherman then was one of Connecticut's first two U.S. senators, and Congress was meeting in New York City.) "The people in this place," Mitchell wrote on Jan. 16, 1790, "have agreed many of them to set up a library and are collecting money to make a small purchase of books." Was it cheaper, Mitchell asked Sherman, to buy books in New Haven or New York? Asking for a list of titles, the Senator replied on February 8 that New York book dealers would sell as low as they could but would not give any "abatement" to the Canaan Parish purchasers. Mitchell reported in March that "We have sent for [books] and are to be received this week," adding that several gentlemen wanted books about the Revolution and would Sherman advise them on the best titles to buy. Apparently housed in Mitchell's parsonage, the private library eventually acquired about 100 titles, to be borrowed only by the "gentlemen" contributors. That the Canaan Parish ladies in the late 18th century also bought and read books can be proved by surviving orders, account books, and correspondence.

The School Society

With a library for themselves and a school for the sons of those who could afford private education, the leaders of Canaan Parish next gave their attention to the matter of public schools—as did every town in the state, because public funds were about to become available. Connecticut in 1795 authorized the sale of its Western Reserve, that huge tract of land which is now the state of Ohio. To buy the Reserve, 35 men put up $1,200,000, and Connecticut intended to deposit the net proceeds from the sale in a special fund, the interest on which was to go to support local public schools.

In the colonial charter granted by Charles II in 1662, Connecticut's western boundary was given as the Pacific Ocean. Although this grandiose claim was relinquished by the state to the new federal government, Connecticut retained title to the bloc of land west of the Alleghenies that it called the Western Reserve. This Connecticut governed until 1800. Along with the sale of the land, Connecticut in 1795 also authorized a settlement scheme for a 25-mile-wide strip of land in the Reserve. This was the "Firelands," so called because the state deeded the land in small parcels to those who had filed claims for losses when the British "fired" Danbury, Fairfield, Norwalk, and New London during the Revolution. (Most of such owners sold their Ohio lands to pioneering settlers, but Thomas Comstock of Valley Road, who had assisted so many Norwalk refugees, sent his son Nathan S. Comstock to take up his grant and help found Norwalk, Ohio. Although Nathan in 1809 built the first house in Norwalk in the Firelands, he soon returned home.)

To obtain their share of Norwalk's potential school money, the people on the Norwalk side of Canaan Parish met on Oct. 29, 1795, and with Capt. Isaac Richards presiding, incorporated the Canaan Parish School Society. In this way, some financial support could be secured for the eight district schools that were functioning on the Norwalk side of Canaan Parish. (The three district schools on the Stamford side were then under the North Stamford School Society, the records of which do not exist for this period.) Captain Richards saw to it that matters were handled properly, and one can find in the records the boundaries of each school district and which families sent children to which school. Possibly as a result of these efforts, Isaac Richards was elected a selectman of Norwalk the next year and in 1799 one of its state representatives. In the legislature he served on a committee that dealt with the regulation and encouragement of public schools. In 1800 and 1801, Dr. Joseph Silliman replaced him as one of Norwalk's two representatives.

Rock School, built c.*1799 for School District No. 2, is New Canaan's oldest schoolhouse, preserved since 1973 on the grounds of the New Canaan Historical Society.*

Township

Some time before the School Society was incorporated the movement to become a town must have gathered momentum, because by early 1796 the proposed boundaries had been surveyed and a carefully written petition prepared for submission to the legislature. Dated "Norwalk, 10 March, 1796" and "Stamford, April 26, 1796," the petition was signed by 172 legal male voters in Canaan Parish.

In well-chosen words, which suggest that Justus Mitchell was the author, the inhabitants of Canaan Parish and "that part of the inhabitants of the Parish of North Stamford...who live on the east side of...Poness Street" stated their desire "to be incorporated into a town and to have and to enjoy the immunities, Libertyes and privileges" the same as other towns. The petition then stated (1) what the boundaries would be, explaining that "a line running through the center of said town from east to west" was four miles "wanting 40 rods" and from north to south, five and a quarter miles; (2) that the population of the area was 274 families and about 1,500 inhabitants; (3) that, based on their 1794 grand lists, Stamford would lose only £3,970 from its total of £32,412 and Norwalk, £7,179 from its £33,425 list of taxable lands (land values still were being recorded in pounds, shillings, and pence), so that the new town would begin with a list of £11,149-0-9. (4) The places in Norwalk and Stamford "appointed to do Public business," the petition continued, were so far from the petitioners' homes (in some cases 9 miles to Norwalk's town house and 12 to Stamford's) and the public roads were "not only uneven and stony" but so often bad and indirect that the people of Canaan Parish were "induced to neglect" freemen's and town meetings, and that while "they & their ancestors have submitted to these great inconveniences and expense," the petitioners considered them a hardship. Furthermore (5), their continued incorporation in Norwalk and Stamford was of no advantage to those towns, while incorporation as a separate town would promote the inhabitants' interests. (6) Besides relinquishing all claim to the public buildings of Norwalk and Stamford, the petitioners stated their willingness to pay their part of all debts of the two towns according to the 1794 lists. "Wherefore your Honours, Petitioners Humbly Pray your honours to take their case into your wise consideration, and order and direct that the Inhabitants of the Parish of Canaan and such inhabitants of the Parish of North Stamford as dwell within the limits ascertained" be incorporated as a town. Nowhere was the name of the new town mentioned.

To consider the petition, the legislature ordered the first selectman of Stamford and of Norwalk to appear at a hearing in Hartford on the second Thursday in May 1796. Thereafter no record or paper can be found to explain why it took five years for incorporation to be achieved. That Stamford had objections is known, because on Apr. 6, 1801, it called a special town meeting to act on a legal proceeding and at that meeting named an agent to oppose Canaan Parish's petition when it came before the legislature the next month.

This move came to nothing, and on an unspecified day in May 1801 Connecticut's General Assembly granted the petition and incorporated the town of New Canaan—*New* because though Canaan Parish had been founded in 1731, the town of Canaan, Connecticut, had been incorporated in 1739—with two conditions. All taxes owed to Norwalk and Stamford on their 1799 (not 1796) lists were to be paid, and the first town meeting was to be held on the last Monday in June at the Presbyterian (meaning Congregational) meeting house. Dr. Joseph Silliman, then one of Norwalk's two representatives, was to draw up and post on the public signboard the warning of this meeting and to preside as moderator. Should he be dead or otherwise absent, Stephen Betts was to preside. When the news reached home, two days after the Assembly's act, it was celebrated by the firing of a cannon.

As the state had ordered, New Canaan's first town meeting was held on June 29, 1801, and a town government was organized with Capt. Isaac Richards, Dr. Joseph Silliman, and Col. Joseph Seely being appointed first, second, and third selectman, respectively. Altogether, 18 men were appointed to offices in nine different categories. Samuel St. John was appointed town clerk, and New Canaan began to function as an incorporated town within almost the same boundaries that Canaan Parish had, since most of the landowners who had put themselves under the North Stamford Society now came back. After exactly 70 years, one month, and 16 days, Canaan Parish was no more. The Society of Canaan, however, survived a full century longer, functioning as the business arm of the Congregational Church.

PART II

New Canaan 1801-1951

Illustrations

	PAGE
Dr. and Mrs. Joseph Silliman	123
Amos Ayres' shoe factory, later known as the "Big Shop"	145
New Canaan's first Town House (Town Hall)	147
The Hanford-Silliman House	148
A typical small shoe shop	154
Church Hill, 1835	158
The Fitch family's boarding house	163
Rev. David Ogden; Rev. Theophilus Smith	177
Steamboat at South Norwalk (Old Well)	179
Stagecoach arriving at the top of Church Hill	180
Noah Wilcox Hoyt; Selleck Y. St. John	192
Lucius M. Monroe; Prof. Samuel St. John	193
Samuel A. Weed; Stephen Hoyt, Jr.	198
The 13th Connecticut regiment at Camp Thibodeaux	200
New Canaan's first bank building	204
Locomotive leaving the New Canaan station	207
J. & J. Benedict's first shoe factory	210
The 1878 industrial scene near the railroad tracks	216
Henry B. Rogers; Dr. Willard Parker, Sr.	223
"Central Park" and the Parker elm	225
Benjamin P. Mead; Joseph F. Silliman	232
Francis E. Weed's coal and lumber yard	235
Map of the Borough of New Canaan	239
The Country Club	247
Center School, *c.*1893	254
Start of the 1901 parade	262
A parade unit on Main Street	263
Main Street, 1906; Forest Street stable; the "third" automobile	269
Elm Street, *c.*1910	273
New Canaan's second and fourth Town Halls	276
Main Street on Armistice Day, 1918	291
Dedication of the Wayside Cross	293
Elm Street, *c.*1935	311
The Birdsall House in its prime; being demolished	318
Philip Johnson's "Glass House"	319
The Mill Pond	323

CHAPTER 6

The Benevolent Despots, 1801-1825

When New Canaan held its first annual town meeting on Dec. 14, 1801, the qualified male voters elected by secret ballot the same three selectmen they had approved in June: Isaac Richards, Joseph Silliman, and Joseph Seely. As third selectman, Colonel Seely represented no opposition party; like the other two he was a Congregationalist and a Federalist, convinced that only large landowners knew how to govern and that the status quo was the best.

For its first 17 years, excepting 1812, New Canaan seems to have been content to leave its affairs in the paternalistic hands of its Federalists. Capt. Isaac Richards served as first selectman until 1824, with the exceptions of 1812 and 1819, and twice was New Canaan's representative to the General Assembly. Dr. Joseph Silliman was elected second selectman for four successive years, and then was representative seven times, while Joseph Seely after four terms as third selectman moved up to fill Dr. Silliman's place. Until he died in 1825, Samuel St. John, Isaac Richards' son-in-law, was annually elected town clerk and treasurer and also served seven terms in the legislature. All the while, the small office-store of Richards & St. John doubled as New Canaan's town hall, where were kept the land records, town-meeting books, and minutes of the selectmen. There, too, apparently were deposited the monies New Canaan collected in taxes, since nowhere closer than New York or New Haven was there a bank.

To finish setting up its government, New Canaan voters at the December 1801 meeting elected two constables by ballot and then by show of hand elected some 40 men to a variety of public offices. Except for the five listers, the equivalent of assessors, who kept the grand list up to date, the offices were not any the town fills today, but they were offices that, successively, the Colony and then the State of Connecticut expected every town to have: grand jurors (3), haywards (6), fence viewers (2), tything men (2), and a pound viewer, a sealer of weights, a sealer of measures, and a leather sealer. Tything men were to work with the constables and grand jurors to make sure the laws were enforced, especially those for the strict observance of the Sabbath; fence viewers, as the name implies, were to make certain that fences—be they stone or wood—were in repair and 4½ feet high; while the haywards' job was to turn over to the pound keeper any swine found wandering at large. The sealer of weights and the sealer of measures once a year checked what was being used by New Canaan sellers against the town's standard weights and measures, for which they had custody, while the sealer of leather (the office was gone by 1807) made sure every "manufacturer of leather goods"—boots, shoes, saddles, etc.—lived up to his "seal" of quality.

Between the organizing meeting in June and the annual meeting in December, the selectmen had settled with Norwalk and Stamford on the poor—two from each town—for whom New Canaan was responsible, and they had compiled a grand list for the town that listed all real and personal property. On this the December meeting voted to lay a tax of 1 cent on the dollar to cover the town's expenses for the coming year. Since no one, not even the selectmen, was paid a salary (the town clerk, poundkeeper, and others collected fees for work done), and school budgets were the responsibility of the parents of children attending the several district schools, New Canaan's expenses were limited to the care of the poor, a few minor items, and potential lawsuits. (If a horse broke its leg when a wooden bridge gave way, its owner would sue.) Highways had a budget unto themselves.

In its petition for incorporation, Canaan Parish had stressed the bad state of its roads. Consequently, the first annual meeting created 17 highway districts and elected a surveyor for each. Then it voted a highway tax of 2 cents on the dollar, double the town tax, stipulating that three fourths of the total collected was to be spent before June 30, 1802. Whereas the job of collecting the annual town tax went to the man making the lowest bid (something under $10), each highway surveyor was obliged to collect from the people in his district and turn the full sum over to the selectmen, who then paid the "highway crews." A man working the roads in spring and summer was paid 75 cents a day and 75 cents more if he supplied a team; in the fall the rates fell to 67 cents; in the winter no work was done, since snow plowing town roads was unheard of.

Winding up its December 1801 meeting, the town named a collector of the state tax and voted the privilege of "insulating" the townspeople against smallpox to Dr. David Richmond, a newcomer who soon moved away.

With that business attended to, New Canaan had a functioning, responsible town government. Because of incorporation, it had its own representative in the legislature. All the money collected in taxes would now be spent right at home. Town meetings were to be held in the Congregational meeting house, across the way from the makeshift town hall in Richards & St. John's store, and never again did anyone have to go to Norwalk or Stamford to vote. Weather permitting, the April and September state elections took place out of doors in front of the Congregational church, for which the county treasurer still collected the "church tax." Incorporation had not eliminated that.

New Activities

As 1802 began, New Canaan was (and would be for years) the scattering of regional settlements Canaan Parish had been. Incorporation could not change that. Nothing resembling a town center or a village existed; no street could yet be called "main." People living in Silvermine or Smith Ridge knew little of the people in Ponus Ridge or White Oak Shade, though the new militia companies were helping to break down some of the regional barriers, and so was trade. But change would come.

The early 19th century saw everywhere a proliferation of the cottage industries that had characterized Canaan Parish's economy. Three fulling mills suggest that sheep raising and weaving were profitable. Grist mills were prospering on a number of streams, and Capt. Isaac Richards bought two as investments: one on Five Mile River near the foot of Parade Hill, the other in Dantown on a branch of the Noroton River. Still flourishing on the

Mill Pond were the former Hanford saw and grist mills, now owned by the Hoyt family. And joining the ranks of shoemakers was Thomas Greenley, a London cockney, who in 1805 was able to settle at what is now No. 64 Silvermine Road once the legislature passed a special law conferring on him as a "foreigner" all the privileges of a native-born citizen, including the right to own land.

At the same time, new industries began to appear. Seth Hamilton found clay deposits on his 40-acre Ponus Ridge farm and started a brick "factory," perhaps to make chimneys and beehive ovens for new homes, since no all-brick house was ever built in New Canaan. William Watson, another Englishman granted citizenship by the legislature, was encouraged by the town fathers in 1811 with a grant of "as much common land as will accommodate him in carrying on the Mechanical business he had commenced on Five Mile River." Watson had started a small tool factory off East Avenue just north of the Mill Pond and needed waterpower to run his machinery; hence New Canaan's gift of riverbank land. He soon earned a statewide reputation for the quality of his crowbars, hammers, chisels, and the hundreds of knives he made for the shoemakers. His edged tools, it was said, were so sharp "you could shave your beard with them." And, though the records for this period are few, what exist suggest that already such large farmers as the Comstocks on upper Smith Ridge and the several Lockwoods on Oenoke Ridge and Canoe Hill were shipping dairy products to New York, as well as quantities of hay, cider, and dried apples.

Evidence of wealth other than landholdings can be found for a few families. Capt. Isaac Richards bought stock in out-of-town banks and in toll roads, and he paneled the upstairs rooms of his house—proving, as was later said, that New Canaan had families of "quality." Elsewhere, stenciling done on plaster walls in this period can still be seen in more than one surviving New Canaan dwelling. Breaking away from the traditional center-chimney colonial house, Samuel St. John in 1808 built a "mansion" which had a chimney on the outer wall of each of its ends. This house stood across the road from the old family homestead (now No. 46 Park Street) and, set well back from the highway, was approached by a semicircular drive. And instead of riding long distances on horseback or in a wagon, a few men indulged in two-wheel traveling chaises (which the state promptly taxed).

Old inventories show that a number of families owned china and housewares imported from abroad, while sometime after the arrival of Edward Nash from Norwalk in 1809, New Canaan had its own silversmith. (Nash's shop stood at the edge of Main Street on the lawn of the present Town Hall.) And Dr. Joseph Silliman had portraits painted of himself and his wife. (The almost life-size Silliman portraits, painted in 1810 by Nathanial F. Wales, now hang in the Connecticut Historical Society in Hartford, which acquired them in Charleston, S.C., in the 1950's.)

Instead of moving west as Canaan Parish families had done a decade or so earlier, New Canaan men in the early 19th century were drawn to New York City by possible jobs in various trades. And since both old and new industries needed raw materials and markets, trade was focused on New York more and more.

The story has come down of a New Canaan man who tanned his own leather, cut out and made up a sack of shoes, and, taking his

Dr. Joseph Silliman (1756-1829) and his first wife Martha Leeds (1756-1822). Courtesy of The Connecticut Historical Society.

food with him, walked to New York City to sell his wares. His expenses for the trip were all of 12½ cents: 6¼ cents for a night's lodging and the same amount for a shave before he walked home. But this shank's-mare story wasn't typical of the way New Canaan was doing business early in the 19th century. To get themselves and their goods to New York most men made use of the sloops that sailed irregularly from the small ports of Norwalk and Stamford, especially those out of Five Mile River harbor at Rowayton.

Early in 1801, just before incorporation, Isaac Richards, Jr., age 21, was lost at sea. Soon afterward, his younger son having died, Capt. Isaac Richards seems to have ended his career as master mariner and ship owner, closed down his shipyard, but retained the Richards' store at Five Mile River, which he now owned in shares with Samuel Comstock and Samuel St. John. It was the trade in and out of this wharfside store that soon made Rowayton "New Canaan's port."

If Captain Richards had no need for seamen, other sailing masters did, and along with the rest of Connecticut, New Canaan had young men to "export" as crew. The Rev. Justus Mitchell's eldest son and his son-in-law left New Canaan to sail Hudson River sloops. They soon owned the 56-ton sloop "Cornelia," berthed at Mt. Pleasant but licensed in 1809 in New York, Sherman Mitchell "master." Two others who went to New York were Israel and Moses Hoyt, sons of the Baptist shoemaker-preacher. Called both "seaman" and "mariner" in old papers, Israel Hoyt died in New York in 1809, necessitating the return to New Canaan of his widow and son. As master of a sailing vessel, Capt. Moses Hoyt with his wife aboard sailed from New York in 1810. He is supposed to have cleared Hull, England (although the Embargo was on), but after that neither he nor his ship was ever heard of again, and his Main Street property passed by probate to his relatives.

The First Stores

Meanwhile, the Hoyts' brother Gould had gone bankrupt in 1802, losing the store at the Firehouse corner that once had belonged to S. Cooke Silliman. Perhaps to fill the gap, Benoni St. John in 1804 built a tiny general store on the south corner of where today East Avenue meets Main Street. There were only five families living in the neighborhood, but Main Street was then on the upper stretch of the "Road to the Landing," which led from Pound Ridge down Oenoke Ridge and White Oak Shade Road (which then began at God's Acre) directly to Rowayton harbor. Over this road passed the men and produce wagons who went to and came from Five Mile River landing. St. John's strategic location may explain why the next year Nathan Seely and Stephen Hoyt opened a general store practically abutting the south wall of the one St. John had built. Stephen Hoyt was another of the "Preacher's" sons, while Nathan Seely, who had been a schoolteacher, was county surveyor and would later (it is said) own a sloop sailing from a Stamford wharf to which he brought back New York goods for New Canaan customers.

In a short time general stores were started in almost every New Canaan neighborhood—on Ponus Ridge near Davenport, out West Road, on upper Oenoke and upper Smith ridges, in Silvermine—helping to maintain the regional character of the town. And at these stores the tax collector would appear on scheduled days, to save people the bother of getting to the still-nonexistent center of town. Since almost every store sold liquor, many can be traced through the book of liquor permits, which the selectmen issued from 1815 to 1838.

Isaac Richards and the Norwalk Road

Because the "Road to the Landing" led to Isaac Richards' Rowayton store, New Canaan was involved in a lawsuit with Norwalk in 1808-09. A petition, dated Dec. 8, 1807, proposed the building of a new road to provide a shorter and more direct route to Norwalk harbor from New Canaan, and had been signed by 49 men, including 9 from New Canaan, 15 from Pound Ridge, 9 each from Bedford and Salem, N.Y., and one each from Dutchess and Delhi counties. The petition read "That at the Port of Norwalk . . . is a very convenient Public Market for the vending of all kinds of Country produce & a fine Harbour connected by its Navigation with the principal seaports in the United States & with foreign ports." For those living in "a very Fertile & well cultivated Trace of Country" northwest of Norwalk, access to the port would be of much importance if Norwalk harbor could be reached by a public road "to accommodate the travel."

In its 1796 petition for incorporation, Canaan Parish had spelled out how circuitous roads made the distances to the centers of Norwalk and Stamford much longer than necessary, but in 1808 New Canaan wanted no part of the proposed direct route to Norwalk. When the selectmen refused to build New Canaan's stretch of the road, Norwalk took Isaac Richards to County Court. Not only did the Court recommend the highway but it ordered it surveyed and laid out—despite the fact that 23 of the original 49 petitioners had withdrawn their names. They had been misled, they told the Court in writing, into believing New Canaan wanted the road.

With Captain Richards as first selectman fighting both Norwalk and the County Court, New Canaan on Apr. 18, 1808, called a special town meeting, which voted 92 to 2 against laying out the road. Among the seven recorded reasons, New Canaan said it "had full conviction and certain knowledge" that the market place at Middlesex (meaning Isaac Richards' store at Five Mile River) gave men a better deal than would the market at Norwalk; the road, if laid out, was for "private Speculation at others expense to fill their own Coffers"; and moreover 1808 was no year to build a highway to a port, "there being an Embargo laid on all articles of exportation and our Country threatened with Immediate War."

Nevertheless, the road was laid out 3 rods wide from the head of Norwalk harbor (at Wall Street) along present Route 123 (to beyond the state armory) and then along what is now called Old Norwalk Road to meet "the Road to the Landing." In December 1809 New Canaan received a bill for $535.71 owed to the town's landowners whose property had been taken for the new road or to widen the existing road (Main Street) that led from the new highway to the Congregational meeting house. How much the new road to Norwalk was used and how much it cut into business at the Five Mile River store was never reported, but some years were to pass before the first house was built on Old Norwalk Road.

A Shaker Community

The year 1808 was also famous for another local lawsuit. The people of Canaan Parish had not led unblemished lives any more than people elsewhere. Drunkenness, as already mentioned, was a problem; not every marriage was a happy one; and baptisms of illegitimate children and confessions of adultery can be found on the Congregational church records. But not until 1808 did New Canaan have a divorce.

After 20 years of marriage and five children, Stephen Fitch of Carter Street had threatened to hang his wife. Charlotte (Selleck) Fitch managed to flee to safety with Selleck relatives farther north on the road, and on Sept. 22, 1807, she filed a petition for a separation with Connecticut's General Assembly, the only body then with authority to grant a divorce. In May 1808 the Assembly acted favorably, and with her decree and $150 annual alimony, Mrs. Fitch settled in Norwalk with two of her children. Stephen Fitch remained in New Canaan on his 130-acre farm with his mother and three other sons. (Stephen Fitch's farm was the nucleus of the later famous Hoyt Nursery, 1848-1970, which was sold to RCA for a proposed executive park, and is now the development known as "Hoyt Farms.")

In September 1809 Stephen Fitch paid a visit to the Shaker community at New Lebanon, N.Y., returning there a month later with two of his sons. Then on Feb. 5, 1810, for $7,000 Fitch sold the Shakers his New Canaan farm and took himself, his mother, and his three sons off to New Lebanon. Already the Shakers had voted to send three brothers and two sisters to New Canaan to "improve the place," and soon others were sent to live there, so that the Census for 1810 shows 12 men and women in residence at the Carter Street "community." Before 1810 was over, the Shakers had bought 11 more acres and agreed to pay Stephen Fitch's $150-a-year alimony to his former wife, to rear his three youngest sons, and to provide a home for his aged mother Abigail. (She died at New Lebanon in 1812.)

Between 1787 and 1794, the Shakers had established 11 communities in New York and New England, earning fame for their excellent goods and produce, especially herbs, for which they had extensive markets in cities or peddled door-to-door through the countryside. Four other Shaker communities had been founded in Ohio and Kentucky in 1806-07, so the New Canaan settlement was their sixteenth. Shaker records show that, usually, both an elder and an eldress were in residence on Carter Street, that a large granary was built, and that considerable energy was expended on the Fitch farm, where "an abundance of stone fences" had to be built. Help and visitors from New Lebanon came and went frequently, but except for two young Hanford girls, the Shakers seem to have made no converts.

Perhaps this was because Ann Lee, who founded the Shakers in 1774 as a Separatist sect with communal principles, believed in celibacy, a doctrine not likely to appeal to the young. Sexual desire, Mother Lee held, was responsible for all wars, poverty, famines, diseases, inequalities, and slavery throughout the world, while mortification of the body led to purification of the soul.

Celibacy, communal sharing—something turned Stephen Fitch against the Shakers, and New Lebanon records show that on Feb. 5, 1811, he was escorted to Albany "to stay there, if he will, for we want no more of him." Three months later, however, he went back to New Lebanon to collect two of his sons being raised there. By June the Shakers were advertising the Fitch farm for sale, but not until the next year did they find a buyer—one of Charlotte Fitch's Selleck relatives. With the $9,000 from this sale, the Shakers paid Stephen Fitch his original selling price. Possibly the Embargo that troubled the Old Norwalk Road opponents, as well as the lack of converts, motivated the sale. From New Lebanon came men and wagons to remove farm implements, furniture, animals, and grain, while the Shakers who had been in residence went to Norwalk, where they boarded a sloop, sailing to New York and then up the Hudson River before reaching the home community.

Except for a very few contemporary land records that name "the Shaking Quakers" as bounding landowners, no public record mentions them. (New Canaan acknowledged their presence in 1953 by naming a new street—in the wrong place—Shaker Road.) Though the Fitches were Congregationalists, the Church took no stand against them or Shaker proselytizing, and seemingly the Shakers made no dent on the town. Yet something happened in 1811 that caused the annual town meeting to turn out of office its first and second selectmen.

In place of Isaac Richards, Enos Weed, a Weed Street farmer who had been third selectman, was elected first selectman, while Nathan Seely, the Main Street store owner, replaced second selectman Isaac Benedict. There isn't a clue to what had happened to overthrow the "old guard"—Shakers, expenses, or something else. In April 1811 Connecticut had, with Episcopalian support for the

Democratic-Republican party, elected Roger Griswold as its first non-Congregationalist governor, but there is no evidence that New Canaan had a new political party, and Enos Weed was a Congregationalist, not an Episcopalian. Whatever had occurred, it had no lasting effect, and one year later Isaac Richards and Isaac Benedict were back as first and second selectmen.

Meanwhile, the Rev. Justus Mitchell had died in 1806, and the Congregationalists waited until January 1808 to chose as their fifth pastor the Rev. William Bonney, aged 29, a graduate of Williams College (1805), who had just been licensed to preach. At the same time, New Canaan's first Methodist Society was formed in Silvermine and met in the district schoolhouse, built on land owned by Capt. Ebenezer Crofoot. When the school district taxpayers voted against Methodist use of their building, Captain Crofoot threatened to prevent the Congregationalists from holding meetings there, and the vote was soon rescinded. When he was converted to Methodism, Crofoot became leader of a "class" that met in his barn.

Wherever they were meeting, the Baptists now had an out-of-town clergyman conduct services for them once a month, and in the ledger of the Seely-Hoyt general store are the names of the ministers, the dates when they preached, and the names of the New Canaan Baptists who contributed toward their pay.

The War of 1812

By 1810 New Canaan's population had risen to 1,596, but its economy was suffering as the Embargo affected shipping and trade, and the only bright spots in the year seem to have been the days on which the militia trained. Next to Thanksgiving, Training Day had become the great holiday, when everyone who could gathered at the Parade Ground to buy cookies, cider, and peddlers' goods and watch the regiments drill. New Canaan had barely been incorporated when in September 1801 Joseph Blatchley, then living in Fishkill, N.Y., signed an indenture with John Carter, captain of the Revolutionary Train Band, giving Carter title to the Parade Ground off Oenoke Ridge. Blatchley's original deed, which gave the acre of land to the "Inhabitants of Canaan Parish" and not the militia, had disappeared, not to turn up and be recorded until 1854. (It is now in the Historical Society's archives.)

After the Revolution, Connecticut had reorganized its military, and New Canaan no longer had a militia company of its own. Instead, with military training still obligatory for most able-bodied men, New Canaan males belonged either to the 5th Infantry Company or to the 2d Grenadiers of the 34th Militia Regiment, serving under officers and with men from a number of neighboring towns. According to William St. John (1815-1884), who as a boy watched Training Days, rivalry between the units was keen and competition for commissions was considerable, while old receipted bills suggest that uniforms were both colorful and expensive.

From the start, Connecticut strenuously opposed the War of 1812, as it had the Embargo, but what effect the War had on New Canaan is a complete blank. The town meeting minutes never refer to it. All one knows is that on an unspecified day in 1812 the townspeople held an "Indignation Meeting" under an elm that once stood on the present Library's lawn.

Neither the federal government nor the state has service records for the men in the War of 1812 comparable to those for the Revolution. (To apply for a pension afterward, a man had to have served 60 days, and few Connecticut militiamen did.) When the war began, Governor Griswold refused to let the Connecticut militia serve outside the state, holding that President Madison's request for troops was unconstitutional. Local defense, however, became vital after the spring of 1813, when the British effectively blockaded Long Island Sound, and large militia units were kept on the alert in case of British attacks.

Surviving military orders show that, as commandant of the 34th Militia Regiment, Lt. Col. Enoch St. John ordered his companies to drill together twice during the summer of 1813, once in New Canaan and once in Norwalk. Lt. Col. Nehemiah Benedict, who became commandant of the 2d Grenadiers on June 2, 1813, was credited with four days of active service in September of that year, along with his adjutant, Jared Ayres. (Joseph Seely, New Canaan's first third selectman, had been commissioned a lieutenant colonel of the 34th Militia in 1804, but he committed suicide in 1811.) Samuel Comstock, the Smith Ridge farmer, was a major of the 34th; Cary Weed was captain of the 5th Company, and Holly Seymour was a sergeant. None of them, it would seem, ever faced the enemy.

One by one, the names of a few enlisted men who served in the War of 1812 from New Canaan have come to light, but there must have been several more. John Weed, son of the Revolutionary soldier Stephen Weed, was lost at sea in 1812 while in the Navy; Austin Hanford, a private, died the same year after ten weeks in camp; and Silas Benedict, who died in October 1814, probably was a soldier in the war. Squire Scofield, from Dantown, out of a job in New York City, enlisted there as a drummer. Fear of a British attack on New London sent Sgt. David Chichester, Corp. Jesse St. John, Jonathan K. Johnson, and Elihu Matthews to duty at Groton, Conn. They served from Sept. 13 to Nov. 1, 1813, but unlike the Revolutionary militiamen, they were not part of a New Canaan unit. All four apparently were drafted, as was James Selleck in 1814, who was sent to defense duty at Bridgeport. The War of 1812 was so unpopular that few Connecticut men would volunteer.

Two men who did see combat were soldiers in the United States Army. Enlisting at Hartford in March 1814, Alanson and John Conley fought in western New York. Alanson was discharged as a sergeant; his brother John was wounded at the battle of Chippewa, near Fort Erie, N.Y., on July 5, 1814. (John Conley later drew a disability pension of $10 a month, but this was not enough to let him support the habits of his mother-in-law, who lived with him and his wife. Deserted by her husband "Aunt Betsy" Benedict first took to drink, and after Conley could not afford her alcoholism, she turned to tobacco and became New Canaan's first known female smoker.)

In January 1815, New Canaan sent Samuel St. John as its delegate to the Hartford Convention. Since that body had already drawn up its now-deplored Articles, St. John was nothing more than a rubber stamp. News of the peace treaty ending the War of 1812 put a quick end to the circulation of the Hartford Convention's Articles, and St. John returned home. In May he was back in Hartford as New Canaan's elected representative.

Town Matters

Before the War of 1812 was quite over, New Canaan's annual town meeting of December 1814 voted for the first time to pay the selectmen "a reasonable compensation for their services"—without putting a figure on "reasonable." A growing responsibility of the selectmen was the care of the sick and the poor, and that same December meeting directed the selectmen to "make a present" of $2.81 to Dr. Samuel S. Noyes for his services in visiting and burying Zachariah Wyllis, "a resident but not an inhabitant of this town." Dr. Noyes had succeeded Dr. David Bouton, Jr., of present No. 38 Main Street, who died in 1812 of "spasmotic fits," and was the first physician in New Canaan to make a living solely from the practice of medicine. He would become the hero of the 1828 epidemic of "putrid sore throats." Well before that, Dr. Lewis Richards, a son of Captain James, had established a practice too—the first New Canaan doctor to have attended a medical school. While Dr. Joseph Silliman was still practicing, New Canaan also had a "summer-resident" medical man: a tall Indian "doctor," who camped seasonally with his tribe at Indian Rocks. Noted for his cures, he had white men, women, and children for patients, but because he prescribed herbs and simples, some people thought he might poison them.

Though the selectmen had been directed by the December 1814 town meeting not to tolerate "foreigners"—anyone from out of state—who were likely to be unemployed and become an expense to the town, on the whole New Canaan treated its poor kindly and allowed them to retain their dignity. Home relief didn't extend much beyond providing wood and medical care and allowing food purchases at the general stores, yet when the Widow Molly Hayes's house burned down, the selectmen built her a new dwelling house (provided that, on her death, house and land passed to the town). But after Austin Hanford died in the War of 1812, a special town meeting directed the selectmen to send his widow and children to the Weston poorhouse, after which his real estate was sold for the town's benefit. (There must have been a good reason that is not evident now for such seeming callousness.) A continuing problem, however, were the slaves who had been freed with no means of support.

In compliance with Connecticut's antislavery laws, many families had freed their slaves, so that only seven were listed on New Canaan's 1810 Census. Properly married by the Rev. Justus Mitchell, some couples had gone to New York, and a few freed slaves had run away, but 12 "free colored" persons remained in New Canaan in 1810. These were largely former house slaves from Canaan Parish days, who were able to make their own way at some trade. (Though it was against the law for blacks to be educated, Dover Comstock and Lewis MacCauley sent their children to District School No. 1 and paid their shares of the school rates.) By 1817, however, the heads of two black families were temporarily too ill to work, and for them the selectmen purchased New Canaan's first poorhouse. This stood somewhere near where Strawberry Hill and Garibaldi Road meet River Street, but the house is gone and the roads in that area have been so changed that it is impossible to pinpoint its exact location.

The Academy and the Post Office

Although he bought Justus Mitchell's home, Mr. Bonney had not continued his predecessor's preparatory school, and those private schools that started under other men were short lived. Education in the one-room district schools was becoming a hit-or-miss affair, dependent upon the qualifications of the men hired to teach the winter term and the young ladies who taught in the summers and on the salaries the school districts were willing to pay. Consequently, in 1816 Samuel St. John and three of his neighbors founded the New Canaan Academy, New Canaan's first parent-owned school, to educate their sons and daughters. Built on St. John land on the east side of Park Street, almost opposite present No. 63 (then the site of District School No. 1), the Academy continued until May 1834 under 13 successive headmasters, all of whom were Yale graduates. (Though the Academy never was a church school, the New Canaan Congregational Church took considerable credit for its success, and 11 of the 13 Academy heads were or became Congregational clergymen.) Offering a wide range of courses for that day—foreign language instruction cost $5 a term, English only $3—the Academy had so many students accepted by Yale that it quickly attracted out-of-town pupils, who were boarded by Richard Fayerweather, one of the four proprietors, at his home (now No. 38 Main Street). Toward the end, when the Academy was no longer self-supporting, it was underwritten by an unnamed benefactor (probably Mrs. Samuel

St. John, whose four sons and one daughter were Academy graduates).

Bits and pieces of evidence other than the founding of the Academy indicate that New Canaan's economy picked up quickly after the end of the War of 1812, enough so to warrant a post office in town. Despite heavy opposition, the legislature in 1817 had changed Connecticut's laws so that mails could be transported on Sundays—contrary to the old Congregational-inspired statute, which prevented travel by anyone on the Sabbath Day. With the beginning of daily mail service between Boston and New York in January 1818, New Canaan was granted a post office—located in the Richards & St. John store on the Park Street hill—and Town Clerk Samuel St. John was named the first postmaster, Jan. 19, 1818. In the beginning mail was brought from Stamford once a week by horseback, but soon it was arriving twice a week, with the recipient paying the postage. After December 1819 postage had to be prepaid, though postage stamps were still a thing of the future.

Then on May 6, 1818, the Norwalk *Gazette* began weekly publication, with a special rider to deliver the paper to New Canaan subscribers. It included some New Canaan items, and it is from the columns of the *Gazette* that one learns that at New Canaan's Fourth of July celebration of 1818 a cannon exploded and killed young Andrew Merritt, resident farmer for Ebenezer Ayres, a leading shoe manufacturer.

The New State Constitution

All the while, a statewide political storm was brewing that was to affect New Canaan enormously. Despite the unpopularity of the War of 1812, the Federalist party had retained control of the state government, though the Republicans gained ground and opposition to the influence of the Congregational church continued to grow. Financial support through public taxation, control of the political and educational systems, political sermons preached from pulpits, and the arrogance of some of its clergymen—all were working against the Established Church. And once the Episcopalians, Baptists and Methodists after the War's end began to work together politically with the Republicans, separation of

Church and State became inevitable. As a Tolerationist, Oliver Wolcott of Litchfield was swept into the governorship in 1817, and one year later Connecticut ratified a new state constitution.

There is no evidence that New Canaan had a Republican or a Toleration faction, but something was happening politically. Isaac Richards had been reelected first selectman in December of 1815, 1816, and 1817, but in April 1817 Samuel St. John, a Federalist and Congregationalist had been replaced as New Canaan's representative by Nathan Seely, the Episcopalian storekeeper. Perhaps seeing the handwriting on the wall, the Rev. Mr. Bonney in 1816 had held the first of his three "revivals," gathering 39 new members into the Congregational Church. At the same time, however, the Methodists in Silvermine officially became part of the Stamford Circuit, and in 1818 the Methodists in White Oak Shade were strong enough to form a second Society, which worshiped in the district schoolhouse and held a "class" in the home of Holly Seymour. (He had just become captain of the 4th Company in the new 24th Militia Regiment, successor to the 34th.) What the Episcopalians and Baptists were doing is not known, but the Methodists had become something the Congregationalists had to reckon with.

Although Nathan Seely was elected representative in 1817, New Canaan bucked the political tide and was one of only two towns in Fairfield County to vote Federalist in the state gubernatorial election. (The other town was Redding.) The next year Seely was New Canaan's delegate to the Constitutional Convention, but when the time came to vote on Oct. 5, 1818, New Canaan voted 96 to 35 against the new constitution. Trumbull was the only other Fairfield County town to vote "No." Norwalk, beginning to industrialize, voted 111 to 21 in favor of the constitution, which was solidly ratified by the state as a whole. Seemingly in defiance of the political trend, New Canaan in April 1819 elected Isaac Richards as its state representative—for the last time. The constitution not only revised suffrage requirements and changed the old Council into the State Senate, but it also eliminated the fall session of the legislature, providing for annual instead of semiannual elections to the legislature, which would sit alternately in Hartford and New Haven until Hartford became the sole capital in 1875. In 1820 Nathan Seely would be New Canaan's assemblyman for a full year, followed in 1821 by the Baptist Capt. Stephen Hoyt, Sr. The new constitution also changed the date of the towns' annual meetings from December to October, though New Canaan did not make the shift until October 1821.

Besides important reforms in the three branches of government, the constitution of 1818 included the controversial Article 7, which disestablished the Congregational church by giving equal rights and privileges to "every society or denomination of christians" (but not to Jews or atheists). For the New Canaan Congregational Church, Article 7 meant that no longer could it (or any church) raise money by a tax laid on the assessed value of property owners, which heretofore the County treasurer had collected and passed along. Furthermore, anyone wishing to "separate himself" from the Society of Canaan (that name was still used), had only to leave a written notice of intent with the Society's clerk and thus avoid liability for future church expense. To raise the money needed for the minister's salary and meeting house repairs, the New Canaan church after 1818 could call only on its parishioners, so to supplement voluntary contributions from members, it turned to renting pews, which hitherto had been free. (Later it built horsesheds and rented those.)

The year 1818 was memorable in New Canaan for other reasons than a post office and the state constitution. Departing the scene was Mrs. Jonathan Huntington, the first of New Canaan's great ladies about whom much is known. Born in 1754 a daughter of Abijah Comstock, Dinah Huntington had been the second wife of S. Cooke Silliman and died in the house he had built *c.*1766, now No. 18 Seminary Street. To her nieces Mrs. Huntington willed silk shawls, silk gloves, a lace cloak, leghorn hat, lace caps, a pair of "earnubs" with semiprecious stones, a string of gold beads, and lots more—many cuts above the wearing apparel most women owned. To her brother Samuel Comstock, she left her sidesaddles, silk umbrella, china snuffbox, wine decanters and servers, 10 glasses, and a china teapot with creamer, sugar, and silver sugar tongs.

Next Dinah Huntington willed $500 each to the Andover (Mass.) Theological Institution and the Commissioners of Foreign Missions, and then to the newly formed Missionary Society of Connecticut she left her residual estate, including her house and homestead land. But, paradoxically, Dinah Huntington willed to her brother "my Black Girl Belinda." Her father had freed his slaves Dover and Rose; Samuel Cooke Silliman by his will had manumitted his slave Phyllis in 1795 (she died in the County almshouse in 1851 at age 101), but Mrs. Huntington did not free Belinda, who appears on the 1820 Census as a Comstock slave, one of four still owned by New Canaan people. Mrs. Huntington did give her brother $200 to pay off the bond she had given to the "masters of the poor of the Town of South Salem . . . at the time my Mullatto Boy Harry was born in said town." Harry was Phyllis's son, born after she had been freed, and was never a slave.

Shoemakers

It was in 1818 that Eliphalet St. John and Elisha Leeds Silliman, one of Dr. Joseph's sons, rented the buildings at the present Firehouse corner and opened the third general store on the "road to the Landing." New Canaan had entered upon its great era of shoemaking, and the "road to the Landing" was seeing more and more traffic as shoemakers as well as farmers went back and forth to the port.

Today it seems ridiculous to think of New Canaan as a shoe manufacturing center, and yet it once was. *Niles Register* for 1818 credited the town with an annual output of 50,000 pairs of shoes—a lot for those days—and the shoe business was to grow and grow. In 1820, when Connecticut had a population of 275,248, only five incorporated cities—Hartford, Middletown, New Haven, New London, and Norwich—had more than 5,000 inhabitants. New Canaan's population was 1,689, of which 271 men were "in agriculture" and 193 "in manufacturing," though not all 193 of these were making shoes.

By 1820 New Canaan's shoe business was dominated by two families—the Benedicts and the Ayres. Atop Brushy Ridge, Caleb and James Benedict (d.1838) carried on the cottage industry that James had started in 1768. In a series of one-story buildings (said to make a factory 100 feet long), "Boss" Caleb and his cutters readied work to be given out to journeymen, while in his house, besides his 15 children, he boarded the young men who were his apprentices. Nearby was Nehemiah Benedict 2d, a distant relative and on Park Street was Caleb's cousin Ezra, while other Benedicts were shoemaking in Walton, N.Y.

The Ayres brothers, the four oldest of the five sons of Jonathan Ayres, a farmer on Greenley Road, had spread their shoe-making operations across the township. On Brushy Ridge, around the corner from James Benedict whose apprentice he had been, Ebenezer Ayres had established a highly successful shoe "manufactorie"; on upper Carter Street Jared Ayres both made shoes and ran a general store; somewhere in the Ponus Ridge area Amos Ayres was making shoes, while Frederick worked in "the old red house" on the "Road to the Landing" just north of East Avenue. In addition, the Ayres owned two tanneries and a bark mill.

In 1809 Ebenezer and Frederick Ayres bought the tannery that stood on East Avenue, just east of where Forest Street now begins. Records don't show just when this tannery was started, but it functioned from about 1790 until after Frederick Ayres died in 1854. With its series of pits and vats dug in the ground, it must have been an evil-smelling affair. Beginning with bark on the bottom, layers of cleaned and scraped hides were alternated with bark until the pits were filled, after which water was poured in up to the top. There the hides soaked, out in the open, for almost a year, being turned now and then. A good tanner knew it took that much time for the bark to be leached and the tannic acid to get into the pores of the hides. No one in New Canaan ever seems to have raised herds of animals for slaughtering, so hides were bought individually from farmers over a wide area, a small source of income for some local families. (When in the 1830's New Canaan got its first butcher shop, its owner lived on East Avenue practically next door to the Ayres' tannery.)

Hides can travel long distances, but in those days tanbark could not. It was both bulky and fragile and in danger of being leached by the rains. Consequently, in the 1820's Frederick Ayres bought and rebuilt the old Eells' bark mill on Five Mile River, just above Watson's ax factory, less than a quarter of a mile from the tannery and close to supplies of the best tanning barks—those of the oak and the chestnut, of which New Canaan then had large stands. The bark mill and its dam have long disappeared as nature and man rebuilt the course of Five Mile River above and below Locust

Avenue, but present Vitti Street more or less follows what once was the "Path to the Barkmill" from the tannery.

The ledger Ebenezer Ayres kept from 1822 to 1839 has recently come back to New Canaan, and it shows that from the opening date Ayres had a steady southern market for his wares. (Later he also had large customers in New York and New Haven.) Each month, in barrels or boxes, he shipped from New Canaan some 900 pairs of shoes to firms in Norfolk, Va., Charleston, S.C., and Savannah and Augusta, Ga. His monthly billings averaged $1,100, making his annual gross income some $13,000, a considerable sum for 1822. From the ledger one learns that Ebenezer Ayres built a business on quality shoes for men (only 24 pairs were made for women in the early years), and a popular item was his "Washington," made of fine calf. The ledger also shows that one order was "Sent by land to New York thence shipped on board the schooner *Telltale*" to Norfolk; that 50,000 sparrowbills (headless wedge-shaped iron nails) cost Ayres all of $3.50; and that if you wanted to make laudanum, the "Rule" was to put 1 ounce of opium into 1 pint of rum.

Where the Ayres built their business on quality shoes, the Benedicts developed a large trade in rough pegged shoes. Ever since the 16th century heels had been fastened to soles by wooden pegs, and early in the 19th century necessity accounted for shoe uppers being also joined to the soles with pegs. An Albany visitor to New Canaan, so the story goes, approached "Boss" Caleb Benedict with a shoemaking problem: lime burners in the Albany district had troubles because lime rotted the stitches in their sewn shoes. Benedict was able to solve the problem by setting a row of wooden pegs inside the stitches. Though the stitches still ripped, the pegs held the soles on until the shoes wore down to their uppers.

The limeburners satisfied, Benedict shipped several dozen pairs —shoes were always marketed by the dozen pairs—of pegged shoes to New York city, where a relative hung them in the window of his general store. Instead of being a curiosity, the pegged shoes were snapped up by city workmen, creating a new outlet for Benedict wares. Never for dress, because they were so stiff, pegged shoes stood up under extremely hard wear, and the Benedicts soon developed a profitable market in Georgia, where plantation owners bought them for their field slaves.

At first pegged shoes were made with wooden pegs whittled by hand, the size of the pegs depending both on the size and the toughness of the shoe. A skilled journeyman could whittle in five minutes enough pegs from a maple slab to peg one pair of shoes. In 1815 a peg-making machine was invented, followed in 1833 by a machine that performed the pegging operation, but this did not replace shoemakers until the 1850's. Ironically, once the pegging of shoes was patented, a group of Norwalk men secured the local franchise to the Hitchcock and Bement patent in 1824, and Caleb Benedict was forced to obtain a license and pay royalties on both the making and vending of pegged shoes, after practically inventing the process.

Canaan Parish and early New Canaan shoemakers followed medieval guild practices, whereby the few men who were master shoemakers taught their trade to boys, who served a seven-year apprenticeship for which their fathers paid. At the end of this period, a young man was considered a qualified journeyman, who eventually might rise to be a "boss" on his own. Not all young men took to learning a trade, whether it was shoemaking, blacksmithing, or carriage-making, and ads appeared regularly in the Norwalk *Gazette* for runaway apprentices, boys 16 and 17, with rewards ranging all the way from 10 cents to 1 mill.

The system apparently worked well for years for New Canaan shoemakers, and 40 to 50 "jours" were employed by both Ebenezer Ayres and Caleb Benedict, some coming from nearby towns to pick up sacks of cut shoes to take home for finishing. Others worked for the smaller shoe manufacturers who were scattered throughout the town. It was New Canaan's reputation for skilled journeymen that led David Law, a Scotsman, to move his shoemaking business from New York to Park Street in 1824. When Trowbridge Benedict opened a watch and jewelry business in New York on lower Broadway, he sold Law his homestead on the north corner of Park and Maple Streets, and to the north of this Law build his "factory." Though little is known of his New Canaan operation, Law was a very successful shoemaker, judged by the size of his estate when he died in 1835. He was the first New Canaan shoe manufacturer to open a branch business in the South—in New Orleans—which he visited regularly by ship.

Stagecoaches, Sloops, and Steamboats

Largely because of the growing importance of its shoemen, New Canaan in 1821 had been connected with New York by two stagecoach lines. In November of that year, a Norwalk-to-New York stage was started, which made stops in Ridgefield and New Canaan, and the next month a Stamford-New York line extended its route to Danbury via New Canaan and Ridgefield. The New Canaan depot for both lines was the Richards & St. John store near the top of the Park Street hill. (The advertised one-way fare from New Canaan to New York was $1.88 via Norwalk and $1.50 via the Stamford route.) The stage now brought the mail from Stamford, the coach driver announcing his arrival with blasts on a four-foot-long tin horn. While mail and passengers were being shifted on or off, St. John's hostler watered the horses, after which the driver took off, cracking a whip over the lead pair of the four-horse team.

Hitherto, New Canaan shoemakers and others going to and from New York had traveled largely by packet sloop—a ship sailing on a schedule—advertisements of sailings being posted on the town's signboards. With the beginning of the Norwalk *Gazette,* ads appeared in its pages, so one knows that Norwalk had two packet lines. One owned the sloops *Eliza, Mechanic,* and *Union,* sailing Tuesday, Thursday, and Saturday, respectively, and returning to Norwalk on Saturday, Tuesday, and Thursday. By 1818 sea travel had become so sophisticated that the second line advertised its *Orion,* "58 and 45/95 tons burthen," as having 16 berths and sailing at night for the convenience of businessmen. All four vessels docked at Peck Slip in the East River. Since passengers, applying at the lines's offices or directly to the captains, often totaled more than 50, the greater part of a sloop's hull was "berthed off," the cabin being divided between captain and passengers, with freight carried below. The *Orion* had no separate staterooms, but "for five lengths" both sides of her cabin were lined with curtained berths, allowing passengers as much privacy as later Pullman cars.

Although she sailed out of Norwalk on Tuesday nights, the *Orion* rarely returned at night, usually sailing home on a Saturday morning to put passengers ashore before sundown, when the Sabbath began. Despite the new state constitution, the old Congregational-inspired law prohibiting travel after Saturday afternoon was still in effect. Sloops advertised that they took passengers across the Sound to Methodist camp meetings on Long Island, but even for this purpose the sloops never sailed on a Sunday.

In season, the sail to New York from Norwalk, Five Mile River, and Stamford could easily be made in under 24 hours, though in bad weather the sail might take up to six days. In winter few sloops ventured out of port, since market goods and passengers were scarce, and as late as the 1850's the Sound could freeze over for as long as 36 days.

New Canaan had barely been made a stagecoach stop when a new mode of transportation became available in summertime. As early as 1821 a steamboat line from Norwalk to New York had been proposed, but it took three years to become a reality. Sponsored primarily by the president of Norwalk's new Fairfield County Bank, the line launched its *John Marshall* in New York in 1824 and noisily welcomed "him" to Norwalk on July 6. Some of the "steam" had been taken out of the arrival by the prior appearance of the *General Lafayette* in April, which made Norwalk a stop on its first New York-to-Bridgeport run. More steam (and money) was lost by the line with the immediate withdrawal of the *John Marshall* for alterations after its maiden voyage.

The *John Marshall* was a low-pressure steamboat, seemingly in need of constant tinkering, but Norwalk and New Canaan hearts swelled with pride when in November 1824 the *Marshall* made the trip from New York to Norwalk in 5 hours and 10 minutes, beating the *Lafayette's* time by 6 whole minutes. By 1825 Stamford had the *Oliver Wolcott* in service, and in summer New Canaan businessmen could schedule their "commutes" to New York City from two or more ports with some degree of certainty. (New Canaan ladies took to steamboat travel as much as the men. Once aboard, they knew they would have the "ladies saloon" to themselves, with a female attendant to care for them.)

Steamboats were larger and faster, though not necessarily safer, than sloops, but they never entirely supplanted the small sailing vessels on the Sound. Until the late 1850's, Five Mile River harbor would be "New Canaan's port," through which produce and goods came and went, though New Canaan ownership of the store came to an end. Samuel Comstock died in 1818, and five years later his widow, Isaac Richards, and Samuel St. John sold the wharf and store, together with land and a house, to Alfred Seely for $2,100. Though born in New Canaan and married to a daughter of Capt. Stephen Hoyt, Sr., Seely had moved to Rowayton, where he operated the first packet sloop as well as the store.

Unlike the sloops, the steamboats did make Sunday voyages to Stamford and Norwalk, bringing New York excursionists, who complained of the ungracious receptions they received. In an effort to enforce the "Blue Laws," the Consociation of Western Fairfield County, meeting in Darien on Oct. 11, 1825, expressed its disapproval of Sunday travel in steamboats in no uncertain terms. In a preamble the Congregational ministers reviewed the sacredness of the Sabbath as inherited from Biblical times, termed the Sabbath "an institution designed to promote the best interests of Society" and "a guardian of morals, public and private." Then they adopted five resolutions, the third of which said "That professing Christians, by taking passages and otherwise encouraging Sunday boats, set an example to the world which weakens belief in the sacredness of religious institutions" (and lots more). The New Canaan Congregationalists delayed until April 1826 before approving this lengthy "report" against Sunday travel, but the Congregationalists were fighting a losing battle. With the spread of industrial and commercial developments, men who worked at trades or in stores in Connecticut usually worked until 8 P.M. Saturdays and had only Sundays to go home. When they did, they had to travel on Sunday.

The Return of Lafayette

As in Canaan Parish days, Norwalk was larger and more important than Stamford, so it was to Norwalk that most New Canaan people went on Aug. 20, 1824, to pay their respects to Lafayette. The aging hero of the Revolution was revisiting the United States, and some New Canaan people could later tell their grandchildren that they had shaken the General's hand. Riding in a coach drawn by four "elegant" gray horses and accompanied by a military escort, Lafayette and his son had left New York City early in the morning for New Haven, but frequent stops and throngs along the Post Road had slowed his progress. He was well off schedule when at dusk he arrived at Norwalk's hotel, to be welcomed by volleys of musketry, roars of cannons, music, and cheers. To be part of the honor guard, the 4th Company, 24th Infantry Militia, and its military band had marched from New Canaan under the command of Capt. Stephen Hoyt, Jr. After a reception and refreshments, Lafayette was on his way at 8:30 P.M., to be entertained at supper in Fairfield before lodging for the night at Bridgeport.

New Ways, New People

Despite their enthusiasm for prolonged religious revivals, held by all denominations except the Episcopalian, the people in New Canaan no longer looked on the church and the Train Band as centers of social life. Some men belonged to the new Fairfield County Agricultural Society, two physicians went out of town to Fairfield County Medical Society meetings, and in 1825 New Canaan had the first of its numerous secret societies. Harmony Lodge No. 67, A.F. and A.M., was chartered in New Haven on May 30, 1825, on the application of Samuel Carter, Jr., John Seely, Eliphalet Weed, and an unspecified number of other men. Although the "Blue Laws" still prevented public theatres, New Canaan men and women went to Stamford and Norwalk for balls, such as the annual affair that celebrated Andrew Jackson's 1815 victory at New Orleans. As a result of the 1823 Jackson balls, $159 was raised ($77 in Stamford, $82 in Norwalk) for aid to Greece, then fighting for independence. Just a year earlier, the newly formed Foreign Mission Society of the Congregational Church had voted to "adopt" and support an orphan boy in far-off Ceylon. There was nothing parochial about New Canaan in those days, although it still lacked a village as a center for the town.

Before the War of 1812 began, Wolsey Burtis, Edward Nash, and Thomas Seymour Husted had begun buying land along both sides of Main Street. Burtis bought a house where the Raymond Block now stands, with farmland stretching to the east, and erected a blacksmith's shop (south of present Burtis Avenue) so close to the "Road to the Landing" that it encroached on the highway. South of Burtis in 1820 was just one house—the home of Stephen Hoyt, who was Thomas Husted's partner in the general store at the corner of Main and East. North of East Avenue stood Frederick Ayres' dwelling and small shoe "factory" and north of that Amos Ayres by 1820 was occupying the house and store at the present Firehouse corner recently vacated by St. John & Silliman. There he, too, was making shoes. On the west side of Main Street, where the Town Hall now is, lived Edward Nash. His silversmith's shop stood close to the road, and his farm extended south to the present Morse Court parking lot, where Stephen Hoyt had built a house for Bradley Keeler, his son-in-law (opposite the blacksmith's shop). On East Avenue Frederic Wright had a tailoring business briefly, for by 1823 he had lost his holdings to Husted & Hoyt and moved to New York. (Wright's claim to local fame came from the cookies he made and sold on Training Day.)

Shoes were bringing enough money to New Canaan to encourage some men to start new enterprises, and the first change on Main Street came in 1822 when, across the road from his house,

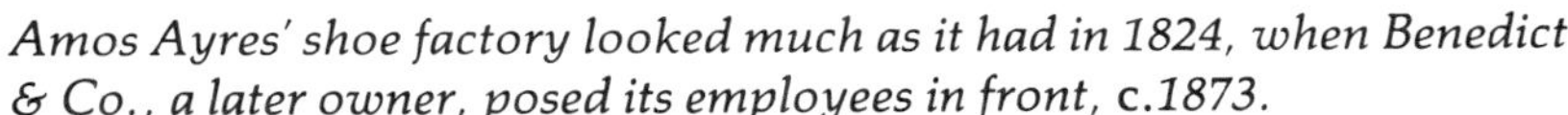

Amos Ayres' shoe factory looked much as it had in 1824, when Benedict & Co., a later owner, posed its employees in front, c.*1873.*

Bradley Keeler erected a carriage works on land Wolsey Burtis rented to him. (At the same time, Burtis took over a blacksmith business on the Darien line and rented his local shop to Edward Nash, who backed David Taylor as the new blacksmith.) Next, in 1823 Stephen Hoyt, Jr., bought out his father as Thomas Husted's partner in the general store, and behind this, on East Avenue, a new tailor set up—Luzerne Gilbert (whose account book survives). Then, in 1824, having bought the Firehouse corner, Amos Ayres tore down the old house that had been the Rev. Robert Silliman's parsonage. In its place he built a four-story structure which, painted white, resembled a meeting house. With a home for his family in the rear, Ayres' new shoe factory accommodated a dormitory for his apprentices, a front-room store, and a public bar. (This was the building, which stood until 1926, and which New Canaan would later call "the Big Shop.") Finally, in 1825 New Canaan built its first town hall—on the "Road to the Landing" but just to the north of Church Hill.

The First Town Hall

After the 1818 Constitution was in effect, the Congregational Church made a little money by charging the town $2 each time its meeting house was used for a town meeting. Talk of New Canaan building a town house (town hall) remained just talk until the issue was forced by the death of Samuel St. John on Jan. 14, 1825, at age 52. Apparently Richards & St. John's store would no longer be available as a town clerk's office and town treasury. By February 1825 a special town meeting had voted to build a two-story town house, 28 x 34 feet wide, and by March New Canaan had acquired a site at the top of God's Acre, where present Main and Park streets meet. This was the southeast corner of the homestead of Joseph Silliman, Jr., which had been given to him 14 months before when his father, Dr. Joseph, remarried and moved to Bedford, N.Y.

To pay for the building and land, the town voted an extra tax of 2½ cents on the dollar for one year and authorized the selectmen to sell the poorhouse, no longer in use, to Ebenezer Ayres. At that time, New Canaan owned at least four pieces of land with buildings on them, all of which were to be sold and the proceeds to go

New Canaan's first Town House, built in 1825, survived a variety of uses and changes before it became the Historical Society Library in 1960.

either "for the use and benefit of the poor" or to finance building the town house. Painted white on the front and gable ends and brown on the north side and roof, the town house was far enough along by the fall of 1825 for the new Masonic Society to offer an annual rent of $20 for use of the upstairs as its meeting hall. (In 1848 the town house was moved back from the road and a few feet to the west. It was sold by the town in 1865, after a new town hall had been acquired; subsequently, after a checkered career, it became in 1960 the headquarters of the New Canaan Historical Society.)

In November 1825, with objections from the land owners at the east end, Maple Street was accepted by New Canaan as a highway. This was the first cross road to connect what would be called Main Street with Park Street. Although it was laid out primarily to provide access to the new private cemetery Ezra Benedict had developed to the south, Maple Street eliminated the necessity of going all the way to the Congregational meeting house to cross from one road to the other.

With the death of Samuel St. John, Edward Nash had been appointed both town clerk and postmaster. With the death of Capt. Isaac Richards on Dec. 29, 1825, at age 66, an era in New Canaan's history came to an end, though the men who would carry on had already proved themselves. Isaac Richards was the last of the men who had been responsible for New Canaan's incorporation and its organization as a town, and his high standards of public service started a tradition that the town still tries to follow. Fame in New Canaan has always been fleeting, and few people today know who Isaac Richards was. Yet as late as 1901 he was remembered for his "determined will for justice," anecdotes about his honesty were still being told, and his ghost was sometimes called to haunt those who sought to cheat the town.

The Hanford-Silliman House, built c.*1764, where Stephen Hanford had his tavern, Dr. Joseph Silliman practiced medicine, and Joseph Silliman, Jr., later held court. The Greek Revival portico was added in the 1830's when Joseph Silliman, Jr., remodeled and enlarged the house.*

CHAPTER 7

The Shoemaking Boom, 1826-1850

From all accounts, New Canaan in the 1830's and '40's was a lively place. With the end of the "old guard," men with very different interests were ready to take charge, and the old ways began to give way. The shoemaking business was booming, and the people who went back and forth to New York and much farther away came back with new goods, new ideas, new political and religious thoughts. While New Canaan was still a deeply religious community, all its hard working people, as one man would later recall, seemed intent on making money and playing politics to the hilt.

A Center to the Town

With Amos Ayres' "manufactory" looming large over a still-rural scene, two businessmen foresaw that the shoemakers who worked there or for Frederick Ayres or for David Law on Park Street would benefit if their homes were nearby. Thomas Seymour Husted and Stephen Hoyt, Jr., in 1826 were partners in the Main Street-East Avenue general store. They also were back-to-back neighbors, since Husted lived on a large tract of land on Park Street just south of present Elm, and Hoyt lived on Main, where the Library is. Pooling their adjoining interior lands, Husted and Hoyt laid out Cherry Street as a second cross road between Park and Main, and in New Canaan's first real estate development sold off eight or more building lots, priced at $500 per acre. Then they deeded the new highway to the town of New Canaan for 25 cents.

The first to buy and build on Cherry Street was Caleb St. John Benedict, who left his father's Brushy Ridge business to become a cutter for Frederick Ayres. His house (No. 41) is the only one standing on Cherry Street today. On the south corner, but facing Park, John Lambert built what today is the Melba Inn Annex. An early Irish immigrant, Lambert was known for his fine shoes and in time he succeeded to David Law's New Orleans' outlets. (He was successful enough to send his son to Yale Law School, class of 1845, the first New Canaan law school graduate.) To the south, on Lakeview Avenue, Abram Crissy, 2d, went into the shoe business on a large scale, while Caleb S. Benedict soon set up for himself in a shoe factory on East Avenue, just east of the general store. Shoemakers soon occupied most of the houses along Cherry Street, though close to Main on the north stood a hatter's shop. New Canaan in a small way was attempting to imitate Norwalk and Danbury by making hats.

Simultaneously, the east side of Main Street began to fill up, initially because Wolsey Burtis, having bought a second blacksmith shop on the Darien line, had land to sell and Thomas Husted had money to invest. After the Cherry Street development, the partnership of Husted & Hoyt came to an end, with Edward Nash, the town clerk, buying Husted's share in the general store. Promptly, Husted formed a new Husted & Hoyt firm, this time in partnership with Benjamin Hoyt, a master tailor, whom Husted backed to make men's fine clothing for the southern trade. A shop was built (about where the Telephone building stands) on land bought from Burtis, but the business was short-lived, and in 1833 Husted sold the shop to a new hatting firm, which rented space to a watch and jewelry dealer. (The building was later moved to the west side of Main, just north of present Elm Street, and seems to have been the post office after Husted became New Canaan's postmaster in 1833.)

Between the hat shop and Bradley Keeler's carriage works, Daniel W. Bouton set up as a currier. Then in 1837 he bought another tract of Burtis land, north of the carriage factory, and there built a shop for D. W. & L. Bouton, leather suppliers. New Canaan's tanneries never could fill the shoemakers' demands for leather, and along with other findings the Boutons imported sole leather by the ton, which they brought by sloop from New York to Five Mile River harbor and by cart to New Canaan.

North of East Avenue the east side of Main Street was developing too. After Elisha Leeds Silliman lost his store on Church Hill (near the Congregational meeting house), Silliman's building was moved to where No. 86 Main Street now is, and there Hezekiah Jennings opened New Canaan's first meat market. To the north, Seymour Comstock, who had quit Raymond & Comstock, had a house and a general store of his own, and between him and Amos Ayres two more small stores were built. Before all these businesses were functioning, New Canaan had developed enough of a town center for the word "village" to be used for the first time in the town records of 1831.

Between 1825 and 1840 too many men and their firms occupied Main Street properties to make interesting reading. Businesses came and went—three blacksmiths, two carriage works, three or four tailors, two or more hatters, a dozen different partners in the general stores—and one is aware that the shoe money pouring into New Canaan led to new enterprises, though some men seem to have miscalculated what could be sold competitively. Those who made clothes, hats, and shoes for distant markets sometimes lacked adequate financing and sometimes were victims of panics and hard times. Collection of notes from southern customers was a slow business in the best of times, complicated by poor mail service and the lack of banks.

In 1824 Norwalk men had established the Fairfield County Bank, said to have been the first bank between New Haven and New York, which made a few loans to New Canaan people. (At the time it was formed, letters to the Norwalk *Gazette* denounced banks as instruments of evil, which took from the poor to benefit the rich.) Ten years later, when the Stamford Bank began in one room of a shabby old house, the role of banks was appreciated, and in one day its $100,000 initial capital was oversubscribed fourfold by would-be investors from as far away as New York. As a result, the $50 shares of stock had to be issued on a pro-rata basis, 17 New Canaan men and firms being allotted $18,500 worth, though they had subscribed for much more. Edward Nash was elected one of the Bank's first nine directors, being succeeded the next year by his partner, Stephen Hoyt, Jr., on Nash's death.

New Canaan, despite talk, made no effort to found a bank of its own, and the general stores (as Richards & St. John had done) continued to loan money on notes secured by mortgages. Often notes went unpaid, and as a result the store partners acquired real estate that they resold at good profits. By the mid-1830's, general stores were regularly advertising the properties they had for sale, thus founding New Canaan's real estate business. All along, the town of New Canaan showed an annual surplus from tax collections, and the thrifty Yankee selectmen were always ready to "put out" this money at interest instead of hoarding it in the town house. One 1827 borrower was Alfred Seely, the New Canaan man who now owned the Five Mile River store and was having built in New London the packet sloop *Enterprise* for his Rowayton-New York run. (When Seely died in 1838 he still owed New Canaan $240, having paid only the interest on his loan.)

New Canaan in 1827-28 knew at least five bankruptcies, two of them shoe manufacturers, but the effects of these seem to have been small. As was the case until the federal bankruptcy law of 1841, bankruptcies were handled by the Norwalk Probate Court, which appointed a committee of trustees to receive not only every claim against a man "in failing condition" but also all his assets—business inventory, raw materials, land and dwelling, personal possessions, and livestock. It is possible that the royalties Caleb Benedict was having to pay on his pegged shoes pushed him into bankruptcy in 1828, but he was rescued by his son-in-law, Stephen Hoyt, Jr., and was soon back in business; he may never have closed his doors.

Shoes

By 1830 New Canaan's shoemaking boom was again under way. More and more people were working at shoes, and those who did not have a separate shop in their front yards turned over a corner room, upstairs or down, to the making of the shoes brought home from the "manufactories'" cutting rooms. About this time, women throughout the United States were employed in a hundred different trades, and in New Canaan some women were to be found working on shoes. Usually, women were employed at "closing"—meaning preparing shoe tops for lasting—or at stitching cloth gaiters, and in either case they worked with a needle and not with a shoemaker's awl.

"Never," wrote an oldtimer recalling this decade, "was there a more industrious and incessantly working population," and he estimated that shoe sales brought a million dollars into the town (though he neglected to say over what period of time). What he also did not say was that the old system was changing radically. No longer did a boss shoemaker teach his apprentices over seven long years. Instead, young men were being trained in just certain shoemaking operations, and in February 1836, when Caleb Benedict advertised in the Norwalk *Gazette* he asked for 50 journeymen but only two apprentices—"boys disposed to conform with duties and instructions of a religious family." (In New York state, once shoemakers were aware that they were not being trained to set up for themselves, the new ways led to the Geneva, N.Y., shoemakers' strike of 1835.)

In New Canaan, while there was plenty of work to be had, a decade of specialization had begun when a White Oak Shade shoemaker would work for months on dozens of pairs of just size 8 shoes, while a man on Smith Ridge worked exclusively on pegged boots. A shoemaker could, however, collect work from more than one boss, and the 1834 account book of a "jour" shows that in two months he worked at fitting and bottoming 83 pairs of children's shoes, ladies slippers, and men's brogans—earning a total of $66.68. No one except store clerks received a weekly salary in those days, though a journeyman who picked up and returned shoes on a once-a-week basis would be paid regularly. But "paid" did not necessarily mean "paid in cash," because by the 1830's all New Canaan shoemakers except Hezron Ayres (who paid in cash) paid for work with "white dogs"—drafts drawn on the general stores. And "white dogs" explain why, when later shoemakers went bankrupt, they owed such large sums to the local merchants.

Orders came from all over the United States for New Canaan's handmade shoes, both turned and welted, so that in an 1839 newspaper a boss advertised for 130 journeymen: 50 to work on women's welts, 50 more on ladies' welt gaiters, and 10 each on fudge halfboots, brogans, and women's turnabouts. The larger New Canaan firms also received requests for such special items as the shoe Caleb Benedict was asked to create. South Carolina in

1832 had passed its Nullification Act, declaring void certain federal tariff acts that affected the state's imports and threatening to secede from the Union. To "celebrate" this, a Charleston customer asked Benedict to design a special shoe, and the resulting "Nullifier" sounds special indeed. It was a man's turned slipper made of boarded goat, cut high in the vamp and quarter, with a goat binding, and it had either a low heel or no heel at all, depending on the whim of subsequent customers. As a Benedict later wrote: "Our neighbors," seeing the quantities sold, copied the slipper and appropriated the name. (Near the Benedicts on Brushy Ridge was the factory of the prosperous Ebenezer Ayres. When Ayres retired in 1836 to live for two years outside Rochester, he sold his business to his sons Hezron and Alvah Ayres, and when H. L. & A. Ayres went bankrupt in 1850, one "Nullifier" showed up in its inventory.)

Instead of the South, Daniel Gesner Weed, who had a shoe shop at what is now No. 86 White Oak Shade Road, saw New England whalers as potential customers. Accordingly, he sent his younger brothers Stephen and Fitch Weed to New Bedford to set up a shoe factory and hire "jours." The whale oil business prospered, but the Weeds' shoemaking did not, and the brothers failed in 1844.

As the shoe business boomed, New Canaan families not only took in journeymen lodgers but also opened their homes to summer boarders, as relatives and friends fled from New York to avoid the heat and the regular plagues of cholera—not to mention the disastrous fire of December 1835, which destroyed some 700 dwellings. Room rent made it possible for people to set better

Daniel Gesner Weed continued the shoe business begun by Ebenezer Carter in this typical small shop—later moved and enlarged into a house.

tables, and Joel Hoyt's semiweekly market cart, which picked up produce, cider, butter, and cheese for sale in New York, brought back from Five Mile River harbor supplies of oysters and fish. Such large farmers as Col. Nathan Lockwood, out Oenoke Ridge, and Samuel Comstock, on Smith Ridge, regularly shipped grain and hay for New York's rising horse population from the same port and were said to have rivaled the general stores as money lenders.

A Stagecoach Line

In 1833 Almaduras Brower bought the house on East Avenue behind Nash & Hoyt's general store, established a livery stable, and started a regularly scheduled stagecoach run from New Canaan to Norwalk. Soon afterward he made his house into New Canaan's first "hotel." Brower had begun his driving career on the Norwalk-to-Stratford section of the New York-to-Boston stagecoach line. In later years, he told colorful stories of fighting off would-be holdup men and of nearly freezing to death when the unheated stage bogged down in a winter storm. In early days, he recalled, when his coach pulled up at a hotel or wayside inn, every passenger piled out, went inside, and took a drink. Invariably someone would ask him to join in, but Brower always refused; he was not a teetotaler, but he took pride in his responsibility for the U.S. Mail and believed liquor and safe stagecoach driving did not mix. Tired of saying "No, thank you," Brower decided to say that he didn't indulge but would take the price of a drink, if it was all the same to the passenger. Although, as he later admitted, the first few passengers were a bit nonplused, paying the driver the "price of a drink" became a regular thing on Brower's run, and his tips for three months, in sixpences, shillings, and "quarter silverpieces," amounted to more than $44.

Brower could not have been a stagecoach driver on the Post Road for very long, because by 1828 he was riding the mail on horseback from Norwalk to New Canaan for the Norwalk man who then had the contract to deliver the mail. Soon he worked up a profitable sideline of his own, delivering to Norwalk the small packages he picked up from New Canaan men before his return trip. Not a man to pass up an opportunity, Brower quit the mail riding to operate a once-a-day, six-days-a-week "express" business, out of which grew his New Canaan stagecoach line.

Always strong on service, Brower established an early morning "commuter" run, picking up businessmen along Oenoke Ridge and on Church Hill and delivering them dockside in South Norwalk in time to catch the morning steamboat to New York. (On the days Norwalk's harbor was frozen, Brower was known to drive his stagecoach all the way to New York.) The stage was a red Concord coach with "New Canaan Diligence" neatly lettered over its doors. And until New Canaan had its own branch railroad line (1868), the town depended on Brower's and subsequent stage lines to get its residents and visitors to and from Norwalk's steamboat and (later) railroad depots.

Temperance and Religion

The people of New Canaan in the 1830's were not so "industrious and incessantly working" as to have no time for talk, and the uppermost subjects of conversation were alcoholism, religion, education, and politics, with a bit of culture thrown in. Samuel St. John, Jr., for one, made a grand tour of Europe following his graduation from Yale in 1834, and New York offered art shows, museums, circuses, and book stores. Theatre was still frowned upon, but dancing was not, and there was many a Saturday night dance frolic along with a general interest in music. Singing schools were the thing. A quartet of instrumentalists was formed to provide music at Congregational worship services; while one or more New Canaan bands participated at a Norwalk celebration and a gala concert in Danbury as well as performing at home.

By the 1830's, like many another town, New Canaan came face to face with the problem of alcoholism. Small legal stills were scattered throughout the town and every general store—in the village and in the outskirts—had a license to sell liquor across the counter, unless the store owners declined to apply for one from the selectmen. A "jour" with shoe money in his pockets, a farmhand, or a clerk could buy rum, whisky, or brandy as easily as groceries—price 3 cents a glass. By 1833, deaths from "intemperance," the number of intoxication cases heard in the J.P.'s courts, and the need for the town to support families of "common drunkards" resulted in the formation of the New Canaan Temperance Society, sponsored by the new Congregational minister.

Though the Temperance movement would not reach its peak until the next decade, the Rev. Theophilus Smith prevailed on the Congregational Church in 1837 to vote that it was an "immorality" for any member to manufacture, sell, or use distilled spirits unless ill. One of the Church members at that time was Edwin S. Seymour, a partner in Ayres & Seymour, son and son-in-law of Amos Ayres, for whom they operated a specially fitted up bar. When in June 1838 Seymour was brought to trial by the Church, accused of selling spirits to "persons in ordinary health," Seymour fought back. Never, he swore, had he sold liquor to an intoxicated man or done anything immoral by selling spirits, and he denied that the Church had the right to pass binding resolutions on what its members should eat or drink or what business they should pursue. Like a weekly serial at a later movie house, daytime hearings in the Seymour case drew 40 to 50 people month after month, until finally in February 1839 the Church backed down and rescinded its vote—but not until the Consociation of Fairfield County West had determined that the Church had the right to change its mind.

If some of the money being made in shoes went into alcohol, much more went into the building of five new New Canaan meeting houses between 1833 and 1843 and to contributions to two more in other towns.

Besides money, the men who went to and from New York or traveled farther afield brought back new ideas and new ways from areas that had never known the domination of the Congregational church. Encouraged by a member who had observed such in New York, the Congregationalists took the lead and in 1827 established New Canaan's first Sunday School. (Since the old meeting house was too small and had no heat, teachers and pupils met first in the Academy building on the Park Street hill.) By then, the town had granted permission to both the Baptists and Methodists to use the new Town House for their worship services, while the growing Episcopal Church still met in its unconsecrated building on West Road. The Methodists in 1832 and the Episcopalians in 1833 both started Sunday Schools.

In 1832 the Episcopalians bought a site at the top of Church Hill, just south of the Town House, and there built a Greek Revival Style meeting house, which was consecrated as St. Mark's on May 6, 1834, by the Bishop of Connecticut. (Although remodeled in the 1850's and now St. Michael's Lutheran Church, this building is the oldest religious edifice standing in New Canaan today.) The Methodists in October 1833 bought on lower Main Street (at the north corner of present Church Street), and by 1834 they too had completed a meeting house—a small two-door one. (Hauled by oxen to a new site in 1854 to become, first, the Concert Hall and, then, the second Town House, this much remodeled and enlarged building today is Nos. 132-138 Main Street—the second oldest local church structure.) Built in 1843, the Congregational meeting house is the third oldest, for neither the Campbellite meeting house nor the Methodist one in Silvermine, built a bit earlier, survive.

Because of poor health, the Rev. William Bonney had resigned as Congregational minister, to be succeeded in August 1831 by the Rev. Theophilus Smith. One of the successive Yale graduates to head the Academy, Smith had just returned to New Canaan to

An 1835 engraving of Church Hill—the first known New Canaan picture. From left to right around God's Acre, the second Congregational meeting house, the schoolhouse, dormitory, and residence of the boy's boarding school, the first Town House, and the new St. Mark's.

marry Hannah, the only daughter of the late Samuel St. John in June. Fresh from Yale Divinity School, he was more "modern" than his revivalist predecessor, but even before his temperance stand Theophilus Smith had battled another church member over freedom of religious thought.

At the adjourned annual town meeting, Oct. 19, 1835, a petition was read and a motion passed that the Town House be opened to *any* religious denomination wishing to hold services there. The only condition was that a 25-cent fee be paid in advance. On the surface, the petition framed by Thomas S. Husted "and others" asked only for the same privilege the Baptists and Methodists formerly had, but, underneath, the petition was an act of defiance of the Congregational Church. Every man voting that day knew that Thomas Husted intended to form a new Protestant denomination.

As New Canaan's leading businessman, postmaster, and Whig politician, Thomas Seymour Husted was a person of consequence. Besides his several Main Street stores, Husted was dealing in shoes in New York, where he had an office and home on Pitt Street. In New York, Husted and his wife had been introduced to new religious thought, and, though members of the Congregational Church since 1817, had in 1832 joined the Church of Christ, then meeting at York Street and St. John's Lane. Popularly referred to as "the Campbellite church" because of its father and son founders, Thomas and Alexander Campbell, the Church of Christ had just ended its affiliation with the Baptist church and become a denomination on its own. The first change Theophilus Smith had made on becoming minister pertained to the dismissal of church members: since the fall of 1831 members who wished to transfer could be dismissed to an Episcopal, Methodist, or Baptist church after years of dismissals only to another Congregational church. But the Church refused to dismiss Mr. and Mrs. Husted to the Campbellites, "the brethren not having sufficient knowledge of the Church mentioned." While a three-man committee sought information "respecting the standing and faith" of the Church of Christ, Theophilus Smith and his two deacons fruitlessly sought to dissuade the Husteds from the step they had taken.

Thomas Husted, however, made it abundantly clear that he now differed with the Congregationalists on several points of doctrine. No longer, he said, could he believe in the baptism of infants; instead he believed in the baptism of adults only, and that by immersion. He could not agree with the Congregationalists that the Old Testament was a rule of duty, because he saw no reason why the laws of Moses prepared anyone to receive the gospel of Christ. Further, Husted contended, all man-made creeds should be abolished because Christianity was for all, and the only confession of faith one needed to make was the affirmation made by Simon Peter to Jesus (Matthew 16:16).

Following the affirmative town vote, the Congregationalists in the spring of 1836 washed their hands of the Husteds and two other members, declaring themselves "discharged of any further watch and care" over the souls of the four. In this way the Church denied the Husteds dismission as members in good standing but stopped short of excommunicating them. For the members of the new Church of Christ in New Canaan, Thomas Husted soon built on Brushy Ridge, somewhere east of Rosebrook Road, a small, steepleless meeting house, which long after it had been converted to a private school would be referred to as "the Campbellite Church." (This branch of the Campbellites apparently ceased when Husted left town in 1844.) Though the whole affair was shortlived, it was proof that by 1835 New Canaan had shaken off the domination of the Congregational church, though it had not gained much religious tolerance.

Episcopalians and Congregationalists looked down their noses at the noisy Methodists, the young "Red Bloods" who shouted Hallelujahs during worship service and whose camp meetings sometimes were disorderly. Taking their cues from their elders, young men were likely to make the Methodists the butt of crude pranks, as in the winter of 1835-36. The Methodists then were holding a revival meeting in their new meeting house that lasted for several weeks, with many members in attendance and much enthusiasm generated. To ridicule these "new methods," a group of young men picked a night when the meeting house was packed to bury a jug of blasting powder at the rear and fire it with a slow match. Panic ensued. Damage was done to the building, but no bodily injuries occurred. (This was no isolated incident, for the next year Anti-Abolitionists blew up the Redding Baptist church.)

Four years earlier, in 1831, another Methodist revival had resulted in tragedy. At the time, Stephen J. Miller, a shoemaker's apprentice living on upper Ponus Ridge, was a member of the North Stamford Congregational Church, where the pastor, the Rev. Henry Fuller, had held a revival. Not satisfied, Miller participated in a "four-day meeting" of the New Canaan Methodists, at which incredible horrors were conjured up. He was returning home from this on September 8, when a severe thunderstorm broke at midnight. Having, as he later said, just experienced "true religion," Miller interpreted the storm as the arrival of the Day of Judgment and, rushing into his house, killed his two small children and nearly murdered his wife. In the subsequent trial, the Superior Court acquitted Miller on the grounds of insanity and bound him over to the care of his friends, but the "respectable" people in New Canaan held the Methodists to blame.

The New Canaan Methodists had internal problems as well, and in 1837 the Methodist Society split, as had the national church, a small group leaving the local church to found a Methodist Protestant Church in Silvermine. On the west side of present Silvermine Road, somewhat south of the district schoolhouse in which New Canaan's original Methodist Society had been formed, the Methodist Protestants built a meeting house, dedicated May 17, 1844. Thereafter they struggled constantly to make ends meet, and their building was not torn down until 1928.

Although Connecticut was decidedly intolerant of Universalism, a convention to organize a statewide Universalist church government was held in Hartford in 1832. At that time, the first of two Universalist preachers appeared in New Canaan, but with small appeal. When Universalists built a meeting house in 1834, it was in Stamford on Long Ridge, and some New Canaan money did go into the building fund.

The year before, New Canaan's Baptist minister, a Mr. Whitney, had resigned and went to Bridgeport, where he committed suicide. Lacking numbers as well as a pastor, the New Canaan Baptists in 1837 united with the Baptists in Norwalk, formed a new church and there built a meeting house, which was dedicated in 1840. For the next 30 years, descendants of New Canaan's earliest Baptists were members and officers of the Norwalk Baptist Church, among them Stephen Hoyt, Watts Comstock, and Cary and Noah Weed.

Adding to denominational proliferation and new religious thought, the Mormons were proselytizing in Norwalk as early as 1842, and soon had New Canaan in an uproar because a local parent claimed his ill child had been cured by the Mormons after a physician had failed. (Mormonism did have some appeal later, and in the early days of the Civil War, when a group of Latter Day Saints left Norwalk for Utah, among them was Seely Griffin, who had been a New Canaan shoemaker.)

Schools

If there was a broadening of religious thought, there was no similar development in education. The almost 600 New Canaan children who attended the nine district schools in the early 1830's were taught reading, writing, arithmetic, and geography from whatever assortment of textbooks were on hand, though here and there they might study a little history, book keeping, and natural philosophy. To teach the summer and winter terms, for a total of 39 weeks, the district school societies were happy to certify any candidate, male or female, who could be persuaded to apply, and to pay pitifully low salaries from the money they assessed parents. When, as in the case of District School No. 1, it became necessary to build a new schoolhouse, money for this also came from the parents in the District.

For years, District School No. 1 (the forerunner of Center School) occupied a building at the corner of Seminary and Park Street that once had been the blacksmith shop of David St. John. When the adjoining acreage was bought in 1835 by members of the Fitch family, who planned to build a new house, an exchange of land was agreed to, with the result that a new building, the "Long School" (now No. 40 Seminary Street), was built. At the corner site, the Greek Revival house that the Fitchs built (No. 63 Park Street) became such a successful boarding house for shoemakers and others working in town that it had to be enlarged within ten years.

Once schools were removed from Congregational supervision, education in Connecticut deteriorated, so that by the mid-1830's something obviously had to be done. A Fairfield County Association for Improvement to the Common Schools was formed, with the Rev. Theophilus Smith being one of the vice presidents, and, thanks to the educator Henry Barnard, the state organized a six-week institute for teachers and a state department of education was set up. By 1840, as New Canaan's School Visitor, Theophilus Smith could report some improvement in local district schools and a greater interest on the part of the parents. Allowing that qualified teachers were yet to be had, he deplored the low standards of the school societies, noting that only three of the 10 district school teachers (4 males and 6 females) had continued after one term, requiring seven replacements. Such turnover, Smith felt, was "injurious."

Not one cent of tax revenue had ever been paid by the town of New Canaan to its district schools. Beginning in 1837, however, the school societies (increased to 10 in 1840) could count on small annual sums to reduce what came out of their pockets for salaries and expense. After Andrew Jackson's distrust of the Second Bank of the United States led to its dissolution for all practical purposes, the national government's money was deposited in a number of "favorite" banks. Called on to pay out the federal surplus to the states on a population basis, most of these banks were unable to make the last two of four payments (which led to the Panic of 1837), but Connecticut got its share. In turn, and again on a population basis, the state "loaned" this money to the towns for the

The Fitch's boarding house as it looked in an 1860's photograph.

support of local education. To manage its share, New Canaan on Jan. 23, 1837, set up the Town Deposit Fund (which still exists), naming five agents to manage it.

With public education so poor, these were the days when everybody and his brother set up a private school, and though they came and went quickly, New Canaan usually had three at any one time. After the famous Academy on Park Street closed, its good will passed to Silas Davenport, who in January 1834 bought the house that is now No. 1 Park Street and some 22 acres of land to the west. There, adjoining the house, he built a dormitory and a schoolhouse (which looked like a meeting house) and in the fall opened the Philopædean Seminary, a boys' boarding school that accepted local girls and boys as day pupils. For $200 a year he offered "board, washing, bedding, fuel and light" and 46 weeks of tuition "in English studies, Latin, Greek and French."

From the start, Davenport was more interested in developing his land than in teaching school, and on paper he laid out his 22 acres into 50 x 150-foot lots along four proposed streets, which he named Main, Grove, North, and South. After a year of advertising these house sites at $150 each, he had not made one sale and so was forced to turn his large tract over to his father and to sell the school plant in April 1837 to David S. Rockwell, an experienced educator. Under a variety of names, principally as Church Hill Institute, Rockwell ran a successful boys' boarding and day school, which drew pupils from as far off as Cuba and Spain. (The Rev. Joseph L. Gilder acquired the school in 1861 and continued it another six years.)

Politics

When you look at the voting record, you can be sure that New Canaan in the 1830's and '40's "had a good deal of politics to the acre," as an oldtimer once wrote. No one today would think that the Republican New Canaan of the 20th century had been a Democratic stronghold or a political bellwether, but in the first half of the 19th century it certainly was. People were sure that the future of the state and the nation depended on their vote—as New Canaan went, so went the Union—until this claim was overturned by the results of the presidential election of 1848. From

1822 until 1838 (excepting 1836), New Canaan was decidedly pro-Andrew Jackson and had a Democratic representative in the legislature to prove it. In local elections the town remained Whig until 1845, with an ever-decreasing majority that in 1840 was down to 12 (201 to 189).

Instead of being large wealthy landowners, successive first selectmen—Jonathan B. Benedict, Stephen Hoyt, Sr., Watts Comstock—were businessmen, and the only man who could be said to have filled Isaac Richards' shoes was Joseph Silliman, Jr. (1786-1850), who though a representative to Whig conventions seldom sought public office. Remembered as a "man of sound judgment and unimpeachable integrity," Silliman had graduated from Yale in 1806 and studied law in White Plains with Aaron Burr. For years he was the only New Canaan man admitted to the bar, but instead of practicing law, he was content to be executor of countless estates, the court-appointed conservator for ailing people, and a justice of the peace. Held in his home (No. 33 Oenoke Ridge), his courts were said to have been models of decorum, at which everyone had to be seated, hats removed, and silence observed by the spectators. As a member of the Society's Committee, Silliman for years ran the financial affairs of the Congregational Church, and though a bachelor until 1839, he was clerk of District School No. 1, in charge of building the new school in 1835 and of hiring the teachers (one of whom he married). He was elected town clerk for five terms (1835-1840), served once as third selectman (1832-33), and was New Canaan's representative in 1850, the year he died. And like Isaac Richards, Joseph Silliman, Jr., was motivated by what he thought best for the town.

Where 250 men might turn out to vote in a local election, 390 men voted for state officers and 541 in the national election of 1840. After its long record of Democratic support, New Canaan went overboard for William Henry Harrison, voting Whig 321 to 220 after joyously participating in a huge Whig mass meeting, held at North Castle, N.Y. In one-horse, two-horse, and four-horse vehicles, the Whigs of New Canaan had lined the length of Oenoke Ridge and, carrying banners, flags, and miniature log cabins in honor of General Harrison, had driven across the state line to the accompaniment of bands. At North Castle, besides speeches, they were treated to free hard cider, bread, and cheese—and an uproarious day. In New Canaan the campaign was the hardest fought in the town's first half-century, for the issues centered on Jackson's removal of deposits from the Second Bank, Van Buren's proposed subtreasury, tariff questions, and the general hard times.

Dominating the Democratic scene in this and many other elections was Samuel Raymond (1784-1865), the son of a wounded Revolutionary soldier. Trained as a shoemaker, Sam Raymond in 1809 bought several acres and a house on the west side of Main Street, below where Maple Street would later meet it, and then at the end of the War of 1812 went off to New York. When he returned in 1821, he bought out Erastus Seely's general store. The next spring as a Democrat he was elected New Canaan's representative, an office to which he was returned annually until 1834 and then again in 1837 and 1841. Later he was elected sheriff of Fairfield County and a state senator.

From the start of his political career, Raymond was opposed to everything the Whigs stood for and supported the cause of the working man. Like all other Democrats, he would be labeled a "Locofoco" by Whig editors, who used the derisive terms that grew out of an 1835 Tammany Hall meeting. (When the Tammany "old guard" was about to be overturned by Reform Democrats, the gas was turned out and the Hall left in darkness until locofoco matches were struck to light candles and the reformers continued successfully—to become known as Locofoco Democrats.) Time and again, Raymond was attacked by his Whig opponents and in newspaper editorials for making no effort in the legislature to secure a bank charter for New Canaan, something he was not about to do. Banks, Sam Raymond insisted, fostered new businesses and new businesses created new jobs, which worked against the laboring man. Workmen, he contended, did better when employment opportunities were scarce, and the opportunities limited to established businesses (such as shoemaking), for which the job seekers had been trained.

In New Canaan, Raymond's political power gradually increased, so that in 1838 he was able to oust Thomas Husted as postmaster and replace Husted with his son Thomas Raymond. (With the Whig victory of 1840, Husted was soon back as postmaster.) Then, beginning in 1842, the Locofoco candidate for the legislature outpolled the Whig candidate for four years in a row, but, because of votes cast for splinter party candidates, no man received a majority, as state law required. As a result, for four straight years, New Canaan sent no representative to the legislature!

When Sam Raymond was elected sheriff of Fairfield County in 1842, he turned his lucrative general store over to his three sons—Charles, Thomas, and William Edgar—but not for a while did he drop out of politics. He had the satisfaction of seeing three of his Loco followers—Hanford Carter, Burling D. Purdy, and Timothy E. Raymond—elected successively as New Canaan's representative, and the Locofocos capture the town government in 1845, 1847, 1848, and 1850.

Bankruptcies—Second Round

There was a very good reason for all this political turmoil. New Canaan was in serious financial trouble, as one leading businessman after another filed for bankruptcy and more and more people were out of work. The situation began when Amos Ayres, the Main Street shoe manufacturer, borrowed $5,000 from Thomas S. Husted in 1836. To pay back this sum, Ayres borrowed $2,000 on Feb. 13, 1837, from the brand-new Town Deposit Fund and other sums from David Brown of Rye (Feb. 22) and Thomas Chatterton of Brooklyn, N.Y. (July 24). In each case he mortgaged not only his shoe factory-home but three other tracts of New Canaan land. As the effects of the Panic of 1837 spread, successive town meetings demanded the Deposit Fund trustees collect at least the interest owed on the Ayres' loan until the 1843 town meeting voted to foreclose on Ayres. During the nine years it took to settle the involved claims of his creditors, Ayres was befriended by Joseph Silliman, who rented him half a Main Street house, and on the 1850 Census Ayres' former shoe factory shows up as a public house, temporarily renting rooms to shoemakers.

Meanwhile, as court judgments were returned against one New Canaan man after another, everyone began scrambling to collect what was owed to him. And, in domino fashion, person after person went bankrupt, a shoemaker taking with him a general store which held his "White Dogs," and the store in turn pulling under a service business. The first to go bankrupt was Jared Ayres, who in 1840 quietly moved out of town, leaving his mortgagees to sell his Carter Street house, shoe manufactory, and general store. Then, in 1841, Jonathan K. Johnson (Amos Ayres' son-in-law) lost his property to a New York creditor. He was followed by Abram Crissy, Jr., the Lakeview Avenue shoe manufacturer, who held the contract to make shoes for the United States Military Academy at West Point, and then by Joseph Scofield, who had left Seymour Comstock's employ to start his own general store near the head of Locust Avenue. In 1842 Caleb Benedict went bankrupt for the second time and closed his Brushy Ridge shoe factory permanently. He was followed by Andrew Ayres, the Cherry Street tailor, William St. John, Main Street tinsmith, and Daniel W. Bouton's currier shop. Three shoemakers—Thomas Carter, George N. Foote, and James Pattison—went bankrupt in 1843, as did Bradley Keeler, the carriage maker. (One of the few who bucked the tide was Seymour Comstock, who branched out from his Main Street emporium to establish general stores in Pittsburgh, Pa., Norwalk, Ohio, and Detroit, Mich., which were supervised by himself or his sons.)

With many people out of work and others out of cash, New Canaan was temporarily in the doldrums. Page after page of the volumes of the Norwalk Probate Court are filled with the lists of shoes in the hands of journeymen, of inventories of leather and shoes on hand, of stock on store shelves, and the claims against individuals and firms. In the case of the big shoemakers, claims were paid off, at best, at 60 cents on the dollar, but even if they soon found new work, "jours" had to swallow a 40-percent loss on work they had already done.

As the situation worsened, Thomas S. Husted declared himself bankrupt, with Watts Comstock as his trustee, although his assets proved to be greater than his debts. Husted for years had loaned money to New Canaan businessmen or signed as surety on any number of notes. Besides his loan to Amos Ayres, he had loaned a considerable sum to Abram Crissy, Jr. In an attempt to stave off that shoemaker's default, Husted had made a trip to New York to deal with Crissy's creditors, only to find on his return that Sam Raymond had attached Crissy's assets, and the arrangements as well as his own claims were valueless. Many papers pertaining to Thomas Husted's bankruptcy have survived and show that he was a partner with his son-in-law Barrett Coon in a New York coal business and a partner in New Canaan in Husted & Ayres, a general store, and Husted & Johnson, a liquor firm, his partners being a son and son-in-law of Amos Ayres. Husted owed fees to Norwalk lawyers who over the years had represented him in 13 lawsuits against the Ayres and others. He also owed considerable sums to Hiram Crissy, a New Canaan builder, while many notes owed to him were uncollectible.

Always the developer, Husted recorded more than 100 transactions on the New Canaan land records, some of the last pertaining to a new highway he had opened in 1839. That year he had bought from the daughters of the late Edward Nash the southernmost part of the Nash homestead on the west side of Main Street, and at the north end of this he laid out a short dead-end road—what in 1848 would officially become the first block of Elm Street running west off of Main. Where Cherry Street had been residential, Husted's new highway opened up new commercial sites in the center of town. To Andrew and Jared Burtis he sold the south corner of Main and Elm, while to the west Husted sold one business site to Jeremiah T. Lockwood and William Dauchy, who started a wagon works, and another to Joseph Hickok and Stephen Holmes, who operated a livery stable. Husted backed both firms in the face of established competition, and since neither was especially successful, he was further out of pocket at a bad time for him. Husted resigned as postmaster, Sept. 18, 1844, and left town, but was buried in December 1848 in the Seely family graveyard on Old Stamford Road.

Among the last to go bankrupt at this time was the elderly Thomas Greenly, whom so many people later recalled with affection. Born in England, Greenly had come to New Canaan from London in 1802 with a wife and three children, to have two more daughters born here after he had acquired land by special act of the legislature. Well known as a shoemaker, though on a small scale, Greenly was also something of a farmer, eventually owning 60 acres of land. Taking advantage of Connecticut's bounty of $1 for every 100 white mulberry trees, in 1832 he planted acres of mulberries and took to raising silkworms, hoping to cash in on the state bounty of 50 cents for each pound of silk that he reeled. Odd though it sounds today, Fairfield County was enough involved with silkworms to have a county Silk Society, but efforts to develop a native industry came to naught, and Connecticut discontinued all silk bounties in 1840.

Greenly was also something of a musician. Though he never joined the Congregational Church, he played bassoon in a small instrumental ensemble encouraged by Theophilus Smith as a choir accompaniment at Sunday services. His bassoon was remembered as "having the length of a fencepost," with a gooseneck and "a couple of rows of flappers on its back and a few on its belly," which was so hard to blow that his face turned bright red.

Greenly never lost his admiration for London, which he called the world's greatest city and where he seems to have acquired a Cockney accent. Full of good humor, he enjoyed his glass of "hale" and constantly amused New Canaan neighbors with such comments as "Give some of these Yankee fellows a hinch and they'll take a hell"—although a neighbor noted that it took a very sharp Yankee to get the better of Thomas Greenly.

Whether New Yorkers were sharper than Yankees records don't reveal, but it was a New York not a New Canaan businessman who put Greenly into bankruptcy in 1845. Called a model of integrity, impulsive, blunt in manner but tenderhearted, Greenly had depended on outsiders to run his New York shoe outlet, because his only son chose to become a farmer on what is now Greenley Road. After a series of judgments against him in Connecticut's Superior court, Greenly turned over his holdings to a grandson, Thomas Nelson Ayres of New York. His house and 60 acres were bought by two New Canaan Ayres, who, in turn, lost them in bankruptcy less than 10 years later. After a local miller had pressed his claim for $26.13 before a justice of the peace on Sept. 16, 1845, all the worldly goods of Thomas Greenly that the constable could find to attach were 35 shocks of oats, 17 shocks of rye, 100 bushels of rye straw, and 10 bushels of rye. Twenty-one days later, due notice having been posted on New Canaan's signboard and a drum beaten to announce the sale, these were auctioned off at the miller's barn, bringing $7.40 more than the costs and the claim. This small sum was promptly attached by another creditor. Nineteen months later Thomas Greenly was dead.

New Businesses, New Moves

In the face of so many bankruptcies, New Canaan's population grew, new shoe firms were formed, new businesses started, and the west side of Main Street began to fill in. The only surviving children of Edward Nash, the former Democratic legislator, postmaster, town clerk, storekeeper and bank director, were his two daughters: Ann Elizabeth, who in 1840 married the Rev. David Ogden of Fairfield, the first resident rector of St. Mark's, and Hannah Nash, who in 1843 married the rector's brother, Capt. Sereno Edward Ogden, a master mariner. Encouraged by their husbands, the sisters sold business sites on the west side of Main Street, north of the parcel they had sold to Thomas Husted. At least three new stores were built there, one of which was occupied by S. & E. Ayres, a general store started by Samuel and Ebenezer Ayres, Jr., with the backing of their father. North of this, Samuel C. Silliman, Jr., in 1845 opened New Canaan's first drug store, which, with changes in name, continued in the original building until that was torn down for the widening of Main Street in 1965.

Like their parents and brothers, the two Mrs. Ogdens died of consumption, as did the Rev. David Ogden, and Capt. S. E. Ogden was left in control of Edward Nash's former properties. In 1850 he sold the land just north of the drug store and directly opposite the head of East Avenue to Noah W. Hoyt. From 112 Fulton Street in New York, Hoyt moved his shirt manufacturing company to Main Street, thus introducing a new kind of employment in New Canaan.

Two years earlier, in 1848, another new enterprise had made its appearance, one that would become New Canaan's longest-lived business and continue until 1970. Capt. Stephen Hoyt, Jr., tired of storekeeping, decided to move "to the country" and in 1836 bought the run-down acres on Carter Street that once had been the Shaker Farm. There for a time he raised onions and turnips as cash crops, to be sold in New York, but a chance encounter changed all that. David Scofield, from New York state, was traveling through Connecticut in search of a suitable farm on which to start a tree nursery. Fired by the thought, Stephen Hoyt impulsively formed a partnership with Scofield, and in 1848 founded the New Canaan Nursery, which began growing fruit tree seedlings on just 15 acres of land. In a relatively short time this became the largest tree nursery in New England and the employer of many New Canaan young men.

Along with H. L. & A. Ayres on Brushy Ridge and C. S. Benedict & Co. on East Avenue, a number of smaller shoemakers stayed busy and solvent. Such was New Canaan's reputation for capable journeymen that Edson Bradley moved here from Westport and in 1840 began building the pillared Greek Revival house that today is No. 46 Main Street. In partnership with William H. Adams of Chicago, Bradley made men's fine patent leather shoes, renting as a factory the former Daniel W. Bouton shop on the east side of Main Street at the south corner of Burtis Avenue. (Known then as the "Great Western," later as "St. John Hall," the building was moved around the corner in 1912 and is now No. 12 Burtis Avenue.) By 1848 Bradley and Caleb S. Benedict had formed the new shoe manufacturing firm of Benedict, Bradley & Co., which rented from the Burtis brothers their new three-story wooden building on the south corner of Main and Elm streets. Adams, also a partner in the new firm, took charge of its Chicago office, while Bradley was sometimes resident agent in New York and at other times in New Orleans. Also engaged in the New Orleans shoe trade was John Lambert & Co. About this time, Roswell S. Benedict reorganized his father Ezra's shoe business at 291 Pearl Street, New York, and also began shoe manufacturing in New Canaan in partnership with Charles Benedict and William A. Hall of Brooklyn, N.Y.

As in earlier days, throughout this quarter century people moved out of New Canaan to seek their fortunes elsewhere. In the 1820's two sons of Samuel St. John had gone south to become cotton factors in Savannah, Ga., and a son of Col. Enoch St. John had settled as a banker in Mobile (where, it is said, he originated greenback currency). He became a financial backer of Texas when it fought for its independence, and Texas was where one of New Canaan's early hatters went. In 1832 Ebenezer Carter, who had been the leading shoemaker in White Oak Shade, moved his shoe business to New York.

Scattering through New York state, as far west as Lockport, other New Canaan men founded stores and grocery routes, while the more adventuresome moved to the new midwestern territories, in particular to Michigan. Like Seymour Comstock with his chain of stores, Samuel Andros Weed, of Weed Street, opened a store in Ohio. Weed had begun his business career in New York City in a small basement store, where he sold peanuts, candy, and cigars, and he invested in New York real estate, which his descendants retained for two generations. Returning to New Canaan, Weed in 1839 bought out Stephen Hoyt, Jr.'s, interest in the Main Street-East Avenue general store, which was renamed Weed & Hoyt (Benjamin Hoyt, this time).

Finished with Yale Law School in 1845, John B. Lambert went off to practice in California, to be followed during the Gold Rush by at least four New Canaan men. One of these was Col. Darius Davenport of Ponus Ridge, whose capable wife foresaw that there would be a crop shortage after so many men left for California. Calling on all available hands in her neighborhood, Mrs. Davenport planted every suitable acre to potatoes, and Colonel Davenport returned in 1851 to find his barns, cellar, wagonhouse, woodshed—every possible storage place—filled with her crop. In short time, he had ox teams hauling wagon-loads of potatoes to Shippan Point for shipment by water to Fulton Market in New York, his wife's tubers bringing in as much cash as the gold he had dug in California.

A Fire Department

Meanwhile, in 1845, the looks of the east side of Main Street had been radically changed. On the night of May 6, Bradley Keeler's carriage works caught fire and burned to the ground, taking with it Daniel Bouton's new dwelling and (perhaps) a shop. The fire forced both men into new bankruptcies, and from Bouton, Darius St. John, who held the mortgage, acquired the "Great Western," which thereafter was known as St. John's Hall. Keeler did not rebuild, and after he moved to Smith Ridge, his former dwelling house on the west side of Main became the nucleus for a hotel that was first known as the New Canaan Hotel and later as the Birdsall House. Not for bachelor journeymen, this catered to out-of-town buyers and salesmen, drawn by business to New Canaan.

Within a week after the fire, the people of New Canaan had subscribed $500 to buy the town's first fire engine, and on July 4,

1845, a volunteer fire company was organized. Incorporated by a private law of the state legislature, the New Canaan Fire Engine Company was authorized to enlist 24 men (soon increased to 40), all of whom were to live "within the distance of three fourths of a mile from the congregational meeting house."

Until an engine was procured, no member of the volunteer fire company was exempt from military duty, and once the hand pumper arrived (later housed in a shed at the foot of Church Hill), no more than 24 volunteers could be excused from militia duty at the same time. But membership in the Fire Engine Company became a satisfying substitute for membership in a military regiment.

Liquor and the Militia

With no military alarms since the War of 1812, the spirit had gone out of the militia companies, and their prestige had so declined that no capable man would become an officer. As a result, the semiannual Training Day became a farce, attended by crowds that wanted to be entertained while drinking hard cider—"the devil's kindling wood." One year an "incompetent" captain, dressed in full military regalia—cocked hat, feathers, huge sword, and all—drilled his militia company dressed any old way and armed with broomsticks, umbrellas, fence posts, and cornstalks (the more ridiculous the "weapons" and uniforms, the more the crowd cheered) on the Meeting House green, not on the Parade Ground.

Incensed by this mockery of a once-proud inheritance, William Edgar Raymond, Sam Raymond's youngest son, organized a new militia company, which he called the Wooster Guards (named for Gen. David Wooster, who died after the Battle of Ridgefield), and for which he had uniforms made to his design. In the fall of 1843, Raymond took the Wooster Guards to Norwalk to participate in a regimental review attended by Gov. Chauncey F. Cleveland. Cleveland was a Democrat, and for two weeks the Norwalk *Gazette,* whose editor was vociferously pro-Whig, had assured its readers that the Governor would not appear. But Cleveland came and so did a large crowd, which the *Gazette* afterward admonished for wasting its time—"as if the sight of a *live governor* was equal to the privilege of looking upon the Pope or his next door neighbor down below." (Like unruly militiamen, newspaper editors knew little restraint.)

It was also in 1843 that New Canaan's Company 2, 3d Regiment Horse Artillery, voted its captain out of office because he refused to pay the Company's grog bills. Then in 1846 the colonel of the 9th Regiment, Infantry, to which other New Canaan militiamen belonged, was cashiered for permitting four intoxicated officers to parade. Partly because liquor and military duty had become so intertwined, Connecticut in 1847 enacted a new militia law that did away with compulsory service. Thereafter, while all men between the ages of 18 and 35 had to be enrolled by the local collectors of state taxes, any man for the annual fee of $1 could have his military service commuted.

Thefts, suicides, and intemperance all increased in New Canaan during the 1840's—and all probably can be blamed on unemployment and hard times. People cried "Murder" when Samuel Monroe of Lewisboro disappeared in New Canaan on Nov. 28, 1845; "death by exposure while in a state of intoxication from the use of spirituous liquors" said the coroner's jury when, some three months later, Monroe's frozen body was found in a melting snowdrift. Accused in newspapers of spending $5,345 annually on liquor, New Canaan had wrestled for years with the problem of alcohol, knowing that when spirits were temporarily unavailable in town men went to Five Mile River harbor to buy.

On Jan. 18, 1841, a special town meeting made an attempt to handle the problem by voting that only a town agent was to be licensed to sell wines and spirituous liquors, which the selectmen would procure, all profits to go into the town treasury. The arrangement was good for just 10 days, when another town meeting voted to license "every Elector" who paid the town treasurer $10, almost immediately reduced to $5. As a result, all the stores who wished were back in the liquor business. Later that year a different attempt was made by 36 young New Canaan men who "took the pledge." They were the founders of the Friendship Division of the Washington Order of Sons of Temperance, part of a national total abstinence society, and enthusiastically met with their counterparts in other Fairfield County towns.

Connecticut in 1845 sought to regulate liquor sales by having each town elect three local commissioners, but by then temperance was mixed up with politics, and several Fairfield County Whigs went down to defeat because of Whig support for license laws, to which the Locos were opposed. Finally, in December 1851, the state enacted the so-called "Maine Law," which prohibited any person from manufacturing and selling by himself, directly or indirectly, intoxicating liquors. Local stills thus became illegal; distilling companies were formed; towns could vote themselves "wet" or "dry"; but intemperance was not cured.

Two Members of the Clergy

In the late 1830's and early '40's, the religious scene in New Canaan was dominated by the Episcopal and Congregational clergymen: David Ogden, first resident rector of St. Mark's (1837-1844) and Theophilus Smith, sixth minister of the Congregational Church (1831-1853). For each man, New Canaan was his only pastorate; each had been a schoolmaster between college and divinity school; each had married a daughter of a well-to-do deceased New Canaan businessman; each had his portrait painted (and both portraits survive); each was obliged to preach funeral sermons over parishioners who died of alcoholism; and each died of consumption. There the similarities cease, and though they occupied adjoining homesteads, there is no evidence that the two ministers ever spoke to each other.

David Ogden, at considerable sacrifice to his parents and brothers, had been sent to Washington (now Trinity) College in Hartford and then to General Theological Seminary in New York. Once settled in New Canaan, he lost no opportunity to assert his authority as rector of St. Mark's and the superiority of the Episcopal church. Before the end of his first year, he had hauled his vestry to the mat and won dismissal of two of its members, because the vestry had approved a secular concert in the church building without consulting him. While downgrading all other denominations, Ogden did much to make St. Mark's a part of the Diocese of Connecticut and proud of its Episcopalian forms. (His successor was the Rev. William Everitt, a high churchman, who came to St. Mark's in 1845 and left in 1846, soon to be converted to Romanism and be ordained as a Catholic priest in New York, which had all New Canaan agog.)

At the time of the dedication of the third Congregational meeting house (1843), Ogden printed in *The Churchman,* the diocesan newspaper published in New Haven, a scathing denunciation of interdenominationalism. The mere presence of an Episcopal rector on any but an Episcopal platform, he wrote, "preaches to the audience that [the rector] considers all ministers to have as good a commission as himself," thus making ordination by a bishop "a mere matter of moonshine." To have respect, he stated, an Episcopal rector must stand on his own ground—meaning his own meeting house—and maintain Episcopal principles. "This dabbling in Temperance Societies, occupying the rostrum with reformed drunkards, attending Bible Societies out of the Church . . . weakens the confidence of a clergyman's own congregation."

This was thinly veiled criticism of Theophilus Smith, who was an officer of two temperance organizations, had helped to form the county Bible Society, not only worked to improve the quality of district-school education, but with his wife taught a small private day school. To improve the appearance of God's Acre, Smith had repaired the stone wall that then enclosed it and with his own money bought maple trees he had planted around the cemetery's edge. Although its membership was declining, the Congregational Church in 1841 voted to build a new meeting house,

The Rev. David Ogden (1811-1845), first rector of St. Mark's, and the Rev. Theophilus Smith (1800-1853), sixth Congregational minister.

and out of his pocket Theophilus Smith paid Minard Lefevre, a New York architect, to draw up the plans. Despite David Ogden's views, Baptists and Methodists contributed to the Congregational building fund, collections being spurred by the considerable damage done in 1842 when lightning struck the old structure. The Baroque Style third meeting house, with its steeple showing the influence of Christopher Wren, was consecrated on June 14, 1843, at an interdenominational service.

The next year, his health failing, his wife and infant son dead, David Ogden resigned from St. Mark's and made a trip to and from Europe by sailing vessel.

Steamboats, Stagecoaches, and Trains

New Canaan people traveled to New York primarily by steamboat on the Sound. But the original steamboat lines out of Norwalk and Stamford had run into competition when in 1829 Cornelius Vanderbilt, "the proprietor of Long Island Sound," started operating "opposition" boats. Two years later the *John Marshall,* Norwalk's boat, was forced off the Sound, and all that can be said for Commodore Vanderbilt's cutthroat methods was that he cut fares when many people had to flee from New York during summer cholera epidemics, lowering the charge to 12½ cents, while the Norwalk steamboat raised its fare to 75 cents. After a relatively brief hassle, a new New York steamboat company was formed, in which some Norwalk men had an interest, and by 1836 Norwalk had two steamboats running to New York, each captained by a Norwalk man. These were the *Nimrod* and the *Fairfield,* making three round trips a week, with the *Nimrod* in 1842 setting a record of 2 hours and 55 minutes from New York to Wilson's Point. That year the *Croton,* also on the New York run, caught fire in May, giving 400 passengers a narrow escape.

As the story has come down, every New Canaan traveler had his or her favorite steamboat and would patronize no other. Bets were made on travel time and arrival, and Almaduras Brower knew that the men waiting at his depot for the arrival of his evening stagecoach were not there to pick up passengers or freight; they were waiting only to learn whether the *Nimrod* or the *Fairfield* had docked first that day and then to settle their bets.

East shore of the harbor at Old Well (South Norwalk), when in the 1830's smoke from new factories rivaled that from the steamboats.

After 1838 Stamford had morning steamboat service to New York, but most New Canaan people were conditioned to traveling from Norwalk, and when that service began to decline, New Canaan, early in 1841, had no trouble in calling a special town meeting at which 101 men signed a petition demanding the steamboat service they felt was their due. The answer was the *Napoleon,* put on the Norwalk run in May, but the boat was soon withdrawn with the explanation that the roads leading to Norwalk were so bad that farmers in surrounding towns could not get to the dock to put their produce aboard—reminiscent of the complaints in the first 19th-century decade when Isaac Richards opposed a new road to Norwalk harbor.

While steamboat travel was fast, it was not always safe, especially at night, and to supplement the rather low lighthouses in the Sound the United States Coast Guard erected tall beacons on land. Beginning about 1834, one beacon stood near the top of Brushy Ridge, described as "something like a brass ball, as large as a kettle, atop a giant mast." With far fewer trees than exist today, people living on Brushy Ridge claimed that with a spyglass they could clearly read the names of every vessel passing on the Sound.

Views of the water were so uninterrupted that many New Canaan people—on Ponus Ridge, Smith Ridge, even at the top of Church Hill—watched the famous steamboat disaster of Jan. 13, 1840, when the *Lexington,* bound for Stonington, Conn., caught fire and sank off Eaton's Neck, opposite Norwalk, with a terrible loss of life. Perhaps in the same year, unaware of its purpose or that they were committing a federal offense, a group of boys toppled the Brushy Ridge beacon. But the Coast Guard righted and relit it, and the beacon stood for another ten years.

While the Norwalk and Stamford papers continued to publish letters from New Canaan about poor steamboat service, their editors gave regular attention to the progress being made in erecting poles for the first telegraph line between New York and Boston and construction of the railroad that would soon change not only the mode of transportation but the entire economy. In 1840, four years after work had begun on the roadbed of the Hartford & New Haven railroad, the New York-New Haven road was proposed. By today's standards, that railroad took a long time to build, but rocks had to be blasted for cuts, inlets of the Sound and rivers had to be bridged, and routes had to be changed now and then. Still

The stagecoach that deposited pupils at the boys' boarding school atop Church Hill belonged to Almaduras Brower and probably was the same stage that brought Mrs. Olmstead to New Canaan in 1848.

the day was approaching when the stagecoach, if not all steamboats, would be obsolete.

On Oct. 19, 1847, Sophia Richards, who had taught a New Canaan district school, married James Olmstead of Wilton, then a New Haven pharmacist. Back in New Canaan the following March on a visit to her father, Dr. Lewis Richards, who lived in the present Roger Sherman Inn, Sophia wrote her husband, describing her stagecoach trip from New Haven to her old home.

> I waited nearly half an hour at Bishops Hotel for the passengers to arrive. There were seven in the stage, four Gentlemen and two Ladies besides myself. Nothing occurred of interest until we arrived at Milford where we changed horses. There I saw some distinguished Gentlemen: Mr. Horace Greeley and the Whig Senators Thompson & Corwin. They were in a private carriage, rode just in front of us, as far as Bridgeport. Did you ever see Mr. Greeley? The most careless in his personal appearance of anyone I ever before saw. I supposed he was a common loafer, a shabby looking hat on, his coat collar turned in, hands in his pocket, hair every which way. You must imagine he did not appear very gentlemanly. I was amazed when told who it was.
>
> I must tell you something about our passengers. One was a Boston Lady, who was going to Mrs. Ward's School in Bridgeport for her daughter. The other female was a coarse appearing person. She stopped in Bridgeport. One Gentleman was from Albany. Another from Norwalk, and a Mr. Whiting, quite a Gentleman in his appearance, rode with us as far as Milford. The other Gentleman who was very kind and attentive to your wife I do not know his name. He left us in Bridgeport.
>
> Now I must return to Milford, a very pleasant ride as far as Washington Bridge. Then there was a little romance about it. You told me we were to cross the river in a ferry boat, I supposed such boats as they have in Brooklyn. We rode quite a winding way down to the water side. I feared we should upset, but we did not just then. We all of us jumped out to make preparations to cross over. Such an amazing scene. The raft as I call it, for it seemed to be nothing but boards, was coming in, or rather toward us. There were some Ladies & Gentlemen crossing and two carriages. As soon as they landed we walked on. They were some minutes putting our luggage on as there so many little kegs of glue, about twenty I think, to remove.
>
> Let me tell you there were no seats to accommodate us on this "boat"—we sat on our trunks. We had a delightful sail. I enjoyed it much. The scenery around looked very wild and beautiful. Our party were all in fine spirits. The coarse female I mentioned was very timid. When she found that we were to cross on the rough looking boat, she exclaimed "I'm scart to death! Oh dear! I wish I had staid in New Haven." We reached the other side safely, found a much better stage to convey us to Bridgeport. We seated ourselves, anticipating a fine ride it was such a charming day. We had proceeded a few steps before the stage broke down. Several men who were working near the bridge

> came to our assistance. We stepped out as quickly as possible, or rather two Gentlemen lifted me out. We sat down on some logs the side of the street until things were ready for us to proceed. The Boston Lady made some amusing speeches. I was thankful that none of us were hurt. We rode about a mile and down we came again. I really was frightened and yet laughed, seeing this timid woman. It was very fortunate that rail fences were near. The driver took every thing in good nature as he ought. We finally arrived at Bridgeport, only tarried long enough to step from one stage to another. I was sorry as I wished to go into the Hotel a moment. Our ride from Bridgeport to Norwalk was very pleasant however. I was rejoiced to reach the Hotel I was so very tired. . . I tried to sleep thinking I should feel better, but there was so much noise I could not rest. . . . About five, or rather half after, the [New Canaan] stage called for us.

One year later Sophia Olmstead, again in New Canaan, wrote to ask her husband whether she should meet "the cars" in Norwalk or Darien when he came to join her.

The first through train from New Haven to New York ran through Norwalk, Darien, and Stamford on Christmas Day 1848. For 20 more years the people in New Canaan who wished to ride a train had to take the stagecoach to a main-line depot, and by 1850 both Brower and his competitor, Dann & Curtis, were advertising twice daily service to Darien. Freight, as before, went by stage to Norwalk. The New York, New Haven & Hartford maintained a respectable schedule, with six trains leaving Norwalk and five coming out of New York every day. A commutation ticket in 1852 from Norwalk, Darien, or Stamford cost $40 for six months or $60 per year, something less than 10 cents a ride. But people didn't relinquish their fondness for steamboats until they were forced to do so, and into the 1920's, if you were in no hurry, you could ride a train from New Canaan to Stamford and transfer to a New York-bound boat, 35 cents one way, 50 cents round trip.

CHAPTER 8

The Best Laid Plans, 1851-1875

If the 1830's and 40's were exhilarating times, the quarter century that followed was filled with unpleasant surprises and unforeseen events, though in 1851 New Canaan could contemplate its 50th anniversary with complacency. The 1850 Census had given it a population of 2,600, an increase of 324 in a decade, making it almost twice the size of Darien, on the Post Road and on the railroad's main line, and almost a third larger than Wilton, on the Danbury turnpike. Norwalk had grown to 4,651, while Stamford had reached 5,003, both as the result of fast-growing industrialization. Trade Street, as Main Street was then called (later it would be Village Street), could boast two large general stores, two jewelers, a druggist, and an oyster dealer, and had just erected an iron-framed signboard in the "square" at the head of East Avenue. In the village lived five clergymen, four physicians, six schoolteachers, and a dentist, and a man calling himself "artist." Employment was so general that, though 44 men were "retired" and 229 women neither kept house nor were employed, the Census listed only one pauper.

Of New Canaan's work force of 729 males over 16 years of age, 355 worked at shoemaking (including 10 tanners) and only 231 farmed; 510 women kept house and 660 children over 5 years of age were "in school," including the 18 pupils at Mr. Rockwell's Church Hill Institute. The old cottage industries were dying out. The fulling mills had all disappeared, and only two weavers and four coopers were listed in 1850. Instead, the Census had recorded 42 men in the building trade and 43 artisans, among whom were 12 blacksmiths, 4 carriage- and 1 wagon-maker, and (locally important) 6 gristmillers. Of the 117 persons providing "Services," 6 were tailors, 5 butchers, 5 hatters, and 95 were female servants, 56 of them Irish girls.

Well ahead of the influx of immigrants from Ireland to other parts of Connecticut, New Canaan could record 113 Irish-born residents, a bit more than 4 percent. The makeup of the town's population had changed radically from earlier days, and besides Ireland the foreign-born came from England, Scotland, Canada, France, Germany, Portugal, and Spain, while eight states other than Connecticut were listed as places of birth. Twenty-four residents were black.

The 1851 Election

Six weeks before its actual 50th birthday, New Canaan men voted in the state election, contested by Whig, Democratic, and Free-Soil parties. Although there is nothing about the election in local records, feelings were running high over the Fugitive Slave Law, and New Canaan had its Free Soil party, which had taken a stand against slavery. Two prominent Free Soilers were Stephen Hoyt, Jr., once a teetotaling Whig, who was running for state senator, and Selleck Y. St. John, a newcomer seeking office as a justice of the peace. From two surviving letters, we now know St. John, while living in Lewisboro, had been a part of the "underground railroad" and responsible for passing at least two escapees through his "station" there.

Newspapers in nearby towns were so solidly Whig that opposing tickets were seldom mentioned, so for the first time in its history New Canaan published a newspaper, *The New Canaan Omnibus & Fairfield County Agriculturist,* dated Apr. 2, 1851. The editor was William D. Snyder, the local part-time dentist. Although the stated purpose of the *Omnibus* was to open its columns to all political parties if they paid for the space occupied by their views, the only party represented was the Free Soil, which listed its state-wide slate. Then, despite the printed objections of S. Y. St. John, Stephen Hoyt and eight other Free Soil men inserted a scathing review of a lecture in support of the Fugitive Slave Bill that had been delivered before the New Canaan Lyceum on February 28 by the Rev. John C. Lord of Buffalo.

Both Free Soil candidates went down to defeat when New Canaan went Democratic that first week in April 1851, and since the first was also the last issue of the *Omnibus,* little more is known of local antislavery activities. The next year, in the presidential election, New Canaan voted 221 for Franklin Pierce, Democrat, against 180 for Gen. Winfield Scott, Whig. The Free Soilers rapidly faded out; the Whigs continued to decline, partly because of support of the Maine Law, and in the wake of the Kansas-Nebraska Act of 1854 were replaced by the American Republican party, in New Canaan as well as in the state.

Town Matters

In 1851, with Thomas Raymond, a Locofoco Democrat, as first selectman, the burning issue before the annual town meeting was the Parade Ground. This piece of public property had not been used since the local militia companies had died out, so Hanford Davenport and John Jones, who lived on Oenoke Ridge to the north and south, took the opportunity to encroach on the land. To add several feet to his sideyard, Jones had gone to the trouble of moving his stone wall boundary to the north side of Parade Hill road, blocking access to Parade Hill Cemetery and the highway leading down to the Five Mile River mills. The town meeting voted for immediate removal of the obstructions, but nothing happened then or two years later when the town voted to take legal action, though by constant travel a new western end to Parade Hill was made across another piece of the Parade Ground. (Special town meetings in 1876-78 were still considering how to regain the Parade Ground, and not until 1957 was the title quieted by the Superior Court in favor of the then owners of Hanford Davenport's land.)

Although the 1850 Census had shown only one pauper, care of the poor was an expense with which successive selectmen had been dealing for years. Time and again since the 1830's New Canaan town meetings had expressed themselves in favor of county support of the poor in a central poorhouse. (New Canaan town meetings had also gone on record in favor of Norwalk as a new county seat, only to have the choice go to Bridgeport in 1853.) Fairfield County was not about to establish a county facility, so, complying with state law, New Canaan's 1851 annual meeting voted to have the town buy property suitable for a poor farm. Hence, on Jan. 2, 1852, New Canaan purchased its second poorhouse—the 82-acre farm of Matthew Kellogg on what is now Laurel Road—and in line with the thinking of the day promptly ordered the purchase of livestock, farm utensils, and seed. The poor were to become as self-supporting as possible and the poor farm to show a profit from the sale of surplus crops. The next year, again conforming to the law, New Canaan ordered a workhouse be provided for delinquents, but there is no evidence this was ever done. Those accused of serious crime were sent to the new jail in Bridgeport. The selectmen were also ordered to provide the town clerk with a day book and ledgers, with the result that—after 51 years as a town—New Canaan finally began to record its births, marriages, and deaths as well as its land records, mortgages, and town meeting minutes.

Shoemaking in the 1850's

New Canaan in 1850 might have 355 men and an unknown number of women working at shoes, but the number of shoe firms was dwindling. In 1851 the firm of H. L. & A. Ayres on Brushy Ridge failed as did Hezron L. Ayres personally as resident partner. Because of Ayres' claims against him, Thomas Carter of Carter Street, who gave out a large quantity of work to journeymen, was forced into bankruptcy, and he was soon followed by his neighbor Thomas Simms, who lost his property and moved to Columbus, Ohio.

When the *Omnibus* reported that New Canaan's annual income from shoes was $300,000, it named Benedict, Bradley & Co. and Benedict, Hall & Co. as "the most extensive manufacturers." The latter firm was a partnership of Roswell S. and Charles Benedict and William A. Hall of Brooklyn, N.Y., and though it had a large outlet at 291 Pearl Street in Manhattan, its New Canaan location in 1851 is uncertain (perhaps in the "Great Western"). By June 1852, however, Benedict, Hall & Co. owned the "Big Shop" at the present Firehouse corner on Main Street. One month before, in settling the claims to Amos Ayres' former properties, the Superior Court had ruled in favor of the Town of New Canaan, and the town promptly sold the Ayres' factory at public auction, Benedict,

Hall & Co. bidding $1,565. Thus, 15 years after the Town Deposit Fund made its unfortunate $2,000 loan, New Canaan got back three fourths of the sum—minus interest and plus considerable legal expense.

The next year (1853) Caleb S. Benedict and Edson Bradley parted company, and Benedict, Bradley & Co., with its factory at Main and Elm streets, continued as C. S. Benedict & Co. Going into business for himself, Bradley bought a store at the head of Locust Avenue next door to his Main Street house and enlarged it into a shoe factory, which today is Nos. 54-56 Main Street. (Bradley's interests, however, were in New York City and by 1855 he was renting this building to the small shoe firm of J. E. Ayres & Son.) While some small-scale shoemakers out in the country might make deals with a New York or southern outlet, New Canaan's three largest employers of journeymen were concentrated on Main Street, and in 1853 this led to New Canaan's one and only shoemakers' strike.

One of the strikers was Benjamin Benedict, a brother of Caleb S., who much later wrote: "Wages were quite low on many kinds of work, and the bosses were . . . pressing the jours with numerous requests to vigorously apply the hammer and hasten the stitches and to hurry up the work." (Possibly this need for haste was because in 1851 the sewing machine Elias Howe had patented in 1846 had been adapted in Lynn, Mass., to the sewing of shoes, while New Canaan continued to make shoes, boots, and slippers by hand.) To consider how to improve their condition, all the shoemakers in New Canaan and the surrounding area met at the Town House and chose a committee to draw up a list of wages. Prices were set for 75 different kinds of shoe work and submitted to the "bosses" of the big firms. When the employers "laughed" at the prices, the jours voted to strike—on the following Saturday after everyone had turned in the boots and shoes he was working on. So it was that the members of the newly formed Cordwainers' Protective Union—lasters, sewers, peggers, stitchers, and crimpers—assembled again at the Town House, and with lasts flung over their shoulders and hides held aloft, marched to music down Church Hill and into the Main Street manufactories. The "bosses" were ready with new offers of their own—a few higher but most lower than the wages the jours had asked. But the bosses' price scales on the whole amounted to better wages than before for "the brothers of the craft," and as one shoemaker after another individually accepted the new rates, the strike collapsed and with it the Cordwainers' Protective Union.

Stating that New Canaan was a modest, thrifty town, second only to Lynn as a shoemaking center and not half so well known as it should be, the New York *Times* in 1856 sent a reporter to the village, who wrote an article entitled "A Day among Cordwainers." More interested in shoemakers than shoe manufacturers, the man reported that a journeyman's pay ranged from 5 shillings to $2 per pair of shoes, depending on size, style, and quality. The $2 top price was paid for a pair of men's shoes of the highest quality; 9 shillings was top for a pair of first-quality gaiters. Although an unusual man in an unusual week might earn $15 and the superior shoemaker $12, the reporter found that most jours averaged $7 weekly over a year, which wage, he wrote, was sufficient to keep a man and his family in comparative comfort. What struck the *Times* reporter as odd was that most journeymen (as had their predecessors) preferred to pile up accounts at the shoe factories and draw on them as need arose, instead of collecting weekly or when work was turned in. Some men who lived at a distance from the village, he noted, came to collect earnings only three times a year. (Some things don't change, and the reporter wrote: "A marked peculiarity of New Canaan is its stone fences. It is commonly understood that every field contains a sufficiency of fencing material for its own inclosure.")

If the reporter was aware, he did not mention that New Canaan still had no bank. Three years before (1853), an attempt had been made to found a commercial bank. A prospectus was published, asking subscriptions of $50 per share toward the proposed $50,000 capitalization of the New Canaan Bank, signed by the intended directors: Samuel A. Weed, Benjamin Hoyt, Nehemiah E. Weed, Sereno E. Ogden, Benjamin N. Heath, George Lockwood, and S. Y. St. John. But subscribers were few and the proposal came to naught, because a year before they became nationwide "Hard Times" had hit New Canaan.

In 1853 Andrew Benedict, a prosperous farmer who was then first selectman, went bankrupt. Next, overextended by his midwestern branches, Seymour Comstock failed. But such was the areawide need for his general store that, on petition of neighbors and others, Comstock & Co. was refinanced. With his son Albert in charge of the store, Seymour Comstock retired from business to raise garden produce on the land behind his house (No. 38 Main Street) until he died in 1902 at age 98. When "Uncle" Fred Ayres died in 1854, the East Avenue tannery came to an end and the Ayres bark mill, which had been leased, seems to have shut down at the same time. Then, also in 1854, just two years after its formation, C. S. Benedict & Co. failed.

Where Caleb Benedict had gone bankrupt in 1841 for $10,500, claims against H. L. & A. Ayres in 1851 had amounted to $58,189, while assets were only $9,951. Claims against C. S. Benedict & Co. totaled $46,980, and assets of finished boots and shoes, leather and other materials, two horses, and a wagon came to $5,942. Instead of local men, as in the bankruptcies of the 1840's, the largest claims against the Ayres and Benedict firms were filed by out-of-town banks, Norwalk and New York suppliers, and an insurance company. Nevertheless, so many failures severely affected New Canaan people. Under probate court order, the small sums Benedict owed to women workers and "for labour done and performed within six months last preceeding" were paid in full; a few large preferred claims, including those of Stephen Hoyt ($9,550) and Edson Bradley & Co., were 50-percent paid; and the remainder were paid off at 6.58 cents to the dollar. (Though not legally obligated, Caleb S. Benedict eventually paid every one of his creditors in full.) Replacing C. S. Benedict & Co. was a new shoemaking firm, J. & J. Benedict, made up of Caleb S. Benedict's brother John and Caleb's son Junius, which took over the three-story manufactory at Main and Elm streets.

Time and again it has been put into print that New Canaan's shoe business declined because the Civil War cut off its lucrative southern markets. Obviously, the decline had begun a decade earlier. On Feb. 10, 1859, when 350 men from the leather and shoemaking trades sat down to a banquet at the Metropolitan Hotel in New York, one of the evening's speakers was William A. Hall of Benedict, Hall & Co. in New Canaan. Just one year before a man in Abington, Mass., had invented a machine to sew soles to shoes, and at the end of his speech Hall predicted that in short time labor-saving machinery operated by steam engines would both boost shoe production and lower costs. When the Civil War created a huge demand for shoes for the Union soldiers, shoe manufacturers rushed to install the new sewing machines so they could meet the large orders in the shortest possible time. New Canaan manufacturers stuck with their hand-made shoes, losing out on most of the wartime market, and it was a good ten years before the "Big Shop" installed a steam engine. J. & J. Benedict never mechanized.

As hard times spread, people complained that prices for necessities were extraordinarily high, wages were low, money was tight, business was in a depression, and the care of the poor cost too much. As a result, New Canaan turned its Democrats out of office and for nearly a quarter of a century elected a Republican first selectman—Peter Smith (1853-1861), William L. Waring (1861-1876). After sending a Whig to the legislature in 1853 and 1854, the town for 18 straight years was represented by a Republican. Though the Union-Republicans had no overwhelming local majority, until the end of the Civil War they had plenty of fervor, especially the young men who were "Wideawakers" in the 1860 presidential campaign. It was during these times that the New Canaan Band participated in all sorts of political parades in and out of town, including New York City.

In the hard-fought presidential campaign of 1856, when Frémont was running against Buchanan, an ardent Democrat at Five Mile River harbor thought to bolster New Canaan's Democrats with the loan of a cannon for the 4th of July rally. A day before, the cannon was set up on the north corner of Main and Elm Streets—Trade and First streets in those days—in front of blind Ben Tucker's toy store, with sacks of powder for the charge put under the bench near the curb. Excited small boys were everywhere, on the cannon, on the sidewalks, in the streets, when a boy threw a lighted firecracker under the bench, unaware of what would happen. Amid sheets of flame from the explosion, a three-year-old was killed, a nine-year-old lingered a few days, and 22 others were badly burned, some maimed for life, despite the care of New Canaan's three physicians, who rushed to the scene. July 4th went uncelebrated that year.

New Leaders

By 1856 Wolsey Burtis, Capt. Stephen Hoyt, Sr., Joseph Silliman, Jr., and the Rev. Theophilus Smith were dead. Never again would a clergyman equal Smith's influence over New Canaan, and though national campaigns would be almost as hard fought as that of 1840, never again would a political leader like Samuel Raymond dictate to the town. Instead, a mixed group of men had come to the fore, who sought to preserve New Canaan's prestige. They did not see eye to eye; their backgrounds differed enormously; but all had money to invest, and their cooperation in attempting to improve New Canaan's condition added to the tradition Isaac Richards had begun.

The oldest of the businessmen in the group was the newcomer Noah Wilcox Hoyt (1817-1880), the successful shirt manufacturer. As a Republican, he was elected not only to the legislature in 1857 and 1858 but as town clerk, 1856-59. Appointed New Canaan's postmaster in 1861, he served in that post until he died (though Andrew Johnson in 1866 appointed another man who never took office). Selleck Y. St. John (1819-1903), already mentioned as an Abolitionist, would become a bank officer, New Canaan's first fire insurance agent, and a leader of the Methodist Church. He had replaced Joseph Silliman as the most respected of the justices of the peace and would be named executor or administrator of countless estates.

The third of the businessmen was native-born Lucius M. Monroe (1825-1916), who early in 1855 bought the drugstore from Samuel C. Silliman, a rather peculiar choice of occupation for him. Having been given one year to live when he was a young man, Monroe put no stock in medicines and to many a would-be customer would recommend only bicarbonate of soda. Nonetheless, Monroe's drug store prospered and continues today as Varnum's Pharmacy at a different Main Street site. Never one to pass up an opportunity, Monroe in the 1860's took on the agencies for Adams Express and Western Union telegraph, and in time added a third Mansarded story to his drugstore dwelling and an ice cream parlor out back. He also operated an ice business from the Mill Pond and later from Monroe's Pond off River Street (now

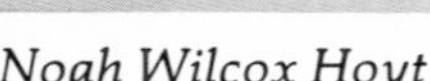
Noah Wilcox Hoyt

Selleck Y. St. John

obliterated by Route 123), became the leader of New Canaan's Democrats, and in the older general-store tradition invested and dealt in real estate.

Returning to New Canaan with inherited wealth were two native-born sons. Alexander Law (1821-1894), son of the Park Street shoe manufacturer, had been in his father-in-law's cast-iron business in New Jersey before he came back to New Canaan in 1854 with enough money to build a private school, the Law Academy (on the site of No. 100 Park Street) and hire a principal so that his only child Emma might be well educated. Two years later, on the death of his mother, Prof. Samuel St. John (1813-1876) returned from Ohio with his two motherless children to share the family fortune and mansion with his younger brother William (1815-1884). (In his quiet way, William St. John had great influence on the town and was a silent partner in various enterprises.) Samuel St. John had been professor of chemistry at Western Reserve and the principal of a young ladies' seminary in Cleveland. Now he was to be professor of chemistry and medical jurisprudence at the College of Physicians and Surgeons in New York, to which he commuted. To the fascination of New Canaan, he built an astronomical observatory to the north of his house, where he and his brother studied the stars through a high-power telescope.

Lucius M. Monroe

Prof. Samuel St. John

One other newcomer was Marvin W. Fox (1800-1882), a New York City schoolmaster, who in 1852 bought the old Ezra Benedict homestead opposite Alexander Law's house. There with his wife he started a girls' boarding school. The school was short lived because Mrs. Fox died, but Marvin Fox remained in New Canaan until his son's return from the Civil War, to become a prominent Methodist and Democrat, hold many town posts, and be responsible for opening Richmond Hill Road.

It is not a cliché to say that all seven of these men were of unquestioned integrity. Depending on the venture, they would be associated with a variety of others, but their judgment was as trusted as had been that of Isaac Richards, grandfather of Samuel and William St. John.

Captain Ogden

Probably the most colorful man in New Canaan in the 1850's and '60's was redheaded Capt. Sereno Edward Ogden (1818-1891), earlier mentioned as a developer of Main Street. As the town's only master mariner, Ogden was frequently at sea, often on the New York to Charleston and Mobile run. Before the Civil War, he was a part owner simultaneously in two or more sailing vessels, including the brigs *Mary Hamilton* and *Eolian* and the barques *Clara, Myrtle, Magnolia,* and *Petrea.* Investing with him in the *Mary Hamilton* in 1855-57 was Selleck Y. St. John. From the records that survive, Ogden was master of the *Eolian,* which made profitable voyages to Oregon in 1854 and 1856, and of the *Magnolia,* which he sailed to Galveston in 1857, but whether he or another captain took the *Myrtle* to Hong Kong via Valparaiso later in 1857 isn't clear. He had a one-fourth interest in the *Petrea* and her cargo, which in 1858 sailed from New York to Melbourne with $64,000 worth of lumber on board.

When ashore, Ogden was something of an opportunist. Besides developing what once had been Edward Nash's land, he and Caleb S. Benedict, the shoemaker, had been among the incorporators in 1851 of the Stamford, New Canaan and Ridgefield Plank Road, which the legislature incorporated to do just that—build a plank toll road from Stamford to Darien and thence through New Canaan to Ridgefield. But toll roads in Connecticut had never paid off; branch railroads already existed; and except for a brief mention in the Norwalk *Gazette* in late 1854 little is known of this enterprise.

Like almost every other man, Ogden was elected to public office in New Canaan. He served frequently as a tythingman; was on the 1851 commission that got nowhere in removing obstructions to the Parade Ground; and was highway commissioner for his district. (Years later his grandson wrote that Captain Ogden did such a crude job of filling in potholes that those whose wagons and carriages were damaged by jolts burned him in effigy.)

In the spring of 1854 fire destroyed the elegant two-story schoolhouse being built for School District No. 1 on Park Street, just north of Cherry Street. Involved in a lawsuit with the contractor, School District No. 1 named Sereno Ogden, a parent of pupils, as a one-man building committee, and as a new school site Ogden in 1855 sold School District No. 1 a part of the property he owned on the south side of Maple Street. There, after much cost-cutting that later proved disastrous, was built the first wooden schoolhouse that was the predecessor of present Center School. While waiting for its new building, District School No. 1 held classes in the Town House for almost two years. But, following that 1854 fire, New Canaan for the first time voted town money for its schools.

New Roads and Meeting Houses

Budgets and financial statements are not parts of the town meeting minutes, but in its Aug. 11, 1857, issue the Norwalk *Gazette* printed grand list statistics for Fairfield County towns. New Canaan's grand list was reported as $1,021,000, with 11,873 acres assessed at $376,000 and 442 houses at $319,000. Merchandise in stores was valued at $43,000 but manufacturers' inventories at only $17,600. Money "out at interest" was $126,000.

It was at this time that, despite its economic problems, New Canaan went overboard for building roads, voting to spend $1,400 in 1857. The year before, the right of way had been bought for a new road that was to run from Cherry Street on a northeast diagonal to where Edson Bradley's shoe factory stood at Main Street and Locust Avenue. Then the whole project was abandoned and, instead, the first block of South Avenue was laid out from Elm to Cherry Street. With the completion of Center School, the town in 1857 extended South Avenue (called Broad Street then) through the school grounds and all the way to the Darien town line—a phenomenon of road planning in this part of the state, for South Avenue was and still is the longest and straightest stretch of road in town.

Next, in 1858 Elm Street was extended westward from Park to meet Seminary Street at the foot of "Weed's Hill," and Forest Street was laid out from East Avenue north to Locust Avenue. Then, just one year later, the much-needed continuation of the highway on Smith Ridge was made southward from Canoe Hill Road to link up with the new Forest Street. While the latter added to business sites in the village, all other roads opened up potential residential sites along direct routes to the village.

Just before the spate of road building began, New Canaan acquired a Concert Hall. Following construction (1851) of a small Methodist meeting house at Selleck's Corners, the Methodists in town first established their own cemetery (1852) and then voted to build a large, steepled meeting house (dedicated Dec. 21, 1854). To make way for this, their original church building was sold to a group of parishioners, who had it drawn by oxen up Main Street to about where Bradley Keeler's carriage works had stood. There, with remodeled galleries, it was enlarged to seat 500 people and renamed the Concert Hall, more often the scene of lectures by prominent outsiders than of musical events. (Further enlarged and much changed on the exterior, this first Methodist meeting house today is Nos. 132-138 Main Street.)

Not to be outdone by the Methodists, St. Mark's in August 1857 voted to enlarge its building by additions at the front and rear, and while the church worshiped next door in the Town House, the original Greek Revival structure was rebuilt in a semi-Romanesque Style, with a steeple above a new vestibule and arched tops to the sanctuary's window frames. As a result of the remodeling, St. Mark's was so much in debt that during the next six years two successive rectors resigned because they could not support their families on a salary reduced below $500 a year.

Despite his months at sea, Sereno E. Ogden served St. Mark's as a vestryman from 1843 to 1865, and while the church was being rebuilt he was contractor for erecting the horsesheds that stood behind St. Mark's until 1952. Although it happened a little later, Ogden as contractor also built New Canaan's first Roman Catholic church. In October 1862 he sold to Francis P. McFarland, Roman Catholic Bishop of Hartford, a piece of former Nash land along the extension of Forest Street north of Locust Avenue, and within a year New Canaan's nearly 200 Catholics had their own place of worship.

The first known Roman Catholic in this area was an Irish-born hat dyer, who settled in Norwalk in 1828. Not until 1851 were there enough Catholics to warrant building a church, but in that year both Norwalk and Stamford dedicated their first Roman Catholic churches, both named St. Mary's. New Canaan was immediately put under St. Mary's in Norwalk (it also had charge of Westport and Georgetown), which twice monthly sent a priest to read mass, first in private homes, next in the Town House, then in St. John's Hall (the former Great Western shoe manufactory), and finally in the Forest Street building. New Canaan remained a mission under St. Mary's until 1896, when a resident pastor was assigned and the church became St. Aloysius. (Today the first Catholic church building is the two-family dwelling at Nos. 104-106 Forest Street.)

The Last Slave

One footnote must be added to the history of New Canaan in the 1850's—the death of Onesimus Comstock on Nov. 17, 1857, at the age of 96. In 1773 Capt. Jonathan Husted of West Road sold his black boy Onesimus to Phebe Comstock of Comstock Hill in Norwalk. When she died in 1840, Miss Phebe willed Onesimus to her niece, another Phebe Comstock. Although slavery had long been outlawed in Connecticut, Onesimus firmly refused to be freed, and on the 1850 Census for Norwalk he recorded himself as "voluntary slave." When the second Phebe Comstock died, Onesimus, well provided for, returned to New Canaan to live on Ferris Hill, and so it is that the last slave in Connecticut is buried in New Canaan's Upper Canoe Hill Cemetery. Anecdotes about Onesimus abound, including two of his participation in the Revolution, as a result of which his grave is decorated with an American flag each Memorial Day.

New Business

When the 1860 Census was taken, New Canaan's population had grown only slightly—to 2,770. From an 1850 total of 231, the number of farmers had risen to 264, while the shoemakers declined by 27 and the number of servants fell from 95 to 41, all reflecting New Canaan's hard times. Town meeting minutes show a growing number of elderly women receiving home relief and the town spending more on home assistance than for those at the poorhouse. Many young men had taken themselves off to factory jobs in Norwalk and Stamford, to professional schools, and to clerkships in New York offices and stores, while a generation of women would grow up and die as maiden ladies for lack of available men to marry at home. Still, the number of new occupations on the 1860 Census suggests a growing sophistication in New Canaan's way of life, especially in the village proper. Services now were offered by a clock repairer, a book binder, a sash and blind maker, and a man who put up lightning rods. For the first time, New Canaan had a hardware store, a "segar" factory, and a basketmaking trade, at which 14 men in the northwest corner of town were employed. And although no man listed himself as "banker," New Canaan at last had a bank.

Samuel A. Weed

Stephen Hoyt, Jr.

On May 20, 1859, the legislature by special act had incorporated the New Canaan Savings Bank. Six of the 20 incorporators had been among the would-be bank promoters of 1853; only three were shoe manufacturers; and though Alexander Law, William St. John, and Marvin Fox were among the Savings Bank founders, so too were farmers, a physician, and a school principal. Storekeeper Samuel A. Weed (1796-1868), who invested in local real estate, was elected the first president, with Sereno E. Ogden as vice president and S. Y. St. John as secretary-treasurer. With deposits limited to an annual $400 by any one depositor, at the end of the first day of business, July 1, 1859, they totaled $2,889. The first loan was made to Stephen Hoyt, whose New Canaan Nurseries on Carter Street already had earned a wide reputation for the fruit tree seedlings it sold to wholesalers in the Midwest.

Besides the New Canaan Savings Bank, two new businesses had been started in 1859 by local men. Albert S. Comstock (1831-1909) with his cousin Henry B. Rogers (1839-1905) had formed Comstock, Rogers & Co. to manufacture men's clothing in conjunction with Comstock's general store on Main Street. There, imitating the shoe manufacturers, overcoats and suits were cut out, to be distributed by wagon through the countryside to women who sewed at home. Finishing touches were added by tailors when the garments were returned. And, though he appears on the 1860 Census as "confectioner," William Edgar Raymond (1821-1890) had gone into the perfume-making business quite successfully. In the mid 1850's, this youngest son of Samuel Raymond, the Democratic leader, had sold the family general store and gone to Oklahoma, intending to enter banking. Instead he had speculated in government land, returning in time to be elected the town's representative in April 1859 as a Republican. It was then that, south of his home (No. 191 Main Street), he built a perfume laboratory. (Tradition has it that he also made patent medicine and soap, though there is no proof of either, but he did become famous for the Bohemian glass bottles in which he packaged his wares, which were distributed by wagon to distant markets.)

The Civil War

When the news of Fort Sumter reached New Canaan on Apr. 13, 1861, the town responded, as did all Connecticut, with flag raisings, church services, and a sense of outrage. There was a rush to volunteer for the Union army and, by mid May, 18 young men from New Canaan had enlisted for three months in Company B of the 13th Connecticut Volunteers. Among them were Apollos, son of Watts Comstock, and William, son of Edson Bradley, both just graduated from Yale, who returned to New Haven to enlist. They would become, respectively, major and captain in the 13th, Comstock being New Canaan's highest ranking Civil War officer. In October more New Canaan men would join Company G of the 10th Connecticut under Capt. Isaac L. Hoyt of Ponus Ridge.

What war might be like was soon brought home to New Canaan, for on Aug. 23, 1861, Lt. Charles Hunnewell died of typhus fever after being mustered out of the Rifle Brigade of the 3d Connecticut Infantry. The first New Canaan soldier to die, Hunnewell's funeral at the Methodist Church attracted an overflow gathering of mourners.

On July 3, 1862, following Lincoln's call for 300,000 nine-month enlistees, Gov. William A. Buckingham called on Connecticut for more volunteers. In New Canaan, William E. Raymond, who two decades before had organized the Wooster Guards, was put in charge of recruiting, and a special town meeting on August 16 voted a bounty of $50 for each volunteer. Eighty men responded by forming Company H of the 17th Connecticut Volunteers.

With Enos Kellogg as captain, they assembled on August 28 on Main Street in front of the New Canaan Hotel, and amid much excitement climbed into wagons that took them to the Darien station where a train took them to Bridgeport to be mustered in. Within a week the 17th was building earthworks outside Baltimore. Before the war ended, a total of 91 New Canaan men enlisted in the 17th, three in Company A under Capt. James H. Ayres. Although some men were mustered out after just three months, Company H remained "New Canaan's Company" throughout the Civil War. It came under fire for the first time at Chancellorsville and ended the war at Jacksonville, Fla. Those in the 13th saw service mainly in Louisiana.

Detail of "Camp of the 13th Regiment Connecticut Volunteers at Thibodeaux, La.," 1865 sketch by Pierre Gentieu of Company B. (Gentieu later married a sister of Francis E. Weed, fellow soldier in Company B.)

The 1860 Census shows that New Canaan had 232 young men between the ages of 16 and 25, yet when the war ended New Canaan had sent 260 men into the Union army. Five were killed in action (including a son of Caleb S. Benedict), 24 died of disease, 68 were discharged for disability, and 21 deserted—which is not the reflection on courage it may at first seem.

As Union defeats mounted, war industries boomed, and volunteering lagged, Connecticut began to draft soldiers on July 13, 1863. Anticipated draft riots in Stamford and elsewhere never materialized, though an innocent bystander James Fairty of New Canaan lost his life in the New York City draft riots of July 13-16. Lincoln's Conscription Act of March 1863 had provided legal ways of avoiding military service, one of which was procurement of a substitute. As the names of New Canaan men drawn in the draft lottery were published, those who could afford $300 went in search of substitutes. Two draftees, chosen simultaneously, were Albert S. Comstock and Henry B. Rogers, neither of whom wanted to leave their new clothing business, which was filling orders for Union uniforms. Since the town on August 4 had voted to pay $300 to each draftee and appropriated $10,000 for such bonuses, substitutes had to be found out of town, so William E. Dann, the Elm Street livery stableman, made trips to Bridgeport to sign up immigrants debarking from incoming vessels. How many substitutes went from New Canaan isn't clear, but those who were newly landed in a strange land could have had but little loyalty to the Union cause, and it's no wonder that some deserted.

By Nov. 28, 1863, after the General Assembly forbade towns to offer bounties, New Canaan was 37 men short of its quota, and Alexander Law and Noah W. Hoyt were two of the three town agents appointed to enlist men. In June of the next year, after Lincoln's call for 500,000 more troops, Stephen Hoyt was a one-man committee to procure certificates for earlier volunteers who had reenlisted, with the town voting a $50 bonus to each veteran volunteer. But, at the same time, the town voted to give $50 to any draftee who furnished "an acceptable substitute." By then, New Canaan was hard put to borrow bonus money, and for the first time in its history the town authorized the issuing of bonds. Yet, despite its financial predicament, the town spent $1,125 to buy the Concert Hall on Main Street, which had gone bankrupt. Thus in

April 1864 the original Methodist meeting house became New Canaan's second town hall, which on October 3 was used for the first time by a town meeting that assembled at the old town house and then adjourned to the new one.

Where Canaan Parish during the Revolution had a large number of Loyalists, New Canaan during the Civil War had no known "Copperheads." But New Canaan was never wholeheartedly behind Lincoln's efforts to preserve the Union, and throughout the state the Democrats, advocating peace, were so strong that Governor Buckingham won reelection in 1863 by just over 2,500 votes. Though the New Canaan Democrats weren't known as a "peace party," chairman Lucius Monroe's Civil War politicking was recorded thus:

> There's a man in New Canaan who keeps a lot of drugs.
> In the rear of his store, you'll find a set of plugs.
> They assemble each night in that rusty old pen
> Known around town as the old traitor's den.

Despite the lack of official evidence, church records and later reminiscences make it clear that the Civil War split some New Canaan families and ended lifelong friendships, especially after the Emancipation Proclamation of September 1862 led some men to make the Union cause into a moral crusade. One man changed his name from Weed to Reed and enlisted in the Confederate army; no congregation took a public stand on the war; and when the Methodist minister, the Rev. William T. Hill, spoke "in behalf of our bleeding country and of the suffering slaves," seven members thereafter refused to attend services.

Nevertheless, on the day of Lincoln's funeral, Apr. 19, 1865, Prof. Samuel St. John and Lucius Monroe had joint charge of a carefully planned memorial service. Led by muffled drums past stores and dwellings draped in black, Masons, Odd Fellows, Sons of Temperance, and hundreds of others, all dressed in mourning, slowly walked to the Congregational meeting house where a resolution was read, choirs sang, and four Protestant clergymen participated in the solemn observations.

More Developments

The Civil War never brought New Canaan to a standstill, and while the young men, the poorer families, and the local stores bore the brunt, the men with money had simply postponed their plans. In February 1864, with Roswell S. Benedict and William Hall electing to carry on in New York with shoemaking machinery, Benedict, Hall & Co. was dissolved. The "Big Shop" continued under Charles Benedict, who soon formed the short-lived firm of Benedict, Webb & Co. with William G. Webb of Elm Street. Then on Jan. 9, 1865, the Hoyt Manufacturing Co. was incorporated by special act of the legislature to become New Canaan's first business corporation. With Alexander Law subscribing to 200 of the 600 shares, the St. John brothers, Albert Comstock, Henry Rogers, S. Y. St. John, William G. Webb, and 10 other men invested some $16,000 in Noah Hoyt's shirt manufacturing business, which by then was also making men's underwear. Law was elected the first president and Noah Hoyt, secretary and treasurer. Retaining its New York office, the new corporation temporarily leased the former Law Academy for manufacturing and bought the old town house at the top of Church Hill to use as its warehouse. (The town house was sold in 1867 to the Ladies Benevolent Society of the Congregational Church, which remodeled it into a parsonage.) The Hoyt Manufacturing Co. was successful enough to pay 6-percent dividends until 1873, and its surviving records show that it had a fair number of women employees.

All the while, Sereno Ogden was busy changing the look of Main Street on the west side. In 1859, opposite the "Big Shop," he had built the turreted Italianate Style dwelling house that almost from the beginning was called "Vine Cottage" and today is a Main Street landmark. This he sold to Alexander Law as a rental property. (At the same time, on small lots on Forest Street, Ogden built two smaller replicas of this house, which he sold off along with the other small dwellings he built there.) Then in 1862, south of his house (which stood behind the present Town Hall), he built a store for William St. John, who with the backing of Alexander Law started a tinsmith business and also sold stoves. Between that store and Noah Hoyt's dwelling-post office, Ogden built a second store that became the meat market of Samuel S. Crissy and Hiram

Terrill. Finally, in 1865, just north of St. John's store, he built a small one-story wooden structure with a front porch to house the New Canaan Savings Bank and the First National Bank.

The Civil War had not ended when, on Feb. 16, 1865, a group of men, well aware that the Savings Bank could not provide the credit needed by New Canaan businesses, met in the store of William St. John to organize a commercial bank. One month later 82 men, 4 women, 2 business firms, and the Savings Bank had subscribed to all 1,000 shares being offered, thus raising $100,000 capitalization. As the largest stockholder with 110 shares, S. Y. St. John was elected cashier and a director. Though he was the unanimous choice, William St. John declined the presidency, which went to the elderly Watts Comstock (1790-1876), who, like Samuel A. Weed, the Savings Bank president, owned considerable New Canaan land. The Civil War was just over when S. Y. St. John went to Washington with a satchel of money and returned with necessary government permit that allowed the First National Bank of New Canaan to begin business on July 1, 1865. The first depositor was Justus Hoyt, the blind miller at the Mill Pond. Today, as its successor, Union Trust Company occupies the original site of the First National Bank, while New Canaan's first bank building, moved in 1911, is No. 19 Locust Avenue.

The first bank was just one of the buildings Sereno E. Ogden erected on Main Street. Another was "Vine Cottage," still standing (upper right).

Charles Benedict and William G. Webb, the shoemakers, Lucius M. Monroe, Albert S. Comstock, and Alexander Law were among the 13 original bank directors, though Law resigned immediately. "Not one of us," says the Bank's 25th anniversary statement, "had had experience. Some have done better; a good many worse." Still, in January 1875, the First National Bank of New Canaan could report that it had earned $30,000 free and clear, paid its dividends, and loaned some $4 million, represented by 10,300 notes. But the decade of 1865-75 was far from prosperous for New Canaan, and some of these early loans had to be written off, including the notes signed by Captain Ogden.

Captain Ogden Again

The Civil War had barely ended when Sereno Ogden, backed by Charles Benedict and S. Y. St. John, his former shipping partner, went to Georgia and bought leases to hundreds of acres of timber land in the vicinity of Reidsville. He intended to make his fortune by cutting down stands of long-leaf yellow pine to make railroad ties, which would be rafted down the Ohoopee River to the Altamaha River to the port of Darien. But Ogden was in trouble from the beginning. There were legal problems with the leases; the sawmills were inadequate for the job and the machinery broke down; and "regulators" appeared to threaten his black employes. (All his life Ogden kept the ropes he had slashed from one black man who had been tied to a tree for a whipping.) Ships to carry ties north were not easily found at the War's end, and when in 1867 the *Sargent* delivered 100,000 feet of ties to a South Norwalk wharf, the customer complained of the small quantity and poor quality. By that time, the directors of the First National Bank were concerned about their loans to Ogden, which amounted to $11,500, And when Ogden sought more money to build a new mill, Charles Benedict withdrew his support. By 1870 Ogden had to give up and the next year deeded all his New Canaan property, already fully mortgaged to them, to Benedict and S. Y. St. John. He moved to Wilton, where he died on June 12, 1891, a bitter one-horse farmer. But before he quit Georgia, Ogden did supply ties to the contractor of the New Canaan Rail Road.

The Railroad

"New Canaan is a happy land," wrote the *Times* reporter in 1856, "It lies, not on the other side of Jordan, but on the other side of the New Haven Railroad tracks." To correct this situation, plans had been long in the making to build a railroad connection between New Canaan and Norwalk or Stamford, as the only way to save New Canaan from insignificance and business extinction. With the end of the Civil War, Stamford had been chosen as the terminus, because with its new canal, passengers and freight had tidewater connections practically next door to the railroad station.

In February 1866, one year after the First National Bank began selling its stock, subscription lists were opened for the $50-par-value common stock of the proposed railroad. As potential shippers, Benedict, Webb & Co., bought 100 shares ($5,000), Comstock Rogers & Co. and Watts Comstock & Son (dealers in lumber and coal) each invested $4,000, while Stephen Hoyt & Sons, who had to cart nursery stock to Norwalk for forwarding by rail or water, pledged $2,000. With building and equipment costs estimated at $150,000, of which Stamford investors were expected to raise half, New Canaan by mid March was sure it could raise $75,000, and on May 30, 1866, the legislature by special act incorporated the New Canaan Rail Road Company. Besides two Stamford men, the nine incorporators included Alexander Law, Noah W. Hoyt, Charles Benedict, Lucius M. Monroe, and Prof. Samuel St. John, who became president.

On the same day as incorporation, the legislature granted the Town of New Canaan permission to invest in railroad common stock, but not until Nov. 2, 1867, did a town meeting, voting 188 against 77, authorize Noah Hoyt as town clerk to subscribe to 500 shares of common stock and to borrow the $25,000 if necessary.

With the end of the Civil War, New Canaan was in debt. After years of surplus, which the selectmen loaned on interest, the budget for 1867 listed $24,578 in loans owed by the town, on which interest charges of $2,547 were due. The total budget for the year was $38,448, which included $4,463 state tax, $1,912 for the district schools, $1,000.91 for the poor farm (which that year sheltered 19 residents and 43 transients), and $838 for 35 people on home relief (food, coal, shoes, burials, etc.). Significantly, $4,407 of the previous year's taxes were still unpaid, and yet New Canaan was ready to invest $25,000 in a branch railroad that was to solve all its problems!

Amid great fanfare, excursions to and from Stamford, and dinners served in the new roundhouse, the railroad opened on July 4, 1868. Instead of $150,000, it had cost $242,348. The expected Stamford subscriptions had never materialized, making New Canaan investors buy more shares than they had intended, and though stock sales raised $162,777, the New Canaan Rail Road had debts of $79,567 bearing interest at 7 percent. Dreams quickly faded of extending the tracks crosslots to Wilton and the Danbury line.

The immediate results of the railroad were rather diverse. Thanks to a federal contract, mail now came into and left New Canaan by train. Replacing the produce wagon that for so many yeas had taken market crops, first to Five Mile River sloops and then to trains at Darien, a produce car was attached to the earliest morning train. New Canaan people now could either sell or consign their cheeses, apples, cider, nuts, and the like to the car's agent for resale in New York. By the end of 1868, 11,000 passengers had used "the cars" to go back and forth to Stamford, some to jobs there and a few, like Prof. Samuel St. John, to commute to New York. From the depot to Main Street a sidewalk was laid along Elm Street, promptly renamed Rail Road and then Railroad Avenue. (The name was not changed back until 1936.) And,

Detail of the locomotive "Stamford" leaving New Canaan's railroad station, from Pierre Gentieu's 1876 sketch. (Cow is grazing where Pine Street is now.)

largely because the railroad was expected to draw customers to Stamford stores, the Stamford *Advocate* published the first issue of the New Canaan *Era* on Oct. 3, 1868. Except for a half column of "Local" items on page 2 and a few New Canaan ads, the *Era* differed little from the *Advocate* and as a local paper left much to be desired.

Taking advantage of the freight traffic, Andrew K. Comstock, son of Watts, built a planing mill just south of the tracks (about where No. 41 Pine Street is), which became his coal, brick, and fertilizer depot as well as his lumber yard. At the same time (1868) William G. Webb broke away from Charles Benedict and, opposite the depot, started a new shoe manufactory in the Law Academy building when Hoyt Manufacturing Co. moved out. Two years later, having sold its general store to J. V. Rockwell, Comstock, Rogers & Co. succeeded Webb as the tenant there.

What New Canaan desperately needed and what the railroad was supposed to attract were new businesses that would employ local people, so that they could stay solvent, pay their taxes, and remain in town. The planing mill perhaps employed 15; Comstock, Rogers & Co. hired new tailors, but from Hartford; and the railroad created just two new jobs: Joseph Lounsbury was night watchman at the roundhouse; Francis E. Weed, a veteran of the Connecticut 10th, was the first stationmaster and freight agent. (Later Albert Weed, a disabled veteran of Company H, would be the freight agent.)

By 1869, when it was obvious that the railroad was not a success, an effort was made to clean up Main Street by planting trees, and a committee was formed to encourage out-of-town businesses to settle here. Lucius Monroe, committee chairman, went so far as to offer to give a 160-foot lot fronting on the railroad to any new manufacturer who would move his business here—but no one accepted. While New Canaan did have a potential skilled labor force, what no one seems to have taken into consideration was that New Canaan, with all its many streams, lacked sufficient water power for large mills and had nothing to equal the tidal falls that had helped Norwalk and Stamford to industrialize. Nevertheless, in 1870, one new business was started in New Canaan.

That June, a new type of sewing machine, invented by Enos Waterbury of Stamford, had been exhibited locally, and this led to the formation of the New Canaan Sewing Machine Co. to build Waterbury machines. William E. Raymond, Samuel St. John, A. S. Comstock, and Stephen Pardee were among the seven directors of the new company, which, according to the *Era,* would be second only to the railroad in improving New Canaan.

Just north of the railroad tracks, on land bought from A. K. Comstock, owner of the nearby planing mill, a factory was built in only three months on a new road called Pleasant Avenue (which today is the driveway into New Canaan Fuel & Lumber's yard). But the venture failed in less than a year, without a single sewing machine being built, because of "insurmountable difficulties in obtaining a license" under dominating patents of another manufacturer. As a result, the factory building and land were turned over to 14 local partners, all of whom had been original investors in the Sewing Machine Co., including Alexander Law, Samuel St. John, Comstock, Rogers & Co., two shoemakers, and William E. Raymond (who had been president of the company). Then, in February 1872, Raymond bought out the others and moved his perfume laboratories into the factory, where he made his wares until he sold his business (but not the property) to a New York concern and retired in 1875.

One new shoemaker did settle in New Canaan. Far out of the village, on the Pound Ridge road just east of Bowery Road, Henry A. Pinney of Pleasantville, N.Y., started a small shoe factory in 1870, giving employment to many in northwest New Canaan, where the basket-making industry was thriving.

Main Street

All the while, Main Street had its share of change. While he was still backing Sereno Ogden in Georgia, Charles Benedict divided the "Big Shop" lengthwise along all four floors and persuaded William G. Webb & Co. to buy the south half, so that the "Big Shop" now housed two shoemaking concerns. (Shortly afterward, to the south, a separate building was erected to house the steam engine that powered the machinery both firms now used.) Down Main Street, at the corner of Elm, J. & J. Benedict in 1870 opened New Canaan's first retail shoe store, on the ground floor of their factory, while next door on the south, the New Canaan Hotel had completed an eight-room wing, anticipating clientele the railroad would bring. Opposite the shoe store, J. W. Burtis started a new grocery store, later known as Burtis & Mead, which as agents for the basket makers filled large out-of-town orders that were shipped by rail. When in May 1871 Edson Bradley left New Canaan, he sold his house, land, barn, and former shoe factory to Albert S. Comstock for $10,000. By then Comstock, Rogers & Co. had opened distant retail stores and was ready to expand its wholesale clothing manufacturing. So, while Comstock moved from "Vine Cottage" to Edson Bradley's Greek Revival house, his firm quit Park Street to move into the former shoe factory across Locust Avenue from the "Big Shop."

More to fill a public need than to give employment, the men who had backed so many business schemes once again had joined forces and incorporated the New Canaan Cemetery Association, Feb. 26, 1868. The number of Civil War dead had pointed up the fact that New Canaan had no adequate cemetery; God's Acre had been closed since 1856, and most of the 27 rural cemeteries were

J. & J. Benedict's shoe factory, built 1848, burned down in 1875 (p. 216). Between it and the lamp post is the east end of Elm Street.

family or church burying grounds. So, with Stephen Hoyt of the Hoyt Nurseries as president, Charles Benedict, Lucius Monroe, Noah Hoyt, William Webb, and S. Y. St. John joined with others to form the Cemetery Association, which in November 1868 purchased the small Methodist burying ground near the Mill Pond dam. Then they began to beautify and enlarge what would become Lakeview Cemetery.

Associated with these men was Russell L. Hall (1832-1928), who had come to New Canaan on Christmas Day 1853 from Warren, Conn., and south of the "Big Shop" in 1856 began making furniture in what is now No. 64 Main Street. (Although the Norwalk *Gazette* of June 8, 1852, carried an ad for a New Canaan firm called the "New York Cabinet, Chair, Sofa & Bedding Upholstery Establishment," which offered "grave digging and interments," the owner of that enterprise is unknown and, in connection with his furniture business, Hall became the town's first identifiable undertaker.)

Life in the Early '70's

Despite the many attempts to bolster the town, the 1870 Census showed that New Canaan's population had fallen from 2,770 in 1860 to 2,473. Though specie payment was resumed in September, meaning that merchants no longer gave postage stamps or fractional paper currency as change, business was generally poor, and both banks were aware that they must soon foreclose on some of the mortgages they held. Then, on Apr. 22, 1871, the *Era* ended publication, blaming unpaid accounts. Once in a while the *Era* had given good coverage to New Canaan stories, in particular to the attempted bank robbery.

With so much thievery—a young man even stole a horse and wagon and abandoned them in Norwalk—and drunken brawling in the village, the merchants banded together and in December 1868 hired Norbert Bossa, a Civil War veteran, as a night watchman. While making his rounds after midnight on Mar. 3, 1870, Bossa was overpowered by six men, who dragged him into the bank. There gagged and bound to a chair, Bossa watched for two hours while the robbers prepared to dynamite the vault that supposedly held $100,000. The outer vault door was shattered, but the inner door held, and the robbers fled empty-handed, while Bossa, unharmed, was released by Lucius Monroe and William E. Raymond who, awakened by the blast, rushed to the scene.

What the 1870 Census, of course, did not show was that money (or lack of it) was dividing New Canaan into "groups," even in churches, and complaints were made that the town had lost its sense of neighborliness. New ways, it was said, meant the end of old customs that once had brought residents together. Yet when Dr. Lewis Richards' horse died in 1869, a subscription started by Dr. William G. Brownson, a newcomer who had been a Civil War surgeon, raised $165 to buy a new horse for the aging doctor and pay for its care. And the next winter at a supper party a purse was presented to Leander Smith, an elderly black who had been a shoemaker. Not all the old ways had changed.

Amid crime, alcoholism, and general discouragement, the year 1871 saw a new interest in religion. Although they could now take the train one stop to attend services, the people in Talmadge Hill in February had the legislature incorporate the Flatridge Hill Christian Union, which built what today is the Talmadge Hill Chapel where they worshiped by themselves. The next month, after discharging three successive pastors in ten years, the Congregational Church installed the Rev. Joseph Greenleaf, who would remain for 15 years. Next, as its representative to the legislature, the town in April elected the Protestant Methodist minister from Silvermine, the Rev. Mark Staples, who ran as a Republican. Finally, in November, between the "Big Shop's" steam engine house and Russell Hall's furniture-undertaking establishment, Watts Comstock bought a small plot of land and founded the First Baptist Society. Tired of driving to Norwalk each Sunday and mindful that his parents, Enoch and Anna, had been among New Canaan's first Baptists, Comstock built a Baptist meeting house, where the first service was held, Feb. 6, 1873. Somewhat enlarged, that building today is No. 62 Main Street (Knights of Columbus hall), while the Victorian house Comstock built as a potential parsonage for a Baptist minister is No. 66 Seminary Street.

New Canaan's cultural and social life in the 1860's and '70's was by no means limited to church gatherings. Despite the financial pinch, a few people went abroad in the summers; some went to New York to see art exhibitions; many more went to the circus in

Norwalk or Stamford; dances were held at the New Canaan Hotel; minstrel shows came to St. John's Hall; and entertainments were put on in the town house and elsewhere. Horse races on South Avenue and the new Shoe Fly Base Ball Club occupied the men. But lectures seem to have been the thing. A hundred or more people would take the train to Stamford to listen to an evening lecture, while in New Canaan in the winter of 1870 a Young Men's Christian Association was formed, before which such men as Prof. Samuel St. John talked. Horace Greeley delivered a political speech in the town hall in March 1871; the Congregationalists heard a lecture on Honolulu, while the Methodists listened to one on China. It was a rare week when New Canaan was without some public speaker.

A popular lecturer was Commodore Robert Wilson Shufeldt, U.S.N., who in 1868 had bought a house and land near the south end of present Lapham Road. Shufeldt, who would go on to a distinguished naval and diplomatic career, was already well known—among other things he had been U.S. consul general in Cuba during part of the Civil War—and New Canaan basked in reflected glory when he was made a captain in 1869 and put in command of the Miantonomah Expedition that surveyed the Isthmus of Tehauntepec for a canal route. He and his family remained in New Canaan until 1876, after Shufeldt became chief of the Naval Bureau of Equipment and Recruiting in Washington and was made a rear admiral.

An earlier admired resident was Hezekiah D. Hull, who had made a reputation and a fortune as the first hide broker in the New York leather trade. Hull became a large landowner after buying in 1852 the former Holly Hanford property along lower Main Street and Old Norwalk Road. There he built the Italianate Style house that is No. 528 Main Street. A year after Hull died of typhus fever in New Canaan in 1866, this house became a boys' military school, run by Nathaniel W. Starr of Yonkers, N.Y., and his son Oliver, a Civil War veteran. Despite the impression made by a corps of uniformed boys marching into the village, the Starrs were gone from New Canaan by January 1869, when Comstock, Rogers & Co., Hoyt Manufacturing Co., Lucius Monroe, and Rockwell's grocery store attached all their property for sizeable unpaid bills. Among other accounts owed by the Starrs was almost $600 to the New Canaan Rail Road.

Education

By then New Canaan was without a private school, for in the spring of 1867 the Rev. Joseph L. Gilder, third owner of the boys school on Church Hill, had sold the seven acres and buildings to Dr. Willard Parker of New York for a summer residence. Thus Dr. Parker became a neighbor of his old friend Samuel St. John, with whom he had traveled in Europe in 1835.

With no private school, Center School—as District School No. 1 was now known—came under attack. It was too large; it needed to be "graded"—that is, divided into grades—so it could provide better education. (Enrollment in the other ten district schools was so small that one teacher could teach pupils of all ages in one room.) Since the spring of 1868, by state law, education in all Connecticut public schools had to be free. Towns, not parents in the school societies, now were responsible for the money to pay teachers, buy two tons of coal, a water pail and two dippers, and one box of crayons, so New Canaan was appropriating one fifth of its annual budget, about $4,500, for education. With Center School receiving the lion's share of this sum—$1,844 in 1870—Prof. Samuel St. John as chairman of District School No. 1 Society, saw to it that something was done. He had the Board hire a principal at a salary of $1,000, who divided pupils into an upper and a lower school, which were taught by the principal and three female schoolteachers, hired at $28 each per month.

But the school budget was soon slashed to $3,500. That was in 1872, when New Canaan decided to refinance its $53,101 debt by issuing 100 bonds of $500, paying 7-percent interest, and constables were out trying to collect the back taxes unpaid for previous years.

Excitement

On Nov. 19, 1873, New Canaan was horrified to learn that Mrs. Sarah Selleck, a widow, had been bludgeoned to death with an ax and her West Road home set afire to conceal the crime. A jury of inquest and three New Canaan physicians hurried to the scene to hear testimony from Mrs. Selleck's neighbors, but beyond identifying the corpse and determining what had been stolen, little was learned. Suspicion fell on several men, including one of the widow's two sons, but all were exonerated. No one was ever brought to trial, and the murder of Sarah Selleck remains one of New Canaan's unsolved homicides.

With the *Era* gone, New Canaan had to learn from the columns of the *Advocate* that Edson Bradley had been reported missing. Bradley had quit the shoe business to become senior partner of Bradley & Co., a cloth house at 495 Broadway, New York, and was then living in Morrisania. He had disappeared on Dec. 20, 1873, while out for a Sunday drive, and foul play was suspected because he was known to have had a good sum of money on his plump person. Not for a week did New Canaan learn that Bradley had converted $70,000 of his firm's assets into gold and absconded to Canada. After his creditors accused Edson Bradley of fraudulent bankruptcy, his son Capt. William Bradley of Civil War fame went to jail in his place, while New York newspapers were full of the hearings and testimony. (Bradley eventually returned from Canada to die in Westport in 1886, while William Bradley and his half-brother Edson, Jr., settled in Kentucky, where they had a controlling interest in a trust that operated numerous distilleries, among which was one making "old Crow," a brand of bourbon still famous and available today.)

Fire

For New Canaan, as for most small towns with many wooden buildings, fire was always a possibility. Fire burned down the Carter Street (District No. 3) schoolhouse in February 1870, and one month later fire destroyed 15 acres of Hoyt Nurseries' timberland on the east side of the same road. Within three weeks of its destruction, a contract was signed for a new District No. 3 schoolhouse—"the Little Red Schoolhouse," which when it was closed in June 1957 was the last functioning district school in Connecticut. (Today it is a private neighborhood museum.)

At the time of the schoolhouse fire, the town's original hand pumper stood rusting and useless in front of Noah Hoyt's factory on Main Street, and the volunteer firemen were reorganizing. On July 6, 1870, the legislature incorporated this reorganized group as the New Canaan Hook & Ladder Co., but not until March 1873 was a secondhand ladder truck acquired from New Haven. This was put to good use in January 1875, when the combined planing mill and sash and blind factory of A. K. Comstock, near the depot, burned with a $10,000 loss. Comstock immediately rebuilt on the same site and then added a plaster mill.

Then, on Feb. 14, 1875, the second of Main Street's three disastrous fires occurred. South of Elm Street, fire broke out in a saloon that was next door to the New Canaan Hotel and spread rapidly north to engulf the three-story wooden shoe factory of J. & J. Benedict. On the opposite side of Main Street, Andrew Burtis' blacksmith shop was so badly burned it had to be torn down. New Canaan had almost hit rock bottom—but not quite.

The 1878 map of New Canaan shows Pleasant Avenue (unnamed) running past the former Sewing Machine factory to Comstock's planing mill on the south side of the railroad tracks. The roundhouse, west of Grove Street, was still standing when World War II began.

CHAPTER 9

The Changing Scene, 1876-1900

The town's cannon had boomed, firecrackers popped, and New Canaan was streaming with bunting when at 9 in the morning of July 4, 1876, groups of boys began to assemble in front of the Town House for the march up Main Street behind the New Canaan Brass Band to the Congregational meeting house. The program for the Centennial had read "The entire community, men, women, and children are respectfully invited to attend, as another opportunity will not occur until the year 1976, and then some of us may not be here." Though a few people had gone to Philadelphia, so many "accepted" the committee's invitation that the meeting house was filled well before 10 A.M., and a hundred or more citizens had to take themselves home to wait for the evening's fireworks display.

For this observation of the 100th birthday of the United States, politics and denominationalism had been put aside. Fifty-eight of the leading male citizens were there, representing the signers of the Declaration of Independence plus Washington and Lafayette; four clergymen, a combined choir, and a soloist from New York participated in the long exercises that culminated in Prof. Samuel St. John's historical address. Omitting any reference to his sea captain ancestors and barely mentioning the shoe industry, St. John misleadingly stressed the "purely agricultural" background of New Canaan, the problems of transportation, and the histories of all the churches and the schools. He did mention the banks and the New Canaan Rail Road, in which so many of his audience had invested and which he called "a determining influence in shaping the future of the town."

Samuel St. John did not live to see what that future would be. He died on Sept. 9, 1876, age 63, and on October 13 the house he had shared with his brother William burned to the ground, taking with it the early Canaan Society and Congregational Church records the Professor had borrowed to prepare his address. He, of course, knew, because he was the largest creditor, that the railroad was in trouble, the unpaid interest on its debts mounting steadily.

"The Year of Misfortune"

By 1877 the financial situation of the New Canaan Rail Road was such that the directors sought (and in January 1878 received) authorization from the state legislature to mortgage the road. Passenger revenue was averaging about $8,000 a year and freight receipts $4,500, but the unpaid interest had risen to $19,251 on a floating debt of $99,878, represented by accounts payable and unsecured bonds. So with the approval of directors and stockholders, on June 1, 1878, the railroad was mortgaged to three trustees—William E. Raymond and Albert S. Comstock of New Canaan and Charles W. Brown of Stamford.

Besides some $15,000 owed to Stamford banks and the Stamford Canal Co. and $6,000 to the New York, New Haven & Hartford, the New Canaan Rail Road owed nearly $75,000 to its New Canaan backers, including $11,860 to the estate of Samuel St. John, $7,694 to Dr. and Mrs. Willard Parker, Sr., and $51,842 to two syndicates in which both the St. John estate and the Parkers were participants. So, too, were S. Y. St. John, Stephen Hoyt, Andrew K. Comstock, and William E. Raymond.

While the creditors agreed to forgive the accrued interest on their accounts and the bondholders to exchange their unsecured bonds for promissory notes, the trustees could not work a miracle, and on Dec. 22, 1882, they foreclosed. Under legislative act, the New Canaan Rail Road ceased to exist on Feb. 1, 1883, to be succeeded by the new Stamford & New Canaan Railroad Co., of which William E. Raymond became president. The noteholders received the equivalent of their debts in capital stock of the new railroad, but the original stockholders of the New Canaan Rail Road Co., including the Town of New Canaan, lost their entire investment—about $165,000. Ten months after its formation, the directors of the new company leased the branch line to the New York,

New Haven & Hartford for an annual rent of $4,000, which was paid out as dividends on the capital stock. On Oct. 1, 1890, it was completely merged into the New Haven.

If 1878, the year the railroad was mortgaged, was locally known as "the year of misfortune," the years just before and just after were no better. Alexander Law, who had backed so many local enterprises, had become financially embarrassed by his attempts to assist a Boston lumber concern in which his son-in-law Charles H. Demeritt was a partner. To cover three promissory notes, Law on May 22, 1877, put up five parcels of New Canaan land as collateral with the First National Bank. Four days later all five were attached by the lumber company's creditors in proceedings in the federal bankruptcy court in Boston. (It was a matter of three years before the First National Bank could establish that it had first claim to the Law property, and Law later had to sell his Park Street residence.)

Next to be embarrassed was the New Canaan Savings Bank. Effective Apr. 20, 1877, the state legislature had set 6 percent as the maximum interest that savings banks could charge on loans, and at the same time it required all savings banks to establish a surplus equal to 3 percent of deposits. The New Canaan Savings Bank then had deposits of $297,000 and loans of $271,000, on which it was collecting 7 percent. So, in a letter to the new New Canaan *Messenger,* S. Y. St. John, then the Bank's president, protested that 6-percent interest was an outrage. Since the law was retroactive, the Savings Bank now had to lose a much-needed 1 percent as it rewrote mortgages and loans already in effect. He thoroughly approved the law pertaining to surplus, though this meant the Bank must omit its 1877 dividends so that the surplus could be quickly built up. As St. John pointed out, the New Canaan Savings Bank in the 18 years of its existence had paid some $21,000 in state and federal taxes, which had cut down its ability to accumulate surplus.

In 1879 the First National Bank of New Canaan had to omit its semiannual dividends. Since 1876 it had lost two presidents by death—Watts Comstock (1876) and Stephen Hoyt (1879), both of whom had previously been presidents of the Savings Bank. Rumors of failure were rife, but both banks weathered these and later crises.

Meanwhile, J. & J. Benedict had had its troubles. After the 1875 fire had burned down their factory at the southwest corner of Main and Elm, the shoemakers resumed business in a new three-story brick building erected on the same site. But the partners still refused to install machinery, and with all shoes, boots, and slippers made by hand, output was low while building costs had been high. So J. & J. Benedict was dissolved on Jan. 1, 1878, to be succeeded by J. & T. W. Benedict, in which Junius Benedict's new partner was Theodore Winfield Benedict, one of Caleb S.'s sons. Most of what this new firm made was jobbed through J. Irving Benedict & Son in New York.

Possibly because he was one of the railroad's large creditors, Andrew K. Comstock went bankrupt in 1878 and sold his planing mill to Francis E. Weed (1842-1915). Weed, the Civil War veteran who was the railroad's first ticket and freight agent, had earlier been a shirt cutter for Noah W. Hoyt, and with Hoyt he had founded the *Messenger,* which began publication on Jan. 13, 1877, New Canaan's first responsible newspaper, about which more will be said. Convinced of the value of the planing mill to New Canaan, Weed resigned his posts with the railroad and the *Messenger* to devote himself to salvaging the planing mill, and save it he did.

Andrew K. Comstock had barely left town for North Dakota when his brother Charles was sued by the town for shortages in his tax accounts. Following a 75-year-old arrangement, Comstock had for four years been New Canaan's tax collector by submitting the lowest bid—$124—to do the job. Now the state, too, brought suit against him; his bondsmen were held accountable for the tax shortages; and the 1879 annual town meeting voted that thereafter the selectmen appoint the tax collector and pay him a fixed salary.

In the five histories of Connecticut that have been published to date, New Canaan rates a mention in only one. That was because in February 1880 a special town meeting authorized the selectmen to offer the state 100 acres of land on "one of our high ridges" on which Connecticut could build an Insane Retreat and to invite the Committee on Human Relations to "visit our town and examine the advantages." The state did not accept, but New Canaan's offer did get into a history book. Other years besides 1878 had their "misfortunes."

The 1880 Census

The 1880 Census, however, did show that New Canaan had ended its population decline and had gained 176 over the 1870 figure to reach a total of 2,673—about 100 under the 1860 figure. Females outnumbered males 1,379 to 1,294; of the 764 children recorded 516 were in school; of its 270 foreign-born inhabitants, 70 came from Germany. Reflecting the economic problems New Canaan had survived was the shift in occupations. From a high of 355 in 1850, shoemaking had dropped to 139, a figure that included 14 female shoe workers and one female clerk. (Of the 988 adult females listed in 1880, 163 worked for a living.) As a source of income, agriculture had almost doubled, with 153 farmers, 143 farm workers, and 50 laborers recorded, while 40 more were employed at Hoyt's Nurseries, which was successfully carried on by Stephen Hoyt's sons James and Edwin. In the village, by far the largest single employer was Henry B. Rogers, who had become sole owner of the men's clothing business in 1878 when Albert S. Comstock sold his interest. Of his 99 employees, 44 were women. Shirt manufacturing accounted for 25 jobs, 22 of which were filled by women. Except for eight grocers, who hired a total of 12 clerks, the stores in the village were primarily one-man affairs: news dealer, hat maker, fishman, photographer, though Lucius Monroe, the druggist, employed two clerks, one of whom was his son. The town had voted "no license" the previous fall, so no saloonkeeper was recorded in 1880.

Outside the village, the Carter Street tannery carried on, employing five men. The grist mills had faltered as grocery stores stocked commercially made flour, and only two millers were listed on the 1880 Census—at the old Isaac Richards' mill at the foot of Parade Hill and at Ponus Ridge, north of Dan's Highway. In Talmadge Hill what had once been a grist and a saw mill now produced wire goods. Aaron J. Jelliff had converted the mill in 1869 to making wooden-rimmed wire sieves, but he had only three helpers: his son George, another man, and a 15-year-old apprentice. Some sawmills would survive into the 20th century, and in 1880 employed a total of eight men. While railroading accounted for 14 jobs, most of these were out of town on the main line.

Just before the 1880 Census was taken, Noah W. Hoyt died in February and, after changing hands twice, his shirt manufacturing company went out of business in 1881, putting two dozen women out of work. But on the 1880 Census one woman was listed as governess, another as seamstress, and four as nurses; seven men were gardeners and six were coachmen. Responsible for these occupations were New Canaan's summer residents.

The First Summer Residents

Ever since the 1830's New Canaan had attracted summer boarders, often whole families who came to enjoy fresh air, wholesome food, and such amusements as could be found in a day's drive in a rented carriage. By 1880 at least 18 households catered to summer guests, including Edwin Hoyt at his Nurseries and Joseph F. Silliman on Oenoke Ridge (in what is now the Hanford-Silliman house). And by 1880, a few well-to-do men from New York and Brooklyn had "discovered" New Canaan and built or remodeled houses into summer residences, asking for and receiving the many kinds of services New Canaan could well provide. (With an assessed value of $11,000, the most valuable house in New Canaan was the year-round Victorian residence Henry B. Rogers built in 1878 on Park Street, opposite Seminary Street, where the parking lot is today.)

Though he eventually lived year round in New Canaan, the first summer resident was Gilbert Birdsall (1823-1886), vice president of the Third Avenue Railroad in New York. In 1861 Birdsall began buying land on Canoe Hill Road, where in time he owned 126 acres and two houses. Something of a horse breeder—he had a stallion named "Prince Albert"—and a lover of animals, Birdsall turned his upper Canoe Hill property into pasture for the aging horses he brought out from New York when they no longer could draw the Third Avenue Railroad cars. (In 1878 he was taxed for 15 of them.) In 1861 he also bought the New Canaan Hotel, of which he became manager when he retired in 1874, though not until later was it renamed the Birdsall House.

Of more importance to New Canaan's future was Dr. Willard Parker, Sr. He was professor of surgery at the College of Physicians and Surgeons and consulting surgeon to five New York

Henry B. Rogers

Dr. Willard Parker, Sr.

hospitals when in 1866 he bought the boy's boarding school at No. 1 Park Street. Before he took title to these seven acres in April 1867, Parker had bought seven adjoining acres from Joseph F. Silliman and 36 from the aging Dr. Lewis Richards, together with the house that now is No. 195 Oenoke Ridge. Brought up on farms in New Hampshire and Massachusetts, Parker made a hobby of farming his New Canaan lands once he retired in 1870. He had begun by remodeling the Federal Style house, tearing down the school building and dividing the old dormitory, part of which he made into a caretaker's cottage (now No. 24 Oenoke Ridge). To the west of his house he built a large yellow barn for his horses and carriages, and farther west was a heated greenhouse. Then from William St. John and Joseph Silliman he bought other land to the west, until he owned more than 100 acres on both sides of Oenoke Ridge.

New Canaan could not have asked for a better ambassador than Willard Parker, Sr., who was soon surrounded by colleagues and friends. To No. 46 Park Street as a summer renter in 1870 came Parker's patient, John Rogers, the sculptor of the enormously popular "Rogers' Groups." By 1877 Rogers had built both a summer home and a studio on the east side of Oenoke just north of the Silliman homestead. North of that, Dr. Parker in 1875 had sold three acres of his land to Dr. Edward W. Lambert (1831-1904), who was the first medical director and chief of the medical staff of the Equitable Life Assurance Society. What Dr. Lambert built as a summer home is the nucleus of the present Hampton Inn. Two years earlier Parker had sold the former Dr. Richards' house to Osborn E. Bright, a prominent New York attorney who resided in Brooklyn. North of Bright, in the summertime lived Edward Delano Lindsey, Princeton University's first professor of art. Rounding out the enclave, Dr. Parker built on the west side of Oenoke, opposite the Sillimans, a summer home for his son Dr. Willard Parker, Jr., who, in time, built summer homes nearby for his three sons. (Of these four, the only one standing is No. 40 Oenoke.)

On the opposite side of town, part way up Brushy Ridge, Dr. William Hanna Thomson, Parker's colleague at Roosevelt Hospital, began in 1875 to acquire what would be a 52-acre estate. From a creditor of the deceased Hezron Ayres, Thomson bought a dwelling and what had been the site of the old Ayres shoe factory. Then, in 1878, at the top of Brushy Ridge, Frederick W. Lockwood bought from the New Canaan Savings Bank the former Caleb Benedict homestead and the start of a 100-acre holding running north along Rosebrook Road. The Savings Bank also sold to George W. Titus of New York two dwellings and 97 acres of land along Weed Street, which would eventually be developed as Marshall Ridge.

Unlike the other summer residents, Lockwood was New Canaan born. He had followed his brother John to New York, where in the 1850's they had become partners in an oil concern on Maiden Lane. This in time led to Frederick Lockwood's association with John D. Rockefeller, who in September 1879 visited Lockwood in his new summer home. (Because he tore down the old Caleb Benedict house, Lockwood aroused resentment, expressed in the *Messenger.* This was further increased when, to straighten out his property line on Rosebrook, he removed all the gravestones from the Benedict burying ground to a specially purchased double plot in Lakeview Cemetery.)

From the start, the first summer residents entered into local life. Besides buying land and employing carpenters, masons, gardeners, coachmen, and maids, they patronized local stores, attended local churches, and even bought adjoining plots in the new cemetery. Dr. Parker not only loaned money to the railroad, but appeared with his friend Professor St. John on the YMCA platform, lecturing on such topics as "The House We Live In," meaning the human body. Elsewhere he spoke on alcoholism, on the treatment of which he had long been an authority. Taking the lead in the effort to improve the appearance of the village, Dr. Parker's wife in 1873 paid for an American elm (planted by Hoyt Nurseries) to replace the signboard in the center of the intersection of Main Street and East Avenue, and later paid for a circular coping of dressed stone to protect the tree roots. This small plot was then given the grandiose appellation "Central Park" by some inhabitants.

At his request, the town in 1877 voted permission to Dr. Thomson to set up the first horse drinking trough in New Canaan—midway up Brushy Ridge Hill—and soon found itself responsible for maintaining more troughs as others were set out at road intersec-

"Central Park," with its Parker elm and watering trough, as it looked in the early 1900's after the Borough had electric lights.

tions. (One stood for years just north of the Parker elm.) At the same time, Dr. and Mrs. Thomson invited all New Canaan to stroll through their landscaped grounds, to use their property as though it were a public park. Thanks to his father, Rev. Dr. William McClure Thomson, once a missionary in the Near East and one of New Canaan's favorite lecturers when he visited here, the Thomson grounds had been planted with cedars of Lebanon and named "Mount Lebanon"—and so labeled on the 1878 map of New Canaan. (The granite frames for the two gateways still stand on Brushy Ridge.) Making their professional presence felt, Doctors Parker and Thomson in 1878 backed Dr. William G. Brownson (1830-1899) in calling a public meeting at which they explained the fever-producing conditions of New Canaan's streams and lakes, especially at the poorly drained Mill Pond. New Canaan too often was subjected to epidemics of malaria, which were attributed to the "miasmatic exhalations" arising from Lake Wampanaw (as the Mill Pond was then called).

The New Canaan Library

The idea for a public library did not originate with the summer residents, but in the end they were the ones who saw it through. The idea began on Aug. 1, 1877, when a committee of three businessmen—Charles E. Hall, cabinetmaker, Francis E. Weed, then editing the *Messenger,* and Benjamin P. Mead (1847-1913), about to be a partner in Burtis & Mead, general store—began asking for subscriptions for the Free Reading Room. With the $70 they raised (and some help from Osborn E. Bright), they opened a Reading Room on the ground floor of a wooden building that stood just west of Main Street on the north side of Elm (then Railroad Avenue). Here they provided chairs, tables, and lamps so visitors could comfortably read the few books and periodicals on the shelves, including volumes that had been in the now-defunct YMCA library.

Except for the Sunday School libraries, New Canaan had had no library, free or otherwise, since 1831 when the Young Peoples' Library, founded in 1811 by the Rev. William Bonney, had closed. But for many people, a Reading Room that was "free to all on the single condition of sobriety and orderly behavior" was not enough; they wanted a library from which they could borrow books to read at home, even if they had to pay for the privilege. So 14 months after the Reading Room began, the three-man committee found its project taken over by a group of 21 men, who had decided that a permanent organization was needed. Only one of the original committee was invited to the initial meeting held in Raymond Hall.

As a lawyer, Osborn Bright drew up the articles of association for the New Canaan Reading Room and Circulating Library Corporation, which were filed with the Connecticut Secretary of State on Nov. 15, 1878. The articles had been signed at the home of Dr. Willard Parker, Jr., and Dr. Parker, Sr., was the first president, while John Rogers and Frederick W. Lockwood were among the incorporators. Others were Henry B. Rogers, Albert S. Comstock, S. Y. St. John, Edwin Hoyt, and William E. Raymond, along with Dr. Brownson and the Rev. Joseph Greenleaf, who succeeded Dr. Parker as president before the year was out.

The articles provided for an entrance fee of $2 and annual dues of $1, with those who paid dues being permitted to borrow books free. Others paid 5 cents a title for the books they took home; all paid fines for books overdue. Though only nine annual dues had been received, the Circulating Library opened in May 1879 upstairs in the building where the Reading Room had begun. To the Reading Room's books and periodicals had been added a number of books donated by many families, over which a part-time librarian had charge.

When it was incorporated, the New Canaan Reading Room and Circulating Library—its name was changed to the New Canaan Library in 1915—intended to raise $3,000 as a permanent fund, but despite annual large gifts from the four summer-resident incorporators only $250 had been put aside by 1883 when Dr. Parker, Jr., proposed that the Library build its own building. Response was almost nil until a year later "a group of prominent gentlemen" —meaning the summer residents—rose to the occasion and underwrote the expense. Whereupon the Library purchased from Junius and T. W. Benedict a site on the south side of Elm Street, adjoining the Benedict shoe factory and almost opposite its original upstairs home. There a tall two-story building was erected, designed free of charge by Prof. Edward D. Lindsay. This was the fourth brick building to go up on the south side of Elm Street since the fire of 1875. (It was torn down in 1952.)

Fire was much on everyone's mind, and complaints had been growing because the town clerk's office and all the town records shared space in the wooden building on Main Street that had been the late Noah Hoyt's shirt factory. So, because the new Library was brick and presumably fireproof, a town meeting voted that the town rent the Library's basement, provided a safe was installed, for five years at $175 per year, and the town clerk's office was moved there on Oct. 1, 1884. Soon afterward the Library opened on the second floor, and remained in the building until 1913.

Main Street also had a new brick building. Cycling had become a national sport in the 1870's, and Henry B. Rogers & Co. was deep into making new lines of bicycle clothing for men and boys. So, opposite the bank, Henry B. Rogers bought and tore down the old Fred Ayres' shoe factory-house and by March 1883 had completed a three-story and basement clothing factory, that stood all by itself. For this he had 650,000 bricks brought to Stamford by boat and put aboard the branch line's freight cars. Fronting on Main and running through to Forest Street, where the basement was above ground, the building was 54 × 80 feet and named the Rogers Block. (Later it was called the Odd Fellows and still later the Ferrara block and today is Nos. 86-92 Main Street.)

When the Rogers Block was built, it was lighted by gas and heated by steam, manufactured in the basement, and out front it had a gas street light, the first in that Main Street block. What's more, the Rogers company had a telephone. As part of the Norwalk exchange, four telephones had been installed in New Canaan in December 1881—at H. B. Rogers & Co., Hoyt's Nurseries, L. M. Monroe's drug store, and Johnson's carriage works, then at the east corner of East Avenue and Forest Street.

A New Fire Company

All the while, fires continued to take their toll and New Canaan continued to spend money to dig and improve cisterns and wells at strategic places around the center of town. But despite the efforts of Chief Burling D. Purdy, the old volunteer fire company, though reincorporated by the state July 6, 1870, as the New Canaan Hook & Ladder Co., had become inactive and the little 1845 engine had been sold for junk. In April 1881 a disastrous fire at Hoyt's Nurseries had taken the life of young Thomas Gray and destroyed eight buildings (including the house once occupied by the Shakers), and soon after that Francis E. Weed took the lead in signing up 41 young men who were ready to form still a new fire company.

On Dec. 8, 1881, the New Canaan Hook and Ladder and Fire Engine Company was organized ("No. 1" was added to its name when the state incorporated it on Mar. 13, 1885), which with a change in name is New Canaan's present volunteer fire company. Before 1882 was out, this fire company had built a wooden engine house on Forest Street just to the north of Johnson's carriage works. The matter of an engine was solved in February 1883 by the purchase of a hand engine for $400 from Stamford, which had just completed its waterworks. Called the "Gulf Stream," this engine was brought to New Canaan by a flat car. When tested, it threw a satisfactory stream and pumped dry the well it was using in five minutes.

A special town meeting of Mar. 5, 1883, not only recognized the New Canaan Hook and Ladder and Fire Engine Company and its several officers, but also voted $800 to buy it a hose carriage or jumper and some necessary fire fighting tools. Otherwise, like their predecessors, the volunteers raised their own funds, bought and owned the engine and engine house.

Liquor and Politics

When the Reading Room opened in August 1877 the three committeemen had every reason to stress that users be persons of "sobriety and orderly behavior." Employment for young men was scarce; village stores and houses were frequently robbed; and in the daytime, then and in later years, people driving in carriages might be spat upon and church services disrupted by drunks. The October 1876 town meeting had voted "no license," so officially 1877 was a dry year. But "license" or "no license" made little difference, because the two saloons, the New Canaan Hotel, and Monroe's drug store always had liquor for sale regardless of the town vote. Hence, at night the center of town was plagued with rowdies and drunks, whom the Citizens' Association's night watchmen had no authority to arrest. The only local "peace officers" with authority to arrest were the elected constables, but though available in emergencies, constables did not do patrol duty.

Throughout the state, however, the temperance forces were again gaining strength, and at their insistence the legislature on June 28, 1876, authorized town selectmen to appoint patrolmen with the power of constables. As a result, a special New Canaan town meeting on Jan. 26, 1877, voted to appoint up to four watchmen as constables—provided they were paid by the Citizens' Association—and the next day Isaac A. Lee and Ezra S. Hall were so designated. This was as far as the town would go toward providing police protection for its residents. They would not call them "policemen," but the swearing in of these two night watchmen as constables marked the unofficial beginning of New Canaan's police force.

Shortly afterward, the young people of the Methodist and Congregational churches formed a new temperance organization called the Band of Hope, though the older Friendship Division of the Sons of Temperance was much in evidence and since 1870 had been accepting women as members.

With the October 1877 annual meeting voting "no license" by 192 to 145, the temperance people in New Canaan this time intended to make the vote stick and called on Anthony Comstock to help. After his brother Samuel died of wounds at Gettysburg (Samuel was a sergeant in Company H, 17th Connecticut Volunteers), Anthony Comstock (1844-1915) enlisted in Company H on Dec. 30, 1863, and served until the end of the Civil War. In 1877 he was living in New York City, where for four years he had been secretary of the Committee for the Suppression of Vice and was on his way toward a national reputation as a "vice crusader." (Anthony Comstock is the only man born in New Canaan to rate a biography in the *Encyclopedia Britannica.*)

What Comstock did was send a detective to New Canaan, who, posing as a hunter, took a room at the Hotel, hired a local man to take him shooting, and patronized the saloons at night. The upshot of this stay was that on Monday, Jan. 7, 1878, the detective and the state's prosecuting attorney with two deputy sheriffs arrived in town with search warrants and orders for the arrest of hotel owner Gilbert Birdsall and saloon keepers Louis Schultz and Charles Scott. The offenders were immediately taken before a justice of the peace, who set bond.

On Wednesday the trials began with Schultz pleading guilty to selling liquor and keeping a house where liquor was sold—his Elm Street saloon, when the town was "wet." He was fined $220. On Thursday Birdsall pleaded guilty to five charges and agreed not to sell any more liquor, provided his stock, worth $1,500, was returned. Scott, thereupon, turned the tables and had the detective arrested on charges of conspiracy. With perhaps 200 men crowded into the Town House, the pro-license people saw their chance and raised a cry of "Hang him." Though the detective was not really in danger, in the ensuing melee, Anthony Comstock drew his revolver and ordered the crowd to stand bank. No one was harmed; the attorney, detective, and deputies, followed by a shouting mob, walked safely across Railroad Avenue and caught the 4:50 train to Stamford.

Sixteen special constables were on hand to keep order in the local court the following Wednesday when Scott was found guilty and the detective cleared. In recognition of what Comstock and the prohibition forces had achieved, a hundred or more men then sat down to "an enormous collation," which "the ladies" had prepared that morning in Raymond Hall. That fall New Canaan again voted "no license" by 211 to 141, but in October 1879 voted "license" 198 to 185—a seesaw pattern that would be followed for a decade.

Similarly, New Canaan vacillated between sending a Democrat or a Republican to Hartford. At home, the first selectman usually was a Republican, though in 1876 and 1879 a Democrat was elected to that office. In 1880, after the usual partisan parades, New Canaan voted 319 for James A. Garfield for president and 300 for the Democrat Winfield S. Hancock. (Garfield had once visited his friend Selleck Y. St. John in White Oak Shade.) Locally, the Republicans had a new leader in Benjamin P. Mead, who had been one of the original Reading Room committeemen.

Mead, after one term (1880-81) as town clerk, was elected first selectman for seven consecutive terms, and at the same time in 1885 and 1887 was also the town's representative. William Edgar Raymond had given New Canaan a touch of political fame when,

Benjamin P. Mead

Joseph F. Silliman

as a Republican, he served as state treasurer in 1873-77. Mead, however, went on from the legislature to the state senate, running successfully in the 12th senatorial district in 1889 and 1891. In 1889 he was also appointed state auditor, to fill an unexpired term, continuing until 1891. Then in 1894 he was elected state controller, and two years later, when he was reelected, he received the largest plurality of any candidate running statewide.

After Mead was elected to the senate, Joseph F. Silliman (1840-1913) served two terms as first selectman. Then the Democrats took over in 1890 and elected their candidate five times, and throughout the 1890's New Canaan voted "license" by large majorities.

Legal sales of liquor were one thing; sales in their homes by unlicensed men were something else. Citizens fumed that because these "kitchen" sales were so profitable, offenders had plenty of money from which to pay fines and then continue in their "wrong ways." Such a man was Joseph Scheele, who lived on the north side of Seminary Street (where Woods Gate condominiums are), whom Constable Louis Drucker was sent to arrest on the afternoon of Jan. 25, 1888.

Drucker, who had led the mob against Anthony Comstock's detective, was a small clothing manufacturer who made local history as the first businessman to give his employees Saturday afternoon off from work. He was first elected a town constable in 1884, the first Jew to hold public office in New Canaan, and because he received more votes (244) than the other three elected constables the *Messenger* jokingly gave him the right to call himself "chief of police." When Drucker arrived at Scheele's house he was greeted with an aimed shotgun, so he went back to the village for assistance, returning with Constable Ezra S. Hall. As the two men approached the house, Scheele fired from a second-floor window, killing Drucker almost instantly. Then, with a pistol, Scheele attempted suicide. Unfortunately for him, Scheele recovered from his wounds in a few days, was taken to jail in Bridgeport, and after a trial was hanged there, but not until June 18, 1890.

New Businesses

In the late 1870's, besides the Citizens' Association, the businessmen had a short-lived Board of Trade, and it was this Board that revived the dream of New Canaan as an industrial Center.

Stephen B. Hoyt, Sr., was New England agent for a weighing scale company in Coxsackie, N.Y., when in the summer of 1880 he let it be known that the company wanted to move its plant closer to New York City. Wasting no time, the Board of Trade sent a committee to Coxsackie and worked out a deal whereby a Connecticut corporation would be formed, if the scale company would lease William E. Raymond's now-vacant perfume factory. (This was the building erected in 1870 on Pleasant Avenue for the ill-fated Sewing Machine Co.) Articles of association for the Perfection Scale Co. were signed in New Canaan on Sept. 9, 1880, and a certificate for a joint stock company was filed October 1 with the legislature.

A major asset of the Perfection Co. was a patent, carried on the books at $5,000, for an improvement in weighing scales that had been issued on Apr. 1, 1879, to David Hallock of Coxsackie, principal owner of the old company and president of the new one. Eventually paying in $15,000, 20 New Canaan men invested in 200 of the 400 shares of Perfection stock, with Russell L. Hall, the undertaker, buying 25 shares and becoming treasurer. William E. Raymond, John Rogers, the sculptor, and Henry Pinney, the shoemaker, each bought 20 shares and Henry B. Rogers, 15. Among those buying 10 shares were Benjamin P. Mead for Burtis & Mead, James and Edwin Hoyt for Hoyt's Nurseries, Dr. Willard Parker, Sr., and Joseph F. Silliman, who became secretary.

Although casting still had to be done at Coxsackie, the Perfection Scale Co. was in business in New Canaan by late October, and predictions were made that it soon would provide jobs for 25 men. (Of Perfection's initial 12 employees, five were men brought from Coxsackie, one of whom was killed the next month in a plant accident.)

After two fairly prosperous years, the Perfection Scale Co. ran into trouble for reasons now unknown and became virtually bankrupt. At the same time, a disagreement arose between Hallock and the other shareholders as to who was to own improvements being made to the original scale design, and the directors removed Hallock as president. Meanwhile, as creditors pressed their claims, factory work was suspended at the end of 1882, with several hundred scales yet to be finished. Then in August 1883, two workmen were rehired to complete the unfinished scales, and business resumed for a while. In the end, the Perfection Scale Co. followed the path of former New Canaan industries and shut down permanently in 1884.

Three footnotes can be added to this story. (1) The Fairbanks Scale Co. of Vermont is believed to have acquired the Perfection patents. (2) William E. Raymond in May 1887 sold the factory building to G. Duff Nichols, a newcomer, who proposed to manufacture corsets there. But Nichols never occupied the Old Sewing Machine-Perfume-Perfection Scale factory, using it instead as security for loans for other deals. In 1901 he sold the building to Irving Lockwood to be used as part of the latter's coal and lumber yard, and it burned down in 1908. (3) Lockwood's business in time became the present New Canaan Fuel & Lumber Co., and on June 13, 1951, a New Canaan special town meeting finally voted to abandon Pleasant Avenue as a town street, since for years it had been only the lumber company's driveway.

Well before Lockwood went into business, Francis E. Weed had developed the nearby planing mill site into a thriving coal and lumber yard. In 1887 he sold this trackside property to the New York, New Haven & Hartford and moved to the west side of the new Grove Street, where his new office and yard was served by a

1,000-foot railroad siding. With a series of partners, Weed continued his business until he died in 1915, when his son took over. Though no longer family owned, it continues today as Weed & Duryea.

Like B. P. Mead, his cohort in founding the Reading Room, Weed was active in politics. In 1884 he was New Canaan's representative to the legislature, where he introduced a bill making it obligatory for towns to pay schoolteachers every four weeks instead of at the term's end. (He voted against reducing the working day from 12 to 10 hours because he found no support for the idea.) As Mead would do in 1892 when he was responsible for opening up Harrison Avenue (named for President Benjamin Harrison), Francis E. Weed was responsible for opening up St. John Place, which he named Prospect Street.

In 1889, from the heirs of William St. John, he bought the 10-acre tract where the mansion house had stood and laid out a highway running west from Park Street and turning south into Seminary Street. Along this he laid out 26 lots, but only two had been sold when the town accepted the road. As his own residence,

Francis E. Weed on the step of his Grove Street office.

Weed in 1896 built the house that today is No. 7 St. John Place, retaining next door the St. John observatory, which his son William F. Weed converted into a photography studio and where he sponsored art exhibitions.

Besides the sieve factory, New Canaan had another new family enterprise. Arthur and Marshall Gray, living on Weed Street just south of Richmond Hill, in 1882 went into the business of manufacturing extracts and bottling soft drinks. (In early days they also made and sold bottled beer.) Gray's products soon became popular throughout the area, and this business flourished until 1922, when it was sold and moved out of town.

The shoe business was another story. In 1884 the First National Bank reluctantly had foreclosed on William G. Webb, thus putting an end to his shoe operations in his half of the "Big Shop." Charles Benedict became the sole owner of that building, and in 1885 the *Messenger* could report his weekly payroll was $600 (adding that this was far below what the predecessor firm had paid out in the 1850's). Benedict later reorganized his firm by turning Benedict & Co. over to his son Charles F. Benedict and his son-in-law George F. Lockwood (who eventually also became president of the First National Bank).

Taking up a bit of the employment slack was a new shoemaking firm, Fancher & Co., which in the summer of 1885 moved from Norwalk to the former Law Academy on Park Street. Induced to move to Bridgeport in 1887, a differently organized Fancher & Co. returned to New Canaan in September 1891 and on the northwest corner of Elm and Park streets erected a three-story wooden factory. Weathering a strike and a serious fire, this Fancher & Co. continued in business until November 1900. (Shortly afterward, its building was moved to the opposite side of Elm Street to become a part of Irving Lockwood's coal and lumber yard. Like the Perfection Scale building, this too burned in Lockwood's 1908 fire.)

Although it had very few employees, the *Messenger* had proved that it was here to stay. For its first issue of Jan. 13, 1877, Noah W. Hoyt had been editor and Francis E. Weed business manager of the *Messenger,* and therein the two men stated that their purpose was to advocate the "well being of Society," their object was "to make money," and their opinions on all matters were "decided." Within three months Hoyt had resigned, and Weed became both editor and business manager, on Jan. 19, 1878, buying out the New Canaan *Herald,* which a Norwalk man had started publishing at the end of 1876.

When as of Jan. 1, 1879, Weed had to decide that the planing mill was of greater importance to New Canaan than the *Messenger,* Lucius Monroe rose to the occasion and put out the paper for seven months until Will W. Kirk (1852-1911) purchased it. Kirk, though born in Patterson, N.Y., had been brought up in Stamford and had worked nine years for the Stamford *Advocate.* As editor, his opinions were as decided as the *Messenger's* founders could have wished. If in his columns he played up his favorite businesses and favorite men, Will Kirk spared no one who disagreed with the cause he was championing, and year after year the *Messenger* supported what Kirk believed was for the good of the town—and time has proved that Will Kirk was usually right.

The Borough of New Canaan

From its start, the *Messenger* had cajoled or nagged for improvement in the looks of the town. A favorite target was God's Acre, the first sight most visitors had. With its stones moved to Parade Hill Cemetery, the abandoned graveyard had been overgrown with briars, while pigs wandered in and out through the breached stone walls. And, though it was cleaned up in 1877 and 1882, it had to be done again in 1895. Then there was always the bad state of the roads, the higgledy-piggledy appearance of Main Street with buildings oriented every which way, the need for more shade trees (answered periodically by gifts from Hoyt's Nurseries), and, of course, crime. The trouble was that most suggested improvements would be in the village, and residents farther out had no intention of voting for higher taxes for the benefit of a few. The answer was to create a borough (as Stamford and Norwalk had done years before) and let a government within a government tax its residents for improvements that would benefit them.

So it was that on Jan. 5, 1889, a petition was submitted to the legislature by Francis E. Weed, Junius Benedict, and others, asking for a charter for the borough of New Canaan for the purpose of properly lighting streets, improving sidewalks, and "guarding the said Borough after dark with a proper and sufficient police force." And with Benjamin P. Mead then chairman of the Senate's Committee on Cities and Boroughs making a favorable report, the legislature passed a bill incorporating the borough of New Canaan on May 9, 1889.

The area over which the borough would have jurisdiction was, roughly, a circle with a diameter of one mile. Its boundary, in present-day terms, began at Lakeview Avenue and Summer Street and ran westward along the then new Bank Street, past Park Street to the railroad tracks; then northward (keeping west of the new Grove Street) across Elm Street to the Nature Center's property; there it turned east to cross Oenoke Ridge (north of Holmewood Lane) and Forest Street to Five Mile River, where it turned south and ran down the west side of Summer Street to the starting point.

As the legislature had required, all the voters within these bounds went to the polls on June 8, 1889, and by a slim majority of 22 voted "yes." Nine days later the borough of New Canaan elected its first officers—a warden and board of six burgesses (including Henry B. Rogers and George F. Lockwood). Other officers were soon sworn in—clerk, treasurer, sheriff, tax collector, three assessors (one of whom was F. E. Weed), and two auditors (one was L. M. Monroe, Sr.)—but until the assessors could get their books in order, the borough had to borrow money to pay its bills.

The first warden was Dr. William G. Brownson, who lived on Main Street just north of Lakeview Avenue in what is now No. 242 Main and whose ability to conciliate disgruntled citizens had already been proved. In 1888 the Connecticut Board of Health had appointed Brownson as New Canaan's first health officer, but with no powers to enforce his decisions, he had had to persuade parents to keep at home any schoolchild who had scarlet fever, measles, diphtheria, or another of the communicable diseases to which New Canaan was susceptible. Quarantine was an outrage; it was an invasion of a man's personal liberties! What right had a health officer to tell a father what he should do with his children? (The same stubborn opposition had greeted fire insurance companies, when, in writing policies, they tried to get people to number their dwellings.) And Dr. Brownson was well aware that as warden he would be dealing with the man who pastured his cow on Borough streets and tackling Lucius Monroe because a faulty drain let the

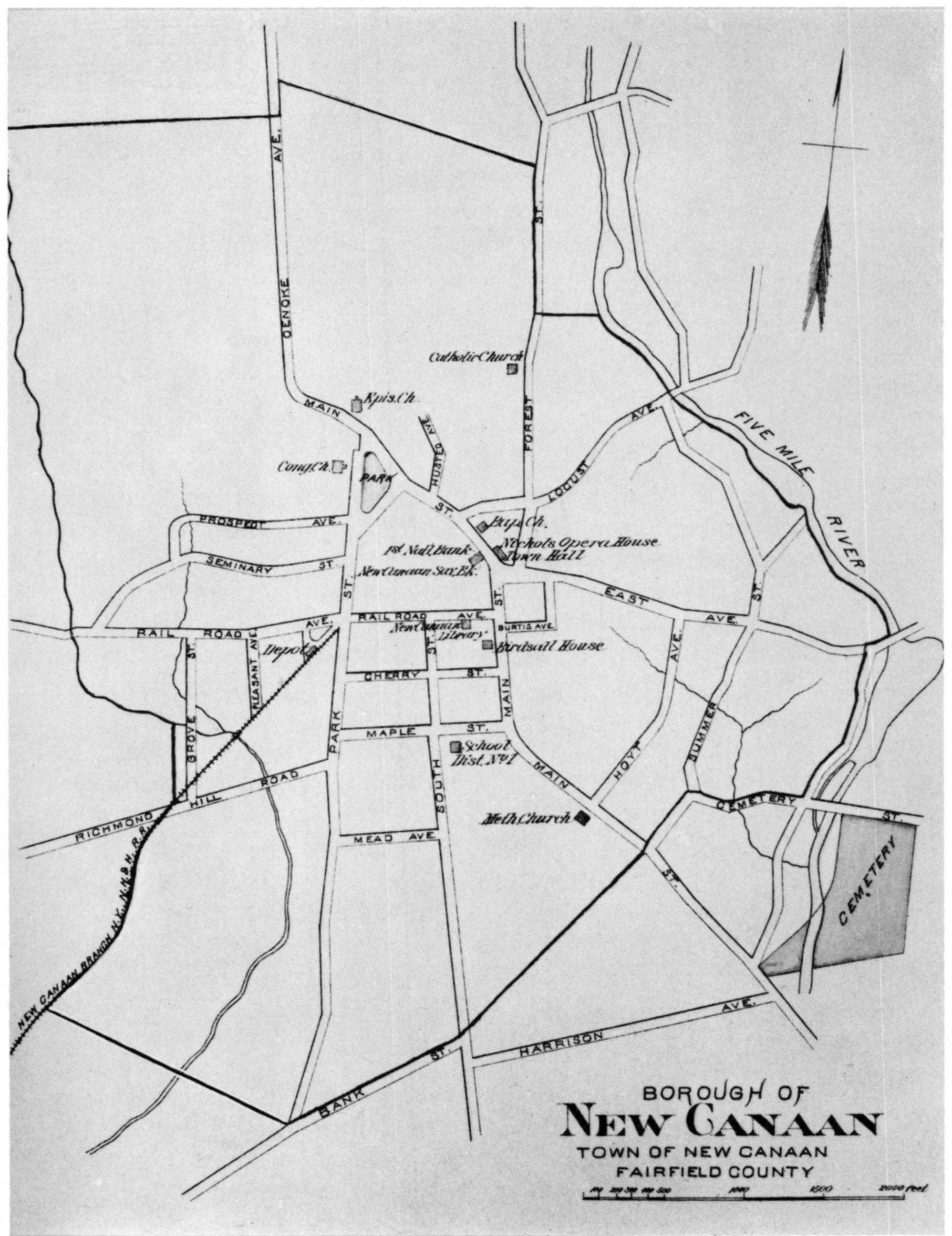

From Hurd's Atlas of Fairfield County, *1893.*

overflow from his cellar spill into Main Street to cause "foul odors."

Saying "We are sure our forefathers could not have selected a more beautiful spot on this whole planet than this little town and Borough," the warden and burgesses set to work. They had been empowered to provide street lighting, lay sidewalks, and pass ordinances of many sorts to prevent nuisances, be they animals at large, discharge of firearms, circus parades, and bicycle riding (not on the sidewalks and at night only with a light), and had the power to enforce the ordinances with fines and, if necessary, tax liens. The warden and burgesses chose to begin with street lights.

In the center of town at that time there were 30 kerosene lamps hanging from poles. These had been privately erected and maintained, but only two owners objected to having their lights taken over by the borough and lighted at its expense. A lamplighter was hired at $60 for each three months, and kerosene was bought at local grocery stores. Although the *Messenger* editorially opposed the expense, saying our forefathers had gotten home safely in the dark, resident after resident wanted a street light near his house, and in short time the borough had 70 of them. The number rose to more than 100, as new streets were opened up and the summer residents on Oenoke Ridge asked for and got lights as far out as the borough boundary.

By 1897 kerosene, repairs, and the lamplighter's wages had topped $1,000 annually, so the borough after considerable dickering made a deal with the Norwalk Electric Light Co. For $1,300 a year, the company would provide 80 20-candle-power street lights, 5 arc lights, and 10 police lights that were to be lit only from 2 to 5 A.M. The other street lights were turned off at 2 A.M. and turned on only 26 nights a month, the full moon supposedly providing light on the other four or five nights. So in March 1898 New Canaan turned on its first electric street lights—and before the year was over the New York, New Haven had electrified the branch line. Even before electric lights burned, the Southern New England Telephone Co. had been granted permission to erect telephone poles, and the Borough was anticipating the start of a trolley car line to Norwalk (which never materialized).

But in 1889 the warden and burgesses had begun making ordinances about sidewalks, telling residents what must be done where and when. Sidewalks were to be made of gravel, flagstone, or concrete, and time limits were set for house owners to comply. (Since the burgesses were aware that the expense of a sidewalk was beyond some house owners' means, now and then the borough absorbed the cost to make sure a sidewalk was continuous.)

For the main street crossings in the village, the borough laid flagstone crosswalks and hired a sweeper to keep them clean, and for $1.50 annually they maintained "Central Park," where Mrs. Parker's elm stood. One week was all the time allowed for an owner to take down a dead tree, and not much more for the removal of brush and high weeds that prevented a carriage driver from seeing around a curve. In 1890 Raymond Hall was ordered temporarily closed when it was determined that some trusses had rotted (and kerosene was stored in tanks under the main stairway). Street signs went up at the ends of most roads, but sidewalks and street lights were the borough's first trademarks.

Despite the need for police protection stated in its petition, the borough made do at first with just one night watchman—and almost made a profit on him. John Tucker was paid $12 a week, but the village merchants contributed almost the whole of that sum. The same was true when his successor John B. Weed was paid $780 annually and Theodore B. Weed, his assistant, got $364; the merchants paid $958.14 of the $1,144 total. John B. Weed had been appointed night watchman in November 1890, and in 1892 the warden wrote in his annual report that "Our peaceful citizens feel a restful sense of security under the protecting shadow of the 275 pounds of active humanity in the person of our popular Chief." Though the force consisted of just two men, one of them part-time, they were thereafter referred to as "the police."

Under its charter, the borough also had the power to "continue a fire company," and this created a situation that took time to resolve. Eventually, in April 1894, having been asked to provide the New Canaan Fire Engine Company with 400 feet of hose, it passed an ordinance adopting the existing fire company as the borough's fire department but leaving the fire company free to manage its own affairs. The year before it had voted to pay the insurance premiums on the new firehouse. The firemen in 1892 had vacated their wooden firehouse on Forest Street and on the south side of Elm Street (where No. 32 now is) built a new wooden firehouse, conveniently across the road from a livery stable that could provide the horses needed to pull the "Gulf Stream."

The new firehouse was barely under way when a proposal was made to install in its hose-drying tower out back a town clock, which would strike 24 times a day. Promptly a subscription paper was circulated, the first (and the largest) contributors being summer residents. Despite a benefit performance of Shakespeare's *Comedy of Errors,* put on by the young people of the Congregational Church, the fund languished while concern for an appropriate location rose. The drying tower was not strong enough to hold a town clock of suitable size; the nearby Reading Room building was too low; if the clock was installed in the steeple of the Congregational meeting house it would have to be larger and more expensive than was first planned—and might turn out to be for the benefit of only "those on the Hill." But the idea wasn't dropped. Slowly, slowly the Town Clock Fund deposited small sums in the New Canaan Savings Bank until in December 1902, prejudice was put aside, and the town clock was installed in the Congregational steeple. (It is a Seth Thomas clock, which cost $350, and it is still the town's clock, not the property of the Church.)

The Water Works

Every time New Canaan appropriated money to dig wells strategically located for the firemen, the cost of a town water supply was brought up. A reservoir for New Canaan had first been mentioned in June 1877 when an engineer from Bridgeport determined that one would be feasible between upper Oenoke and Smith Ridges. If Five Mile River were to be dammed well north of what is now Country Club Road, it would back up the River as far north as the old sawmill (near where Michigan Road then crossed to Oenoke) and make a 7-million-gallon reservoir. (Nearly ten years before, the borough of Norwalk had made Grupe's Reservoir in New Canaan by damming the Silvermine River west of upper Valley Road and under legislative charter in 1870 had been given the power to pipe water to Norwalk through New Canaan land.) Even in those days some people had running water in their houses, usually pumped from springs or wells to rooftop cisterns by small steam engines, but 1877 was a bad year for New Canaan and the cost of a water system was estimated at almost $30,000. The *Messenger,* then under Francis E. Weed, had been quick to point out that "it is not creditable to ourselves to sit down and whine about our poverty"; outsiders were interested in the reservoir and New Canaan should be too.

It was Lucius M. Monroe, F. E. Weed, and B. P. Mead who kept the idea alive, and it was Monroe, with 27 others, who proposed to a special town meeting on Aug. 4, 1891, that New Canaan build and own a system of water works. This would be constructed under a charter granting certain individuals the privilege of taking water from Five Mile River, as already surveyed, and laying mains and pipes. The proposal was voted down, and instead of a town-owned water supply, the private New Canaan Water Co., capitalized at $40,000, was incorporated by the state legislature in 1893.

At the first corporate meeting, held in Monroe's drug store on May 20, 1893, Lucius Monroe was elected president and George F. Lockwood, vice president of the Water Co. The offices of secretary and treasurer went to two New Haven men, representing the New England Public Works Co., which owned the controlling interest. The *Messenger* said there was "no use crying over spilled milk," but New Canaan had lost its second opportunity to own and control its water supply, since in 1891 it had let the Stamford Water Co. buy Lake Siscowit—or Anthony's Lake or Tom Mead's Pond as Mud Pond has been called—on its northern boundary.

Land purchases and a right of way across private property along the planned spillway had first to be attended to, so it was not until November 1894 that some 30 Italians began the work of clearing the reservoir and building a 24-foot-long dam. This was a experienced "gang," brought to New Canaan from Vermont (where the New England Public Works Co. had just finished another reservoir) to work under L. N. Farnum, the engineer who was the New Canaan Water Co.'s first manager.

Working only with hand tools, the men had the last ditch dug and the last main laid by Aug. 9, 1895. In the center of town the pressure was tested at the new hydrant in front of H. B. Rogers' factory, and when the stream from a hose rose 75 feet in the air, both engineer and the volunteer firemen were satisfied. In short time, the borough agreed to rent the hydrants within its bounds from the New Canaan Water Co. for $1,000 a year, and with hydrants making the hand pumper unnecessary, the Fire Company sold the "Gulf Stream" and bought a second hose cart.

Although the reservoir covered some 12 acres of land and already was two thirds full, many a doubting Thomas predicted that once the mains were filled the reservoir would go dry. Nevertheless, in anticipation of water mains, at least 10 percent of New Canaan's householders had installed bathrooms and kitchen sinks, and there followed a plumbers' paradise as house after house was connected to the mains. The first house to have Water Co. water was that of Frank L. Comstock, now No. 241 Main Street.

Once the water system was complete, many of the Italians who had worked on the job remained in New Canaan as stone masons, gardeners, or laborers, and established families whose descendants have made important contributions to the growth of the town.

More Summer Residents

Although running water was still in the future, the *Messenger* in the 1880's was stressing the charms of New Canaan as a place of summer residence—its elevation, its views, its healthful climate, its available land—as a decade before New Canaan's industrial potentials had been praised. Since the paper was rarely read outside the town, the *Messenger* was hardly responsible for the next wave of New York and Brooklyn families that "discovered" New Canaan.

Although Dr. Parker, Sr., had died in 1884, Oenoke Ridge retained its appeal. William E. Bond, a New York businessman, bought No. 195 Oenoke from Osborn E. Bright, while on the opposite side of the road Bright remodeled an old house into a new summer home (now the Presbyterian Church's Bliss House) and developed the estate that eventually would become the New Canaan Nature Center. Immediately to Bright's south, John B. Gerrish of Brooklyn built a large verandahed wooden house, a design much favored by the newcomers, while between Dr. Edward Lambert and John Rogers, Dr. James Wood McLane in 1898 built his home (where St. Mark's Church is today). That same year, Payson Merrill, a New York lawyer, bought where the old Parade Ground had been and at the north corner of Oenoke and Parade

Hill built the house that is now No. 289 Oenoke. Earlier, in 1886, not far from where the reservoir would be, the Rev. Charles Riley Abbott had built the brick verandahed house that is No. 757 Oenoke Ridge. Like Frederick Lockwood, Abbott was New Canaan-born and had become superintendent of Brooklyn's No. 1 School District.

As more and more summer residents arrived, other areas of New Canaan began to have their vogue. Luciano Fabbricotti, part owner of a Carrara marble quarry in Italy, in 1888 bought eight acres on South Avenue at the north corner of the new Bank Street and there built the house that, in Newport style, was for years called the "Fabbricotti Cottage." He impressed New Canaan not only by installing the first artesian well but by arriving here in his private railroad car. The next year John R. Downey, the New York contractor who had built both the Waldorf and the Astor hotels, bought Frederick Lockwood's summer home on Brushy Ridge, while at the same time Franklin W. Anderson, a Brooklyn paper manufacturer, bought and enlarged the colonial farmhouse on West Road that once had belonged to James Hait. Around the West Road site that Hait had given to the professors of the Church of England, Lewis P. Child in 1893 began putting together a 71-acre estate. Child was a railroad executive from Red Bank, N.J., who had summered in New Canaan before deciding to build and had acquired local recognition because, together with O. E. Bright, he had presented the American flag that was raised at Center School on Sept. 1, 1890, on the occasion of New Canaan's first Labor Day celebration. (Rumor had it that they were two capitalists working hand in hand with labor!)

Smith Ridge, with its magnificent unobstructed views of the Sound, also was soon to become a favored site, and the first summer residence was built there in 1894, at the north corner of Canoe Hill Road, by William E. C. Bradley, a New York textile man. The next year, at the opposite end of town, Thomas W. Hall, of New York, president of the American Hide & Leather Co., began buying the 175 acres he would call "Prospect Farm." (This in 1904 became the nucleus of the estate that Lewis H. Lapham, also of New York, called "Waveny," and which today is New Canaan's extensive park.) Then, although they could hardly be called summer residents, the rector, warden, and vestry of Grace Church in

New York in 1899 acquired from the New Canaan Savings Bank the 178-acre former William Y. Davenport farm at Ponus Ridge and Frogtown Road. There, as a summer vacation spot for city mothers and children, they built Grace Home in the Field—what today is the central structure of the New Canaan Country Day School. No wonder that an oldtimer complained to the *Messenger* that the farmers had quit working and only sat around waiting for their farmland to turn into "real estate." Needless to say, both local banks were delighted to dispose of the farms on which they had foreclosed during the hard times in earlier years.

Unlike the first summer residents, most new families knew no one before they built in New Canaan and began by making friends among themselves. Once they became acquainted, the Downeys and the Halls alternated Sunday afternoon visits, each family driving out in its tallyho, because they knew no other family to call upon. (Dr. Willard Parker, Jr., earlier had owned a tallyho, and stories have come down about what it took to hold him on the box when he insisted on driving while drunk!)

Because they needed a place to gather, the summer residents in 1893 decided to form a club with grounds that would be "a convenient and pleasant resort." So with Dr. Parker, Jr., as president, William E. Bond vice president, and John R. Downey as treasurer, the Oenoke Field Club came into being on land made available by Mrs. Bright. Where the Presbyterian Church's parking lot is today, a tennis court and a pavilion were built by midsummer, and tennis tournaments became "the thing."

But tennis was not enough; a golf course was wanted, and Dr. Edward Lambert undertook to find a suitable site. Near at hand (at the head of the road later named for him) was the little-worked farm that once had been Capt. Isaac Richards' homestead. The heirs of William St. John, Capt. Richards' grandson, were willing to rent these 186 acres to the newly incorporated New Canaan Golf Club, of which Dr. Lambert was president. By the summer of 1897, four holes of a nine-hole golf course were ready for play, and the Oenoke Field Club faded out of existence when the Golf Club built tennis courts. Soon trap shooting and croquet were available to members, who used the old farmhouse as a clubhouse. When the land was finally bought in 1904, the Golf Club was reincorporated as the Country Club of New Canaan.

Ridgefield also had summer residents, some of whom commuted from New Canaan, where a summer stagecoach could drive them to Ridgefield if they were not met by their coachmen. As early as February 1884, the New York, New Haven & Hartford had begun catering to New Canaan passengers by adding a car, called a compartment smoker and baggage car, to the branch line train. Then on June 1 it attached a through New York car to the morning train, but this was withdrawn after just two weeks. On May 30, 1887, however, the railroad introduced the first through train, which consisted of an engine, baggage car, and coach. This ran nonstop from New Canaan to Stamford, where other coaches were added for passengers boarding the New Canaan and New York Local Express at Greenwich and three other stops. On the return evening run only two stops were made before Stamford. Partly because the New Haven was having trouble fitting the New Canaan Express into its crowded main-line schedule, but largely because only 40 New Canaan commuters made use of it during the winter months, the train was discontinued on May 15, 1892. (The New Canaan Express was revived on May 30, 1904, and, except for a temporary withdrawal in October during the Panic of 1907 and a very rare strike, has since operated continuously.)

Capt. Isaac Richards' house converted into the Country Club's clubhouse.

Other Clubs and Social Life

On the whole, the newer summer residents went their own way. Their large formal teas and garden parties gave the town something to talk about, but they also divided New Canaan by setting apart those local families who were invited to attend—not that anyone cared very much. By then many New Canaan families had their own social life at their "summer residences." Dr. Willard Parker, Sr., and Dr. Lambert may have set a fashion when in the 1870's they bought Tavern Island off Rowayton and restored part of it as a "Brighton adjunct." (Much later Tavern Island was the summer retreat of Billy Rose, the New York producer.) Be that as it may, by the early 1880's Belle Island and Hickory Bluff at Rowayton were filled with summer cottages, owned or rented by as many New Canaan families as could afford them—and endure the smells of inadequate drains.

At home, clubs and secret societies had begun to proliferate. Besides church groups for old and young, there were baseball, bicycle, fishing clubs and a Gentlemen's Driving Association. There were glee clubs, a choral union, drum corps and bands, a whist club, a chess club, a debating society, and a literary club. The Farmers' Club began in 1883 to be followed in 1886 by the New Canaan Grange, No. 38, Patrons of Husbandry, still in existence. The Civil War veterans, led by Francis E. Weed, organized the Samuel P. Ferris Post of the G.A.R. in 1883, while in 1894 a group of women, led by Mrs. Albert S. Comstock, founded the Cornelia Carter Comstock Chapter of the D.A.R., which continues today.

In imitation of the much older Masons and Oddfellows were Weiland Lodge, No. 20, Sons of Hermann (1890), which drew many German-born men, and the Ponus Tribe of Red Men (1896). For the working man there was the Commodore Perry Council No. 44, Order of United American Mechanics, organized in 1889 by William G. Webb, George H. Jelliff, Will Kirk, and others, and in 1893 the Oenoke Tent No. 8, Knights of the Maccabees, to which Dr. Brownson belonged. (This offered low-cost life insurance plans to its members.) Any week would find a dozen or more scheduled meetings listed by the *Messenger,* all of which apparently were well attended.

A quite different "club" had also been founded in 1889, when 65 men and women, most of them descendants of the town's founders, met at the home of Mr. and Mrs. Albert Comstock (No. 46 Main Street) to form the New Canaan Historical Society. With the exception of Mr. and Mrs. Frederick Lockwood and Charles R. Abbott, New Canaan natives who were summer residents, the founders were the leading year-round residents—among them Alexander Law, S. Y. St. John, James and Edwin Hoyt, Lucius Monroe, Sr., Francis E. Weed, Mr. and Mrs. Henry B. Rogers, and Mr. and Mrs. Joseph F. Silliman.

When on Jan. 1, 1891, New Canaan moved its town offices out of the Reading Room and Circulating Library building, the Historical Society moved into the vacated ground-floor room. But the $75 annual rent that it paid was not enough to solve the Library's financial problems, and late in December 1892 the Library was forced to close. Public opinion, however, was strong for the Library's continuation, and a special town meeting was called for May 27, 1893. For the first time in the town's history that meeting voted town money for the Library's support—$200. Then, beginning in 1895, the town budgeted $100 a year for the Library, which had reopened in August 1893, whereupon the Reading Room and Circulating Library became a "free library"—free to all without payment of dues. In return, although the Library corporation retained control of its building, the town had the right to elect its board of directors, provided the names proposed were acceptable to the corporation. So it was that, until rescinded in 1947, Library directors were elected at annual town meetings—and from the start a woman was one of the directors.

The Opera House

When New Canaan quit the Library building on Elm Street, it moved its town offices to Nichols Opera House, which had just been completed on Main Street. (Needing repair, the Town House opposite the Birdsall House was seldom used for town meetings and frequently rented out.) Ever since he had arrived in town, George Duff Nichols had a finger in a number of business pies, reminiscent of Capt. Sereno E. Ogden. Two years before he bought the Scale factory, Nichols in October 1885 had purchased a rood of land on Main Street to the north of the Rogers' Block, and there in 1890 he built a 50 × 150-foot building, running through to Forest Street.

Prof. Edward D. Lindsay, who had designed the Reading Room building, had prepared free of charge plans for a new New Canaan town hall. When this failed to materialize, Nichols asked Lindsay to give him the plans, and what had been designed to be a town hall became Nichols Opera House, a wooden building with an auditorium capable of seating 850 people. To either side of the entrance hall opening on Main Street was a store, and though it took two special town meetings in July 1890, New Canaan authorized its selectmen to rent the southern one at $350 per year—double what had been paid to the Library—provided Nichols installed a fireproof vault. (In the basement he had also to provide a lock-up with three iron cells.) Until 1910 this store was New Canaan's town clerk's and selectmen's office and doubled as a courtroom, while the auditorium was regularly rented for town meetings.

When it was built, Nichols Opera House was as fine as any in the state, with a good stage, backdrops, and dressing rooms. Underneath was what Nichols initially tried to promote as a banquet hall, but which soon became the workroom for his corset and children's underwear manufacturing operation. When it opened on Dec. 23, 1890, the Opera House was the first public building in New Canaan to be lighted by electricity, but electricity was expensive to manufacture and in less than two months Nichols removed all the electric fixtures and installed a gas-making machine.

The Churches

Despite the fanfare that preceded its opening productions, the Opera House was far from a success, and Nichols was soon renting it out for benefit concerts for the Library, amateur plays, and Center School exercises as often as he booked entertainments. If the third-rate traveling companies and minstrel shows that came to New Canaan attracted small audiences, their ribald jokes, tasteless productions, and drunken performers attracted the attention of the churches, whose ministers condemned them in sermons.

By then, the Methodist Church had the largest membership and provided the greatest support for the "no license" vote. The Congregational Church in 1883 had celebrated in style its 150th anniversary, but attendance at its services had dwindled. The Rev. Joseph Greenleaf had proved to be a dull preacher, and in 1886 he was asked to resign. (This was a year after Greenleaf had been attacked in print by Francis E. Weed who, resentful of the credit given Greenleaf as a Library founder, accused the pastor of trying to attact summer residents to his church on the strength of his Library presidency.)

Except for the Parkers, the first summer residents attended St. Mark's. They not only made it the "fashionable" church but contributed enough to a building fund that a rectory, planned since 1847, finally became a reality. In 1881, St. Mark's for $600 bought a half acre of land on Main Street just north of Vine Cottage, and there their first rectory was dedicated on Dec. 3, 1881, by the Episcopal Bishop of Connecticut. Today this is No. 51 Main Street, an example of the Stick Gothic Style, and is the headquarters of the New Canaan Chapter of the Red Cross. To St. Mark's and this rectory in 1890 came the much-loved Dr. Robert Howland Neide, who would be rector until he died in 1918.

When he left New Canaan in 1889 Frederick W. Lockwood, in memory of his son, gave St. Mark's a pipe organ, the first in the town. Then, following the death of Osborn E. Bright in 1892, also as a memorial, his family gave the church the second and third bells of a three-bell peel. (These and additional bells were recast in 1948.) And with help from summer residents a Parish Hall was built in 1893.

One year after Dr. Neide came, the Congregational Church called the Rev. James Howard Hoyt, who would serve as minister, until 1922. To the many farmers still in the community, Dr. Hoyt endeared himself by joining the Grange. (For 18 years he was chaplain of the state Grange.) The last week in January 1891 had also seen two members of the Church of Jesus Christ of the Latter Day Saints preaching each evening in the town house and drawing audiences of 50 or more.

Then in 1896, having outgrown its mission status, the Roman Catholic church on Forest Street became St. Aloysius parish, with its first resident pastor, who immediately had built the rectory that is now No. 98 Forest Street.

Mail Service

Nineteen months after the borough began to operate, residents of the borough (because they had sidewalks) received two mail deliveries a day. New Canaan thus became the first town in the United States with a population under 5,000 to have free mail delivery—even though, contrary to law, the town had yet to number the buildings along its streets.

Upon the directive of the Postmaster General, mail was to be delivered free of charge within the borough limits, beginning on Feb. 1, 1891 (a Sunday). A single carrier would start with Main and Elm streets about 10 A.M. and continue along a route of his own making, repeating this walk in the afternoon. Although none had yet arrived, four mail boxes had been assigned to the town, from which mail would be picked up in time to be canceled at the post office and sent out on the next delivery. Mail was again coming into and leaving New Canaan by wagon, four times a day, and not by the railroad. Those who since 1878 had rented boxes at the post office were, however, advised to retain them—a wise precaution because free mail delivery temporarily ended on July 1, 1896, after Congress failed to vote an appropriation.

Credit for this mail delivery went to Lucius M. Monroe, though on Feb. 14, 1891, he would be succeeded as postmaster by Selleck Y. St. John, once the Republican President Benjamin Harrison (1889-93) got around to making the appointment. Monroe as a Democrat had been appointed by Grover Cleveland. The office of the Postmaster General has been unable to supply the exact date, but some time before 1860 (probably in the late 1840's) the volume of mail entering and leaving New Canaan was enough to give it a "Presidential" post office. This meant that New Canaan's postmaster was appointed by the President of the United States, and until the 1930's as a "political plum" the office changed with the politics of the incumbent president. When free delivery resumed in July 1899 New Canaan had branch post offices—on Smith Ridge and in Silvermine—which existed for years.

Education

It had taken 16 years, but New Canaan in 1893 at last took its first step along the road toward the quality public school education for which it is now famous. As early as 1877, Lucius M. Monroe had proposed to a town meeting that the schools be consolidated—and was soundly voted down. Except for District School No. 1, the idea of a central school board was anathema to parents in the other ten school societies—another invasion of private rights.

As a result, the district schools societies went on hiring such teachers as they could find to teach six or more grades in a one-room schoolhouse and make do with such equipment as it possessed. (In 1878 the School Visitors reported that all children under 14 who were employed in local factories had had the required three months' schooling for that year—a sad commentary on the state of New Canaan's education and child labor.) When in 1881, new English and arithmetic books were available for 35 cents and the turn-in of the existing hand-me-down texts, objections were loud. The textbooks being replaced had been in use only 15 years; textbooks should last a whole generation; parents should not be put to such expense—and besides, the new arithmetics were too difficult. No wonder that those parents who could afford to do so sent their children to private schools.

Boys usually were sent to Stamford to be educated at the King School, while both boys and girls could be pupils at the New Canaan Institute. This had been founded (probably) in 1874 by Mrs. Edward F. Ayres, a remarkable educator for those days, in her house at what is now No. 117 Seminary Street.

In 1887, ten years after Monroe's resolution, New Canaan had 535 pupils, aged 4 to 16, attending district schools. One hundred and seventy-six went to Center—which got $2,425 of the town's $5,500 appropriation for all 11 schools—and only 7 pupils attended District School No. 7 (called Raymond Street School) on upper Oenoke Ridge. That year consolidation was again voted down, though it was recommended by the Board of School Visitors, which had been authorized three years before to prepare a school plan.

Despite state and local efforts to get all teachers to attend summer normal school, the quality of New Canaan's public school education remained poor, while equipment and libraries were just about nil, except for Center School. (Only four of the 11 schools had a dictionary.) Lack of interest on the part of parents was blamed when consolidation lost again in 1892 by a vote of 106 to

133. But finally New Canaan woke up to the advantages of a good education, and consolidation won at the annual town meeting of Oct. 2, 1893, by a vote of 206 to 112. After a special town meeting held in May 1894 decided that the school board was to be composed of nine men, New Canaan's first Board of Education was elected the next month. (Among the nine members were Benjamin P. Mead and Edwin Hoyt.) For the first time women had gone to the polls, because by state law, effective Aug. 1, 1893, women were given the right to vote for school board candidates, though they still could not vote for other public officers.

What consolidation meant was that the Board of Education took over the schoolhouses (and the debts) of the now-defunct district school societies, that all teachers were hired by the Board, insuring improved teaching in the rural schools, and that the 1894 annual meeting was confronted with a school budget of $10,000. (This did include a $2,500 addition to Center and repair to the other ten schoolhouses.) As elsewhere, 1894 was a depression year for New Canaan. Business was poor generally (Rogers had had to again lay off cutters), and Alexander Law had died.

At the end of its first full year, in June 1895, the Board of Education could report that it was "proud of its success," although the results were not wholly satisfactory and truancy was up to 48 per-

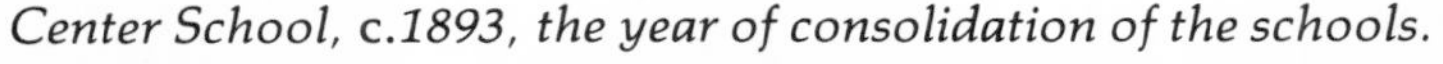

Center School, c.1893, the year of consolidation of the schools.

cent of enrolled students. The outlying schools had been graded through seventh grade to conform with the work being done at Center School, while Center had added an 11th and 12th grade, offering bookkeeping, commercial law, Latin, astronomy, physics, and botany. In 1896, with the town spending $18 per pupil, B. P. Mead as chairman of the Board of Education presented her diploma to Margery Henry, the first graduate of the New Canaan High School at the exercises held in the Opera House. (The next year eight students graduated.) Despite its name, this was not a true high school, and those who went on to attend Stamford High School were penalized with one year of tutoring before they were accepted there.

Much of the credit for improved education was given to George W. Gamble, who became superintendent of schools in 1895. But Gamble believed in corporal punishment, and parental complaints led to his ouster in 1900. He was succeeded then by Henry W. Saxe, who immediately offered the Board of Education a series of plans to induce pupils to continue their studies and went far to eliminate truancy.

The Town

Though it was doing its best to improve its image, New Canaan was still a small town and the village center, with its misarray of wooden houses and stores interspersed with a few red brick structures, was far from picturesque. The year 1888 had seen a building boom when 15 new dwellings and 5 barns were put up at a total cost of $62,000. Out on the ridges large summer homes were to be found between well-kept and tumbledown farmhouses, while in town smaller Victorian-Style residences had been built on South and East avenues and on Elm Street. More would come as new streets opened up—Bank (1885), Grove (1887), Hoyt, Harrison, and St. John Place (all 1892). Still, the 1890 Census gave New Canaan a population increase of only 13 over 1880—up to 2,686—and though a strong minority were sure that the old ways were best, New Canaan as a whole believed its future lay in sales and services to summer residents.

(To avoid panicking the town and driving summer boarders and residents away, the selectmen in 1881 successfully concealed the fact that New Canaan had four cases of smallpox. Dr. Brownson had diagnosed that a maid at Hoyt's Nurseries, returned from a visit to New York, was ill with confluent smallpox—the most virulent form—while a mother and daughter had variloid smallpox. At the same time, Dr. William Willis Cummings, interning with Dr. Brownson, came down with a light case of variloid. Courageously, Cummings offered to be isolated with and care for the other three. So, secretly one night, Brownson and the selectmen moved all four to an unoccupied house on Ferris Hill Road, well removed from any inhabited home, and then closed off the road. Of course rumors circulated, but not until all four persons were cured did the truth get into print. For years afterward Ferris Hill was known as "Pockhouse Hill.")

With the borough spending its money on sidewalks and street lights, the selectmen concentrated on the town's roads. All highways, of course, were then dirt roads—almost as winding as when they were laid out, rutted and muddy during spring thaws, inches deep in dust in the summertime—and they needed reworking. By the end of the 1880's, New Canaan was spending as much on its roads as it did on its schools, something over $5,000 on each. The Blizzard of 1888 had immobilized the town for days (and given those aboard the snowbound branch train some rather scary hours), and it also decided the selectmen that hereafter they must budget a bit for snow removal. But, long before that Blizzard, heavily loaded wagons, such as those from Hoyt's Nurseries, found it almost impossible to climb the Elm Street hill en route to the railroad station.

We are so used to Elm Street as it is today that it is hard to realize that midway between South Avenue and Park Street originally was a short, steep hill. As something of a trial run, the selectmen in 1888 had lowered the Cherry Street side of this hill, before a special town meeting on May 5, 1890, voted to lower Elm Street and widen the entire road.

Accused by some of "ruining the town," First Selectman Joseph F. Silliman hired crews to do the job, blasting through rock, working with picks and shovels and horse-drawn plows, since no power machinery was available. When the job was done, Elm Street's roadbed had been lowered several feet (Main Street was raised somewhat by the gravel deposited there), while a strong retaining wall was built along the south side of the block between South and Park in front of the only house there (then the property of the First National Bank by foreclosure). Silliman's thanks for doing this much-needed job was to be voted out of office; he had spent too much, and 540 voters turned up to say so—the largest number in years. (At the end of three terms, his Democratic successor, Samuel H. Raymond, was defeated because he spent too little, and Silliman then served another two terms, 1893-95.)

One thing Raymond did accomplish was to put gravel on Main, Elm, Park, and Cherry streets "to make the streets in the vicinity of the Depot as attractive as we could," and then to claim at the 1892 town meeting that the new sidewalks along the lowered Elm Street were "one of the greatest improvements in the history of this town"!

Which roads were rebuilt seems to have been decided by where the summer residents lived, and in 1892 and 1893 New Canaan, having bought a rock crusher, spent thousands of dollars on Oenoke Ridge—near the new Field Club. In 1895 a special "Oenoke Avenue Improvement Fund" of $2,500 was voted so that upper Oenoke (near Rev. Mr. Abbot's house) would have a rock foundation covered with earth and gravel as "common convenience and necessity require." The year before it had been Dr. Thomson's turn, and Locust Avenue was rebuilt as far east as his residence; in 1898, Mrs. L. Dade Alexander, a new summer resident, got the selectmen to rework Wahackme Road. Meanwhile, in 1895, the town applied to the new state road maintenance fund for $3,000, which was spent on improving South Avenue "from Maple Street south as far as the appropriation will go."

With more than 100 men working on the roads each summer and gravel, rock, and equipment being bought locally, road-building had become "big business." So in 1893 the town meeting voted that no selectman thereafter should have any interest in any contract for labor or supplies. This must have pinched more than one selectman, since as private contractors they were receiving more than the $400 then paid the first selectman and much more than the $100 annual salaries of the second and third selectmen.

One road Samuel H. Raymond as first selectman had refused to work in 1891 was Cheese Spring Road. Mrs. Susan Anderson, a newcomer from Wilton, had inherited a house near Benedict Hill and found it impossible to drive to New Canaan to shop because Cheese Spring Road was only an overgrown cart track. (Cheese Spring, in those days, had a different route to Valley Road than it does today.) When the selectmen declined to reopen the road, Mrs. Anderson took her case to the Court of Common Pleas; when she won, the town appealed. The matter dragged on until March 1898, when having lost their suit in the Supreme Court of Errors and piled up legal bills, the selectmen were forced to reopen and repair Cheese Spring Road—for the owner of the sole house on a long stretch of highway. Hence no one was especially sorry when the body of Mrs. Anderson was found buried in her pig sty. She had been murdered on Oct. 30, 1898, by her hired man, who committed suicide on November 15, after setting fire to the house, which aroused attention. Instead of sympathizing, New Canaan enjoyed all the grisly details and the publicity given the town in New York newspapers.

By then, the brief Spanish-American War was over and a peace treaty ready to be signed. Despite two calls on Connecticut for artillery and an infantry regiment, the state never filled its quotas, and the only man from New Canaan who volunteered was Frank Humphry. He joined Battery A, 6th U.S. Artillery on June 1, 1898, and on June 18 was drowned at Fort Clinch, Fla., attempting to rescue a fellow recruit when the two had gone swimming while off duty. In New Canaan, the new D.A.R. set up a receiving center from which to forward periodicals, delicacies, pajamas, and shirts to the men in the army, while during the summer the Red Cross Auxiliary No. 41 of New Canaan, formed in July, raised more than $400 by benefits given by schoolchildren and the churches.

As Will Kirk pointed out in the *Messenger* of June 25, 1898, the Spanish-American War did have its effects on New Canan's real estate. Just when the new golf course was expected to act like a magnet and draw even larger numbers of summer visitors, far fewer than the usual number of houses were available for rent. Rumor had it that Spanish gunboats would appear on the Sound and "blow all the cottages to smithereens," and the result was that the local families who ordinarily summered at Belle Island and Hickory Bluff stayed home, refusing to rent their New Canaan residences.

The End of the Century

All New Canaan was saddened when on Jan. 3, 1899, Dr. William Brownson died of pneumonia. Brownson had resigned from the borough board in 1891 to become superintendent of the Fitch Home in Noroton Heights, a refuge for Civil War veterans that had been founded in 1864 by Benjamin Fitch, a son of the Stephen Fitch of long-ago Shaker fame. Living so close to his former home, caring for several of New Canaan's war orphans and veterans, Doctor Brownson had retained all his old friends, who flocked to his funeral.

During the second week of February 1899 the temperature dropped below zero. Strong winds began to blow, and on February 12 a blizzard began. The next night about 7:30 the Raymond Block was found to be on fire. All through the night in the snow and the cold the firemen fought the blaze with the help of water from the new hydrants. When morning came and the fire at last was out, the only structure standing on the east side of Main Street north from opposite Elm was the town's oldest store building at the corner of East Avenue. This third disastrous Main Street fire had destroyed not only the Raymond Block but also the old red store of Samuel Raymond and two other businesses.

Joseph F. Silliman had started a general store business in 1867 with his friend Chauncey Weed in the old East Avenue-Main Street "Weed Block," owned by Weed's father. When a few years later he bought out his partner, Silliman moved to a store in the Raymond Block, from where he sent his helpers or his sons out into the country two times a week, first to take grocery orders and then to deliver the orders by wagon or sled. In time, Silliman added a line of hardware, dividing his store into two departments. It was among the hardware supplies in the basement that the Raymond Block fire began. (Although it moved to first one and then another new site, the business was run by Silliman descendants until February 1977 and continued under the Silliman name until it closed its doors in January 1981.)

When William Edgar Raymond died in 1890, he left his wife as lifetime beneficiary of his estate, and it was Mrs. Raymond who insisted that the estate assets be used to build a new Raymond Block. So by May 1899, at a cost of $15,000, Raymond's executors had contracted for the three-story yellow brick building that, minus its original cornice, is now Nos. 108-118 Main Street. Ninety-six feet along Main Street and 74 feet deep, with offices and a banquet or dance hall above the street-level stores, the new Raymond Block was completed in seven months, and, ready to continue business, J. F. Silliman & Co. moved back on December 21.

After Mrs. Raymond's death in 1905, the assets of the W. E. Raymond estate became the "Mission Fund of the Congregational Church of New Canaan"—a fund unique in the history of American Protestantism. As a result, since 1911, as accumulated income paid their salaries, the Congregational Church has appointed successive ministers-at-large, who have served some 70 Congregational churches throughout the state of Connecticut.

As the end of the 19th century neared, New Canaan could regret that Mrs. Ayres had closed her school and that the Baptist Church had become a mission, its Main Street property deeded to the Connecticut Baptist Convention. But Dr. Joseph C. Wyckoff, the man Alexander Law had hired as a schoolmaster fifty years before, had returned and opened a school on St. John Place. New Canaan's healthful climate was now so recognized that Dr. Myron J. Brooks of Stamford in December 1899 bought a building on South Avenue (now No. 299 at the north corner of Brooks Road), where for some 30 years he had his well-known tuberculosis sanitorium. The town had achieved the self-respect the *Messenger* had pleaded for, but the paper was so hard put to fill out the "events" of the year 1899 that, in addition to all births, marriages, and deaths, it had to include the resident who had sprained an ankle.

Edwin Hoyt had just succeeded Russell L. Hall (served 1879-1897) as president of the First National Bank, which by the century's end had assets of $278,955. The Savings Bank had deposits of nearly $80,000. New Canaan could list 92 farms and a total of 655 houses, and in the fall saw 610 of its 709 registered voters go to the polls to give the McKinley-Roosevelt presidential ticket 405 votes to Bryan's 190. But New Canaan was bitterly disappointed to learn when the 1900 Census was taken that it had not passed the 3,000 mark. It had gained 267 inhabitants since 1890, but the total population was only 2,968. Still, though the Census couldn't count them, the summer residents continued to come—and to buy.

CHAPTER 10

Growing Up—Slowly, 1901-1931

In 1901 New Canaan was 100 years old, and months ahead of time the town set out to celebrate in style. Russell L. Hall, former president of the First National Bank and then president of the Historical Society, was chairman of a 12-man "working committee," which included such town notables as Edwin Hoyt, Will Kirk, L. M. Monroe, Sr., Henry B. Rogers, Joseph F. Silliman, and Francis E. Weed. Dozens of other people served on 10 specific committees, including, of course, one for finance. When the four-day holiday finally arrived nothing had been left to chance. The principal buildings had been professionally decorated by an outside company; houses and highways streamed with bunting and flags; the borough thoughtfully had watered those streets—all dirt ones—over which anyone would march; and the weather cooperated beautifully.

The celebration began on Sunday June 16 with a union service, held in the Congregational meeting house, in which the Baptist, Congregational, Episcopal, and Methodist clergymen participated. (Simultaneously, at St. Aloysius Church Father Byrne gave a historical talk.) Under the direction of H. R. Humphries of New York, a summer resident of Canoe Hill Road, a grand chorus led the singing in the flower-decked, flag-draped sanctuary, and instead of a sermon the Rev. C. M. Selleck of Norwalk delivered a historical address. That afternoon 600 Sunday School children, including those from Selleck's Corners, Silvermine, and St. Aloysius, met and, led by a Danbury band playing Sunday School hymns, held another service at the Congregational Church, featuring Sunday School histories delivered by adult leaders.

Monday's celebration honored New Canaan's schools and New Canaan's schoolchildren. That day's holiday began with the New Canaan Cadet Corps's welcome at the railroad station of the Boys Band from the state reform school at Meriden, whose appearance had been arranged by Benjamin P. Mead, then chairman of the Board of Education. Following speeches on the green near the Congregational meeting house, food was served to the children in the St. John Grove, that great stand of pines which stood on the former St. John homestead between Seminary Street and St. John Place (where the Christian Science meeting house is now). That afternoon an exhibit of school work was on display at the Opera House, where in the evening commencement exercises were held for the 11 pupils graduating from Center School.

Tuesday June 18 was the day everyone had looked forward to—the parade. "Homecoming" had been stressed by the Committee on Invitations, and 10,000 spectators were on hand. Whether they were New Canaan-born or not, people had come from neighboring towns, New York, and elsewhere to watch the celebration, and the branch railroad sold 4,500 tickets that day. Once again the Borough had watered the streets and, to be on the safe side, had hired several "special detectives."

Marshals Scofield and Weed leading the 1901 parade into Main Street.

Nearly half an hour behind schedule, the Tammany Hall cannon (loaned by Franklin W. Anderson of West Road) boomed at 11:55 A.M., and the first division of the parade, led by Francis E. Weed on horseback, stepped off from South Avenue, to turn east into Elm Street and pass under a huge laurel arch into Main Street. Behind Weed in carriages were the invited guests. The second division was led by Loomis Scofield, a Civil War veteran of both army and navy, while John Davenport, a Ponus Ridge farmer, and E. G. Cunningham, an East Avenue dentist, were marshals of the third and fourth divisions, respectively.

Besides invited guests, the first and second divisions of the parade included the Ponus Tribe of Redmen and visiting "chiefs" portraying the town's original settlers, members of other secret societies representing the Train Band and the Revolutionary militia, and local men and women dressed as a colonial clergyman and his wife, a town crier, an 1801 doctor, and other personages. Amid a considerable shifting of bands and drum corps to provide music for the marchers were old carriages, wagons, and sleighs, and much more. Nine floats made up the third division, with two spectacular ones from Hoyt Nurseries. But it was the fourth division that everyone had waited for—the firemen.

"Revolutionary soldiers" marching up Main Street.

With horse-drawn and hand-drawn chemical engines, trucks, hose carts—even a police patrol wagon—and bands and drum corps, firemen had come all the way from Bethel, Danbury, Ridgefield, Norwalk, East Norwalk, South Norwalk, Westport, Darien, Stamford, and Greenwich to march that day with New Canaan's 50 volunteers in New Canaan's parade, and $150 had been set aside to entertain all these men at the Elm Street firehouse.

To allow the crowd of onlookers to spread out through the town, the parade followed a route that led from South Avenue to Elm Street to Main, north on Main to the Big Shop, down Locust, Forest and East Avenue, across Summer Street to Lakeview to Main, north on Main and Oenoke Ridge as far as the triangle at West Road, where the only jam-up of spectators watched the parade countermarch. Then back down Oenoke to God's Acre, down Park Street to Bank Street, to South Avenue, to Cherry Street, across Cherry to Park, south to Richmond Hill, across Richmond Hill to Grove, up Grove Street to Elm, then east across Elm to disband at South Avenue—a distance of nearly six miles. "It was a long tramp," as a reporter wrote, but those were the days when everyone walked—to Broad River to take a trolley to Roton Point, to Lake Waccabuc, 12 miles north in New York state, for a summer swim. And except for visiting firemen and some dignitaries, the 1901 parade was a parade of New Canaan people. Summer residents along Oenoke Ridge might have front-row seats on their lawns, but the place to countermarch had been chosen so that Mrs. Lewis Provost, a venerable New Canaan lady no longer able to walk, could see the whole parade from a chair at her residence at 16 West Road.

Finished by 3 o'clock, some 3,000 marchers and riders on floats sat down to lunch in the St. John Grove, where they were served in three shifts at long trestle tables. Four hundred pounds each of beef and ham, 500 quarts of strawberries, and 5,000 cups of coffee were served that day—the coffee being brewed in a 2,500-cup "coffee pot," which was the invention of Stephen Hoyt (1870-1950), a third generation Hoyt of Hoyt's Nurseries. He had run steam coils around the inside of a huge zinc receptacle, which he hitched to the boiler of a steam roller that belonged to Joseph F. Silliman, groceryman turned contractor. Once the steam was up in the roller, it heated the coffee to the boiling point—which had to be done twice that afternoon.

The fourth day of the 100th anniversary, Wednesday June 19, saw everyone back at the Congregational meeting house for a two-part literary and historical celebration, presided over by Russell L. Hall. Speakers in the morning included Anthony Comstock, the vice crusader, and Homer Cummings, then mayor of Stamford, who would live in New Canaan during World War I and be attorney general of the United States under President Franklin D. Roosevelt. For the afternoon session, Prof. Edwin Hoyt Lockwood had returned from Yale to deliver a historical address. Poems written for the occasion were read, while outside the meeting house was an exhibit of "relics" that had earlier been on display at the old post office. For this some 65 people had loaned 200 old objects, ranging from Bibles and books through such household items as andirons and snuff boxes to farm implements, artisans' tools, and ancient weapons.

When the celebration ended with a banquet at the Congregational church and evening serenades of several prominent citizens, little New Canaan was surprised with "the magnitude of its one hundredth birthday party" and the newspaper coverage it had received far outside the town.

Excitement

Although the New Canaan Baptist Church had been reduced to mission status, it had been represented at the union service of June 16 by its pastor, the Rev. Edward Bell, newly arrived in town. The centennial celebration had barely ended when Bell found himself in the Bridgeport county jail. George Duff Nichols, proprietor of the Opera House, former J. P., and former member of the Board of Education, had been easily recognized as the man "who had not drawn a sober breath in six months" whom Bell mentioned in a temperance sermon on the night of Sunday August 11. As soon as the minister's remarks reached him, Nichols sued Bell for slander, demanding $1,000 in damages. Since Bell was a newcomer in town, no one was willing to post a $1,500 bond for him, and as a result the minister was jailed for several hours in the town's cell under the Opera House and then, handcuffed to a convicted drunkard, marched to the railroad station. In Bridgeport, Bell was again paraded through the streets, but after 30 hours in the county jail, he was released on promise of making a public retraction of his remarks.

At about the same time he was suing Bell, Nichols began publishing a new weekly newspaper called the *Fairfield County Republican* in the Forest Street end of his Opera House. The printer he hired was an outsider named Fred Clark, who boarded at Nichols' house, where apparently he became attentive to Mrs. Nichols. By now Nichols was thoroughly in debt and his intemperance worsened to the point when, following a family quarrel, he ordered everyone (including Clark) out of his house. That was on Jan. 8, 1902, and the next day Nichols left town, only to return at night somewhat inebriated and determined to shoot the printer, who had taken a room at the Birdsall House. Arming himself and his 17-year-old son George with revolvers, Nichols strode to the hotel, found Clark in the billiard room, and fired at him point blank. But the revolver failed to discharge. So, using it as a club, Nichols knocked Clark to the floor with four blows to the head. Bystanders interfered and got Clark to his feet, whereupon at Nichols' orders, young George fired his revolver. Though Clark was hit in the head, the bullet flattened instead of penetrating his skull, and the two Nichols were quickly subdued and rushed off to jail in their Opera House.

Needless to say, when Russell L. Hall as J. P. presided over their hearing, the town clerk's office, turned into a courtroom, was jammed. Because Clark was now out of danger and because Nichols' defense was a hinted reflection on his wife, Hall ordered both Nichols freed on bail. But no one came forward to post the $5,000 bond set for G. Duff Nichols, and he was transferred to the Bridgeport jail. (New Canaan was further enraged when it learned that Nichols had been secretly removed from his cell and, unhandcuffed, driven in a carriage to Norwalk en route to Bridgeport.) Nichols remained in jail for almost a month, until a bondsman was found who would post bail, then reduced to $3,000. But before Nichols could be brought to trial for attempted murder, he died of a heart attack in November 1902 at age 47. The similar charges against his son were later dismissed.

None of Nichols' enterprises was a success except his original corset and underwear business, which his sons soon moved out of town. With Nichols' death, the mortgages on his various properties were foreclosed, and the Opera House, once his pride and joy, was sold by the South Norwalk Savings Bank to Samuel Kuriansky of Stamford in 1904. Thereafter until 1923 the Opera House was New Canaan's first motion picture theatre under lease to a series of out-of-towners. In 1915 it took the name "Colonial Theatre."

Although both male and female inebriates were occasionally locked up in the jail, thanks to the police the center of town was so free of crime that the borough's annual report could consider two incidents a year as unusual. One has to realize that, from the creation of the borough in 1889, the police force was solely a borough institution, while the rest of the town was protected by elected constables, deputy sheriffs, and eventually the state police, who were called to perform special services.

Until 1909, John B. Weed, the first chief of police, had only one assistant, who after 1900 was Marvin F. Merrill. Both men were on duty seven nights a week, 52 weeks in the year, and never seem to have been given a raise, for Weed's salary for years was $726 and Merrill's for shorter hours, was $426.

At 3 o'clock in the morning of Jan. 18, 1908, Weed and Merrill met while making their rounds, and were standing outside the Opera House when they heard what they thought was the report of a gun. For several nights they'd been aware of "suspicious characters" in the center of town—after all they knew everyone and could easily spot a stranger in the dark—so when they saw a man backed against the store at the East Avenue corner they ran toward him. Threatening to blow off their heads, the man began firing, then ran down East Avenue where a second man joined in the shooting. Although Weed had been hit in the right leg with a bullet, both policemen pursued their suspects, some 25 to 30 shots being exchanged. Another bullet hit Weed in the head, but out of ammunition and dizzy, he was able to reach "Central Park" and pull the newly installed electric switch attached to the big Parker elm. This activated the alarm in the firehouse, whereupon the gang, now made up of five men, made their escape down East Avenue.

In response to the fire bell, several men arrived on the scene, and while Weed was taken to Dr. Edmund J. O'Shaughnessy to have his wounds dressed, Postmaster Alexander McKendrick and

Patrolman Merrill discovered that the post office safe had been dynamited. The robbers, whoever they were, had stolen sledges and tools from Johnson Brothers' garage on East Avenue, put a ladder to the back wall of the Raymond Block, where the post office was then housed, and climbed through a window. Though the outer door of the safe was shattered, the inner door held, and all the men got for their efforts was $12.91 from the stamp drawer and $1.50 from a cash box.

Although he reported for duty the next night, Chief Weed was sent home to recuperate on full pay, while the Borough hired John L. Stevens as his temporary replacement and paid Dr. O'Shaughnessy's bill of $48 for treating Weed. The next January the police force not only was increased to three, but for the first time it was uniformed—the Borough immediately disputing the bill of the local tailor who made the uniforms. Weed was 63 years old when because of poor health (due partly to his head wound) he resigned as chief of police in July 1910. As his successor the Borough on July 16 swore in Otto Schmidt, who would serve for the next 39 years as New Canaan's second police chief. In short order the force was increased, hours were reduced from 12 to 10 per day, and because "the advent of so many summer residents made it necessary to direct traffic," summer found Chief Schmidt on daytime duty. New Canaan was willing to admit that the automobile was here to stay.

Automobiles

At the very end of the third division of the centennial parade was a "steam carriage," owned and driven by F. C. Parson of Stamford. It was the only automobile in New Canaan on June 18, 1901, but if it were the first car to be driven over New Canaan roads, the fact was not mentioned by the *Messenger.* Nevertheless the day of the automobile had arrived, and New Canaan horses and New Canaan pedestrians would soon have to cope with cars. So would the town and borough governments.

Thomas W. Hall, Jr., always claimed that he owned the first car in New Canaan, the Stanley Steamer he bought in April 1904. But DeWitt R. Merritt, jeweler and bicycle shop owner where 91 Main

Main Street in 1906. The Post Office was in the rebuilt Raymond Block (beneath the awnings), and in the distance (right to left) were the Rogers Block and the Opera House, then also the Town Hall.

Raymond & Stevens' livery stable is now No. 17 Forest Street.

"Ned" Fairty in the 1904 Northern that was his sixteenth-birthday present from his father. (Courtesy of E. Raymond Fairty.)

Street now is, was agent for the Northern Company, and he had received a Northern car one month earlier. (There is no record of to whom Merritt sold it.) One month later Dr. Clarence H. Scoville purchased a Locomobile. What has long been called the third car in New Canaan is another Northern, sold by Merritt to C. E. T. Fairty on Aug. 9, 1904, which the two men picked up in New York and drove to New Canaan in 3½ hours. Owned today by Fairty's son Raymond, this Northern occasionally is driven in local parades.

The Connecticut Motor Vehicle Department, however, has a different record. In 1934 it issued a list of owners of the first registration plates, and this shows that on Aug. 1, 1903, license plate No. 735 was issued to young Marshall S. Driggs for his Mechaley. He was the son of Silas Driggs, president of the Williamsburg Savings Bank of Brooklyn, N.Y., who rented the Lockwood house on South avenue for several summers, which may explain why Driggs has been overlooked as the first of New Canaan's car owners. By the end of 1905, New Canaan could claim nine of the 2,155 automobiles registered in Connecticut.

Before any automobile was locally owned, Will Kirk wrote an editorial for his *Messenger* against speeding, and he did not change his mind after Dr. Scoville gave him his first auto ride. Kirk, however, had been succeeded as borough clerk by his printer, John E. Hersam (1872-1949), when on Sept. 5, 1905, the Board of Warden and Burgesses ordered the clerk to notify T. W. Hall, Sr. (who owned a Thomas Flyer), Guy McLane (Locomobile), Stephen Hoyt (of the Nurseries), and Nelson King that "they or their chauffeurs must keep within the Borough speed limit (12 miles per hour) and to announce or give warning of their coming." Mr. King was further warned to "carry some kind of light at night on his motor cycle," so by then motorcycles were also on the local scene.

Despite warnings and hazards—accidents occurred from the start—New Canaan residents bought automobiles, and by 1913 the town was taxing 204 cars and 8 motorcycles. Many summer residents now arrived in chauffeur-driven automobiles, while at least two summer-resident ladies could be seen driving their glass-encased electric runabouts. And in the fall of 1912 New Canaan had its first auto fire engine, a Locomobile that was a combination hose and chemical truck. This was the $6,000 gift of Alfred H.

Mulliken, a summer resident on West Road, who probably was the largest single landowner in the history of the town, owning approximately 1,000 acres that he bought over a period of years.

Town and Borough

As though highways had not been a continuing headache, automobiles forced the town and the borough to spend even more tax money than before on the roads, most of which were made of gravel and dirt. At the turn of the century the borough had shelved a proposal to put aside money to pave Main Street eventually, convinced that macadam or any other paving surface could not stand up to the horseshoes of the large number of horse-drawn vehicles that came into the village each day. But as cars and trucks replaced carriages and wagons, the borough in 1916 (after a bitter fight) paved Main Street and Elm Street with concrete. Eighteen months later it was the turn of the selectmen to complain that "With the present amount of auto traffic it is impossible to keep the roads even in fair condition," while justifying the money they'd spent to fill in low spots and mudholes "so that the roads will be passable for autos the year round."

In 1904-05 new streets were opened up in the borough—Church, Oak, Green, East Maple—calling for new sidewalks and more street lights. But by then an arrangement had been made whereby the town paid over to the borough 15 percent of New Canaan's highway budget for work on borough streets.

Usually borough elections aroused little voter interest, while with no burning issue to contest, town elections often turned on personalities. Though he was consideed a "spender," Joseph F. Silliman was again elected first selectman in 1905 and 1906, but when he was chosen in 1908 as the Republican candidate for the 26th senatorial district, he was at first written off as a "figurehead." His opponent was Jeremiah Donovan, a powerful Democrat from South Norwalk seeking his third term. Silliman, although 68 years old, went out and waged a vigorous campaign and won by 300 votes, giving New Canaan a state senator for the second time.

Few people attended the special town meeting on July 6, 1911, that voted to create a Board of Finance—in accordance with an act passed by the legislature. Connecticut towns had a habit of getting themselves into debt and then refinancing with bond issues, and New Canaan's bonds then totaled $250,000. It now became the job of the bipartisan Board of Finance—six taxpayers who held no other office—to put New Canaan on a pay-as-you-go basis by specifying how a proposed appropriation was to be financed—a special tax or a bond issued for a specific purpose.

One of the six men on the first Board of Finance was Thomas W. Hall, Sr., a New York businessman who by then had become a year-round resident. Another was native-born Hanford S. Weed (1868-1937), a lawyer practicing in both New Canaan and New York, who with Francis E. Green, the real estate agent, had replaced L. M. Monroe as head of the Democrats. In 1912, in an all-New Canaan contest for senator from the 26th district, Weed ran against Benjamin P. Mead and won. Though New Canaan went Republican—228 to 223 Democratic and 57 Progressive votes—Connecticut went for Woodrow Wilson for president, and the Democrats carried the 26th. (New Canaan, incidentally, has not had a Democratic first selectman since Rodney Light in 1919-20.)

Business Changes

Just before the panic of 1903 began, Henry B. Rogers in January ended his manufacture of men's clothing, because of his failing health, and sold the Rogers Block to the Lane Shoe Company of Brooklyn. Shades of the Perfection Scale Co., local men had raised $6,000 to induce Lane to open a shoe factory in New Canaan and take up some of the unemployment slack. But five years later the Lane company failed, leaving Benedict & Co. in the "Big Shop" as New Canaan's sole makers of shoes. And on June 30, 1913, the "Big Shop" closed its doors, putting an end to the shoemaking trade, begun in the 1730's, that had once made New Canaan famous. (As surviving partner of Benedict & Co., George F. Lockwood retained ownership of the empty factory until 1920. By 1926 it had become such an eyesore that it was torn down, and the land was given to the borough by Samuel H. Watts, a public-spirited newcomer, as a site for a future firehouse).

Although they were never large-scale employers, new furniture businesses had appeared on the scene. On Jan. 1, 1893, in the second town house, Edward B. Lawrence (1870-1936) opened a furniture business and undertaking establishment in competition to Russell L. Hall. By 1900 Lawrence had formed the New Canaan Couch Co. and sold his retail furniture business to Herbert L. Scofield, who moved it to the nearby "Great Western" building. Lawrence moved the Couch Company to the former Law Academy on Park Street, but in 1904, having discontinued manufacturing, he moved the Academy building to Elm Street opposite South Avenue. There it housed his undertaking business, while he opened a livery stable in a huge barn next door.

To the east, on the opposite side of Elm Street, in the New Canaan Reading Room's building, John E. Hersam on July 25, 1908, published the first issue of the *Advertiser.* An ardent sportsman who played baseball on Chief Otto Schmidt's team, Hersam went into competition with Will W. Kirk, his former employer, because he thought the *Messenger* never gave adequate coverage to either sports or fraternal activities. In 1911, when the *Advertiser* and his printing business were proven successes, Hersam moved to larger quarters on the opposite side of Elm. (The *Advertiser,* still a weekly and now New Canaan's only newspaper, is published by John Hersam's grandson.) In poor health, Kirk had sold the *Mes-*

Elm Street c.*1910. To the left of the awning is the Library, where the* Advertiser *began, and two buildings beyond is the Firehouse. The three men were standing outside the* Advertiser's *second home.*

senger in February 1910, but that paper ceased publication under that name with the issue of Oct. 16, 1913; three years later its successor, the *Messenger-Leader,* was gone.

On Main Street, J. & J. Benedict's former brick shoe factory had been turned into a bakery. If not exactly thriving, local stores did a brisk business; livery stables came and went, to be supplanted by garages, while grocery stores had a habit of changing ownership frequently. One new grocer was Walter Stewart, who in 1907 had bought the grocery store founded decades before by Seymour Comstock south of the "Big Shop." Two years later Stewart bought out the grocery store of W. A. Smallhorn (where the New Canaan Savings Bank is today), moved to that site, and acquired a second store in the Raymond Block nearby. With both a "charge" and a cash-and-carry store, Walter Stewart Co., formed in 1911, was probably the first merchant to cater especially to the summer trade. (Like the *Advertiser,* Stewart's grocery business is continued today by a grandson.)

1911 was also the year when a gas company received borough approval to pipe its product under New Canaan streets and when enthusiasm for a Norwalk-New Canaan trolley line reached a peak. Voters, however, thought that neither gas mains nor a trolley line were in the best interests of the town, and neither project materialized.

Though New Canaan had lost most of its manufacturing and the village was filled with small shops, the artisans were prospering. Carpenters, masons, electricians, and plumbers—anyone connected with the building trade—were fully employed, because well before 1911 New Canaan was launched on a building boom.

A Building Boom

Always mindful of fire, the borough in 1901 had set up a "building district" in the center of town and passed an ordinance making it "unlawful to erect, elevate or enlarge or remove any wooden structure without permission of the Warden and Burgesses." (By 1912 it had a building inspector.) A building permit had to be obtained, and thereafter one can follow in the minutes of the borough Board the changes made to wooden buildings along some eight streets south of Husted Lane. New buildings, however, were mostly built of brick.

The building boom that was to alter radically the looks of Main Street began around the corner on East Avenue in 1906, when the Johnson brothers tore down the wooden building at the Forest Street corner that once had been the Ayres' brothers tannery. In its place they built a two-story brick garage, since they were now agents for the Ford car and were phasing out their carriage works and blacksmith shop. Then in 1908, with a borough permit, Dr. James W. McLane at the head of a group of summer residents remodeled the former Baptist meeting house at No. 62 Main Street, adding the present portico on the front. There, for five years the Doctor and his friends underwrote a Young Men's Club, but when interest waned they deeded the property to the New Canaan Library as a contribution to its building fund. At first the former church was rented out as a movie theatre in competition to the Opera House, but eventually the Library sold it to Francis E. Green, who in turn sold on Jan. 2, 1917, to the Harmony Lodge, which converted it into its Masonic Temple.

Two blocks to the south, the town of New Canaan in 1908 sold to Benjamin P. Mead its second Town House, the building that had begun as the Methodists' first meeting house. This Mead turned into the "Mead Block" (Nos. 132-138 Main Street), with stores below and offices and apartments above, by adding a third story and encasing the front in a bay-windowed, concrete-block-faced shell. Next door in 1910 Herbert L. Scofield built a three-story red brick building for his furniture business, installing the first elevator in New Canaan of which there is record. With business booming, Scofield in 1912 moved the "Great Western" building, which had housed his first store, around the corner to become No. 12 Burtis Avenue, and erected a three-story brick addition (now No. 126 Main).

Meanwhile, the town of New Canaan had gone on a building spree and simultaneously in 1909 was completing a new Center School and the present town hall. Jacked up on skids and drawn eastward, the old wooden Center School building saw daily use while a new two-story brick schoolhouse rose on the original site. (By 1914, with several district schools closed, Center was so crowded an addition had to be made.) Although the need for an adequate, fireproof town hall had been recognized for many years, not until 1908 was a site bought—on the west side of Main Street, almost opposite the Opera House, where the town clerk's office was. Thereupon, a committee of five—Francis E. Weed, Joseph F. Silliman, Edward B. Lawrence, Hanford S. Weed, and Frank Dawless—took charge. Advised by Hobart H. Weekes, a New York architect whose summer home was the pink stucco residence at No. 370 Oenoke Ridge, they considered the 17 plans submitted by architects from New York to Boston. That of Edgar A. Josselyn of New York was chosen and built for $3,000 less than the $45,000 appropriated for it. (The committee found it was cheaper to remove the town's cells from the Opera House basement than to buy new ones.) Although the building has been enlarged several times, the town hall's entrance is much the same as it originally was, with the town clerk's office on the right.

Next, in 1912, two more red brick buildings went up on Main Street. Filling the triangle just south of the Rogers Block, between Main and Forest streets, was the new four-story home of Silliman Hardware Co., which was incorporated in the fall by the three sons of Joseph F. Silliman. A good three blocks to the south, the Southern New England Telephone Co. in the fall began building its

The Methodist Church-Concert Hall-second Town Hall as it appears today, and the fourth Town Hall after it was built in 1909.

first telephone exchange. (Heretofore, equipment had been operated from private homes.)

Not to be left out, the First National Bank of New Canaan, after first rejecting the idea, decided it too must have a brick building. (A second attempted robbery had been foiled on Jan. 7, 1913, only because the bookkeeper, going back in the evening to finish his work, had surprised burglars inside.) So the original small wooden bank was sold (and moved to Locust Avenue, where with a coating of stucco it is today No. 19), and a Greek-porticoed brick building was erected (enlarged in 1924, 1941, and 1952). Until then the First National Bank had shown only small growth, but now it began to expand steadily. When in 1924 Edward B. Lawrence succeeded George F. Lockwood as president, the bank presidency for the first time became a full-time job. (The bank changed its name to First National Bank & Trust Company in 1929, became part of Fairfield County Trust in 1958, which was absorbed in turn by Union Trust Company.)

The New Canaan Reading Room for years had sought to move from Elm Street, where proximity to the Birdsall House barns, Elm Street livery stables, and Elm Street saloons detracted from its use. But for a full decade the Library had troubles acquiring a new site and raising the money to build. After several disappointments, in 1910 it bought the southwestern corner of Main and Cherry streets—where stood the house built in 1823 by Capt. Stephen Hoyt, Jr. (later moved to No. 39 Richmond Hill Road)—but not until Jan. 25, 1913, did the Library have the money to break ground. By July it had completed the granite building, which, porticoed like the First National Bank and the Masonic Temple, is standing today. (The original building was enlarged in 1936 and 1952 and more than doubled in size in 1978 by the addition of the Lewis H. Lapham wing.)

In the neighborhood, one more brick structure was built. Since 1907 the Roman Catholics had owned the northwestern corner of South Avenue and Maple Street, and there on June 25, 1916, was laid the cornerstore for a new church edifice. Completed the next year, the second St. Aloysius Church was dedicated on Sunday July 15, 1917; by then its rectory on Maple Street had also been built. (The third and present St. Aloysius on Cherry Street was built in 1967.)

New Residents

The 1910 Census showed that New Canaan's population had risen to 3,667, with almost half of this total residing in the borough. At the end of 1912, New Canaan could report that it now assessed 945 houses (up 53 from the year before), with a value of $2,859,560. To the satisfaction of both banks and any number of land owners, real estate had sold well ever since the Centennial, both for summer residents and for new dwellings along the new borough streets.

On Smith Ridge, Dr. Percy E. Williams of New York, Judge Edward E. Thomas of Brooklyn, and others had built summer homes; Dr. W. Robinson Townsend was on Lambert Road, while Dr. James E. McKernon, another New York physician, had acquired the former Watts Comstock farm on Weed Street. Nearby, at the top of the Elm Street hill, lived Richard B. Kelly, a New York lawyer and banker, and south of him more summer residences were being built along Weed Street. Out West Road in 1904 Prof. William H. Burr began to build what is now No. 260. Burr was a noted engineer and college professor who, reminiscent of Commodore Shufeldt, had served on both President McKinley's and President Theodore Roosevelt's commissions for a canal across the Isthmus of Panama. More new summer residents bought on Brushy Ridge, Canoe Hill, Oenoke Ridge, and Lambert Road, where at No. 281 the last true summer residence was built in 1913 by Adrian Van Sinderen of Brooklyn. That same year Julius Kruttschnitt, chairman of the Southern Pacific Co., bought a summer home on Oenoke Ridge, while Lewis H. Lapham, who had bought Prospect Farm from Thomas W. Hall in 1904 and renamed it Waveny, was completing the brick mansion New Canaan now calls "the Castle."

Those summer visitors who cared neither to buy nor to rent now had a choice of two inns. The Ardsley opened for business in 1906 in the old Alexander Law house on Park Street, offering year-round accommodations and fabulous meals, while in 1908 the former Dr. Edward Lambert home on Oenoke Ridge was converted into the Hampton Inn (still in existence). North of the Ardsley soon would be the forerunner of the Melba Inn.

Although the newer summer residents, especially the doctors and Professor Burr, were active in civic matters, the newcomers who made New Canaan their year-round home played more active parts. Foremost among those were Harry B. Thayer and Dr. Walter C. Wood. Mr. Thayer was president of Western Electric Co., when in 1903 he bought a house and the old mill at Valley Road and Huckleberry Hills Road, later acquiring much more acreage in that area. Until he died in 1936 he was one of New Canaan's large benefactors. Dr. Wood (1864-1953) was a Brooklyn surgeon when he came to New Canaan in 1912 to regain his health. After starting a dairy farm on Cascade Road, he went on to become a figure in Connecticut's agricultural affairs (a dormitory at the University at Storrs is named for him) and New Canaan's representative to Hartford in 1923-31.

As might be expected, children of some summer residents stayed in New Canaan once they had married—Robert H. Bradley, Lawrence P. Frothingham, Thomas W. Hall, Jr.—to be joined by lawyers, bankers, brokers, bond salesmen, who like them commuted to offices in New York. Like the original founding settlers of Canaan Parish, these newcomers were mostly couples in their 20's and 30's, who had more on their minds than playing golf at the Country Club. Several ran and were elected to the unpaid office of borough Burgess; others had their say at town meetings; but because they were new in town they were sometimes resented by the older local residents, who for years retained the major town offices, and considered as upstarts all those who had not been a resident for at least 20 years. But there had been another change in the composition of New Canaan's population. Subtly, almost unnoticed, the town had become home for a number of architects, artists, and literary men.

When it was ready to start building in 1912, the Library called on five local architects to submit designs. Unlike Prof. Edward Lindsay, who had designed the Elm Street Reading Room, three of these architects were permanent New Canaan residents—Alfred H. Taylor, whose design was accepted, Woodruff Leeming, and Frederick H. Mathesius. Like Hobart Weekes, the other two—Electus D. Litchfield and Austin W. Lord—were summer residents. Besides heading his own New York firm and being professor of architecture at Columbia, Austin Lord had been the first director of the American Academy in Rome (1894-96) and he lived in Silvermine in the summers near his friend Solon Borglum, the sculptor.

Though the house he bought in 1907 and the barn he converted into his studio actually stand in Wilton, Solon Borglum was the leader of the artists he quickly attracted to the Silvermine region of New Canaan. There, to name but a few, settled painters Addison T. Millar, Hamilton Hamilton, Bernhard Gutmann, and Richard Gruelle (whose son John became famous as author and illustrator of *Raggedy Ann*); the illustrator Frederick C. Yohn, and the cartoonist John Cassel. D. Putnam Brinley, a landscape painter, settled farther north on Valley Road in 1909, while Howard Hildebrandt, the portrait painter, and his wife Cornelia, a miniaturist, lived on Silvermine Road. These and other artists soon were meeting regularly in Borglum's studio to study together and to criticize each other's work.

New Canaan considered itself "cultured," but it had little opportunity to admire more than the elaborate amateur theatricals produced by summer residents, listen to musicales and poetry readings at the Woman's Club, or attend the annual flower shows of the New Canaan Garden Club founded in 1909 primarily by wives of summer residents. Local exhibitions of painting and sculpture had never been seen before Borglum held open house in his studio in the summer of 1908. That was the beginning of 13 successive annual exhibitions in the studio by what became the Silvermine Group of Artists, drawing an ever-increasing number of critics and visitors.

Childe Hassam had painted a brook scene in New Canaan as early as 1902, but he was then summering in Cos Cob. Probably the first painter to settle in New Canaan was Augustus M. Gerdes, who built in 1904 on what is now called Gerdes Road. The next decade saw the landscape painter Ernest Albert open a studio on Old Stamford Road, and Howard M. Hartshorne move from Paris to Park Street. Since the Silvermine Group restricted itself primarily to artists in the Silvermine area, these painters and others joined the New Canaan Society of Artists, founded shortly before the turn of the century by William F. Weed, son of businessman Francis E. Weed and well known locally as a photographer. (Weed's uncle, incidentally, was the Frenchman Pierre Gentieu, an artist who worked in New Canaan in the 1870's.) The second exhibition of this Society of Artists was hung in the New Canaan Library in 1916, with some of the painting sold for the Library's benefit.

Although the great influx of authors and publishers would not come until after World War I, by 1910 the tall figure of Bliss Carman, the poet, was a familiar sight. Carman, who would become poet laureate of Canada, delivered the address at the dedication of the Library, and was often in residence at the East Avenue home of his patrons, Dr. and Mrs. Morris L. King; otherwise he boarded on Cherry Street. And well before the War, New Canaan had become home to M. Farmer Murphy, editor of the *Chicago Tribune*, and Robert R. LaMonte, the Socialist.

Health Problems

New Canaan constantly prided itself on being a healthful town, but the facts contradicted the claim—two deaths from typhoid in 1901, seven cases in 1904, and epidemics of malaria and such communicable diseases as scarlet fever, measles, and diphtheria. Annual reports of successive health officers roundly condemned the unsanitary conditions physicians were sure contributed to the spread of disease, and at the top of their list were the lack of garbage collection, lack of sewers, and "Rockwell's Swamp."

In those days people disposed of their garbage by burying it in their yards or dumping it any old where; in the borough, where houses were close together, flies swarmed around uncovered receptacles. The only garbage collection was in the business district, from which refuse was carted to outlying farms to be used for fertilizer. Polluting the air, summer after summer, carloads of manure shipped from New York City for farmers' fields stood for days on the railroad siding in the broiling sun. Finally, in 1908, with seven unloaded cars of manure and 40 more expected, this matter was turned over to the County Health Officer, who ordered immediate unloading—to be done at night.

In those days too, sewage disposal was into individual cesspools, which usually were unsatisfactory and unhealthful, while all too often one family's privy drained into another family's well. As early as 1890 the borough had recognized in its first annual report that a sewer system was its greatest need, but the Board quickly learned that the borough charter was "conflicting in almost every particular," and that it had no legal power to build a sewer system. Not until 1901 did a vote of borough taxpayers authorize the laying of sewer pipes "along streets and highways to a filter bed or to discharge into streams." An amendment to the borough charter was submitted to the state legislature but was quickly withdrawn, as a $1,000 survey and inspection of sewer systems in nearby towns convinced the Warden and Burgesses to forget about "streams," and build a filtration bed.

Though a 10-acre site was decided on in 1905—off lower Main Street south of the Cemetery—purchase was held up for two years by a suit asking damages for the heirs of the deceased owner of the property. Not until 1907 did the work of building a filter bed and laying sewer pipes down the middle of streets get under way, and only after the legislature enacted amendments to the borough charter in 1903, 1905, and 1907. The next May, however, the Warden could report to the annual borough meeting that 4½ miles of sewer pipe had been laid and 75 houses connected to it. To finance this, the borough had issued $75,000 in bonds and assessed property owners along the sewer routes at the rate of 80 cents a running foot.

After long delay, "Rockwell's Swamp" had been drained in 1903, but not satisfactorily. Called the Dismal Swamp in Canaan Parish days, this swamp lay west of Park Street and largely south of Richmond Hill Road. Once a cranberry bog, it took its name from David S. Rockwell, a former owner, who had resided on Park Street after selling his boys' boarding school atop Church Hill, but since 1895 it had been owned by Benjamin P. Mead. On the west side of these 20 acres, along the railroad tracks, was a gravel and sand bank, but, fed by three small streams and criss-crossed by ditches from Park Street, the rest of the Swamp was a tempting public dump, an outlet for sewage from Richmond Hill, and a prime breeding ground for malaria-carrying mosquitoes. All attempts to drain "Rockwell's Swamp" were only temporary, and the health officer of 1909 called on the legislature to abolish it. At the same time consideration was being given to locating a second sewer bed there. Then in 1914, Frank A. Shutes, who lived at present 205 Park Street overlooking the Swamp, proposed to the

Men's Club of the Congregational Church that "Rockwell's Swamp" be made into a park.

All New Canaan then had to offer in the way of public recreation was winter coasting on designated public streets, ice skating on privately owned ponds, swimming (for boys only) in the "Glory Hole," the remnant of Isaac Richard's mill pond off Parade Hill, and baseball on neighbors' lots or the South Avenue baseball field (where Grace and Crystal streets now are), which existed as a kindness of its owner, Charles P. Fish, first selectman in 1903-05. Benjamin P. Mead had died in March 1913, and as the park proposal gained backing, his widow rose to the occasion and offered to give the Swamp outright to New Canaan. So on the night of Apr. 12, 1915, some 350 men and women crowded into the town hall auditorium to hear the pros and cons of the offer, to which strings were attached. But with 136 yeas and 110 nays, New Canaan accepted Mead Memorial Park, agreeing to budget $300 annually for improvement and to establish a six-man Park Board. (One of the original six was Hanford S. Weed, Mead's political opponent; two others were newcomers.)

Although no large-scale improvements would be made until federal money was available in the 1930's, the first year saw a "clean-up day," a dam of sorts raised to make a skating pond, and work begun on an almost unuseable baseball field. But no change in name could eradicate the health menace to the town, though the first Park Board was able to kill a proposal to have Mead Park used as the town's garbage dump. Then the Civic League came forward and offered to try to beautify the Park by planting shrubs and flowers along the high ground near the railroad track.

The Civic League

The Civic League had been founded early in 1910 as another New Canaan "improvement society." Although such native-born women as Mrs. H. B. Rogers, Mrs. William F. Weed, and Mrs. Irving Lockwood joined, its membership came largely from the new families in town—Mrs. Marshal Stearns, Mrs. Raymond E. Streit, Mrs. Louis H. Hall, Mrs. Lida B. Ellsworth, Mrs. Francis H. Adriance, Miss L. Winifred Hall, Miss Olive Reamy, to name only a few. The matter of health was very much on the League's collective mind, for nothing was being done about garbage collection, purity of the water in the mains was under attack, and privies still existed because the filter beds were inadequate and more houses could not be connected to the sewer pipes.

The League went into action almost immediately and, having raised the necessary funds, sponsored two innovations. It began by purchasing covered garbage cans—the first shipment had to be returned because they arrived labeled "New London"—which were set out along village streets. Then in 1914 the League, having mapped out a collection route and invited bids, paid a garbage man with a wagon to make regular collections from June through September, which were taken to a dump on Forest Street. This was the beginning of New Canaan's private trash collecting. Despite a study and professional recommendation, the borough in 1917 and again in 1919 declined to provide municipal garbage collection, though it did order that all garbage carts must have covers.

Also in June 1911 the Civic League hired New Canaan's first visiting nurse, a graduate of New Haven Hospital. For 10 to 50 cents per visit, she gave a helping hand and professional care to anyone in need of her services—not just charitable cases as rumor first had it. And during the epidemics of that first summer, the visiting nurse proved invaluable to the hard-pressed physicians, as she was in 1916 when the polio epidemic struck New Canaan. Despite a rigid quarantine that began on August 1, shutting Sunday Schools and necessitating the Library's re-covering all its books, New Canaan had 13 cases and at least one death from this crippling epidemic.

Out of the Visiting Nurse Committee of the Civic League grew the Visiting Nurse Association of New Canaan, and its Thrift Shop (now on Locust Avenue) had its origins in the "rummage sales," by which the Civic League raised part of the money it needed to pay the visiting nurse's salary.

When a public hearing was held in Hartford in November 1912 to investigate the New Canaan Water Co., the League forces were on hand to testify. Though the reservoir had been enlarged, three successive summers of drought had played havoc with the water supply. Center School had been closed in October 1910 for lack of water to flush toilets. At times water was rationed by shutting off the mains during certain hours, forcing some people to go to friends who had wells to take baths or get drinking water. And as the water level fell, algae coated the reservoir, and the water drawn from the lower gates was stagnant and so objectionable in taste that "even the horses wouldn't drink it," and its purity was widely questioned. The upshot of the Hartford hearing was that the Water Co. was ordered to install a filtration plant, begun in 1913.

All along the borough was having problems with its sewer filter bed, which overflowed at times and otherwise seeped into Five Mile River. In line with Professor Burr's expert opinion, changes had been made and a second filter bed completed in 1911. Then in 1913 the filter beds burst and a new filtration plant had to be built.

Suffragettes

Although it had no connection with the Civic League, the suffragette movement had reached New Canaan by 1910—and so had anti-suffragette activity. (Under the two headings the *Advertiser* soon was publishing a weekly column of "canned" news.) Mrs. Herbert Knox and Mrs. George E. Frank, new summer residents from Brooklyn, were suffragette leaders in New York, and the wife of Dr. John Rogers made New Canaan news by parading in Washington, D.C. So it wasn't long before New Canaan suffragettes (including Mrs. Solon Borglum, Mrs. Marshal Stearns, Mrs. W. F. Weed, Miss May Fairty, and Miss Edith Bartow as well as Mrs. Knox) were participating in suffragette rallies in Hartford. At the same time, led by Miss Florence Gerrish, another summer resident from Brooklyn, an Anti-Suffragette League was formed in 1910 and listened to out-of-town speakers enumerate all the reasons why women should not have the vote. By 1916, although they could vote only for Board of Education members, 41 New Canaan women had registered to vote.

The Community School

Besides getting behind Mead Park and becoming involved in civic matters, the new families with children took an interest in education. Though Mrs. Louis H. Hall was elected to the Board of Education in 1917, the immediate answer seemed to be a new private school. So in the fall of 1916 a group of parents founded The Community School, which opened in a rented house at No. 46 Seminary Street. It not only took over the private kindergarten started in 1910 by Miss Helen Rogers, but it had Mrs. Solon Borglum, a native of France, as the French teacher. (After several moves, the school in 1936 changed its name to New Canaan Country School, having purchased the former Grace Home in the Field property on Ponus Ridge, and continues there today.)

Christmas Carols

The Civic League lost its fight to preserve the "Parker elm," which was cut down in 1916 when "Central Park" was eliminated at the head of East Avenue for the paving of Main Street. But before the year ended the Civic League had another tree and was responsible for establishing one of the nicest traditions New Canaan has ever had.

As sponsors of the town's first community carol sing, the League brought to God's Acre a Christmas tree that had been cut and donated by the South Norwalk Light Co. Around that decorated tree townspeople gathered on Christmas Eve 1916 to sing carols together for the first time. The next year the Civic League bought and had Hoyt's Nurseries plant a live Christmas tree, and though now forgotten that Scotch pine still stands near the southwest corner of God's Acre—New Canaan's original Christmas tree. In 1917 carol singing took place on Sunday December 23, with everyone very much aware that since April 6 the United States had been at war with Germany.

World War I

Long before war was declared, New Canaan had held patriotic services, made and sent bandages overseas, and supported relief programs for Belgium and France. At least two young New Canaan men (Henry E. Kelley was one) working in New York had joined the later famous 69th New York Regiment and were serving in Mexico. In February 1917, on orders from the legislature, New Canaan compiled a military census, and the next month 34 men joined the National Guard. One week before war was declared, 74 New Canaan men drilled in the town hall under Capt. John D. Fearhake, a Texas-born lawyer, who had been living on Valley

Road since 1908. Many of this first group of recruits became commissioned officers, on active duty in Washington or overseas, while some 106 older men formed Company H, 6th Separate Battalion, Connecticut State Guard—the so-called "Home Guard" —which drilled regularly off South Avenue at Woodland Road and went in the summers to Smith Island Camp.

From the beginning, threatened shortages in the world's food supply loomed large everywhere, and New Canaan set out to do its part. The newly formed Plant, Flower and Fruit Guild registered some 200 children who wanted to garden and provided "borrowed" plots for those who did not have space at home. At the poor farm, additional acres were plowed, and some 25 boys and girls worked there under a supervisor. Sponsored by the Civic League, a Canning Club was started, which in the summer took over the kitchen at Center School. The New Canaan Auxiliary of the Stamford Branch of the American Red Cross was reactivated and by May was hard at work in the assessor's office in the town hall, sewing, knitting, and making comfort bags for servicemen. At 24 daily sessions during July, 765 workers had shown up, and by year's end the Red Cross had 805 members.

By the end of May, mass meetings for the First Liberty Loan drive were familiar events. Patriotism not income (3.5 percent interest) was the watchword as New Canaan topped its quota in just two weeks, 538 people subscribing $157,050. For the Second Liberty Loan in October, school bells and church bells announced the start of a parade of the Home Guard and the Boy Scouts led by the Town Band. The rally speaker was an ambulance driver from France, and the town raised more than twice its quota.

Draft registration day on June 5 was a townwide holiday, celebrated by the ringing of church bells at 7 A.M., 1 P.M., and 7 P.M. All stores were closed, and an afternoon parade saw 1,000 participants. When the day was over, 342 New Canaan men between the ages of 21 and 35 had received registration pins, including four who were totally disabled, 83 who were aliens, and 145 men who were likely to be exempt. Already six others, not waiting for a draft, had enlisted and gone into the army, the navy, and the air force, while before the first draft numbers were drawn, New Canaan was claiming it had 49 men in the service. (Since this figure included such summer residents as Dr. James F. Miller and Dr.

Percy H. Williams of New York, it wasn't strictly accurate.) When the first Honor Roll was published on September 16, the total had risen to 76.

By then a county YMCA had been formed and was launched on a fund-raising drive; books were being collected for soldiers' and sailors' libraries; prizes had been given to the "Soldiers of the Soil," those 83 boys and girls who had stuck with summer gardening—and milk had jumped one cent to 11 cents a quart.

In September, 11 New Canaan men went off to Camp Devens in Massachusetts, but not until all the draftees from the area had been given a huge reception in Norwalk, attended by Gov. Marcus Holcomb, and a shore dinner at Dorlan's. At 7 in the morning of October 4, nine more men left for camp to the ringing of church bells and a big demonstration at the New Canaan railroad station. By December New Canaan knew that John T. Kelley, one of its first draftees, was overseas; by January 1918, so were 17 other men (including artist D. Putnam Brinley), and the Honor Roll totaled 108.

In December Connecticut had organized a state Council of Defense in an effort to coordinate the proliferating war efforts. Hanford S. Weed was put in charge of New Canaan's defense and became head of the Draft Exemption Board. Under him, H. B. Thayer served as president of the local War Bureau, charged with merging local committees on food conservation, health, and sanitation. At the same time, Mr. Thayer also headed a highway survey made for the town.

With the beginning of 1918, New Canaan, like the rest of the east, faced a coal shortage. To conserve fuel, the Library closed for two months; classes at Center School were merged so that some classrooms could be shut; and the Congregational meeting house was kept so cold that its pipes burst and the church forced to hold Sunday services upstairs in Raymond Hall. Everyone and every organization did its best. Nevertheless, beginning January 21, New Canaan initiated "heatless and lightless Mondays," when even candles and oil stoves were forbidden. Except for six places (such as the town hall), everything was dark, though street lights did burn at night. Banks and stores closed Mondays at noon and the railroad went on a holiday schedule. As Mr. Thayer pointed out frequently, New Canaan coal yards were almost empty, and scheduled shipments often were rerouted elsewhere. But there was wood, and the Board of Education authorized burning wood at the schools. By February, New Canaan was in the midst of a measles epidemic, which spread from the army camps to undernourished children in underheated schoolrooms for a total of 167 cases. (The heatless Mondays lasted until March.)

On February 21, when New Canaan held another war rally in the town hall, the town had just learned of its first war casualty—Albert Tompkins and 11 other firemen on the *U.S. Grant* had been smothered under coal being loaded into bunkers—and New Canaan put up its first gold star on its outdoor Honor Roll. Designed by Augustus M. Gerdes, the Honor Roll was a gift of the Poinsettia Club and stood on the town hall lawn for all passersby to see. Well before that, the town knew that M. Farmer Murphey was in Paris, heading his newspaper's war bureau, while two of its local physicians were in uniform—Dr. O'Shaughnessy and Dr. Ralph E. White (who soon would be overseas).

Besides a Third Liberty Loan drive in April 1918—quota $105,600, amount raised in one month $230,200—a National War Savings Committee had been formed under Mrs. Francis H. Adriance, appointed by the state director. No school child was considered too young or too poor to fill a book with savings stamps, and to encourage one and all there was a war stamp rally and later a Thrift Stamp Gala. Girls who could knit were recruited into a Junior Red Cross, while some ladies who weren't working daily for the Red Cross formed a uniformed motor corps, called the Women's Relief Corps. Though New Canaan had fingerprinted its resident "enemy aliens," it also had established a night school for the foreign-born, taught by volunteers.

After a 1918 state survey had shown New Canaan intended to have fewer acres under cultivation than the year before, 225 children were enrolled in a Junior Food Army, again under the Plant, Flower and Fruit Guild, which created small plots on land on lower Main Street and on Prospect Heights (off Bank Street). With so many young men in the service, more hands were needed on New Canaan's remaining farms, so under Mrs. Lewis H. Lapham, 10 members of the Woman's Farm Movement were installed (and chaperoned) in the old Nathan Comstock house on Valley Road (now No. 393), from whence they hired out as helpers to farmers and other large gardeners.

The food situation worsened as summer neared, and Mrs. Adriance, now also New Canaan's food director, set limits of two pounds of sugar for families in town and five pounds for rural residents. (Later a 15-pound bonus was allowed for canning.) Every week demonstrations of wartime recipes were held in the town hall, with prizes offered for "Hooverized dishes." (Herbert C. Hoover, the U.S. food administrator, had proclaimed "Food will win the war.) By August "lightless nights" had been adopted for Mondays through Thursdays; in September came "gasolineless Sundays." Since June the Canning Club was in full swing, this time under a trained home economics director, while every woman with a spare minute was engaged in some sort of war work. In his annual report in September 1918 the first selectman could write, "the Town Hall is used almost constantly in connection for war work from which, of course, no income is derived or desired," although wear and tear was beginning to show. And by fall orders had come from the War Industries Board through the Red Cross that everyone was to save and turn in platinum (!), tin, fruit pits, and nut shells. By then the Red Cross was spending $400 per month on materials.

Red Letter days in New Canaan in 1918 included a showing of U.S. war films at the Colonial Theatre (April); a visit of the 20-mule team of Borax Bill from Death Valley, promoting Liberty bonds; a glimpse of an observation dirigible that landed in Wilton, the first dirigible New Canaan had ever seen (both in May); and the arrival of a special four-car train carrying trophies captured at the Battle of the Marne, plus an unexpected view of a DeHaviland warplane out of Mineola that crashed in Vista, with no casualties (both in September). But as more and more New Canaan men reported to army camps, word reached New Canaan in August that, first, Alfred Taylor, a machine gunner in Co. C, 165th Infantry, and then Capt. Henry E. Kelley had been wounded at the front. In October Lt. George R. Stevens, Jr., was wounded and two other New Canaan men died of pneumonia in camps in this country.

One fund-raising drive was hardly over when another began, and New Canaan was just starting a United War Work campaign when on Nov. 7, 1918, pandemonium broke loose as the town celebrated the false armistice. The firebell rang and rang; business came to a standstill as everyone poured into the streets; children let out of school formed an impromptu parade, followed in the evening by an organized one—all adding up to a never-to-be-forgotten day. Celebration of the real armistice on November 11 began at 3 A.M. as church bells rang out, bonfires were lit, and as much noise as possible was raised all over town. Again there were two parades, each again led by the Town Band, some 500 children marching in the afternoon. Joy was obviously unrestrained, and for good measure the Kaiser was burned in effigy.

The end of the war didn't mean the end of wartime conditions for the town. More servicemen were to die from pneumonia or flu, and on the Honor Roll, then totaling 244 names, a gold star was affixed to seven of them. (In subsequent reports to the State Adjutant General the figures were changed at least twice.) Food shortages continued, with Victory gardens being pushed, and postwar inflation was about to send prices skyrocketing. Despite the arrival of a whippet tank for display, the Victory Loan of April 1919 dragged, though New Canaan got behind the Near East Relief drive.

Main Street on Armistice Day 1918, when the schoolchildren's parade had ended. Capt. H. E. Kelley (in trench coat) is behind his father Postmaster Henry Kelley (upraised arm) in the parked car.

The Wayside Cross

Ever since June 1917, when a Soldiers' and Sailors' Fund was started with a benefit in the town hall, New Canaan had been preparing to welcome its returning men. Banquets had been given for individuals or groups of veterans, but the big celebration came on Sept. 30, 1919, an all-day holiday. Originally, the committee headed by Police Chief Schmidt and C. E. T. Fairty had intended to honor only the men who had seen service overseas, but as plans for the celebration grew Spanish American War veterans and the 12 surviving members of the G.A.R. were included. As for the 1901 centennial, streets and buildings were decorated with bunting; horns and confetti proliferated; and at 2 P.M. a parade began. While eight of New Canaan's wounded veterans rode in cars, some 120 uniformed veterans marched behind Col. Marshal Stearns over flowers children had strewn in the line of march. Among the hundreds of participants were Red Cross ladies in cars and the Women's Relief Corps. This time the route was short and ended on South Avenue, so that the men could easily reach the ball park where a special baseball game was played. Late in the afternoon some 175 soldiers and sailors were photographed behind the town hall, where a festive clambake was afterward served to them. The evening ended with a gala carnival and dance.

Despite the hard work of several committees, no memorial to the soldiers of World War I ever materialized—but not for lack of plans. A commemorative plaque on a native boulder did not seem enough, and the addition of a wing to the town hall was voted down. An offer of land on South Main Street led to the design of a much-needed community center, complete with gymnasium, lockers, and stage. (The auditorium in the town hall was all that New Canaan could then offer for basketball games, and the newly formed Veterans of Foreign Wars and American Legion post were in need of a meeting place.) But by 1921 a depression had set in, and the necessary money simply was not available to build a center.

After the idea of a granite shaft to stand in front of the town hall was rejected, such money as was on hand was turned over to a committee, headed by H. B. Thayer, which settled on a stone cross in memory of New Canaan's veterans of four wars. Designed by

Frances Adams Kent, a sculptor who had been a student of Gutzon Borglum, supervised by W. Frank Purdy, a local architect, and D. Putnam Brinley, and executed by Presby, Leland Co., New York monument company of which Ernest Leland of St. John Place was a member, the Wayside Cross was unveiled at the foot of God's Acre on Sunday, Sept. 9, 1923. Some 2,000 civilians and veterans were on hand for the impressive ceremony at which Maj. Gen. John F. O'Ryan, who commanded the 27th Division in France, and Adm. Robert P. Forshew, commandant of the 2d Naval District, spoke. (To provide a backdrop for the Cross, Stephen Hoyt of the Nurseries gave New Canaan a second Christmas tree, which was planted on God's Acre in 1926, where the fourth and present Christmas tree now is.)

Growth

By the end of World War I, the attractions of New Canaan as a residential town were well recognized. The war years had seen several more summer families turn into year-round residents, and they were soon followed by friends and strangers, who quit New

Citizens, soldiers, and celebrities gathered for the unveiling of the Wayside Cross at the foot of God's Acre.

York and its suburbs to raise their children in the country. Padraic Colum, the Irish poet, Robert Flaherty, Arctic explorer, and John Erskine, Columbia professor and author now lived in New Canaan, and they were followed by Maxwell E. Perkins, editor, William Rose Benet, poet, and by artists, engineers, bankers, inventors, lawyers, corporate presidents—the list could go on and on.

Besides an increase in the number of real estate firms, this influx meant the breaking up of some of the former summer estates, beginning in 1928 when the property of the late John B. Gerrish on the west side of Oenoke Ridge was subdivided and Gerrish Lane opened up. By 1929, the year in which some 50 new houses were built, New Canaan counted a total of 1,800 property owners and had a grand list of $16,000,000. By 1930, New Canaan's population had grown to 5,431, an almost 40-percent increase over the 1920 Census figure of 3,895, and commuters to New York now represented almost half of the working male population.

One result of the 1930 Census figure was that New Canaan, with more than 5,000 residents, automatically was entitled to two representatives in the state legislature. That fall Mrs. Nellie D. Stewart, wife of Walter Stewart, won election as a Republican—New Canaan's first woman representative—while John L. Stevens, another Republican, was endorsed by the Democrats and elected on that ticket; hence he had to sit on the Democratic side of the legislature.

It wasn't long before New Canaan's activities proliferated in answer to the wants of older and newer residents—a music week and a Community Orchestra with its concerts, the Bird Sanctuary and a weekly bird column in the *Advertiser,* a story-telling hour at the Library, a Republican Women's Club, dancing schools, a French club, and affiliation of the Civic League with the state League of Women Voters. Solon Borglum died in 1922, and that year the Silvermine Guild of Artists was formed, its exhibits soon replacing those of his Silvermine Group of Artists. Two new country clubs and a swimming club opened in the area, and New Canaan formed a Bridle Path Association and a skating club. In and outside the town, horse shows and polo matches were regular summer events, while for several successive years the state women's tennis championship was played at the Country Club of

New Canaan. Where its first college students had attended Yale, New Canaan by 1926 could say that its 38 resident Harvard graduates gave it more Harvard men per capita than any other town in the country, and a Harvard Club was formed.

The town also had two new religious denominations. In 1922 the African Methodist Episcopal Church (now the Community Baptist Church) began as a mission and worshiped in Raymond Hall until its building on Cherry Street Extension was completed in 1931. In 1923 the Church of Christ, Scientist began holding regular services in the Playhouse, before occupying a building on Elm Street. (Its Park Street edifice was completed in 1954.)

Elm Street

One immediate result of so many new people was a new movie theatre—this time on Elm Street. From South Avenue to Park Street, Elm Street was vacant land, except for one residence on the south side, and opposite this lone house the New Canaan Playhouse opened on Sept. 19, 1923, with a showing of "Down to the Sea in Ships."

This cupolaed building was designed by Calvin E. Kiessling, a new architect in town, as part of an orderly development of Elm Street. Foreseeing the need for new stores and offices, a group of local men formed the Village Improvement Co., and the red brick and white trim Playhouse, suggesting a modified colonial structure, established the style for the future buildings that eventually filled in both sides of Elm. On Main Street the Colonial Theatre closed, and in 1925 the Civic League bought the old Opera House building it had been occupying and renamed it the Village Hall, renting it out for dances, women's gym classes, prizefight bouts, and various other events. But the Civic League could not meet its mortgage payments and the Savings Bank foreclosed in 1928. The Opera House later was torn down, and a one-story building (Nos. 78-80 Main Street) erected on the site.

Opposite the Playhouse, Alfred Mausolff, Silvermine architect and son-in-law of Austin Lord, designed a compatible building, also with a cupola. Into this on July 1, 1930, moved the New Canaan post office and there it remained until 1958, when lack of parking forced it to move to Pine Street. (This building is now No.

94 Elm Street, occupied by State National Bank.) By then, Elm Street had been widened nearly 20 feet on the south side, and just west of the Playhouse the *Advertiser* in 1927 had moved into a one-story brick office and printing plant. Then, in 1931, between South Avenue and the post office, ground was broken for the Colonial Building (Nos. 136-164 Elm). But completion of this building and the other Elm Street stores was delayed for some years by the depression and the bankruptcy of the Village Improvement Co.

Town and Borough

What was not keeping pace with all the new developments was the town government and services. On Dec. 17, 1920, a special town meeting had voted 214 to 98 in favor of consolidating the town and borough governments. Months of work had gone into preparing a plan which eliminated all borough officers and, in addition to the three town selectmen, added a town manager, directly under the Board of Finance. By July 1921 opinion had shifted—too much power, it was said, would be put into the hands of one man (the town manager)—and in a large turnout consolidation was voted down by one vote—356-355.

The number of votes reflected the fact that the 19th amendment to the U. S. Constitution had gone into effect on Aug. 26, 1920, and by election time 379 New Canaan women had registered to vote, bringing the town's electorate to 1,580. (With the 1920 presidential election, which saw Warren G. Harding become president, New Canaan gave itself a small claim to fame—Mrs. Harding's mother, Louisa Bouton, had been born in New Canaan in 1835 and been married from the Main Street house that later was Dr. Brownson's home.)

In 1925 consolidation again came up for vote, the legislature having approved another charter that called for an eight-man town council and the usual three selectmen, with the first selectman being the equivalent of a mayor. Again it went down to defeat amid rumors that the Civic League ladies were planning to elect themselves constables. So for another ten years New Canaan would retain its two governments and the police would remain under borough control.

The 18th amendment to the constitution was also in effect, and since January 1920 New Canaan and its police had been coping with prohibition. New Canaan was no better and no worse than other towns in obeying the Volstead Act. Though saloons were closed, former bartenders brewed beer in home kitchens; grocery stores (for known customers) carried their "private label" brands of gin and applejack (you made a cocktail by mixing equal parts of applejack, grapefruit juice, and maple syrup); and flasks and bottles were seen at private parties and dances—until May 1933, when beer was legal again. As a result, sometimes the local police but more often the state police stopped trucks and raided premises of those suspected of bootlegging, the borough going so far as to hire detectives on occasion to produce evidence. As in the earlier "dry" years, those arrested paid their fines and went right on making and selling illegal liquor and wine.

Back in November 1919, the Board of Warden and Burgesses had threatened to ignore police calls outside the borough, where its small force was spending the better part of its time. The police force then consisted of three men, who in March 1920 were given pay increases: Chief Otto Schmidt to $37 from $30 a week, and patrolmen Charles Kaiser and LeRoy Reynolds were raised from $95 to $120 a month. The next month a special town meeting voted to give the borough $178.50 towards its police expenses, and in May the borough, in return, voted to appoint Patrolman Kaiser to be town dog warden under the borough chief of police. (Do you wonder why consolidation was needed?) Although the town budgeted around $1,000 for the Library and $1,500 for the fire company, this special 1920 appropriation was the first support given the police. Thereafter the annual appropriation increased steadily.

All along the police had no headquarters but operated from Chief Schmidt's home, the second-floor apartment over Fairty's feed and grain store in the building that stood where No. 125 Main Street now is. From his bay window the Chief or his men could look up and down Main Street and respond immediately to trouble or traffic jams. After 1927 the police headquarters were theoretically in the courtroom in the town hall, but the policemen on duty were never there. They were out on the street, and if you had an emergency, you asked the telephone operator to ring 81.

That was a police telephone on a Main Street pole, which would be answered only if someone heard it ring.

A special act of the legislature had made a radical change in New Canaan's system of justice, and on July 1, 1927, the historic justice of the peace court was replaced by a town court. This was presided over by an appointed judge who, in turn, appointed a prosecuting attorney. The old system of fees gave way to fixed salaries, and instead of being irregularly held in some J. P.'s office, New Canaan's town court sat regularly, usually one evening a week, in a new courtroom in the town hall. The first judge was John D. Fearhake, who was appointed by the state legislature on the recommendation of Dr. Walter C. Wood, then New Canaan's representative, who was relaying the decision of the Republican Town Committee. The first prosecuting attorney (and the second judge) was Stanley P. Mead. And from 1927 on, most of the cases they tried were related to bootlegging. Appeal from decisions could still be taken to the Fairfield County court of common pleas.

Along with bootlegging came an increase in thefts and a large increase in juvenile delinquency, so that in the fall of 1926 the town offered the borough an annual contribution of $2,000, if the borough would hire another policeman. This the borough did, and in 1928 purchased its first patrol car and a police motorcycle. In 1929, with its police budget up to $16,000, the borough withdrew police protection from the town. Constables and the state police could cope with calls outside the borough limits—unless the town appropriated the $4,000 recommended by its Finance Board for the borough's police force. The borough did get this sum from the town, but not until it had agreed to have one of the selectmen serve *ex officio* on its police committee.

Education

What was definitely not keeping pace with the town's growth were the schools. When the war ended, School Superintendent Henry W. Saxe could report that Center School had a lunch program and a school nurse (paid by the Red Cross), who could call on a school physician when need arose. But, he warned, Center School was badly overcrowded. Although the town in 1919 bought the adjoining property to the south, no money was appropriated to build an addition to Center School, and by 1922, with the kindergarten and six classes on a part-time schedule, a portable building had to be set up in the schoolyard. Not until 1924 was a four-room addition completed.

By then, besides some 110 New Canaan students attending high school in Stamford, 884 children were enrolled in the town's public schools, with 176 attending the remaining three district schools: Church Hill school on West Road, the Talmadge Hill school on lower Weed Street, and the Little Red Schoolhouse on Carter Street.

The next year (1925) Stamford forced New Canaan's hand by voting that 1925-26 would be the last academic year when its high school would accept nonresidents. New Canaan had no choice but to build its own high school, and where to build was the question before a whole series of town meetings beginning in September 1925. From six possible sites, the town meeting of October 9 picked Mead Park—and two weeks later the next town meeting rescinded the vote. Then, on November 18, another town meeting accepted the gift of four and a half acres of land on the east side of South Avenue, between Church and Oak streets. The donors were Mr. and Mrs. Bardend Van Gerbig, who since 1912 had been summer residents on Smith Ridge. (The *Advertiser* several times had reported the large gifts made by Mrs. Van Gerbig to the Association against the Prohibition Amendment, because she thought prohibition was a farce. Unreported was her generosity to almost every local sports team, though stories are still told of how she could always be counted on for a contribution.)

Work on the new high school (not to cost more than $150,000) was well under way when the United States celebrated its 150th anniversary. Because July 4, 1926, fell on a Sunday, New Canaan celebrated the Sesquicentennial on July 5 with an impressive parade and the dedication of its first high school. Marchers and floats made an early start so that the parade would arrive on South Avenue in good time for the ceremonies that began at 11 A.M. With the basement nearly complete and the brick walls of the auditorium-gymnasium half up, the cornerstone was laid by Francis E. Green, chairman, and Henry Kelley, a member of the Board of Education.

When the first Board of Education had been elected in June 1894, ten candidates had run for the nine places, Henry Kelley (1861-1949) losing out, though only by three votes. The next year he was elected to the Board on which he thereafter served continuously until he died. A tree nurseryman, who would do more than any other individual to beautify the town, and one of the original members of the Mead Park board, he had just completed 10 years as New Canaan's postmaster, having been appointed by President Woodrow Wilson in 1915. (When the Little Red Schoolhouse, which he had attended, closed in June 1957, his daughter Mary J. Kelley was the schoolteacher.)

In the cornerstone Kelley helped to lay is a list of historic events in New Canaan between 1876 and 1926, as compiled by the Historical Society and the D.A.R. The principal speaker that 1926 day was John Erskine, English professor at Columbia University. (After years of disuse, the porticoed red brick building they dedicated was converted into New Canaan's police station in 1980-81.)

Until the new high school was useable, some New Canaan high school seniors had to finish their courses at Stamford, while others attended classes in a town-owned residence on South Avenue. Hence the class that graduated in 1930 was the first that spent all four high school years in New Canaan. But, despite the large sums New Canaan thought it was spending on education—$86,852 out of a total town expenditure of $290,128—state figures for 1928 showed that New Canaan spent only $85.56 per pupil, almost $10 under the state average of $94.90 and far below the figures for Greenwich and Darien.

When it opened, the New Canaan high school had 349 students in six grades, with 160 in grades 7 and 8. Overcrowding soon was evident so grades 7 and 8 were sent back to overcrowd Center School. This time New Canaan did not delay an appropriation for a junior high school, and by 1931 ground had been broken immediately north of the high school on the Van Gerbig tract. When the Henry W. Saxe Junior High School opened in 1932, it was composed of grades 7, 8, and 9, grades 10 through 12 attending the high school. In his annual report for that year, Mr. Saxe stressed that the New Canaan schools now offered manual training and other practical courses on a par with its college-preparatory ones. The depression was pointing up the need for vocational skills.

CHAPTER 11

A Sense of Community, 1931-1951

The impact of the stock market crash on New Canaan had been reported in the *Advertiser* for Nov. 14, 1929, with gratuitous comments on the foolish speculations of people unnamed who had been wiped out. Unquestionably, some people in New Canaan were hard hit by the crash, but, as elsewhere, it was a while before the effects were felt as a growing depression. Salaries were cut, spending was curtailed, unpaid taxes began to mount, and men lost their jobs as factories and businesses in the area were forced to cut back. By the winter of 1930-31, New Canaan had more than 100 men unemployed and 20 families in serious need.

The Depression

New Canaan was no better prepared to meet the depression than any other community, but it was still a "Yankee" town with traditions of caring for its own. New Canaan had neither a social worker nor a department of welfare, so when the selectmen were inundated with appeals for help, private citizens and private organizations stepped into the breech.

For its 1930-31 fiscal year, the town had budgeted only its usual $5,000 for "Outside Needy"; the poor farm was no more. Because of the expense, talk of closing the farm had begun at the turn of the century, and from 1913 on the Finance Board had denounced the growing deficit. But not until March 1921 did a New Canaan town meeting vote to close the poor house. Although by the summer of 1923 the last three inmates had been transferred to the Norwalk almshouse, the farm and its buildings had not been sold until 1928. Now, with families facing eviction for nonpayment of rent or lacking money to buy coal, the town could not relocate them, and the selectmen were faced with a shortage of needed funds.

On Dec. 1, 1930, the Visiting Nurse Association opened its first thrift shop in a rented room, to sell donated warm clothing and shoes at the lowest possible prices to those in need. (Two months later the Thrift Shop was operating rent free in a store next to the Main Street post office in the old Rogers Block.) One week later the League of Women Voters set up a winter Employment Bureau to register men who wanted work. At the same time, the privately organized New Canaan Unemployment Committee also listed unemployed men, and every morning, in a shed behind S. B. Hoyt's greenhouse opposite the Library, assigned men to such jobs as had been listed with it. (This committee also had some money for relief, for it had raised $1,750 from individuals and through a "Golden Rule" Sunday collection in the churches.) New Canaan people and firms did respond to committee pleas to hire New Canaan's unemployed, but in four months the League of Women Voters could provide only 372½ hours of work for a total of 139 men, while jobs given out by the Unemployment Committee amounted to less than two days of work per week for the men listed with it.

Anyone who can remember the depression knows how gloomy were those days. Men wanted work, not charity, and when work was not available, morale sagged. So, cooperating with the private committees, the selectmen obtained an additional $3,000 appropriation, transferred monies from other accounts, and put some 60 men temporarily to work on the highways and Mead Park, well aware that the jobs would be performed better and more economically by trained workers.

If New Canaan was prepared "to care for its own," care of its black residents was given grudgingly. Though consistently just under 1 percent of its population had been black, descendants of the original black families were gone, most dying from tuberculosis, and the newer families had come here as servants from New York or in search of work from the South. Yankee prejudice was so strong that black residents were not welcome in local stores, restaurants, or the Playhouse (though young men who were athletes were popular members of sports teams), and doors were slammed in the faces of blacks seeking to rent. That situation was cracked by Clarence King of Silvermine Road, on the faculty of the New York School of Social Work, who with his wife quietly bought up housing along East and Baldwin Avenues, which they resold to black families. Nor were Jews welcomed as residents. Since the days when Constable Louis Drucker was a small-scale clothing manufacturer, New Canaan accepted as part of the business scene the stores run by Jews, but *Gentleman's Agreement*, that novel about real estate discrimination, was written as much about New Canaan as Darien, where it presumably was laid.

Foreseeing another difficult winter, the Visiting Nurse Association called a meeting on July 6, 1931, at which eight prominent men and women agreed to form the New Canaan Committee on Relief, to coordinate public and private efforts. This committee also appealed directly to the churches and other benevolent organizations, raising $8,587 in the next six months. But by then New Canaan had 156 men and 6 women unemployed, who were responsible for 361 dependents.

Amid hardship and despair, private charity was enormous and largely anonymous, while those who had the means created such jobs as they could. To give work to carpenters, masons, and painters, Mrs. Merrill F. Clarke, wife of the Congregational minister, had a 1795 house at Harwinton, Conn., carefully taken down, moved to New Canaan, and reassembled on her father's former summer estate at 585 Canoe Hill Road (where it still stands). Another private citizen commissioned a sculptor to create two outdoor statues, which were given to the Bird Sanctuary, while others became patrons of hard-pressed artists. Amid criticism, debutante parties were held, making a bit of work for florists, musicians, and caterers, but the depression was too widespread for individual spending to have much effect.

As the situation worsened, New Canaan organizations mobilized much as they had in World War I, but cooperation was lacking until in December 1932 the New Canaan Committee on Relief hired Miss Violet Babcock, a trained social worker, to interview, investigate, and determine the needs of all applicants for relief. By the following June she had been put on the selectmen's payroll, and at the same time the town voted a special tax of 1 mill for unemployment relief and established a bipartisan Board of Charity, which soon became the Department of Welfare. When the 1932-33 fiscal year ended, New Canaan had spent $41,000 on rents, fuel, clothing, food, and medical care plus another $25,000 in work relief on highways and the park.

Toward Consolidation

Spurred by the need to cut every possible expense, consolidation of the town and borough government again came to the fore. The town, but not the borough, had voted down consolidation in August 1931, but a special town meeting of Mar. 16, 1933, authorized the selectmen to appoint a five-man committee to draft one more charter, and Representative Stanley P. Mead introduced a skeleton charter bill in the legislature. Doing an about-face, many people now realized that borough improvements and services benefited everyone and that borough taxpayers, few of whom were wealthy, bore the entire expense.

Although consolidation would not be voted until June 5, 1935—509 for, 360 against in the town poll, 291 for and 67 against in the borough—the adjourned annual meeting of Oct. 7, 1933, voted $15,000 for police and traffic light expenses for the coming 10½ months, after which both would be turned over to the town by the borough. To this the borough agreed, and that month turned over the functions and property of its police committee to the town's new police commission, composed of the three selectmen and an appointee from each of the two major parties. Since then, New Canaan's police department has functioned under the town.

All along the police had been busy investigating crime all over the town. The depression had caused a huge increase in robbery and in juvenile delinquency, for the many closed residences were easily entered and often so isolated that burglaries went undiscovered for weeks. Until the men were caught, at least one ring operated out of Westchester County, looting silver, linens, and rugs from a number of houses. Closed houses also offered a temptation to boys, as much in search of something to do as of cash, and juvenile delinquency grew so serious during the depression that Connecticut established the first of its juvenile courts, starting July 1, 1935, with those for Fairfield and Windham counties. As its first psychiatrist, the Fairfield County Juvenile Court appointed Dr. Daniel Blain of New Canaan. He had come to New Canaan to join Dr. John A. P. Millet, formerly of Riggs sanitarium in Stockbridge, Mass., and on Nov. 14, 1932, both men were incorporators of Silver Hill, the private psychiatric hospital still functioning on Valley Road. (In 1943, Stanley P. Mead, one of the prime legislature movers of the juvenile court bill, was named judge of the First District Juvenile Court, covering both Fairfield and Litchfield counties.)

Federal Funds

Just before welfare became "an almost unbearable burden on our small community," federal funds became available with the organization of the first of the "alphabet" agencies started by the Roosevelt administration to get people back to work.

New Canaan as a whole had no love for Franklin D. Roosevelt, and like the state had given Hoover a majority of its votes in November 1932—Hoover 1,426, Roosevelt 746. (Not as a reward for its vote but because a close friend lived here, Herbert Hoover on Mar. 5, 1933, his first day out of office, drove from New York to lunch in New Canaan with Edgar Rickard at No. 481 Canoe Hill Road. While she was first lady, Mrs. Hoover had paid two visits to New Canaan, on the occasions of the weddings of the Rickards' two daughters.)

When the NRS (National Reemployment Service) started in the fall of 1933, 450 New Canaan unemployed registered for work, and when the CWA (Civil Works Administration) began in November, funds were available to employ 126. Because New Canaan had already prepared a long list of approved projects that would put people back to work, this quota was upped to 275 within three weeks. Outside the quota, funds were available for 40 more to work as teachers, county census takers, and on art projects.

CWA was abolished on Mar. 31, 1934, and the FERA (Federal Emergency Relief Administration) took over. This, in turn, was succeeded in 1935 by the WPA (Works Progress Administration). By 1935, though the number had fallen, New Canaan still had 1,130 individuals in 262 families on welfare—1 out of every 8, the same as the rest of the country. The town had spent $64,903 of its own money on relief, while CWA and FERA funds totaled $73,704 more.

New Canaan had every reason to be proud of how these (and future) federal grants had been spent, primarily on needed town and borough projects that otherwise would have been delayed for years. Roads had been greatly improved, several dangerous curves had been eliminated, and to avoid head-on collisions, the town in the course of its road work had created the small triangles at several intersections (now planted and maintained by the Garden Center). (Toward the end of the WPA in 1939-40, Laurel Road was improved and a new Mariomi Road built to join Cheese Spring road, though together they made a different route than the one over which Susan Anderson and the town had battled nearly 50 years before.) Woods had been cleared of dead trees, providing some firewood for needy families; Dutch Elm disease and mosquito spraying had been accomplished; the town hall, the firehouse on Elm Street, and the schools all had been repaired and painted, but what happened at Mead Park came close to being a miracle.

A hole in that problem swamp had been dynamited to form a lake with an island, after which the land around the lake had been filled in. Roads and retaining walls were built; the baseball field got a backstop and the athletic teams, a stone locker house; tennis courts were improved; a summer park director was hired to keep an eye on nearly 90 children who were sent to Mead Park to play while parents worked; and trees and shrubs were planted, the gifts of generous nurseries and individuals. But that wasn't all.

Since New Canaan had the unenviable record of having the highest number of unemployed white-collar workers per capita of any town in the state, other WPA projects were designed for them. As a result, a sewing room was set up (which continued until 1939), where women made garments for the town's needy from government-supplied materials. Surveyors and other engineers mapped the entire town, setting up boundary markers, while teams were sent to the Norwalk and Stamford town clerk's offices to copy all pertinent land records antedating incorporations in 1801. These now comprise four volumes and an index on the New Canaan's town clerk's shelves. With artists and sculptors hard hit, the town commissioned art projects, the results of which were publicly exhibited. Many works of art later were placed in the school buildings and in the town hall, where today a collection of water colors hangs in the Board of Finance room. In the town hall auditorium still are two decorative maps of New Canaan, though a large mural on the east wall had to be removed when the auditorium ceiling was lowered. (Half of that is now in East School.)

A severe recession in 1937 sent relief rolls up, tax collections down, and had the Welfare Board complaining that too many children were born while families were on relief and that relief money was not spent properly. Of a total budget for 1937-38, 10 percent went to welfare (including a $3,000 milk fund that provided 29,831 quarts of milk to 351 undernourished children). Next year, with the town hard put to find suitable employment projects, welfare accounted for 11.9 percent of the annual budget. The depression really did not wane until the national defense efforts in 1939 created private employment in this area.

One project proposed by the selectmen for WPA funds never materialized—a town-operated water supply through purchase of the New Canaan Water Co. But, in 1937-38, the town with WPA money did build the present firehouse on the Main Street-Locust Avenue corner and added two wings to the front of the town hall. From its shared quarters with the town court the police department then moved into the basement of the left wing—only to find itself so removed from other town offices that it had to hire a clerk to take messages and calls. (Previously, the town clerk, across the hall from the court, had done that when the policemen were out patroling.) By then, the town hall also housed New Canaan's new probate court.

The Probate Court

In Canaan Parish days the estates of those who died on the Norwalk side of the Parish were probated in Fairfield and those on the Stamford side in the Stamford probate court. Then in 1802, one year after it was founded, New Canaan together with Wilton was put under the new Norwalk probate court and was annually assessed a small sum for the court's operation. Along with consolidation, a bill to create a town probate court had been introduced in the legislature, but died in committee. Convinced that, despite the depression, New Canaan was developing fast enough to warrant its own court, supporters of the proposal made a second try, and on June 22, 1937, a legislative act created the New Canaan probate court. With both parties promising to run a layman and not a lawyer for judge, the Republicans nominated Lawrence P. Frothingham, who for years had served the borough as a burgess and was then the unpaid chairman of the town's department of welfare. He was elected, Oct. 5, 1937, and sworn in the following January as New Canaan's first judge of probate.

New Developments

For the 90 percent of the people who retained their jobs and their incomes, money went a long way during the depression, and New Canaan real estate sales and rentals held up. At least 20 new roads were built during the 1930's, primarily to open up property for development. By 1935 Turtleback Road had been started through former Mulliken land on the west side of upper Oenoke Ridge, while custom-built houses went up along Dan's Highway and Pinney Road. In 1937 Miss Ruth M. Child subdivided what had been her parents' estate at West Road and Weed Street by laying out Sunset Hill Road. Sunrise Avenue opened up land on the east side of Marshall Ridge. "Kelly's Woods," once owned by Richard Kelly of Weed Street, whose vision of timbering profits was ruined by the chestnut blight, saw Wood's End Road and Dogwood Lane laid out at opposite ends of the tract, while in the Valley Road section, Colonial Road and Deer Park Road opened other properties as did Briscoe Road off North Wilton. And Chichester Road, which had become impassible, was given a new lease on life by Robertson Ward, a new architect in town.

Neither his own house nor those he designed for others are among those that today make Chichester Road a showcase of the contemporary architecture for which New Canaan is so famous, but Ward was architect of New Canaan's first "modern" house, built in 1937 at No. 909 West Road, and called "Five Wells." Few people remember today the curiosity and the acid remarks called forth by this house, as old timers and newcomers alike drove out to "sidewalk superintend" its construction, all feeling qualified to comment—unfavorably. The "what-was-good-enough-for-grandpa" school dominated ("It looks like a jail"), although a few sophisticated observers ("I still don't think I'd like to live there") were content to point out that a white cinderblock house did not belong in a New England landscape. Overlooked today on the map of New Canaan's modern houses and more properly termed "transitional" rather than "contemporary" architecture, what Robertson Ward designed was a house on six levels to fit the contours of an unusual site—a steep bank at the edge of the Rippowam River where the remains of a mill pond dam could still be seen—once owned by the counterfeiting Slauson brothers.

New Canaan had adopted zoning before "Five Wells" or any contemporary houses were built. Only a little behind Stamford and Darien, a special town meeting on Feb. 27, 1932, voted to create a Town Planning and Zoning Commission and a Board of Zoning Appeal. Members of both were appointed in March, and on May 23 the Commission approved the first zoning map, which identified three residential, a business, and an industrial zone. Outside the borough center and its existing streets all land was put into a two-acre zone. The four-acre zone would come later; the industrial zone would be eliminated; many changes would be made and controversies and lawsuits arise, but New Canaan had taken its first step toward planning an orderly development that would maintain the good appearance of a town that attracted more and more new residents.

When zoning was adopted, New Canaan was not served by either New Norwalk Road (Route 123) or the Merritt Parkway, though the state was at work on the former. To create a Norwalk-Pound Ridge through highway, Connecticut in 1931 had bought a long strip of land from Hoyt Nurseries, running from the east end of present Old Norwalk Road to the east side of the Mill Pond, and from there laid out the route to the upper end of Forest Street. How the road was to run from Forest Street to Pinney's Corner at the upper end of Oenoke Ridge, the state left for the town to decide.

Three possible routes were proposed—(A) along Parade Hill to Oenoke, (B) up Smith Ridge to turn west across a part of Michigan and undeveloped land, and (C) diagonally northwestward from Forest Street across virgin land, Lambert Road, and the Country Club to the east side of the Reservoir—and all hell broke loose. No one wanted a state highway anywhere near their home. A very vocal special town meeting on Aug. 10, 1931, voted 235 for B, 231 for C, and 7 for A, and the town meeting of August 25 rescinded that vote by 468 to 430. The next meeting on September 4 voted 814 in favor of C, 668 for B, and 17 for A—the rising number of votes reflecting the rising tempers. There the matter rested for three years.

By 1935 the state, using FERA money, had completed New Norwalk Road, paying 35 cents per hour for unskilled labor. New Canaan followed suit and reduced the pay of its unskilled from 50 to 35 cents, causing irate petitions from those affected. If today these wages sound like "slave labor," in the 1930's such hourly rates were not out of line. And every man working on a project involving federal funds could work only up to the limit of his need as certified by the Welfare Board, after which another man was put to work. That certified need took into consideration the food prices of the day—27 cents for a pound of coffee, 5 cents for a large can of evaporated milk, 19 cents for two boxes of shredded wheat, 25 cents for three cans of pork and beans. In the end, how Route 123 was continued boiled down to dollars and cents. When the Board of Finance in 1934 recommended acceptance of plan B, only 99 people turned out to vote (63 yes, 36 no) because the town had no other choice. The cost of connecting with Smith Ridge would amount to $103,870, with the federal government paying $47,729 of the sum. New Canaan's share was to be $9,300, but since it already had allocated $7,615 for the road, the town actually had to pay only $1,694.90 for the road. So Route 123 never linked Norwalk to Pound Ridge but instead runs across Vista, N.Y.

As first proposed, the route of the Merritt Parkway would have crossed New Canaan much farther north than where it now runs—across the southern tip of the town. The first route would have crossed Cascade Road and then Oenoke Ridge, well north of the borough line, but by 1932 the state had settled on the present route, though no federal funds were yet available. Instead of condemning property, Connecticut bought the land for the Merritt outright, and it wasn't long after construction began late in 1933 (at the western end in Greenwich) that New Canaan was again up in arms, as accounts of profiteering appeared in newspapers, followed by trials of some agents.

The Merritt Parkway is named for Schuyler Merritt of Greenwich, then U. S. congressman from this area, and it was built largely with federal money to be paid back from tolls. Some of that money went to employ sculptors and craftsmen who designed the Parkway's many overpasses. Next time you travel over the Merritt, look at these, for no two bridges are alike. When the Merritt Parkway was opened in 1938, New Canaan, linked by Old Stamford Road, South Avenue, and Route 123, was far more accessible than before, when motorists had to use Route 1.

Pleasant Days

In 1933 the Congregational Church spread over six months the celebration of its 200th anniversary, with large audiences flocking to its play, its pageants, and its special services, such as "Civic Sunday" honoring many of the town's institutions. (To create employment, the Church also spent $2,500 on alterations, and promptly found itself involved in a strike when a delivery man pitched in to help!)

In 1935 Connecticut celebrated its tercentenary, and for a week there were tours of and teas at historic homes, on-site dramatizations of local historic events, and a grand and glorious Labor Day parade. In the wake of this 300th celebration, a town meeting on

When it took back its original name, Elm Street looked like this. Not until 1939 would buildings fill the gap west of the Playhouse.

Apr. 26, 1936, changed Railroad Avenue's name back to Elm Street. Too many towns had a "Railroad Avenue" in a slum area, while "Elm Street" was much better suited to the "colonial" look being created as stores went up westward from the Post Office and Playhouse. One year before, following the town's improvement and paving of Stamford Avenue, residents along that road had petitioned successfully to change its name to Old Stamford Road.

My parents always maintained that New Canaan was nicest when its population was 3,000, but New Canaan in the 1930's was a good place to live. With a population of just over 5,000, it was still a small town where everyone knew everyone else. You might not call Lincoln McVeagh of Marvin Ridge by name, but you knew President Roosevelt had just appointed him U. S. minister to Greece, just as you knew Paul Manship of Weed Street had been commissioned to make the "Prometheus" fountain sculpture for the new Rockefeller Center plaza. If you didn't recognize H. T. Webster, a Stamford resident, you certainly recognized the New Canaan people he put into his "Bridge" and "Golf" cartoons, just as you could spot the ridiculous ladies and ridiculous situations in Helen Hokinson's drawings for the *New Yorker.* (Both generously made special cartoons for local drives.) Certainly you recognized Gregory Mason, the Central America explorer, and likely as not had watched last Sunday's softball game when his team played Lowell Thomas's team from Pawling. On New Canaan's team was Izzy Cohen, later proprietor of Pierre's restaurant on Elm Street, and Paul Webb, whose cartoons of the "Mountaineers" were nationally popular and who would often be toastmaster at the firemen's banquets.

The fire department in those days had 60 active members and a long waiting list, though equipment and training were not what they are today. New Canaan had no fire-alrm code; the siren wailed, you picked up the telephone and asked the operator where the fire was, and—seldom helpfully—everyone went. I can remember, however, a Sunday telephone call when the telephone operator said: "Tell your brothers to take brooms and shovels and get over to Valley Road. A brush fire is out of control near Benedict Hill." Dozens of people pitched in to help that day.

Since only a few young people were lucky enough to find jobs on leaving college or school, bridge and home entertainment abounded or if you went to the movies, you went "dutch," lest someone with no pocket money be embarrassed by inability to pay for others. You bowled—5 cents a game in the afternoons—with Capt. William F. Verleger, who had taken Admiral Byrd to the South Pole and would become third selectman, with a bookkeeper from a local garage, the plumber, the vice president of the bank, and everyone enjoyed everyone else. And if you were feeling smug, you might say "I saw Flush this morning"—proving that you knew Katharine Cornell and her spaniel were spending the summer on Smith Ridge, taking a vacation from "The Barretts of Wimpole Street."

Everyone certainly knew Margaret Emerson Bailey (1885-1949), author, poet, and schoolteacher. For 32 years she was head of the English department at the Chapin School, commuting to New York from the home at 41 Cherry Street she shared with her artist brother. (To Whitman Bailey New Canaan is forever indebted for some hundred sketches that appeared in the Stamford *Advocate* and the *Advertiser* and which preserve so many local scenes and buildings now gone.) Miss Bailey was a member of the Board of Education and president of the Roosevelt Club, so New Canaan was not too surprised when as a Democrat she was elected third selectman in 1934. But her election caused a furor throughout Fairfield County, for never before had a woman been elected a town selectman.

Interim

By 1939, when war was declared in Europe, New Canaan was almost back to normal. Of a budget of $427,000, the schools with 1,241 pupils received $148,000. Welfare took $43,857, but this total included some $9,000 for those in institutions and hospitals and another $4,000 spent on medical and dental care. Crime had been considerably reduced, and the police budget of $26,451 included purchase of a car that would convert into an ambulance, and installation of a teletype. As their most pressing problems the selectmen listed parking and garbage disposal. To solve the latter an incinerator was built the next year near the sewer beds—and almost immediately proved so inefficient that it had to be redesigned.

In 1940 WPA shut down, as employment opportunities mounted at area factories already engaging in war manufacturing. All eligible New Canaan men had been registered in the Selective Service Draft, and some had been called up by the Norwalk draft board under which New Canaan had been placed. The town had conducted not only a successful USO campaign but its first aluminum salvage drive, and it was involved in "Bundles for Britain" and similar kinds of war relief.

World War II

A year before Pearl Harbor, the U. S. Army began setting up along the northeastern seaboard a grid of observation posts. Manned by civilian volunteers, these were to warn the metropolitan area of potential air raid attacks, and in New Canaan the American Legion was in charge. By October a make-shift observation post had been set up on the highest point of Oenoke Ridge, and there the first of the round-the-clock teams were on duty the morning after Pearl Harbor was attacked. When the Army closed the post on Oct. 4, 1943, 225 New Canaan men and women—businessmen, commuters, housewives—had served as ground observers, taking two-hour shifts through the 24 hours of every day.

According to the 1940 Census, New Canaan had a population of 6,221, composed roughly of 3,700 children and 2,500 adults. Yet when World War II ended in 1945, New Canaan had sent 1,054 men and women into the armed services, plus 12 more on duty with the Red Cross, and a total of 1,345 volunteers had served on the home front. For a small town, the figures are incredible.

Thirty-eight of the men in the Army, Navy, Marine Corps, Coast Guard, and Merchant Marine lost their lives, 24 of them overseas. Of the 29 women who volunteered, 13 joined the WAVES, 8 joined the WACS, three were Army nurses, while the women's branches of the Marines, Coast Guard, and Air Force accounted for the rest. Well aware that, after 20 years, the state had not been able to compile accurate records for its World War I servicemen and that Civil War and Revolution lists were far from complete, New Canaan in 1942 set up a War Records Committee to keep track of and in touch with everyone who went into the armed services. The result was publication in 1946, 1948, and 1951 of three volumes that come close to containing New Canaan's entire World War II service records (They are still in print.). Yet, by the war's end, mobility was evident; some who entered the service here were discharged elsewhere, and so a very few have only their names recorded.

Back in 1940 the New Canaan branch of the Red Cross, still under the Stamford Chapter, had organized a war relief committee, first aid courses, and a blood bank, while under federal directive the town had its Office of Civilian Defense. Under Judge L. P. Frothingham, this became successively the Defense Council and then the New Canaan War Council, with a protective and a service division.

Anyone who remembers World War II will remember the air raid wardens, auxiliary police, disaster committees, canteens, the Food-in-War programs, nurses' aides, Red Cross motor corps, home services, and fund raising. Just what New Canaan's 1,345 volunteers accomplished in a variety of capacities is detailed in Volume III of the town's war record books.Unlike World War I, there was no need for coordinating directives, for as the preface says: ". . . the record as a whole is of a remarkably harmonious and efficient organization, where patriotism, intelligence, cooperation and hard work was the rule." While New Canaan wasn't a community of saints, rationing was accepted philosophically, there was very little cheating, and almost no black market sales.

After tires and then gasoline had been rationed, New Canaan established a bus service for its commuters and another for shoppers coming to the village. Beginning in May 1942, the churches, with services set for 9:30 and 11:15 A.M., rented buses to pick up and return some 300 members who could not walk to Sunday service. Throughout the war people gathered on God's Acre for the Christmas caroling, but New Canaan was on the fringe of the metropolitan brownout area and the War Production Board had ordered energy be conserved, so in 1942 and 1943 the Christmas tree was not lighted except for the star at the top.

By 1942 New Canaan had a war industry located here, Boots Aircraft Nut Corp., which with town permission first functioned in a Ponus Ridge mansion and then in 1944 moved into the former telephone building on Main Street. Most aircraft then being built used Boots nuts and bolts.

Roton Point

Partly because of the owner's age and largely because of wartime restrictions, Roton Point, that mecca of every New Canaan Sunday School picnic, came up for sale in 1942. On Long Island Sound in the Rowayton section of Norwalk, Roton Point had since 1892 been an amusement park, its roller coaster, games of chance, dance hall, picnic area, and beach attracting not only those within driving distance but steamboat loads of New Yorkers. Unless families could be accommodated at Peartree in Darien, New Canaan residents still had no public swimming place, so the selectmen appointed a committee to consider buying and operating a part of Roton Point as a town beach. Already an option had been taken on behalf of the town by interested citizens on 13 acres of land at the east end of the Point. The cost would be approximately $45,000, while income would come from rental of 300 bath houses.

Despite gas rationing, some 450 people heard the details at a town meeting on Aug. 25, 1942, and voted 230 to 206 to acquire the 13 acres at Roton Point. Then, because New Canaan could not legally own land outside its boundaries, a group of six private citizens took up the option while the town waited for Senator Stanley P. Mead to get Private Act No. 1 through the legislature. Signed by the governor on February 4, 1943, that act empowered the town not only to buy land outside its territorial limits but to spend money on developing a shore-front recreation area.

But taxes and wartime conditions prevailed—who would have the gasoline to get to a rented bath house?—and in the end New Canaan declined to buy, 356 against 103. Roton Point eventually became a private club and it was left to Kiwanis Club in May 1946 to buy a gravel pit off Old Norwalk Road and develop Kiwanis Park by creating a pond and a beach. (In 1960 the Club gave Kiwanis Park to the town.)

In the Wake of the War

Wartime shortages of materials and spare parts had played havoc with the town's maintenance of buildings, highways, and equipment, and as early as May 25, 1943, the selectmen had enacted a

Post War Planning commission. This was to prepare plans for meeting New Canaan's postwar problems, including those of the servicemen being discharged. Even before World War II was ended, a Veterans' Advisory Center was operating from a store opposite the town hall, giving help on such matters as employment, insurance, the GI Bill of Rights, and, in particular, housing —which for the next five years was spelled with capital letters.

Almost no new houses had been built in New Canaan during the war, and with shortages in materials continuing, housing was an acute problem, especially for newly married veterans starting their first jobs. Though a Town Housing Authority was set up, the first response to the shortage came from a group of private developers, who before the war had acquired from Hoyt Nurseries a tract of land on the west side of South Avenue. There in 1945-46 Gower and Douglas Roads were laid out and small houses built, with purchase priority going to veterans. Similarly, Fairty and Orchard Drives followed in 1948.

Meanwhile, the Housing Authority, after problems and delays, had purchased four wartime buildings from the Army barracks at Taunton, Mass., and moved them to Route 123 between Locust and East Avenues. By 1947 they had been remodeled into 16 apartments, which disappeared after other and more permanent apartments were built in 1950 on Millport Avenue.

As soon as materials and power lines were available, more new families sought to settle in New Canaan, with the result that among the new roads were Bayberry, Indian Rocks, Rippowam, Wahackme Lane, Hidden Meadow and Cecil Place. Though many more roads and developments were still to come, by 1950 the 35 farms that had totaled 4,021 acres in 1930 were gone.

New residents meant new parking needs, which the town had foreseen. In July 1944 New Canaan had bought from Samuel H. Watts, the man who had made the "Big Shop" property available for the firehouse, the Park Street land opposite Seminary Street. Until wartime conditions ended, the Victorian mansion that Henry B. Rogers had built there in 1876 (later the home for Community and then St. Luke's schools) served as the town's salvage depot. Derelict by war's end, the house was demolished and Rogers parking lot was made, the first parking facilities for commuters other than the station grounds. Later New Canaan acquired the corner land at Main and Cherry streets, and in July 1950 tore down the famous old Birdsall House, which had become a firetrap, in order to make Morse Court parking lot.

By 1950 six rising architects had chosen to build homes for themselves in New Canaan. Eliot Noyes, Marcel Breuer, John J. Johansen, Landis Gores, Philip Johnson, and Victor Christ-Janer

The Birdsall House had been made by a huge front addition to Bradley Keeler's house. All was demolished in 1950 (P.R.B. Dixon photo).

would be responsible for at least 28 of the contemporary houses for which New Canaan now is famous—including, of course, Johnson's "Glass House" built on Ponus Ridge in 1949. And in 1949, Eliot Noyes, as a benefit for the New Canaan Library's building fund, arranged the first "modern house" tour, which attracted a thousand outsiders and coverage by the New York *Times.* (As the town's architectural fame grew, the Library staff, to avoid having to give specific directions to visitors, prepared a map showing the location of 57 contemporary private homes.)

During the war years, New Canaan's school population had remained almost constant, but from 1945 to 1950 it jumped by 414 to 1,450 students, filling the junior and senior high schools to capacity. By then, education took $428,694 of the town's million-dollar budget, and a new elementary school, South, opened in the fall of 1950 on Gower Road.

Unhappily, also by 1950 the United States was involved in the Korean War, and in July the town reactivated many of its former civilian defense groups and began registering young men for the draft.

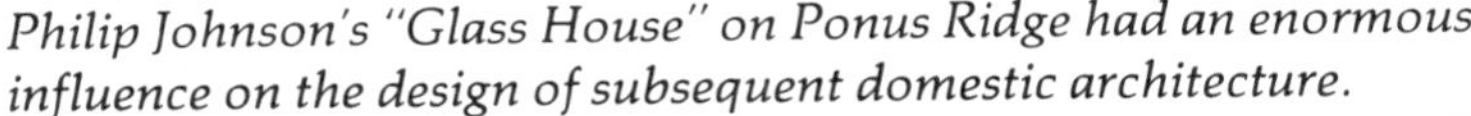

Philip Johnson's "Glass House" on Ponus Ridge had an enormous influence on the design of subsequent domestic architecture.

The next year saw one more town celebration as on July 4, 1951, New Canaan celebrated its 150th anniversary as an incorporated town. This time an enormous parade, which drew an estimated 10,000 watchers, was held in the afternoon, with a reviewing stand for officials and honored guests in front of the Town Hall. And this time the celebration ended at Mead Memorial Park, where even more thousands gathered for an evening band concert and fireworks.

After 1951

What happened in New Canaan in the next three decades is too close in time to be put into proper perspective. The future will have to judge whether the changes were, in the long run, good or bad for the town, whether decisions were wise or foolish, and which leaders will be remembered in history.

In the 30 years between 1950 and 1980, New Canaan's population more than doubled, from 7,968 to almost 18,000. But neither figure reflects the thousands and thousands of other people who moved in and out of the town, in a turnover estimated to be at least 25 percent annually. So many people created demands for services—more police, more fire engines, new roads, new businesses—and put unanticipated pressures on everyone, but especially on the school system. Following acrimonious debate, a town meeting in May 1953 turned down the proposal to locate a new high school on Oenoke Ridge in favor of a site on the east side of South Avenue at Farm Road. There a new high school was built in 1956—and immediately proved too small so that a 23-room addition had to be made in less than five years. Following the opening of South elementary school in 1950, first West and then East schools had to be built. Then, just when the school population began to decline, the third (Lapham) high school was opened in 1971, on the opposite side of South Avenue on an extension of Farm Road, and Saxe Junior High School moved into the former second high school.

During these two decades, reapportionment deprived New Canaan of one of its two state representatives, state law eliminated the town court, and New Canaan in 1969 voted to replace its historic town meeting—that hallmark of New England towns—

with an elected town council (as envisioned in the consolidation charter proposed in 1925).

In 1955 an unexpected flood altered the town's landscape drastically in several areas, washing out bridges, devastating pavements, and eventually changing the routes of some roads. Though in need of more parking, New Canaan in 1959 and again in 1961 voted down a proposal to relocate the station and parking lot in "Fairty's orchard" off Old Stamford Road. As a result, the station remains in the building it has occupied since the railroad was started in 1868.

By then, the town was giving some thought to preserving its landmarks. The New Canaan Historical Society in 1957 had purchased the Oenoke Ridge house built by Stephen Hanford *c.*1764, which it now preserved as the Hanford-Silliman museum. John Rogers' studio, scheduled for demolition, was moved to those grounds in 1960, and to the east the Historical Society in 1963 acquired New Canaan's first town house as its library and headquarters. Then in 1964, thanks to the efforts of Judge Stanley P. Mead and others, a New Canaan town meeting voted to preserve the outward appearance of the area around Church Hill by creating a Historic District, set up under state law.

The religious revival of the 1950's led to a large addition to the Congregational meeting house, the formation of the First Presbyterian Church, the building of a new Christian Science, a new St. Aloysius, and a new St. Mark's, with St. Michael's Lutheran Church acquiring St. Mark's original home. Out of ministerial cooperation in 1963 came the Committee for Common Concern, which championed equal rights and opportunities for minorities at home as well as in the South, and out of this Committee came New Canaan's first ecumenical service in 1966.

By 1970 the character of the town had undergone change. As corporations moved their headquarters outside New York City, the number of residents who drove to work outnumbered those who commuted by train (though parking problems remained). After the mid-1970's, when the Cherry Street extension was complete, four-story office buildings and executive headquarters were built near the center of town. There, too, changes had been numerous as new buildings replaced older structures and new businesses were started to cater to the needs of new residents.

After a spate of two-family dwellings had been built wherever zoning laws would allow, Heritage Hill Road was opened in 1964, to be lined with two tiers of apartment buildings and town houses. Soon these rental properties were converted into condominiums amid a general decline of premises for rent. Beginning in the 1960's, one after another of the older private homes had been torn down to make way for condominiums and cooperatives within walking distance of the town. And the owners of these often were retired couples from out of town, who had no children to be educated.

In the course of these 30 years, the civic and political leaders of mid-century died or moved away, and new people appeared to take their places. New causes drew generous support from many people, but the recent large benefactors of the town were two women, both of whom were summer residents. Miss Susan Dwight Bliss often visited her aunt, Miss Catherine A. Bliss, who in 1899 had purchased the former Osborn Bright estate on Oenoke Ridge; Mrs. Ruth (Lapham) Lloyd had been brought to New Canaan as a child in 1904 when her parents, Mr. and Mrs. Lewis H. Lapham, began summering at "Waveny." In 1959 Miss Susan Bliss divided the estate she had acquired in 1915, following her aunt's death, between the newly formed Presbyterian Church and the Town of New Canaan. On its 48 acres and eight outbuildings, the town established the New Canaan Nature Center, and on their five acres the Presbyterians in 1970 dedicated their new church edifice. Bliss House, Miss Bliss's 22-room summer home, was retained as a parish hall after it was no longer necessary to hold services there.

Beginning in 1969, Mrs. Lloyd gave to the town land on the west side of South Avenue where the third high school was built. Later that same year she offered New Canaan almost the whole of the 300-acre "Waveny" estate on too favorable terms for the town to decline. In April 1972, with a million-dollar gift, she was responsible for the founding of Waveny Care Center, a skilled nursing facility also built on Farm Road. Then in 1978, because of her matching gift of $750,000, the New Canaan Library was able to complete the Lewis H. Lapham wing.

Perhaps it is true, as others have said, that history clings to the land. If so, then everyone who now lives in New Canaan inherits the traditions that, over 250 years, have made New Canaan the unique community it is. Since the days when the first settlers built their homes in every corner of Canaan Parish, there has never been a "wrong side of the tracks" as, actively or passively, residents have added their bits to creating a community. And if any one tradition can account for the growth of the Parish and the town that tradition is service to others in the community. Let us hope that it is embedded in our soil to be inherited by all generations to come.

As it has from the beginning, Five Mile River flows into the Mill Pond, though the grist mill and saw mill are long gone.

Sources

Books, Pamphlets, and Articles

Abbot, Charles Riley, "Historical Address delivered at the Centennial of St. Mark's Church, New Canaan, Nov. 15, 1891."

Andrews, Edward D., *The People Called Shakers.* New York: Oxford University Press, 1953.

Bartow, Edith M., "Dan Town: The Lost District," New Canaan Historical Society *Annual,* Vol. II, No. 1, 1947.

Bayles, Lois B., *Canaan Parish and the American Revolution.* New Canaan: New Canaan Historical Society, 1976

_____, "The Danbury Raid," New Canaan Historical Society *Annual,* Vol. VIII, No. 3, 1977-78

Benedict, Theodore W., "Before the Turn of the Century," New Canaan Historical Society *Annual.* Vol. V, No. 2, 1960.

_____, "The Shoe Industry in New Canaan, Conn.," New Canaan Historical Society *Annual,* Vol. IV, No. 1, 1955.

Bidwell, Percy Wells, and John I. Falconer, *History of Agriculture in the Northern United States, 1620-1860.* Carnegie Institution of Washington Publication #358, 1925; reprinted New York: Peter Smith, 1941.

Bolton, Robert, Jr., *History of the County of Westchester,* 2 vols. New York: Alexander S. Gould, 1848.

Burr, Nelson Rollin, *The Story of the Diocese of Connecticut.* Hartford: Church Missions Publishing Co., 1962

Butler, Lemuel C., "Letters," New Canaan Historical Society *Annual,* Vol. II, No. 4, 1950.

Canaan Parish, 1733-1933. New Canaan: The Congregational Church, 1935.

Centennial Papers published by the Order of the General Conference of Connecticut. Hartford: The Case, Lockwood & Brainard Co., 1877.

Clark, George L., *A History of Connecticut.* New York: G. P. Putnam's Sons, 1914.

Cockran, Louis, and Bess White Cochran, *Captives of the Word.* Garden City, N.Y.: Doubleday & Co., 1969.

Collections of the Connecticut Historical Society, "Law [Gov. Jonathan] Papers," 3 vols. Hartford: The Society, 1907, 1911, 1914.

_____, "Rolls of the Connecticut Men in the French and Indian Wars, 1755-1762," 2 vols. Hartford: The Society, 1903, 1905.

Collier, Christopher, "Justus Mitchell and New Canaan's First Library," New Canaan *Advertiser,* Mar. 16, 1961.

Connecticut Common School Journal, Vol. III, 1840-41.

Connecticut State Register and Manual, 1935. Prepared by the Secretary. Connecticut State Tercentenary. Hartford: State of Connecticut, 1935.

"A Concise History of the Various Secret Societies of the Town of New Canaan, Conn." E. C. Bross, ed. Ridgefield, Conn.: no date.

Contributions to the Ecclesiastical History of Connecticut. New Haven: William L. Kingsley, 1861.

Crofut, W. A., and John W. Morris, *The Military and Civil History of Connecticut during the War of 1861-65.* New York: Ledyard Bill, 1868.

Cutler, Carl C., *Queens of the Western Ocean.* Annapolis, Md.: United States Naval Institute, 1961.

Davies, A. Mervyn, *Solon H. Borglum.* Chester, Conn.: Pequot Press, 1974.

Dickore, Marie, "The Order of the Purple Heart, An Account of Sergeant William Brown." Cincinnati: Society of Colonial Wars in the State of Ohio, 1943.

Feinstein, Estelle S., *Stamford from Puritan to Patriot; The Shaping of a Connecticut Community, 1641-1774.* Stamford: Stamford Bicentennial Corporation, 1976.

Frothingham, John G., "The Country Club of New Canaan," New Canaan: The Country Club, 1968.

Garcia-Mata, Lucy A., "Seventeen Days Dead, Seek and You Will Find," New Canaan Historical Society *Annual,* Vol. VI, No. 4, 1970.

Hall, Clifford S., *Benjamin Talmadge, Revolutionary Soldier and American Businessman.* New York: Columbia University Press, 1943.

Hall, Clifford W., "History of the Methodist Episcopal Church of New Canaan, Conn.," *Canaan Parish, 1733-1933, op. cit.*

Hall, Edwin, *The Ancient Historical Records of Norwalk, Conn.,* New York: Ivison, Phinney, Blakeman & Co., 1865.

Hersam, V. Donald, Jr., "The Early Years of Fire Companies in New Canaan," New Canaan Historical Society *Annual,* Vol. VII, No. 1, 1971.

_____, "History of the New Canaan Fire Company No. 1, 1896-1916," *Annual* Vol. VII, No. 3, 1973.

Hill, Carlton, "New Canaan's 150th Birthday," New Canaan Historical Society *Annual,* Vol. III, No. 2, 1952.

Hinman, Royal R., compiler, *Historical Collection, from Official Records, Files, etc., of the Part Sustained by Connecticut During the War of the Revolution.* Hartford: E. Gleason, 1842.

Hoyt, James S., "Historical Discourse," *One Hundred and Fiftieth Anniversary of the Congregational Church, New Canaan, Conn.* Stamford: Gillespie Brothers, 1883.

Huntington, E. B., *History of Stamford, Connecticut.* Stamford: the Author, 1868.

Keeler, Stephen E., "An Historical Address Delivered in St. Mark's, New Canaan, May 13, 1934, on the Centennial of the Consecration of the Present Church," *Canaan Parish, 1733-1933, op. cit.*

Landmarks of New Canaan. New Canaan: New Canaan Historical Society, 1951.

Marvin, Arba B., "A Child of Canaan Parish" [Walton, N.Y.], New Canaan Historical Society *Annual,* Vol. II, No. 4, 1950.

Mead, Stanley P., "Roton Point," New Canaan Historical Society *Annual,* Vol. IV, No. 2, 1956.

Montgomery, Marshall H., "The Branch's Best Customer in New Canaan—The 100-Year History of Weed's," New Canaan Historical Society *Annual,* Vol. V, No. 6, 1968.

_____, "The Oblong, Otherwise Known as the Equivalent Tract," *Annual,* Vol. III, No. 1, 1951.

Moore, W. T., *Comprehensive History of the Disciples of Christ.* New York: Fleming H. Revell Co., 1909.

Morse, Abner, *A Genealogical Register of Descendants of Several Ancient Puritans* [Richards genealogy]. Boston: H. W. Dutton & Son, 1861.

Morse, Jarvis M., *A Neglected Period of Connecticut's History, 1818-1850.* New Haven: Yale University Press, 1933.

Munger, John D., "The New Canaan Railroad, 1868-1968," New Canaan Historical Society *Annual,* Vol. V, No. 6, 1968.

New Canaan, Town of, "Annual Reports," 1890-1979.

Norcross, Frank W., *A History of the New York Swamp.* New York: The Chiswick Press, 1901.

Norwalk After Two Hundred & Fifty Years, compiled by a Committee. South Norwalk: C. A. Freeman, 1901.

The Papers of Sir William Johnson, prepared by James Sullivan, 3 vols. Albany: The University of the State of New York, 1921.

Pennypacker, John G., *St. Mark's and Its Forebears.* New Canaan: St. Mark's Parish, 1964.

Private Laws of Connecticut, Vols. III-XII, 1857-1897. New Haven or Hartford: The State.

Public Records of the Colony of Connecticut, 1636-1776, 15 vols. Hartford: The State, 1852-1890.

Public Records of the State of Connecticut, 1776-1803, 11 vols. Hartford: The State, 1894-1967.

Purcell, Richard J., *Connecticut in Transition: 1775-1818.* Middletown: Wesleyan University Press, 1963.

Record of Service of Connecticut Men in the Army and Navy of the United States during the War of the Rebellion. Compiled under the direction of the Adjutant General. Hartford: 1867.

Record of Service of Connecticut Men in the War of the Revolution. Compiled under the direction of the Adjutant General. Hartford: 1889.

Records of the Colony or Jurisdiction of New Haven, 2 vols. Charles A. Hoadley, ed. Hartford: Case, Lockwood and Company, 1857, 1858.

Records of World War II, 3 vols. Compiled and published by the War Records Committee of the Town of New Canaan and the New Canaan Historical Society, 1946, 1948, 1951.

Rockwell, A. D., *Rambling Recollections.* New York: Paul B. Hoeber, 1920.

St. John, Samuel, "Historical Address. . . July 4th, 1876," New Canaan: 1876.

Salmon, Genevieve C., "One Hundred Years of School District Number One," New Canaan Historical Society *Annual,* Vol. I, No. 3, 1945.

Schlesinger, Arthur M., Jr., *The Age of Jackson.* Boston: Little Brown & Co., 1945

Scott, Kenneth, *Counterfeiting in Colonial Connecticut.* New York: American Numismatic Society, 1957.

_____, *Counterfeiting in Colonial New York.* New York: American Numismatic Society, 1953.

Selleck, Charles M., *Norwalk.* Norwalk: the Author, 1896.

Sweet, Joseph C., "Nostalgia Corner," New Canaan *Advertiser,* Jan. 10, 1980, Nov. 6, 1980.

Swiggett, Howard, *The Forgotten Leaders of the Revolution.* Garden City: Doubleday & Co., Inc., 1955.

Tallmadge, Benjamin, *Memoir of Colonel Benjamin Tallmadge,* 1858. Reprinted in Eyewitness Accounts of the American Revolution series. New York: New York Times & Arno Press, 1968.

Van Dusen, Albert E., *Connecticut.* New York: Random House, 1961

Manuscripts and Documents
(Unless otherwise specified, items are in
New Canaan Historical Society Library)

Ayres, Ebenezer, Account Book, 1823-1839.

Bayles, Lois B.: Census of Canaan Parish, *c.*1772; Comparative Employment Statistics from New Canaan Census Records, 1850 through 1880; Fairfield County Court Cases; Loyalists of Canaan Parish; Loyalists of Norwalk; Loyalists of Stamford; Norwalk's Upper Division; Tavernkeepers of Fairfield County; U.S. Census Records for Canaan Parish, 1790, 1800; U.S. Census Records for New Canaan, 1810-1880.

Congregational Church of New Canaan, Records of, Vol. 1, 1A, 2, in Connecticut State Library (photostat copy at New Canaan Historical Society).

Congregational Church of New Canaan, Records of, Vol. 3, 4, in Congregational Church.

Consociation of Fairfield County, West, files on Rev. William Drummond, Rev. John Eells, Daniel Keeler, Rev. Justus Mitchell, Edwin S. Seymour, Rev. Robert Silliman, Rev. Theophilus Smith, in Congregational House, Hartford, Conn.

Davenport, Sarah, Journal, May 1, 1849-May 16, 1852. (Reprinted in New Canaan Historical Society *Annual,* Vol. II, No. 4, 1950.)

Drummond, William: Account Book, Jan. 19, 1773-Oct. 2, 1777; Diary, Feb. 1, 1772-June 16, 1772; Journal of Family Visitation, Dec. 7, 1772-Jan. 29, 1773; Remarks and Observations on Voyage from Cowdon to St. John's Island, Apr. 5, 1770-May 12, 1771. (Parts reprinted in *Canaan Parish, op. cit.*)

Fairfield (Conn.) Probate Court records, in Fairfield Town Hall and Connecticut State Library.

First National Bank of New Canaan, minutes of, 1865-1925.

Fitch, Theophilus, Account Book, 1770-1800; Justice of the Peace record book, 1755-1765.

Fuller, Clement A., The History of the Southern Commons or Sequest Land in Stamford, Conn., unpublished paper read to Stamford Historical Society, 1934.

Gilbert, Luzerne, Account Book, 1820-1824.

Green, Erna F., The Public Land System of Norwalk, Connecticut, 1654-1704, unpublished Master of History thesis, University of Bridgeport, 1972.

Hoyt Nursery Collection, 30 files, 12 ledgers, maps.

Law, Alexander, Receipt Book, 1852-1892.

Mead, S. P., Abstracts of Stamford Church Records (microfilm).
New Canaan, Town of, Abstract of Assessment, 1856-1914, 8 vols. in New Canaan Historical Society; Borough Meeting minutes, 2 vols., Land Records, Probate Court Records, Town Meeting minutes, 3 vols., in Town Hall.
New Canaan Cemetery Association, minutes of, at Lakeview Cemetery.
New Canaan Savings Bank, first minute book, at New Canaan Savings Bank.
Norwalk (Conn.) Land Records, Proprietors' records, Book 2 (Book 1 missing), Town Meeting minutes, Vol. 1, in Town Hall, South Norwalk; Probate Court records in Probate Court, Main Street, Norwalk.
Ogden, David, Autobiography, 1833, journal, Voyage to Europe and Return, 1844, with heirs of S. Clerc Ogden (photocopies with Mary Louise King).
Olmstead, Sophia (Richards), copies of her letters.
"Reminiscences," file and clippings in Scrapbooks, Series I and II.
"Richards, Isaac, vs. Jabez Gregory, etc.," photocopy and typescript of Fairfield County Court case in Connecticut State Library, bound as 2 vols.
Salmon, Genevieve C., draft of nine background chapters for unfinished history of New Canaan.
School District No. 1, records, 2 vols.
School Society of Canaan Parish and New Canaan, minutes.
"Shakers," file, including copies made by Gerald C. Wertkin of original papers relating to the "New Canaan Family."
Silliman Collection, 48 files, photographs.
Stamford (Conn.), Land Records, Probate Court Records, in Stamford Town Hall; Town Meeting minutes (microfilm).

Newspapers

New Canaan *Advertiser*, 1908-
Era, 1868-1871.
Gazette, 1932-1934.
Omnibus and Fairfield County Agriculturist, 1851.
Norwalk *Gazette*, 1818-1868 at Lockwood House, Norwalk.
Stamford *Advocate*, Aug. 5, 1840-1877 (microfilm).
Intelligencer and successors, 1829-1840 (microfilm).

Index

(Numerals in italics indicate illustration.)

Abbott, Aaron, 79; Charles R., 245, 249; Deborah, 106; John, 35-36
Adams, William H., 172
Advertiser, 273, 296
Adriance, Mrs. Francis H., 283, 289, 290
Alarm List, 78, 86, 96
Albert, Ernest, 280
alcoholism, 60, 103; in 19th century, 156-57, 174-76
Alexander, Mrs. L. Dade, 257
Ambler, James, 76
American Revolution, and Canaan Parish, 85, 86, 88, 93-96, Canaan Parish men in 75-80, 81, 82-84, 85, 86, 88, 91-92, 96-97, 100; causes of, 43, 73-75; end of, 98
Anderson, Franklin W., 245, 263; Mrs. Susan, 257-58, 306
André, Major John, 94-95
architecture and architects, 44, *148*, 178, 279-80, 308-09, 318-19
Ardsley Inn, 278
Armistice Day, 1918, 290-91
Arnold, Benedict, 82, 83, 94
artists, 280-81, 294, 306-07
Association of Fairfield County West, 67, 68, 80-82. *See also* Consociation
automobiles, early, 268-71
Ayres, Alvah, 154; Amos, 138, 145, 146, 149, 151, 157, 167, 168, 186; Andrew, 168; Ebenezer, 134, 138, 139, 140, 146, 154, 171; Ebenezer, Jr., 171; Mrs. Edward F., 253, 260; Frederick, 138, 145, 149, 150, 189; Hezron L., 153, 154, 186, 224; James H., 200; Jared, 130, 138, 167; Samuel, 171; Thomas N., 170
Ayres, H. L. & A., 154, 172, 186, 189
Ayres, J. E., & Son, 187
Ayres, S. & E., 171
Ayres & Seymour, 157
Babcock, Violet, 303
Bailey, Margaret E., 313; Whitman, 313
Baker, Dr. Samuel, 70, 80, 102, 110
Band of Hope, 230
banks and banking, 151, 166, 188, 204, 219. *See also* names of banks
Baptist Church, New Canaan, 212, 260, 265, 275
Baptists, 103, 104, 105-06, 129, 161
bark mill, 138, 189
Bartlett, Samuel, 41
Bartow, Edith, 285
basket making, 209, 210
Bayles, Lois B., 70
Beecher, Eliphalet, 54-55
Belden, Samuel, 62
Bell, Rev. Edward, 265-66
Benedict, Andrew, 188; Benjamin, 187; "Aunt" Betsy, 131; Caleb, 137, 139-40, 153, 154, 189, 224; Caleb S., 149-50, 172, 187, 189, 194, 201; Charles, 172, 186, 203, 205, 206, 209, 211, 236; Charles F., 236; Daniel, 42, 77, 78, 79; Ebenezer, 88; Ezra, 138, 148, 172; Isaac, 128; J. Irving, 220; James, 137, 138; John, 24-25; John, Jr., 31; John, 3d, 31; Jonathan B., 165; Junius, 189, 220, 227, 237; Nehemiah, 61, 67, 68, 76, 107; Nehemiah, 2d, 130, 138; Roswell S., 172, 186, 203; Silas, 131; Theodore W., 220, 227; Trowbridge, 140
Benedict & Co., 236, 272
Benedict, C. S., & Co., 172, 187, 189
Benedict, J. & J., 189, 209, *210*, 216, 220, 274
Benedict, J. & T. W., 220
Benedict, Bradley & Co., 172, 186, 187
Benedict, Hall & Co., 189, 203
Benedict, Webb & Co., 203, 206
Betts, Dr. Azor, 70; Stephen, 92, 110

"Big Shop," 146, *147*, 186, 190, 203, 209, 236, 272
Birdsall, Gilbert, 222, 231
Birdsall House, 173, 222, 266, *318*
Bishop, Person, 43
blacks, in Canaan Parish, 32, 34; in New Canaan, 133, 302
Blain, Dr. Daniel, 304
Blatchley, Joseph, 88, 129
Bliss, Catherine A., 322; Susan D., 322
Bolt (Boult), William, 29, 42, 71
Board of Education, 254, 285, 300
Board of Trade, 233
Bond, William E., 244, 246
Bonney, Rev. William, 129, 133, 135, 158, 226
Boots Aircraft Nut Corp., 315
Borglum, Solon, 280, 294; Mrs. Solon, 285, 286
Borough of New Canaan, 237-42, 256, 271; building district of, 274; and cars, 270, 271; consolidated with Town, 304; garbage collection, 284; health problems of, 281-83; mail delivery in, 252; map of, *239*; police of, 267-68, 297-98, 304
Bossa, Norbert, 211-12
Bouton, Daniel, 96; Daniel W., 150, 168, 172, 173; Dr. David, Jr., 132; Eleazer, Jr., 64, 68; John, 24, 25, 27, 30, 33-35, 36, 64; Louisa, 296; Nathaniel, 64
Bouton, D. W. & L., 150
Bradley, Edson, 172, 187, 189, 210, 215; Edson, Jr., 215; Robert H., 279; William, 199, 215; William E. C., 245
Breuer, Marcel, 318
Bright, Osborn E., 224, 226, 227, 244, 245, 251; Mrs. Osborn E., 246
Brinley, D. Putnam, 280, 288, 293
Brooks, Dr. Myron J., 260
Brower, Almaduras, 155-56, 178
Brown, Benjamin, 72; William, 100, 102-03
Brownson, Dr. William G., 212, 226, 227, 238, 248, 259, 296
Buckingham, Rev. Stephen, 24
Burr, William H., 278, 279
Burtis, Andrew, 169, 211, 216; J. W., 210; Jared, 169; Wolsey, 144, 145, 146, 150, 191
Burtis & Mead, 210, 234

calendar reform, 46
Campbellite church, 159-60
Canaan, Conn., 38, 115
Canaan, Society of. *See* Society of Canaan
Canaan Parish, area reduced, 104-05; becomes New Canaan, 114-15; division proposed, 66; founding of, 4, 21-27; map of, *26*, and Perambulation Line, 8-9; settlement of, 10-14, 17; Train Band of, *see* Train Band
Canaan Parish School Society, 112-13
Canaan Ridge, 22-23
Caner, Rev. Henry, 37
Carman, Bliss, 281
Carter, Ebenezer, 25, 31, 33, 71; Ebenezer (2d), 172; Hanford, 167; John, 75, 79, 83, 100, 129; Samuel, Jr., 144; Thomas, 168, 186
Cassel, John, 280
cemeteries, 148, 195, 210-11, 224
Census. *See* Population
Centennial, of New Canaan, 261-65; of U.S., 217
Center School, 162, 194, 245, 275, 298, 299, 300
"Central Park," *225*, 241, 267
Cesar, 34, 72
Cheese Spring Road, 258, 306
Cherry Street, 149-50, 256, 321
Chichester, David, 131
Child, Lewis P., 245; Ruth M., 308
Christmas carols, 286, 315
church bells, 103, 251
Church of Christ, Scientist, 262, 295, 321

Church of England, 21, 37, 61-63
Church Hill Burying Ground, *62*
Church Hill Institute, *158*, 164, *180*
Cincinnati, Ohio, settled, 102
Civic League, 283-85, 286, 287, 295, 296
Civil War, 190, 199-202, 210, 230, 259
Clark, Fred, 266
Clarke, Mrs. Merrill F., 303
Cogswell, Dr. James, 96
Cohen, Israel, 312
Colonial Building, 296
Colonial Theatre, 290, 295
Colum, Padraic, 294
Committee of Safety, 75, 76
Community Baptist Church, 295
Community School, The, 285-86
Compo Beach, 82, 96
Comstock, Abijah, 65, 72, 109, 110, 136, 137; Albert S., 189, 198, 201, 203, 205, 209, 210, 218, 221, 227, 249; Mrs. Albert S., 248, 249; Andrew K., 208, 209, 216, 218, 220; Anthony, 230-31, 265; Apollos, 199; Charles, 220; Dover, 133; Enoch, 105-06; Frank L., 244; Moses, 30, 35, 71, 76; Nathan S., 112, 289; Onesimus, 71, 197; Phebe, 71, 197; Samuel, 109, 124, 130, 136, 137, 143; Samuel (Jr.), 155; Samuel (3d), 230; Seymour, 151, 168, 188, 274; Thomas, 112; Watts, 161, 165, 199, 204, 206, 212, 219, 278
Comstock & Co., 189
Comstock, Rogers & Co., 198, 206, 208, 209, 210, 213
Concert Hall, 158, 195, 196, 201-02, *276*
Congregational (Established) Church, 17-22, 24, 35-37, 103-04, 134, 136, 142
Congregational Church, New Canaan, 103, 135, 136, 143, 144, 159-60, 170, 177, 203, 212, 251, 311; formed, 25, 26, 29-31; interim, 98-99, 103; ministerial problems at, 33-35, 37, 38, 63-66, 68, 80-84; Raymond Fund of, 260; trials held by, 52-53, 157
Congregational meeting house, first, 28-29; second, 46, 103, 178; third, 176, 178, 242, 288; town celebrations in, 202, 217, 261, 265; town meetings in, 121, 146
Conley, Alanson, 131; John 131
Connecticut, Colony of, antislavery law, 71; capital, 7, 135; charter, 7, 18; and Church of England, 63; economy, 43, 58; first game law, 12; French and Indian Wars, 53-57; Louisburg expedition, 41-43; Pequot War, 5; religion in, 18-22; settlement, 4, 5; smallpox law, 70
Connecticut, State of, and Civil War, 199, 201; 1818 Constitution, 105, 134-36; first non-Congregationalist governor, 129; General Toleration Act, 103, 105; last slave in, 197; Maine law, 176; militia law, 175; and Protestant Episcopal Church, 106; and Second U.S. Bank, 163; tercentenary, 311; and Western Reserve, 112
Consociation of Fairfield County West, 20, 24, 34, 35, 52-53, 63, 64, 65-66, 81-82, 84, 99, 143, 157
consolidation, of schools, 253-55; of town and borough, 296, 304
constables, 230
Coon, Barrett, 169
Cordwainers' Protective Union, 187-88
counterfeiting, 47-53, 54-55
Country Club of New Canaan, 246, *247*, 294
courts, J. P., 60, 165, 266, 298; juvenile, 304-305; probate, 307-08; town, 298
Crissy, Abram, 150, 168; Hiram, 169; Nathaniel, 68, Samuel S., 203
Crofoot, Ebenezer, 129
"Culper Spy Ring," 90, 91
Cummings, Homer, 265; Dr. William W., 256

Cunningham, Dr. E. G., 263

Dan, Nathan, 77; Nehemiah, 77; Squire, 76, 77
Danbury Raid, 82-84
Dann, William E., 201
Dantown Methodist Church, 104
Darien, Conn., 6, 7, 22, 57, 183
Dauchy, William, 169
Daughters of American Revolution, 248, 258
Davenport, Darius, 173; Deodate, 68, 76; Hanford, 185; Hezekiah, 57, 68, 76, 83; Rev. James, 36; Rev. John, 5, 24; John, 36, 263; Joseph, 68; Silas, 164
Dawless, Frank, 276
Delavan, Timothy, 55
depression, the, 301-307, 310, 313
divorce, first in New Canaan, 127
dog warden, first, 297
Doolittle, Ichabod, 50
Downey, John R., 245, 246
Driggs, Marshall S., 270; Silas, 270
Drucker, Louis, 232-33
drug store, first, 171, 191
Drummond, Robert, 87-88; Rev. William, 67-73, 80-82, 84, 87-88; William (2d), 88
Dutch, the, 4, 5, 13, 15, 33

Eaton, Theophilus, 5
economy, bankruptcies, 152, 167-70, 173, 188-89, 218-20; early, 41, 43, 61; and hard times, 190, 197, 218-20; late 19th-century, 206-11, 233-37
education, in 1830's, 162-64; in 1870's, 214; in 1890's, 252-55; after World War I, 298-300. *See also* schools
Edwards, Rev. Jonathan, 35-36
Eells, Rev. John, 29-31, 33-37, 38, 58; house of, *30*
Ellsworth, Mrs. Lida B., 283
Elm Street, 256, 271, *273, 311;* begun, 169; buildings on, 227, 236, 241-42, 295-96; extended, 195; renamed, 207, 312
Episcopal Church, 106, 134, 135
Episcopal Society of Canaan Parish, 106, 110; *see also* St. Mark's Church
Era, 208, 209, 211
Erskine, John, 294, 300

Fabbricotti, Luciano, 245
Fairfield, Conn., 5, 92
Fairfield County Association for Improvement of Common Schools, 162
Fairfield County Republican, 266
Fairty, C. E. T., *269*, 270, 292; James, 201; May, 285
Fancher & Co., 236
farming, in Canaan Parish, 39-40; early, 12-13; in Gold Rush, 173
Fayerweather, Richard, 133
Fearhake, John D., 286, 298
Finch, Daniel, 72; John, Jr., 42; Peter, 57; Samuel, 10
fire companies, 174, 215, 228-29, 244, 264
fire engines, 173, 229, 270
firehouses, 241, 242
fires, 173, 215, 216, 229, 234, 236, 259, 312
Firelands, the, 112
First National Bank of New Canaan, 204-05, 211-12, 219, 260, 277
First Presbyterian Church, 244, 246, 321, 322
Fish, Charles P., 283
Fitch, Abigail, 127; Benjamin, 259; Charlotte, 127; John, 25, 27, 41; Stephen, 127, 128, 259; Theophilus, 60, 64, 67, 88, 100; Gov. Thomas, 52-53, 54, 61, 65, 68, 69
Fitch Home, Noroton, Conn., 259
Fitch house, Park Street, 162, *163*
Five Mile River harbor, 8, 16, 58-59, 81, 102, 107, 108, 125, 142, 150, 155, 175
Five Mile River store, 59, 107, 124, 125-26, 143

Flaherty, Robert, 294
Flatridge Hill Christian Union, 212
Foote, George N., 168
Fox, Marvin W., 193, 198
Frank, Mrs. George E., 285
Free Soil Party, 184-85
French and Indian Wars, 42-43, 53-57
French Spoliation Claims, 108
Friendship Division, Sons of Temperance, 175, 230
Frothingham, Lawrence P., 279, 308, 315

Gamble, George W., 255
garbage disposal, 281, 284, 313
Garfield, James A., 231
Gentieu, Pierre, *200, 207,* 280
Gerdes, Augustus M., 280, 289
Gerrish, Florence, 285; John B., 244, 294
Gilbert, Luzerne, 146
Gilder, Rev. Joseph L., 164, 214
"Glass House," the, *319*
Gold Rush, 173
God's Acre, 29, 70, 71, 110, *158,* 177, 237; Christmas tree on, 286, 293, 315
Grace Home in the Field, 245-46, 286
Grand Army of the Republic, 248, 292
Gray, Arthur, 236; Marshall, 236; Nathaniel, 83; Thomas, 229
Great Awakening, The, 35-37
"Great Western," 172, 273, 275
Greeley, Horace, 181, 213
Green, Elijah, 42; Francis E., 272, 275, 299; John, 79
Greenleaf, Rev. Joseph, 212, 227, 251
Greenley (Greenly), Thomas, 122, 169-70
Greenwich, Conn., 6, 13-14, 90, 91, 95
Griffin, Seely, 162
Griswold, Gov. Roger, 129, 130
Gruelle, John, 280; Richard, 280
Gutmann, Bernhard, 280

Hait, James, 34, 62; James, Jr., 85; Jonathan, 42; Joseph, 54, 57, 75-76, 77, 79, 85, 86, 94, 110; Joseph, 5th, 77; Silvanus, 68, 79, 85; Warren, 76
Halfway Covenant, 20, 36, 103
Hall, Charles E., 226; Ezra S., 230, 233; L. Winifred, 283; Mrs. Louis H., 283, 285; Russell L., 211, 233, 260, 261, 265, 266; Thomas W., Sr., 245, 246, 270, 272, 278; Thomas W., Jr., 268, 279; William A., 172, 186, 189-90, 203
Hallock, David, 233, 234
Hamilton, Hamilton, 280; Seth, 122
Hampton Inn, 278
Hanford, Austin, 131, 132; Holly, 213; Samuel, 29, 53, 55; Samuel, Jr., 72; Simeon, 57; Stephen, 60, 73; Theophilus, 12
Hanford-Silliman House, 60, 73, 110, *148,* 222, 321
Harding, Mrs. Warren G., 296
Harmony Lodge No. 67, A. F. and A. M., 144, 147, 275
Hartford, Conn., 4, 7, 135
Hartford Convention, 131
Hartshorne, Howard M., 280
Harvard Club, 295
Hayes, Molly, 132
Haynes, William, 7
Haynes Ridge, 7
health problems, 226, 238, 256, 281-85; *see also* smallpox
Heath, Benjamin N., 188
Henry, Margery, 255
Hersam, John E., 270, 273
Hickok (Hickox), Ebenezer, Jr., 97; John, 70
highway districts, 120-21
highways and streets, 39; in 19th century, 126, 195, 235, 255, 256-58; in 20th century, 271, 306, 308, 309-10, 317, 321, 322
Hildebrandt, Mr. and Mrs. Howard, 280
Hill, Rev. William T., 202
Historic District, 321
Hokinson, Helen, 312

Hoover, Herbert C., 290, 305
Hopkins, Rev. Samuel, 98
hotel, first, 155; *see also* New Canaan Hotel
houses and housing, 44-45, 317, 322
Hoyt, Abram, 50; Benjamin, 150, 188; Edwin, 221, 222, 227, 234, 249, 254, 260, 261; Gould, 109, 124; Isaac L., 199; Israel, 124; James, 221, 234, 249; Rev. James H., 251; Jared, 91; Joel, 155; Justus, 105-06, 109; Justus (2d), 204; Moses, 124; Noah W., 171, 191, *192*, 201, 206, 211, 220, 222, 236, 237; Stephen, Sr., 109, 125, 136, 143, 145, 161, 165, 191; Stephen, Jr., 144, 146, 149, 151, 171-72, 173, 184, 189, *198*, 201, 211, 218, 219, 277; Stephen (3d), 264, 270, 293; Stephen B. (Sr.) 233; Stephen B., Jr., 302
Hoyt, Stephen, & Sons, 206
"Hoyt Farms," 127
Hoyt Manufacturing Co., 203, 208, 213
Hoyt Nurseries, 127, 221, 225, 228, 234, 256, 263, 286, 309, 317
Hubbard, Dr. Nathaniel, 70
Hull, Hezekiah D., 213
Humphrey, Frank, 258
Hunnewell, Charles, 199
Huntington, Mrs. Jonathan, 136-37
Husted, Jonathan, 29, 71, 197; Thomas S., 144, 145, 149, 159-60, 166, 167, 168-69, 171
Husted & Ayres, 169
Husted & Hoyt, 145, 146, 149, 150
Husted & Johnson, 169

illicit trade, 91, 93-97, 98
Indian doctor, 132
Indians, 5, 6, 7, 12, 13-14, 17, 33
Ingersoll, Rev. Jonathan, 85, 99
Irish in New Canaan, 184
"inimicals," 100, 106
Italians in New Canaan, 243, 244

Jacklin, James, 34; Robert, 32; Samuel, 34
Jackson, Andrew, 144, 163, 165, 166
Jelliff, Aaron J., 221; George H., 221, 248
Jennings, Hezekiah, 151
Jews in New Canaan, 233, 303
Johansen, John J., 318
Johnson, Henry, 108, 109; Jonathan K., 131, 168; Philip, 318, 319
Johnson's carriage works, 228, 229, 275
Jones, John, 185

Kaiser, Charles, 297
Keeler, Bradley, 145, 146, 150, 168, 173, *318*; Daniel, 47-53, 55, 60
Kelley, Henry, *291*, 299-300; Henry E., 286, 290, *291*; John T., 288; Mary J., 300
Kellogg, Asahel, 76; Enos, 200; John, 30; Matthew, 186
Kelly, Richard B., 278, 308
Kent, Frances A., 293
Kidd, William, 17
Kiessling, Calvin E., 295
King, Clarence, 30; Morris L., 281; Nelson, 270
King Philip's War, 15, 33
Kirk, Will W., 237, 248, 258, 261, 270, 273
Kiwanis Club and Park, 316
Knox, Mrs. Herbert, 285

Lafayette, Marquis of, 143-44
Lake Siscowit, 243
Lake Wampanaw, 226
Lakeview Cemetery, 211
Lambert, Dr. Edward W., 224, 246, 248, 278; John, 150; John B., 173
Lambert, John, & Co., 172
LaMonte, Robert R., 281
land, colonial purchases, 6; developments, 149, 164, 294, 308; as mortgage security, 60, 152; "Upper Division" of, 39; use of, 39-40

Lane Shoe Co., 272
Lapham, Lewis H., 245, 278; Mrs. Lewis H., 289
Law, Alexander, 192, 198, 201, 203, 205, 206, 209, 219, 249, 254, 260, 278; David, 140, 149, 150
Law Academy, 192, 203, 208, 236, 273
Lawrence, Edward B., 273, 276, 277
League of Women Voters, 302
Lee, Ann, 128; Isaac A., 230; Jesse, 104
Leeds, Elisha, 110; Gideon, 62; John, 16; Martha, 110, *123*
Leeming, Woodruff, 279
Leland, Ernest, 293
Lewis, Rev. Isaac, 85, 99
libraries, 111-12, 226-27. *See also* New Canaan Library
Light, Rodney, 272
Lindsay, Edward D., 224, 227, 250
liquor sales, 125, 156, 157, 229-31, 232, 297; regulation of, 175-76
Litchfield, Electus D., 279
Little Red Schoolhouse, 215, 300
Lloyd, Mrs. Ruth (Lapham), 322-23
Lloyds' Neck, N.Y., 93-94
Lockwood, Edwin H., 265; Frederick W., 224, 227, 249, 251; George, 188; George F., 236, 238, 243, 272; Irving, 234, 236; Mrs. Irving, 283; Jeremiah T., 169; John, 224; Nathan, 155
Locofoco Democrats, 166, 167, 185
Lord, Austin W., 279-80, 295
Louisburg Expedition, 41-43, 57
Lounsbury, Joseph, 208
Loyalists, 76-77, 85, 96, 100; raids by, 81, 88, 94-95
Ludlowe, Roger, 5, 6

MacCauly, Lewis, 133
mail delivery, 134, 155, 252
Main Street, developed, 150-51; 203, 209-11, 228, *263*, *269*, 275-77; fires on, 173, 216, 259; paved, 271
Manship, Paul, 312
Maple Street, 146-47
Marvin, David, 38, 41
Mason, Gregory, 312
Masonic Order. *See* Harmony Lodge
Mather, Rev. Moses, 68, 85, 87, 93, 96
Mathesius, Frederick H., 279
Matthews, Elihu, 131
Mausolff, Alfred, 295
McKendrick, Alexander, 267
McKernon, Dr. James E., 278
McLane, Guy, 270; Dr. James W., 244, 275
McVeagh, Lincoln, 312
Mead, Benjamin P., 226, 231-32, 234, 235, 238, 243, 254, 255, 262, 272, 275, 283; John, 90, 91, 95; Stanley P., 296, 304, 305, 316, 321; Thaddeus, 57
Mead Memorial Park, 283, 299, 300, 306, 320
Melba Inn, 150, 278
Merrill, Marvin F., 267-68; Payson, 244
Merritt, Andrew, 134; DeWitt R., 268, 270; Schuyler, 311
Merritt Parkway, 310-11
Messenger, 220, 236-37, 273-74
Methodist Church, Dantown, 104
Methodist Church, New Canaan, 129, 135, 160-61, 202, 251; cemetery of, 211; Sunday School, 157
Methodist Church meeting house, 158, 160, 195, *276*
Methodist Protestant Church, Silvermine, 161, 212
Methodists, 103, 104, 134, 135
Militia companies, 130-31, 135, 144, 174-75. *See also* Train Band
Mill Pond, 122, 191, 226, *323*
Millar, Addison T., 280
Miller, Dr. James F., 287; Stephen, Jr., 160-61
Millet, Dr. John A. P., 305
mills, 121-22, 221
Mitchell, Rev. Justus, 99, 103, 110-11, 112, 114, 124, 129
Monroe, Lucius M., 191-92, *193*, 202,

205, 206, 208, 211, 212, 213, 221, 228, 229, 237, 238, 243, 249, 252, 253, 261, 272; Samuel, 175
motion picture theatres, 267, 275, 295
Mud Pond, 243
Mulliken, Alfred H., 271
Murdock, Rev. Jonathan, 85
murders, 161, 214-15, 233, 258, 266
Murphy, M. Farmer, 281, 289

Nash, Ann Elizabeth, 171; Edward, 123, 144, 145, 146, 148, 150, 151, 169; Hannah, 171
Neide, Rev. Robert H., 251
New Canaan, description of, 121-25, 255; and 1818 Constitution, 135-36; growth of, 293-96; incorporated, 114-15; 100th anniversary of, 261-65, 268; 150th anniversary, 320; and Perambulation Line, 8-9; port of, 124, 143; *see also* town
New Canaan Academy, 133, 158, 164
New Canaan *Advertiser*, 273, 296
New Canaan Bank, 188
New Canaan Cemetery Assn., 210-11
New Canaan Couch Co., 273
New Canaan Country Day School, 246, 286
New Canaan *Era*, 208, 209, 211
New Canaan Express, 247
New Canaan Fuel & Lumber Co., 209, 234
New Canaan Garden Club, 280
New Canaan Grange No. 38, 248, 251
New Canaan *Herald*, 237
New Canaan Historical Society, 249; buildings of, *147*, *148*, 321
New Canaan Hook & Ladder Co., 215
New Canaan Hook and Ladder and Fire Engine Co., 229, 241
New Canaan Hotel, 173, 209-10, 216, 222, 229
New Canaan Institute, 253
New Canaan Library, 105, 226-27, 249, 275, 277, 279, 281, 319, 322
New Canaan *Messenger*, 220, 236-37, 273-74
New Canaan Nature Center, 244, 322
New Canaan Nursery, 171-72, 198
New Canaan Omnibus & Fairfield County Agriculturist, 184-85
New Canaan Rail Road, 206-07, 213, 218-19
New Canaan Reading Room and Circulating Library. *See* New Canaan Library
New Canaan Savings Bank, 198, 219, 224, 246, 260, 274
New Canaan Sewing Machine Co., 209
New Canaan Society of Artists, 280-81
New Canaan Water Co., 243, 244, 284-85, 307
New England Public Works Co., 243
New Haven, Colony of, 4, 5, 6, 7
New Haven, Conn., 7, 92, 135
New Lights, 36, 63, 64, 65
New Norwalk Road, 309-10
New York, N.Y., in Revolution, 75, 77-79; trade with, 123-24
New York, New Haven & Hartford Railroad, 180, 182, 218-19, 247
newspapers. *See* specific names
Nichols, George Duff, 234, 249-50, 265-67
North Stamford Parish and Church, 98, 104, 114, 115, 161
Norwalk, Conn., 61, 71, 143, 144, 151, 183; Canaan Parish officers of, 113, 115; and churches, 21-22, 37, 161, 162; early history of, 4, 5, 6, 7-8, 10-11, 13, 15, 17, 33, 39; and French and Indian Wars, 56; lawsuit with New Canaan, 125-26; and Revolution, 75, 76-77, 86, 92-93, 100; steamboats to, 142, 178-80
Norwalk, Ohio, 112
Norwalk *Gazette*, 134, 151; ads in, 140, 141, 153; quoted, 174
Noyes, Eliot, 318, 319; Dr. Samuel S., 132
"Nullifier," 154

Oblong, The, 8
Observation Post, 314
occupations, colonial, 41, 72-73; early 19th century, 121-23, 151; after 1850, 183-84, 197, 221, 233-37; *see also* shoemaking
Oenoke Field Club, 246
Oenoke Ridge, 7, 240, 257
Ogden, Rev. David, 171, 176-78; Sereno E., 171, 188, 193-94, 196, 198, 203, 205
Old Lights, 36, 64
Old Norwalk Road, laid out, 125-26
Old Stamford Road, 312
Old Well (South Norwalk), Conn., 14, *179*
Olmstead, Nathan, 71; Sophia (Richards), 181-82
Opera House, 249-50, 265-67, 275, 276, 295
Onesimus, 71, 197
O'Shaughnessy, Dr. Edmund J., 267, 268, 289

Parade Ground, 88, 129, 244; encroachment on, 185, 194
Pardee, Stephen, 209
Parker, Dr. Willard, Sr., 214, 218, 222-23, 225, 226, 227, 234, 244, 248; Mrs. Willard, Sr., 218, 225; Dr. Willard, Jr., 224, 227, 246
parking lots, 317-18, 321
Parsonage Land, 39
Pattison, James, 168
Perambulation Line, 7-9
Perfection Scale Co., 233-34
Perkins, Maxwell E., 294
Philopædean Seminary, 164, *180*
Pinney, Henry A., 209, 233
planing mill, 208, 209, *216*
Plant, Flower and Fruit Guild, 287, 289
Playhouse, 295, *311*
Pleasant Avenue, 233, 234
"Pockhouse Hill," 256
Poinsettia Club, 289
police, under Borough, 241, 297-98; first chief, 241; under town, 304, 313
politics, before 1820, 118, 128, 135; colonial, 61, 63, 65; in 1830's and '40's, 164-67; later, 184-85, 190, 260
Ponus Tribe of Redmen, 248, 263
poor, care of, 120, 132, 301-04
poorhouse and poor farm, first, 133, 146; second, 186, 206, 301
population, of Canaan Parish, 38, 70, 114; of New Canaan (1820), 137; (1850), 183-84; (1860), 197, 201; (1870), 211, 212; (1880), 221-22; (1890), 255; (1900), 260; (1910), 278; (1930), 294; (1940), 314; (1950), 320; (1980), 320
post office and postmasters, 134, 150, 166, 191, 252, *269*, 295-96, 300, 302; dynamited, 268
Pound Ridge, N.Y., 7, 91, 104
Powers, Andrew, 79, 107, 110
probate court, 307-08
prohibition problems, 297-98, 299
Proprietors, 10, 39
Provost, Mrs. Lewis, 264
Purdy, Burling D., 167, 228; W. Frank, 293
Purple Heart decoration, 100

Quebec Act, 74-75
Queen Anne's War, 17

Radical Party, 61, 63, 65
Railroad Avenue. *See* Elm Street
Raymond, Charles, 167; Samuel, 166-67, 168, 191, 199; Samuel H., 257; Thomas, 166, 167, 185; Timothy E., 167; William Edgar, 167, 174, 199, 209, 212, 218, 227, 231-32, 233, 234, 259, 260; Mrs. William E., 259, 260
Raymond Block (and Hall), 231, 241, 259-60, 268, 269, 274, 285, 295
Raymond & Stevens livery stable, *269*
Reamy, Olive, 283
recreation facilities, 283, 292, 316
Red Cross, in New Canaan, 251, 258, 287, 289, 290, 298, 315
Reed, Timothy, 73, 80; William, Jr., 96

reservoirs, 242, 243, 244, 284-85
Revolution. *See* American Revolution
Reynolds, LeRoy, 297
Richards, Edmond, 86; Gershom, 108; Isaac, 107-08, 109, 111, 113, 115, 118, 121, 122, 125-26, 128, 134, 135, 141, 143, 146, 148, 193, 246; James, 57, 58-59, 75, 76, 81, 86, 102, 132; Jesse, 109; Dr. Lewis, 132, 181, 212, 223; Samuel (1st), 58-59; Samuel, Jr., 68, 69, 81, 107
Richards & St. John, 109, 118, 121, 134, 141, 146
Richmond, Dr. David, 121
Rickard, Edgar, 305
Ridgefield, Conn., 17, 83, 85, 99
"Road to the Landing," 125, 126, 144, 146
Rockefeller, John D., 224
Rockwell, David S., 164, 282; J. V., 208, 213
"Rockwell's Swamp," 281, 282
Roger Sherman Inn, 111, 181
Rogers, Helen, 286; Henry B., 198, 201, 203, 221, 222, *223*, 227, 234, 238, 249, 272, 317; Mrs. Henry B., 249, 283; John, 223, 227, 233, 321
Rogers, Henry B., & Co., 228, 243, 254
Rogers Block, 228, 272, 302
Roman Catholic Church, in New Canaan, 196, 251, 277, 321; in U.S., 106
Roton Point, 316
Route 123, 309-10
Rowayton, 6; *see also* Five Mile River harbor

Sacket, Rev. Samuel, 64
St. Aloysius Church, 251, 277, 321
St. John, Benoni, 124; Darius, 173; David, 73, 99, 109, 162; Eliphalet, 111; Enoch, 130, 172; Jesse, 131; Samuel, 109, 118, 122, 124, 131, 133, 134, 135, 143, 146, 148, 159, 172; Prof. Samuel, 156, 192, *193*, 202, 203, 206, 207, 213, 214, 217-18, 225; Selleck Y., 184, 188, 191, *192*, 194, 198, 203, 204, 205, 211, 218, 219, 227, 231, 249, 252; Stephen, 56; William, 130, 168, 192, 198, 203, 204, 218, 235, 246
St. John Hall, 172
St. John's Church, Stamford, 37, 63, 85
St. Mark's Church, 158, 176-78; burying ground of, *62;* horse sheds, 196; rectory, 251; Sunday School, 157
St. Mark's Church meeting house, first, 158, 196, 251; second, 244, 321
St. Michael's Lutheran Church, 158, 321
St. Paul's Church, Norwalk, 37, 63, 85, 92
Sanford, David, 47, 48, 51, 52
Saxe, Henry W., 255, 298, 300
Saxe Junior High School, 300, 320
Saybrook Platform, 20
Scheele, Joseph, 232-33
Schmidt, Otto, 268, 273, 292, 297
schools, military, 213
schools, private, 133, 158, 164, *180*, 192, 193, 253, 286; first, 111
schools, public, appropriations for, 206, 214, 300, 319; in Canaan Parish, 31, 60, 112-13; in Connecticut Colony, 19; consolidation of, 252-55; district or grade, *113*, 162-64, 194, 214, 215, 253, *254*, 299, 300; high, 255, 299-300, 320, 322; junior high, 300, 320; last district, 215, 300; in wartime, 288-89
Schultz, Louis, 231
Scofield, David, 171; Herbert L., 275; Joseph, 168; Loomis, 263; Squire, 131
Scott, Charles, 231
Scoville, Dr. Clarence H., 270
secret societies, 248
Seely, Alfred, 143; Ebenezer, 31; Eliphalet, 67; Erastus, 166; John, 144; Joseph, 115, 118, 130; Nathan, 124, 128, 135; Samuel, 79; Wyx, 77

Selleck, Jacob, 75, Jonathan, 15; Mrs. Sarah, 214-15
Selleck's Corners Church, 195
Separatists, 18
Sesquicentennial of U.S., 299
sewers, 282, 285
Seymour, Edwin S., 157; Holly, 130, 135
Shakers, 126-28, 171
Sheldon's Light Horse, 88-89
Sherman, Rev. Josiah, 99; Martha, 99; Roger, 99, 111-12
ships and shipping, 15-17, 58-59, 107-09, 124, 193-94; beacon for, 179-80
shoemaking, early, 41, 123-24, 137-40, 150, 152-54; last, 272; later, 172, 186-90, 203, 209, 220, 236; report on, 188; strikes, 153, 187
Shufeldt, Robert W., 213
Shutes, Frank A., 282
sidewalks, in Borough, 240-41
silk industry, 169-70
Silliman, Elisha L., 151; Gould Selleck, 82, 83, 95; Dr. Joseph, 109-10, 111, 113, 115, 118, *123*, 132, 146; Joseph, Jr., 146, 165, 167, 191; Joseph F., 222, 223, *232*, 234, 249, 256-57, 259, 261, 264, 271, 276; Mrs. Joseph F., 249; Rhoda, 64, 66, 70; Rev. Robert, 37-41, 43, 52, 60, 63-66, 67, 68, 70, 72, 100, 110, 146; Samuel Cooke, 64, 66, 72, 76, 80, 87, 89, 95, 109, 110, 136, 137; Samuel C. (2d), 171, 191; Thomas, 66
Silliman, J. F., & Co., 260
Silliman Hardware Co., 276
Silver Hill, 305
Silvermine Group of Artists, 280
Silvermine Guild of Artists, 294
Slauson (Slawson), Eleazer, 41, 50-51, 52, 309; Eliphalet, 41, 50-51, 52, 309; Jonathan, 57
slaves, in Canaan Parish, 32, 34, 61, 71, 72, 110, 137; last in Connecticut, 197; in New Canaan, 132-33, 137
sloops, *102*; packet, 141-42, 143
Smallhorn, W. A., 274
smallpox, 29, 60, 65-66; in New Canaan, 121, 256
Smith, Daniel, 111; Ebenezer, 42, 62; Ephraim, 62; Joseph, 96; Peter, 50-51, 52, 111; Peter (2d), 190; Rev. Theophilus, 157, 158-59, 163, 176-78, *177*, 191
Smith Ridge Road, 195
Society of Canaan, 25, 28-29, 35, 39, 65-66, 67, 68, 80, 99, 115, 136
South Avenue, 195, 257
Southern New England Telephone Co., 276-77
Spanish-American War, 258
stagecoaches, 141, 155-56, 178, *180;* travel by, described, 181-82
Stamford, Conn., 125, 142, 144, 183, 206; and churches, 22, 24, 37, 105; early history, 4, 6, 7-8, 10-11, 13-14, 15-17, 33; and French and Indian Wars, 56, 57; objects to Canaan Parish, 22, to New Canaan, 115; and the Revolution, 74-75, 76-77, 86, 95, 96, 100
Stamford Bank, 151
Stamford & New Canaan Railroad Co., 218
Stamford, New Canaan and Ridgefield Plank Road, 194
Staples, Rev. Mark, 212
Starr, Nathaniel W., 213; Oliver, 213
State National Bank, 296
steamboats, 142-43, 156, 178-80
Stearns, Marshal, 292; Mrs. Marshal, 283, 285
Stevens, David, Jr., 42, 67; Ezra, 76; George R., Jr., 290; John L., 268, 294; Zephaniah, 47, 50, 51
Stewart, Nellie D., 294; Walter, 274
Stewart, Walter, Co., 274
stills, 109, 156
street lighting, 240
streets. *See* highways and streets
Streit, Mrs. Raymond E., 283
suffrage, women's, 254, 285, 296

suffragettes, 285
Sullivan, Owen, 48-50, 54-55
summer boarders, 154
summer residents, 222-27, 244-47, 257, 278-79, 322
Sunday schools, 157, 226, 261

Tallmadge, Maj. Benjamin, 89, *90*, 91, 92, 93-94, 96, 99
Talmadge, Thomas, 30, 64
Talmadge Hill Chapel, 212
tanneries, 138, 189, 275
Tarleton, Banastre, 91
Tavern Island, 248
Taylor, Alfred, 290; Alfred H., 279
telephone buildings, 150, 276
telephones, first, 228
temperance movements, 151, 175, 230-31
Terrill, Hiram, 204
Thayer, Harry B., 279, 280, 292
Thomas, Edward E., 278
Thomson, Dr. William H., 224, 225, 226; Rev. William M., 226
Thrift Shop, 284, 302
Titus, George W., 224
toll road, proposed, 194
town finances, assessments, 278, 294; Board formed, 271-72; bonds, 201, 272; budgets, 214, 313; in depression, 301, 304; grand lists, 114, 195; and railroad, 206-07, 218; school appropriations, 214, 253, 300; tax shortage, 220; taxes, 120, 125
town government, care of poor, 132, 185-86; and 1818 constitution, 135; and fire company, 229; housing authority, 317; incinerator, 313; last Democratic first selectman, 272; lawsuits of, 125-26, 258; Library support, 249; and liquor, 175, 229-31; and Nature Center, 322; officers of, first, 115, 119-20, later, 128, 131-32, 164-67, 231-32, 235; and police, 297, 298, 304; and road building, 195, 256-58; and Roton Point, 316; salaries for selectmen, 131-32, 257; and State Insane Retreat, 220; and steamboat service, 179; third selectman, first woman, 313; welfare department, 303, 307, 310; zoning boards, 309
town hall (town house), first, 146-47, 203, 321, use of 159, 194; second, 158, 201-02, 275; third, 250; fourth, 275-76, 307, site of, 123; use of, 290, 292, 298, 307
Town Clock Fund, 242
Town Deposit Fund, 164, 167, 187
Townsend, Dr. Platt, 70; W. Robinson, 278
trade, early, 41, 43, 60-61; illicit, 93-96; and Louisburg Expedition, 43-45; maritime, 14-17, 58-59, 93, 107-09, 124
traders, 61, 87
trades. *See* occupations
Train Band, formed, 31; in French and Indian Wars, 53-57; history of, 32-33; and Louisburg Expedition, 41-43; made 9th Militia Co., 33; Parade Ground of, 88; in Revolution, 74, 75-80, 95
training days, 33, 129, 145, 174
travel and transportation, 18th century, 101-02, 123; restrictions on, 134, 142; by sloop, 141-42; by stage, 141; by steamboat, 142
Trumbull, Gov. Jonathan, 89, *90*
Tryon, William, 82-84, 92
Tucker, John, 241
Tuttle, Daniel, 42; Levi, 76

Underhill, John, 13
Union Trust Co., 204, 277
Universalist Church, 161
"Upper Division" of Norwalk, 39

Van Gerbig, Mr. and Mrs. Barend, 299
Van Sinderen, Adrian, 278
Verleger, William F., 313
Village Hall, 295

Village Improvement Co., 295, 296
"Vine Cottage," 203, *204*, 210
Visiting Nurse Association, 284, 302, 303

Walton, N.Y., 101, 102
War of 1812, 129-31
War Records Committee, 314
Ward, Robertson, 308-09
Waring, William L., 190
Washington, George, 77-79, 90, 96, 99, 100
Washington, 108-09
water problems, 242-44, 284-85
Waterbury, David, 96
Watson, William, 122
Watts, Samuel H., 272, 317
"Waveny," 12, 110, 245, 278, 322
Waveny Care Center, 322
Wayside Cross, 292-93
Webb, Paul, 312; William G., 203, 205, 208, 211, 236, 248
Webb, William G., & Co., 209
Webster, H. T., 312
Weed, Abraham, 65, 66, 68, 106, 110; Albert, 208; Brush, 76; Cary, 130, 161; Charles, 74; Chauncey, 259; Daniel G., 154; Ebenezer, 57; Eliphalet, 144; Enos, 128, 129; Fitch, 154; Francis E., 208, 220, 226, 229, 234-35; 236-37, 238, 243, 248, 249, 251, 261, 263, 276; Hanford S., 272, 276, 283, 288; John, 131; John B., 241, 267-68; Josiah, 72; Nehemiah E., 188; Noah, 161; Samuel A., 173, 188, *198*, 204; Stephen, 79, 131; Stephen (2d), 154; Theodore B., 241; William F., 280; Mrs. William F., 283, 285
Weed & Duryea Co., 235
Weekes, Hobart H., 276, 279
Welles, Rev. Noah, 85, 98
Wethersfield, Conn., 4, 6
Whig Party, 165, 175
White, Dr. Ralph E., 289
"white dogs," 153, 167
Whitefield, Rev. George, 36
Williams, Dr. Percy E., 278, 288
Wilton, Conn., 17, 51, 83
Windsor, Conn., 4
Woman's Farm Movement, 289
Women's Relief Corps, 289, 292
women, as shoemakers, 152-53; voting rights of, 254, 296
Wood, Dr. Walter C., 279, 298
Wooster, David, 82, 83
Wooster Guards, 174
World War I, 286-92
World War II, 314-17
Wright, Frederic, 145
Wyckoff, Joseph C., 260
Wyllis, Zachariah, 132

YMCA, early, 213
Yohn, Frederick C., 280
Yorktown, battle of, 97, 98, 100
Young People's Library, 226
Youngs, Abraham, 72; James, 71, 76

zoning, adopted, 309